BARKER, John. Strange contrarieties: Pascal in England during the Age of Reason. McGill-Queen's, 1976 (c1975). 336p ill bibl index 74-81661. 15.00. ISBN 0-7735-0186-6

This is a well-documented and thorough study of what British intelligentsia thought of Pascal during the 18th century. Unfortunately the soundness of the scholarship is not matched by either novelty of approach or arresting conclusions. Indeed there are very few conclusions at all, and one is left to speculate about the importance of such a study. We can hardly be surprised to learn that Hume mocked Pascal or that Priestley admired him — the slightest acquaintance with the works of any of the 18th-century spokesmen here represented would allow us to guess what each one made of Pascal. The author of this type of study should make the implications of influence tracing more explicit than Barker does. Perhaps different organization would emphasize such implications. Still this work represents substantial scholarship and it should be praised for general intelligence. It will not reveal much to a specialist, but it will specify what we expect Pascal's influence to have been in 18th-century Britain. Excellent bibliography. Readership: undergraduate.

Strange Contrarieties

PASCAL in England during the Age of Reason

JOHN BARKER is Associate Professor
of History at Trent University,
Peterborough.

Religion

les Provinciales
Ore.
the Mystery.
of.
Iesuitisme

Δ ὐτεραν Θοουλιδες οοφωτεραν.

By Louis de Montalte;

Ro. Vaughan sculp. 1657

PLATE 1 Frontispiece from *Les Provinciales: or, The Mysterie of Jesvitisme* (London, 1657)

Strange Contrarieties

PASCAL in England during the Age of Reason

JOHN BARKER

MCGILL-QUEEN'S UNIVERSITY PRESS   MONTREAL—LONDON 1975

©McGill-Queen's University Press 1975
International Standard Book
Number 0 7735 0186 6
Library of Congress Catalog
Number 74-81661
Legal Deposit third quarter 1975
Bibliothèque nationale du Québec

Design by Peter Dorn, RCA, FGDC
Printed in Canada by
The Hunter Rose Company

This book has been published with
the help of a grant from the
Humanities Research Council of
Canada using funds provided by
the Canada Council.

TO ROSALIND

Contents

VIII *Plates*

IX *Preface*

XIII *Acknowledgements*

XV *Form of Citations*

1 CHAPTER ONE
The Mystery of Jesuitisme

35 CHAPTER TWO
*The Ingenious
Monsieur Pascal*

65 CHAPTER THREE
*The Greatest Genius on
the Greatest Subject*

97 CHAPTER FOUR
Plac'd on this Isthmus

131 CHAPTER FIVE
*What a Hideous Monster
is Fanaticism!*

167 CHAPTER SIX
*The Absolute Need of
Continual Light*

203 CHAPTER SEVEN
This Strange Combination

235 *Appendix* Pascal in America

249 *Notes*

291 *Bibliography*

317 *Index*

Plates

1 Frontispiece from *Les Provinciales: or, The Mysterie of Jesvitisme* (London, 1657): Cambridge University Library. *Frontispiece*

2 Frontispiece from *The Mystery of Jesuitism* (London, 1679): Cambridge University Library. 22

3 'Figures du traité de l'équilibre des liqueurs,' from Pascal's *Traitez de l'équilibre des liqueurs et de la pesanteur de la masse de l'air* (Paris, 1664): Cambridge University Library. Figure XVII portrays one of the experiments principally questioned by Robert Boyle in *Hydrostatical Paradoxes*. 45

4 Title-page of the second edition of Basil Kennett's translation of Pascal's *Pensées* (London, 1727): British Museum Library. 95

5 Frontispiece from vol. I of *The Life of Mr. Paschal, with his Letters Relating to the Jesuits*, trans. William Andrews (London, 1744): Cambridge University Library. 149

6 Title-page of John Wesley's edition of the *Pensées* in his *Christian Library* (Bristol, 1749–55), vol. XXIII: British Museum Library. 188

7 Plate from the *Encyclopaedia Londinensis* (London, 1810–29), vol. XVIII: Cambridge University Library. 230

8 Tomb of Governor William Stoughton of Massachusetts (d. 1701), in the Burial-ground, Dorchester, Mass. 237

Preface

Blaise Pascal was born in 1623 and died in 1662. Though living amid many distinguished contemporaries, the strength of his versatile gifts was widely acknowledged, and most of his achievements have conspicuously stood the test of time. Quickly attaining fame in the area of mathematics, he produced notable work on conics, the cycloid, and in the development of calculus; also, as a physicist, his discoveries relating to air and water pressure and his research into the vacuum inspired many further investigations. Drawn towards the Jansenist interpretation of Christianity, partly in reaction from the fashionable Catholicism of his day, and partly, it seems, by the daunting prospect offered by the unrestrained exercise of human reason, he became a leading protagonist for that party, and, in the *Letters provinciales*, brilliantly and humorously attacked the Jesuits in a work which has been hailed as inaugurating modern French literature. Never strong, his health began steadily to fail, but his intellectual activities nonetheless continued, and, as a member of the Jansenist community at Port Royal, he planned an apology for the Christian religion which might convince free-thinkers and sceptics of its truth. The fragments of this project were found in his room after his death, and later published as the book by which he is best-known today, the *Pensées*.

A life so full of accomplishments within so brief a span would arouse interest at any time; but Pascal, like Socrates or Machiavelli, is one of those figures who, by the nature of the themes they touch upon and their telling conclusions, create lasting arguments of a most fundamental kind. An opinion upon Pascal, and especially upon his assessment of man's powers and deficiencies and the consequent need for salvation, is indicative of an individual's attitude upon a variety of issues. He also provides a means by which we may conveniently measure the thought of an age; and in no age or place, perhaps, did he stimulate such divergent opinions as in France during the eighteenth century. The conflict between the *philosophes* and the legacy of Pascal was one of the great features of the French Enlightenment. Since the *philosophes*, and Voltaire, in particular, sought to condemn much of the Christian religion on grounds of irrationality, they naturally came to regard as one of their principal enemies this genius who had so perversely defended Christianity with compelling logic by exposing man's limits and inadequacies. Their attacks upon Pascal in some respects lay at the heart of that wider eighteenth-century confrontation between Augustinian Christianity and the forces of Reason, which, in varying degrees, affected the development of opinion in most European countries.

With this in mind, it has seemed appropriate to enquire to what extent attitudes towards Pascal entered into the conflict between faith and reason as it occurred in England from the seventeenth to the early nineteenth centuries. Owing to political and social factors, English intellectual life flourished more freely than French during this period, and striking attempts to refute or defend Pascal are not as immediately apparent in the less exacerbated English contest. Christianity in England was, on the whole, less vulnerable to criticism than the Church in France, and there was no English equivalent to Voltaire. Nevertheless, an inspection of the available material would suggest that the English reception of Pascal may offer useful insights into the related forms the great eighteenth-century debate sometimes assumed in both countries, and provide some contribution to an understanding of this episode in French and English intellectual history. On other grounds, too, such a study would appear to be warranted, for, throughout an era of changing thought, Pascal acts as a prism for drawing out the colours of the English mind. His impact may not have been as great as that of some other contemporary French figures, but he constitutes a useful centre for observing the patterns of English ideas, offering also many a glimpse into English reading habits and the standards by which judgments of character and achievement were made.

To some extent, precedents for this kind of study exist in such works as *La vie posthume des Pensées* by Bernard Amoudru (Paris, 1936), Dorothy M. Eastwood's *The Revival of Pascal: A Study of his Relation to Modern French Thought* (Oxford, 1936), and *Les Pensées de Pascal en France, de* 1842 à 1942 (Paris, 1959), by Raymond Francis. Each of these authors has, however, primarily examined Pascal's reputation during other periods in the history of his own country; and, though some writers have commented on the familiarity of Locke, Pope, or other English figures with Pascal, no published study appears to have been devoted in detail to the comprehensive knowledge of him in England or to the part played there by opinions of his life and writings during the Age of Reason. Taking into account comparable and relevant works, the attempt has here been made, through the information presented by books, letters, journals, library catalogues, and other contemporary sources, to form a picture of the fluctuations in Pascal's fortunes among his English, and sometimes Scottish, readers; and, through having asked what drew men and women to Pascal or repelled them from him, the results of this enquiry may serve to clarify several leading issues of the time, as well as illuminating aspects of Pascal himself. Research into Pascal's impact on English readers inevitably uncovers signs of an American audience, too, linked as the distant colonies were to intellectual life across the Atlantic; yet, interestingly, the scraps of evidence give the impression that the American reaction to Pascal may have differed markedly at times from the types of response called forth in the parent country, and these findings are brought together in an appendix.

Although certain conclusions are set down from the evidence accumulated, the many-sided genius of Pascal—scientist, mathematician, literary stylist, polemicist, philosopher, and devotional writer—the wide-ranging implications of his thought, and the varying depths to which his writings permeated as an intellectual force, have, of necessity, dictated limits to the nature of this study. Several themes associated with Pascal, for instance that of the greatness and insignificance of man, soon became a shared ingredient of English speculation, and seem often to have merged with similar views proceeding from Montaigne and other French thinkers. This study would have been too extensive and too conjectural had it tried to follow the assimilation of these themes by the English mind, or had it attempted to estimate the less determinate importance of Pascal as a literary or theological influence. Instead, there has been a concentration upon examples of definite knowledge of Pascal's life or works, and an endeavour to obtain factual grounds for the analysis of his reputation.

Pascal's achievements in mathematics and physics played a very important part in establishing his fame in England, but the principal changes in attitude towards his life and writings during these years reflect the attention paid the *Letters provinciales* and the *Pensées*. Although English admiration had commenced before Pascal's death, the arrival of the *Provinciales* and, later, the *Pensées*, introduced the elements central to any understanding of his subsequent reputation by making available the particular versions known during this time. In fact, the dates of appearance (or non-appearance) of successive editions of these works have provided one kind of scaffolding around which this study has been built. The year 1830 has accordingly seemed the most suitable moment to end, shortly before the numerous and improved editions of the Victorian era began to be published. To pursue this topic further into the nineteenth and twentieth centuries, reviewing the opinions of such representative figures as Newman, Arnold, Stephen, Pater, T.E. Hulme, Eliot, and Auden, with a host of others, would have been to embark upon a new phase in evaluations, and the period examined in these pages forms a natural entity.

Each chapter heading bears a phrase from a contemporary author, held to incorporate the character of that section of the study under consideration. Chapter 1 carries the title given to early English translations of the *Lettres provinciales*; chapter 2 recalls the description of Pascal by Boyle and other English scientists; and chapter 3 draws from Kennett's preface to his version of the *Penseés*. The heading of chapter 4 is from Pope's *Essay on Man*. The exclamation which introduces chapter 5 concludes an essay in the *Gentleman's Magazine* for 1789, probably by Boswell; the words for chapter 6 come from a pastoral letter of John Wesley; and chapter 7 represents the verdict of Coleridge. The title of the book itself is derived from the heading to the twenty-first chapter of Kennett's *Pensées*, which seems to have forecast the essence of the eighteenth-century's perplexity upon the issues raised by Pascal: 'The strange Contrarieties discoverable in Human Nature, with regard to Truth, and Happiness, and many other things.'

Acknowledgements

In preparing and writing this book I have received assistance at every stage which has exceeded anything I might have anticipated; and I am very glad for the chance to offer my thanks here to the many friends and insitutions who have given of their time, interest, and generosity in advancing this work towards its finished form.

I think the idea of studying a figure such as Pascal to illuminate events in intellectual history first grew in my mind when studying church history at Yale under that most delightful of scholars, Professor Roland H. Bainton. Such an interest was further stimulated at Toronto by Professor Richard M. Saunders of the Department of History, who opened up the eighteenth century for me and, in fact, suggested Pascal's reputation in England as a topic for my doctoral dissertation. To both Professor Saunders and Professor Kenneth Maclean of the Department of English, Victoria College, I am very much indebted for advice during the research and writing of the dissertation, and for continuing helpfulness as it was gradually transformed into a book. I must express my thanks as well to Professor W.H. Nelson of Toronto for some useful suggestions about Pascal's readers in colonial America, and how his audience might compare with that in England. To all these gentlemen, as teachers and as guides, I owe a great deal.

While at Toronto, the Province of Ontario assisted me financially during the later period of my research in the University library, and I must also thank the Canada Council for a predoctoral fellowship which allowed me to spend a summer at Harvard looking for further material. The staffs of the Widener and Houghton libraries, and of the Sterling Library at Yale, made available all I asked for from their vast collections, and met a number of specialized requests.

This book could not have been easily brought together in its early form, though, without the surroundings provided me, as a Junior Fellow, by the Master and Fellows of Massey College in the University of Toronto. To a cell as tranquil as any at Port Royal itself, I should add the advantage that, among Massey's friendly, inter-disciplinary membership, it was splendid always to be able to find someone at short notice who could answer a question when any detail needed settling.

Rice University, Texas, awarded me research grants for two successive summers to travel to England and look for further evidence of Pascal's influence in the libraries of, mainly, Cambridge University and the British Museum. The staff of both libraries helped me considerably, and the early parts of the book in particular profited. The Department of History at Rice kindly defrayed part of the cost of typing the book manuscript, which was carried out by Mrs. Mary Russell of Trumpington. I also wish to record my warm appreciation here to my parents for enabling myself and my family to set up a second home in Cambridge during these visits.

In 1970 portions of the second chapter, entitled 'The Royal Society and "The Ingenious Monsieur Pascal",' were presented at the Canadian Historical Association's annual meeting, and later printed in that Association's *Historical Papers*; and I delivered a paper in similar form on Pascal in America at the Association's meeting in 1972.

Following the book's acceptance by McGill-Queen's University Press, the manuscript received the additional attention of Mrs. Joan Harcourt, who made several practical comments on matters of style and the arrangement of references within a manageable system. Trent University generously gave me funds to recheck certain sections, and for the preparation of an index compiled by Miss Marcia Rodriguez. I am also most grateful to the Humanities Research Council of Canada for making the publication of the book possible by granting a subvention using funds provided by the Canada Council; indeed, my appreciation cannot be expressed too much.

Harvard University, Yale University, and Victoria University, Toronto, have all kindly permitted me to quote from manuscripts in their collections; and I am grateful to the libraries of Cambridge University and the British Museum for allowing materials in their possession to be reproduced as plates. For a different service, I must also say thank you to the City of Boston Parks and Recreation Department for arranging that the gate of the Burial-ground, Dorchester, be specially unlocked so I might photograph Governor Stoughton's tomb.

I have left my deepest gratitude till last. My wife has encouraged this work from the beginning, and I have benefited in countless ways from her lively interest and support. From the book's inception I have looked forward to dedicating it to her, and my pleasure is immense in being able to do so now.

Form of Citations of Pascal's Works

An attempt has been made to trace all quotations from Pascal's works and other references to him to their original source, and insert an informative note. Perfect consistency has not been possible, however, since the words of Pascal were often summarized in a manner which embodied a specific theme for which he was known, rather than being drawn exactly from a passage in his published writings. In the case of the *Pensées*, there has been the additional problem of identifying such passages in a work with an exceedingly tangled history. In order to assign references to French and English editions then available, but also take advantage of modern scholarship, it has seemed best to supply several sources on each occasion and relate them to the edition of Léon Brunschvicg. Although the edition of Louis Lafuma, based on more recent research, is increasingly regarded as a more authoritative treatment of the papers left by Pascal, Brunschvicg's version has a longstanding record of acceptance, and his enumeration is listed in every leading concordance. Moreover, complications are lessened if, for all writings by Pascal mentioned in this study, the reader is referred to his *Oeuvres*, edited by Brunschvicg and others (Paris, 1908–21, 14 vols.). Besides the section number given by Brunschvicg to each fragment, that denoted in the Port Royal edition of 1678 according to chapter and paragraph has been quoted, knowledge of the *Pensées* being estimated from its contents until the appearance of new versions beginning late in the eighteenth century. Page numbers from the English translation by Basil Kennett (London, 1704), the edition which became most familiar to English readers, have also been added. Thus, a reference to Pascal's argument of the wager appears in a note as: Pascal, *Oeuvres*, XIII, 147, sec. 233 (P.R., ch. vii, para. 1, 2; Kenn., pp. 57–65).

Readers interested in a more detailed comparison between the texts of the Port Royal and modern editions may turn to the excellent study by M.M. Vamos, 'Pascal's *pensées* and the Enlightenment: the Roots of a Misunderstanding,' *Studies on Voltaire and the Eighteenth Century* (ed. Besterman), XCVII (1972), 7–145.

CHAPTER ONE

The Mystery of Jesuitisme

[I] Apart from some slight knowledge of his discoveries in mathematics and physics, Pascal's reputation in England may be said to have begun, as it principally did in France, amid the heat of religious controversy. The fortunes of the spiritual community at Port Royal had been approaching a crisis ever since its leader, Antoine Arnauld, had published in 1643 *De la fréquente communion*, upholding the necessity of genuine readiness when receiving the sacraments. Such a view deriving from the teachings of Cornelius Jansen, Bishop of Ypres, was opposed by the Jesuits, and the issue deepened when the Syndic of the Sorbonne compiled five propositions which were claimed to embody the essence of Jansenism and placed them before the university. In 1653, Pope Innocent x condemned these propositions and, by implication, the *Augustinus* of Jansen also; and two years later the Sorbonne followed suit, the forces who favoured the scholastic tradition of theology combining in hostility to the Jansenists' theories of divine grace, which emphasized an experiential Christianity of the kind exemplified by St. Augustine. Arnauld's endeavours to interpret his position in a more popular way met with little success; but his suggestion to Pascal, who had increasingly associated himself with Port Royal, that he might write a defence instead, produced the famous *Lettres provinciales* which were presented as a series between January 1656, and March 1657.

The *Provinciales* were immediately recognized by a wide circle of opinion as an outstanding contribution to the defence the Jansenists were making at that time against the Jesuits. The first three letters described the astonishment of one, Louis de Montalte, an educated man but with slight knowledge of theology, at the little difference that seemed to exist between the two parties. Writing to a friend in the country, he discussed with wit and irony the definitions of grace and ridiculed the arguments put forward by the Jesuits and their allies. Before the third letter had appeared, however, the censure of Arnauld had officially taken place, and in consequence the remaining letters pursued a relentless attack upon the Jesuits for a wide range of conspicuous failings. Their verbal ingenuity was shown to be an offensive substitute for the original teachings of the Church, and their system of morality often conflicted outrageously with the law of the land. According to their double standards, the Jesuits were prepared to defend lying, revolution, and even murder if these seemed justified by the intention of the person indulging in them. More exclusively religious in content as they progressed, the *Provinciales* contrasted the harsh insistence of the Jesuits upon orthodoxy and obedience to ecclesiastical authority with the spiritual understanding of Christianity advocated by Port Royal; and, though obviously relevant to a dispute already arousing attention, the letters were also acclaimed as a masterpiece of satire and literary style.

The *Provinciales* were quickly placed on the Index and ordered to be publicly burnt, but their fame spread fast until, as Macaulay was later to write, 'all Europe read and admired, laughed and wept';[1] and it is a particularly striking sign of their success that, apparently by August 1657, a few months after the last instalment had come from Pascal's pen, an English translation of the collected letters had been published in London, well ahead of any other translation into a foreign language.[2] It was almost inevitable the contents of the *Lettres provinciales* should appeal to an England so dominated by religious ferment; but, even so, the rapidity with which the first English translation was made is still surprising. Although the government had been informed of the progress of the dispute and there was some awareness in religious circles, it does not seem any general knowledge existed in the country of the conflict between the Jansenists and their opponents. The sympathy English Protestantism would later express for Port Royal had not yet begun to develop, and the fundamental reason for the speed with which the *Lettres provinciales* were translated and rushed into print is best exemplified by the language of the title-page: 'Les Provinciales: or, The Mysterie of Jesvitisme, discover'd in certain Letters, written upon occasion of the present differences at Sorbonne, between the Jansenists and the Molinists, from January 1656. to March 1657. S.N. Displaying the corrupt Maximes and Politicks of that Society. Faithfully rendred into English. Sicut Serpentes.'[3]

Such phrases clearly indicate that, in the emotional religious atmosphere of Commonwealth England, the *Lettres provinciales* had been quickly recognized by those responsible for their translation as a valuable new polemic which could be used in the warfare Protestantism was constantly waging against the Jesuits and against the Roman Catholic Church in general. In thus presenting the *Provinciales* to the English public, giving the book a new sub-title not found in the original and stressing its controversial nature, it must have been hoped the work would make the greatest possible impact. These expectations were largely assured. English readers might not share the involvement of the French in the disputes at the Sorbonne, but an extreme fear of Popery as a danger to church and state ran through almost all levels of society and shades of opinion in seventeenth-century England, singling out the Jesuits for special unpopularity. The accumulation of hatred aroused by the efficiency of their organization, their high standard of ability, and, perhaps most of all, their reputation of being agents of foreign powers – a charge often implied in the *Provinciales* – made certain that a work by description hostile to the Society of Jesus would have a ready audience.[4]

It seems, however, that the purpose behind so rapid an appearance of the *Lettres provinciales* was more specific than merely to stir up anti-Catholic feeling once again. That this was the case has been revealed by enquiries into the identity of the man who translated the text of the *Provinciales*, possibly as each letter in turn was issued,[5] and who also adapted for English readers the preface which Pascal's associate, Pierre Nicole, had written for the French edition printed at Cologne in 1657. In the late seventeenth century, Anthony à Wood attributed this first English translation of the *Provinciales* to John Davies of Kidwelly (1625-93), who had at one time studied at St. John's College, Cambridge, learned French, and then had spent much of the remainder of his life making translations of French books, among them several other works relating to the Jansenist controversy.[6] Recent investigation has centred upon the prefaces to each of the first and second editions of the *Provinciales* in English (1657 and 1658 respectively), and to *A Journall of all Proceedings between the Jansenists, and the Jesuits* (1659), which, taken together, provide a sequence. Whereas the earlier prefaces were anonymous, the *Journall* announced it was 'publish'd by a Well-Wisher, to the distressed Church of England,'[7] who, at the end of that preface, signed himself 'H.H.' It has been speculated that the writer was Henry Holden, an English Catholic living in France, who sympathized to some extent with the Jansenists.[8] The research of Mlle. Paule Jansen has now, it seems, firmly established that Davies was indeed the translator of the *Provinciales*,[9] but that responsibility for their publication and for the three prefaces referred to rests with Henry Hammond (1605-60), an Anglican divine, who habitually made his signature in this fashion.[10]

Hammond had been one of the chaplains to Charles I during the latter part of the Civil War, and afterwards became a leading exponent of the claims of the Anglican Church under the Commonwealth. Also recognized by some as the founder of English biblical criticism, he wrote a number of treatises defending his church against the Presbyterians on one side and Catholicism on the other; and his design in introducing the *Provinciales* to English readers would appear to have proceeded from this polemical interest. With the loss of its favoured status and with numerous clergy deprived of their livings or in exile abroad, the Anglican Church was finding great difficulty in maintaining its position during the interregnum; and, with no restoration of their Church apparently in sight, acceptance of Rome could present an attractive and practical alternative to many. In the circumstances, the appearance of the *Provinciales*, with their sensational exposure of the Jesuits, happened to coincide with attempts being made by Hammond and other divines to launch a new attack upon Roman Catholicism, and, in doing so, to strengthen and more clearly define the *via media* of the Church of England. The Anglican purpose behind the early publication of the *Provinciales* in English is further suggested by the fact that the book's printer was Richard Royston, from whose press also came the *Eikon Basiliké*. In 1645, Royston had been imprisoned for publishing scandalous books against the Parliament, and he was known as a strong adherent of the Anglican and royalist cause.

Viewing the *Provinciales* for a purpose ultimately different from that which their author had intended, it seems that Hammond considered the work a welcome ally which could assist in checking the drift of many Anglicans towards Rome – the Jesuits being in the forefront of the Church of Rome, and the group with which prospective converts would likely first become acquainted. Moreover, he came to believe the Jansenists were destined to be the spearhead of a new Gallican Church, which would break with Rome and enter into some kind of close relationship with the Church of England. In his preface to the *Journall*, after describing himself as 'an afflicted Member of a late flourishing Church,' he blessed God for 'these happy beginnings, opening a way we never thought on,' which might produce in time 'an union among us all.'[11] By making the English public aware of the Jansenist controversy, Hammond may well have imagined he would hasten possible ecclesiastical developments. A few years earlier, enquiries of this nature had been directed to the Jansenists by two Anglicans, and the hope of union between the Anglican and Gallican Churches would recur into the eighteenth century.[12]

Since the *Lettres provinciales* play an important part in the course of

Pascal's reputation in England, it is appropriate to examine in some detail the manner in which this work of his was first introduced to an English audience. The contents of the preface Hammond wrote for the first English edition were largely drawn from the *avertissement* written by Nicole; but especially at the beginning and conclusion he proceeded to give Nicole's introduction a decidedly personal touch, and he generally omitted remarks which viewed the Church of Rome with favour. Undoubtedly most English readers would have carried away an impression of the preface as a whole, irrespective of its composite nature; and its outstanding characteristic, as far as this study is concerned, lies in the extent to which it established, at the very outset of Pascal's career in England as a writer and thinker, one of the most durable of the themes which contributed to the appreciation of him in the future – Pascal as the brilliant exposer of the Jesuits and of the evils of Roman Catholicism.

With a sense of dramatic effect, Hammond began in his own words by declining to unmask the character of Jesuitism himself. Some readers might consider the form of satire chosen by the author inadequate for writing about

> ... a sort of people pretending to such a transcendency of holinesse above all others, as not to content themselves with any other name then that of the holy Jesus, degenerated into such Monsters both as to Religion and Morality, as Barbarisme it self cannot parallel. But this is the main design of the whole Treatise, and what it does with such life and conviction, as must needs work a strange alteration in mankind; that is, a body so powerfull as that of the Jesuits, and so scattered over the face of the earth, will be looked on hereafter as the most abominable and most despicable thing in the world.

Instead, 'leaving therefore the Reader to discover what ever may be of horrour, impiety, and extravagance in their Maximes, out of the Letters themselves,' Hammond stated his intention of including only what he thought necessary for the preface: a brief account of the events occasioning the *Provinciales,* a survey of each letter in turn, a few words about their author, and, finally, something about the effect the *Provinciales* had had in France. He justified presenting so much information by a concern for those, who, 'in regard the scene lyes in another Country, being unacquainted with some circumstances, would haply be glad of such satisfaction.'

A description was then given of the proceedings against Arnauld at the Sorbonne which had come to centre upon the doctrine of grace, the subject of the first four letters; the next six letters 'explicate the Morality of the Jesuits, by certain discourses between the Author and a Casuist of theirs.' Hammond explained this form of dialogue had been chosen so that 'the Author does not onely acquaint us with the maximes of the Jesuits, but also with the subtile insinuating wayes whereby [t]hey poison the world therewith'; and from these discussions the resulting conclusion might clearly be drawn:

The main design of their Morality we find to be this; viz. to draw all the world to themselves by accommodation and compliance. To this end are their maximes levelled to the severall humours of men. And because these contrary inclinations oblige them to have contrary opinions, they have been forced to change the true rule of manners, and foyst in another that should be like a nose of wax, subject to any sense, and capable of all formes, a Monster, called The Doctrine of Probability.

After giving an outline of the remaining letters in answer to the defence Père Annat had made for the Jesuits, 'questionlesse the weakest of their productions,' Hammond continued with a brief note on the author. Pascal's pseudonym, Louis de Montalte, had been omitted from the title-page, and, as elsewhere, the *Provinciales* were first presented to the English public in a somewhat anonymous form. The allegorical frontispiece engraved by Robert Vaughan carried a small portrait of a clerical figure – certainly not Pascal – to whom the fictitious name had been given; but some explicit reference to the author must have seemed desirable, and, greatly condensing Nicole's remarks, Hammond tried to describe him in the following words:

Something would be said of the Author, but there's no more known of him then what he hath been pleased to afford us of himself. He hath lately appeared under the name of Louis de Montalte. He hath often declared that he is neither Priest nor Doctor, which the Jesuits would interpret, as if he were no Divine; but how well he is acquainted with true Divinity, there needs no more then his own Letters to prove.

Hammond thus openly shared in the general bafflement about their authorship that attended the first appearance of the *Lettres provinciales*, and to have known only what Nicole was prepared to disclose. He went on to describe the effect the *Provinciales* had had upon religious affairs in France, and brought his preface to a close on an original note that recalled his opening remarks. The case against the Jesuits was complete:

From what hath been said, may be, not impertinently, started this question, viz: What Idea men should conceive of these excellent Jesuits and other Casuists? To which it may be justly answered, That, it being proved against them, that they not onely maintain these extravagant Maximes, but dayly brood such as are yet more horrid and monstrous, they ought to be looked on as the vermine of Religion and humane Society, and consequently accountable for all the inconveniences and mischiefs occasioned thereby.[13]

A glance at what happened subsequently reveals that the appearance of the *Lettres provinciales* in England established their author almost overnight as a valuable protagonist in the drawn-out struggle against Rome and the Jesuits, and whetted the appetite of a wide section of the reading public for more news about the conflict in France. The translation was not good, concealing plenty of the wit and spirit of the original; but it erred, too, on the side of the colloquial, and this no doubt helped create the apparent immediate demand for sequels and further news, which in turn aroused interest in the writings of other prominent defenders of the Jansenists' position. The number of books connected with the Port Royal controversy that were published in English are too many to describe here in detail;[14] but some deserve attention, and the general effect of the majority of these works was, in all likelihood, to enhance through association the fame of Pascal as a supposed witness to Jesuit practices and morality.

In October 1657, Royston printed a volume of *Additionalls to the mistery of Jesuitisme*, 'translated out of French by a person of quality';[15] and in the following year, no doubt pleased by the success of the *Provinciales*, he brought out a second edition, 'corrected; with large Additionals.' Corrections to the text itself were minor, but the manner of presentation was much more forthright. The reader was now confronted by the portraits of five prominent Jesuits — Lessius, Molina, Loyola, Vasquez, and Escobar; and to this visible target, placed immediately before the first letter, was added a scurrilous 'Jesuiticall Creed,' which Royston stated had been sent to him by 'a Worthy Divine, of my acquaintance in the Countrey' on hearing a second edition was planned.[16] Hammond contributed a new preface, rather confidently proclaiming at the outset that victory had been won: 'To presse too much upon a broken Enemy argues in the Conquerour a want of that Generosity, which might justly be expected in him, as a pure consequence of the successe of his arms. The extravagances of the Casuists are come to that height, that there needs nothing of satyre or aggravation to make them more horrid then they are in their own dresse.'

A short account of recent events in the dispute then followed; but, although sounding a triumphant note, Hammond was later at pains to settle certain doubts that had arisen regarding the book's veracity. There had been some, 'who, though such as were no great friends to the Jesuits, thought it not impossible they might be unjustly charg'd,' and they 'could not be guilty of such an excesse of impiety.' He proceeded to advise such waverers how best to repel the arguments being used by the Jesuits in their defence:

For if they quarrell at the Obscurity of the Author of the Letters, and would thence insinuate that his work hath some affinity with a Libell, because he dares not owne it. Tell them it was but a necessary prudence in him to conceale himself, so to elude the mischiefs he might well feare must be the dreadfull effects of their exasperation and revenge. Do they complain that some things are impos'd upon them, others maliciously represented. Tell them, it is more probable, that the Author of the Letters, knowing he had to do with a sort of people eminent for nothing so much as their calumnies, impostures, and evasions, is the more strict and faithfull in the citations of passages.

Moreover, 'an Association of most of the Curez and Pastors of France' had found that propositions in the works of the Casuists agreed 'in all things with what was brought upon the stage by the Author of the Letters'; and this 'can signifie no lesse then a certain authentication of the Letters.' Hammond's conclusion was the same as before. The Jesuits should be looked upon 'as the vermine of all Humane Society, and accordingly as such as ought to be accountable for all the inconveniences and mischiefs occasioned by this so deplorable a degeneration.'[17]

The Additionals, 'Englished By the same Hand,' which followed the text constituted the most striking departure from the previous edition. Mostly consisting of various letters and petitions occasioned by the controversy in France, and of the opinions of recognized theological authorities on the issues concerned, Royston had first thought of restricting them to the papers included in the Cologne edition of the *Provinciales* in 1657. However, two further pieces 'coming so opportunely to hand' seemed so likely to interest the reader that 'I had to file them up.'[18] These were the *Factum pour les curés de Paris* and the *Second écrit des curés de Paris*, both since attributed to Pascal;[19] their importance in strengthening the Jansenists' case had also been noticed by Hammond earlier in the volume. Seeking to add to the exposure of the 'pernicious Maximes' revealed by 'the Authour of the Provinciall Letters,'[20] *A further Discovery of the Mystery of Jesuitisme* also appeared in 1658, presenting a miscellaneous collection of provocative anti-Jesuit writings.

The actual nature and extent of this expanding popularity of the *Provinciales* will be reviewed shortly; but, as Hammond's later remarks have demonstrated, their reputation was not being allowed to increase entirely unchallenged. During and after publication they had been repeatedly attacked by the Jesuits in France, and, in September 1657, were condemned by Pope Alexander VII. Their success in England did not escape the Society's attention either, and eventually, in 1659, English readers were given their first full opportunity to hear the other side when *An Answer to the Provinciall Letters . . . Made by some Fathers of the Society in France* began to arrive from its printers in Paris. Written by two Jesuits, Nouet and Annat, this translation was by Martin Grene (1616-67), an Irish Jesuit, who, after an association with several Jesuit colleges on the Continent, was at the time engaged in the English mission.[21]

Accompanied in this instance by a short history of Jansenism, the *Answer to the Provinciall Letters* was one of the more prominent replies the Jesuits had yet made, and the thoroughness of its arguments demanded some consideration. Our interest here centres on Grene's direct attempt in his preface to challenge those specifically English aspects relating to the appearance of *The Mysterie of Jesvitisme* and its successors. Wishing to blacken indiscriminately both the 'counterfeit Name of Lewis Montalt' and the reputation of his translator, Grene gave to all Englishmen a Jesuit's view of the general circumstances which surrounded the arrival of the *Provinciales* across the Channel:

These infamous Letters then, branded with the ignominy of so many Censures, and banisht [from] all Catholique Countreys, came for their refuge into England. And they found a Translatour, who either for his hatred to the Catholique Church, or private spleen to the Jesuites, or for love of Jansenisme, or for desire of gain, (for nothing sells better then a Libell) set them out in an English dresse: And that they might the better please those ears, which itch to hear something against the Jesuites, he baptized them by a new name of the Mystery of Jesuitisme; it being common to Fugitives that are forced to flye their Countrey, to change their name.

Apparently seeing but one hand in the English edition, Grene ridiculed the remarks in its preface which forecast 'a strange Metamorphosis' would follow in the world through the revelations of the *Provinciales*:

For speaking of his Book he saith, It must needs work a strange alteration in mankinde. *What* Alteration? *This. The Jesuites hitherto by all men held in esteem for Learning and Vertue, (if we believe this Translatours Poeticall Prophesie)* will be looked on hereafter as the most abominable and despicable thing in the world. *Surely this man taketh the Jesuites for an Army of Philistims, which he is to conquer with the Jaw-bone of an Asse.*

The world in general, Grene claimed, held the Jesuits in high esteem, and it was now being asked to reverse its opinion. 'But Why? How? by What Means must this *strange Alteration* be wrought in Mankinde? let's hear':

The reason is, because a French man, whose Letters this Translatour hath done into English, saith so. But who was that French man? A man that by his own confession is no Church-man, no Priest, no Doctour, no Protestant, no Catholique. A man, of whom all the good that's known, is that he can write a Libell well, and challenge others boldly, without ever heeding whether what he saith be true or false, Catholique or Heterodox, sense or non-sense. A man, that's ashamed of nothing, but of himself; for in all his daring Propositions he dareth not say who he is: in all his desperate adventures he will not venture to shew his face.

It was absurd to think such a libellous work coming from such an unprincipled author could change the minds of the wise and reasonable; and, with an excess of confidence equal to Hammond's, Grene went on to declare its effect had been negligible. ''Tis two years since the Book hath been out, and the world hath seen no alteration wrought by this Work: the Jesuites have not lost one Friend by means of it.' The Jesuits did not claim to be impeccable, and some criticism might be allowed; but to describe their general doctrines as 'a monstrous Source of all Irregularities,' and themselves as 'the most abominable and despicable thing in the world,' only invited scorn upon the accuser. In spite of all its efforts, Jansenism had yet to produce a substantial case against its opponents; and, wishing, it seems, to dispel the growing English sympathy for the Jansenists, Grene expanded upon the weaknesses of their position:

All the whole Book of the Provinciall Letters, which casts so much durt on the Jesuits, that the Translatour calls it The Mystery of Jesuitisme, is a false and groundlesse Censure, given by an Heretique to Doctrine, which hath the generall Approbation of Schools. When I say an Heretique, I would not have our Protestants of England think themselves concern'd. I understand the Jansenian Heretique, who dissents as far from the Protestant, as he doth from the Catholique. This then is the aim of these Answers, to shew that the Censures, which the Provinciall Letters lay on the Jesuites Doctrine, are groundlesse Censures, and false Calumnies, and meer Impostures: and so the Translatour hath his Mystery revealed. It is but a Pacquet of lying Letters, which he calleth the Mystery of Jesuitisme; he might better have called it the Misery of Jansenisme. For it is the greatest misery of the world to be reduced to such streits, as that one cannot say any thing, either for himself or against his Adversary, which is not false. Now this is the Jansenists case.

Grene's mounting attack upon those responsible for the English edition reached its climax when he vigorously objected to the final description of the Jesuits in the preface as 'the Vermin of all Humane Society.' He began by hurling the invective back at the author of the *Provinciales*, before letting it rest with its originator:

I do not desire to use foul language; yet if I may use this term of Vermin to any Christian, I conceive it cannot agree with any man so well, as with the Authour of the Provinciall Letters. For who is the Vermin of Mankinde in matter of Faith, but he that denieth, that Christ is the Redeemer of all men; and so openeth a way to desperation, and neglect of Christian duty? This Montalt doth. Who in matter of Learning can be called Vermin, rather then the Writer of Libells against Learning? who is but a Scold in print, and like a Moth, doth but corrode and disgrace learned Books; or like a Fly sucks at others sores; or like a Serpent, extracteth poison, where he might have suck'd honey. This Montalt doth. Who in civill community can be termed Vermin, but the Detractour? This Montalt is evidently proved to be; and so was he judged by the Parliament of Aix. Finally who among all men, noble and ignoble, deserves the name of Vermin, as unfit for any humane Society, either Christian or Heathen, but the Liar? This Montalt is convinced to be. Now if the Authour of the Provinciall Letters deserveth these Titles, his Translatour may judge, what part of these commendations reflects on him. I will not deal him any part; all I say as to him is, that I am sorry to see him mislead, and I wish him hereafter a better employment to practise his pen on, then the translating of condemned Libells.

In a more temperate vein, Grene concluded by requesting the 'Learned Reader' to give a fair hearing to both parties, but to pay special attention to the citations supporting the arguments in the *Answer*; while the unlearned, 'or those that will not take the pains to look into Books of Divinity,' should be ready to credit the strength of such arguments rather than the words of 'an idle Pamphleter.' As for those who could not overcome their deep-rooted hostility to Catholicism, 'I commend them to the Man in the Moon to cure their Phrensie.'[22]

At the end of the volume, Grene made a few further remarks, suggesting that, although it should now be clear that the author of the *Provinciales* 'ought not to be believed in any thing,' the reader should still proceed to examine the Jesuit doctors in their own writings; and, if the following story were typical, there would be no doubt whatever as to who possessed the truth:

It was thus a Lawyer of our Nation not long since did. For having read the Provinciall Letters, he, who knew it was not a legall nor rationall way to judge before both Sides were heard, took some pains to turn to the Authours that were taxed. And he was soon satisfied. For having looked on three or four Citations, and found them all false, he gave no more credit to the Provinciall Letters, but esteemed all of no credit; and cited a Maxime of the Law, That he that is once convinced a Lyar, ought never to be believed. *In this manner I appeal to all the men of England.*[23]

As for the unlearned, applying another legal maxim, that of 'Quis quem accusat? Who accuseth whom?' should give them a sufficient verdict.

Grene also sought at this point to make some reply to the Additionals that had accompanied the second English edition, although he found them himself 'of such a nature, that they need no answer.' In his opinion, the Jesuit creed was 'a very fit Frontispice for so fabulous a Work,' while only 'a Mysterious Fool' would have included a censure of the books of Caramuel, a member of the Order of St. Bernard. It was not hard to imagine the underlying reason:

But I understand, he that printed this Book wanted not onely Grace, (which 'tis evident he did) but (which he was much more sensible of) money; and hoped to gain by the bulk of his Book, and so thrust in every thing to make so many more Sheets. And I suppose he is resolved, so long as this way will yield him money, to trade in Mysteries. We have seen a second part of the Mystery of Jesuitisme; and we are to expect a third, and a fourth, so long as there is hope of gain, the true Source of these Works, and the Mystery of all these Mysteries.[24]

Among other papers selected for brief discussion and ridicule, particular attention was given to the two which Royston had made a late decision to insert. Lastly, Grene announced that several friends had urged him to meet the charges contained in 'another Pamphlet, called, A further Discovery of the Mystery of Jesuitisme.' This was 'so senslesse a Piece, that it deserveth not to be taken notice of'; but, as in the case of the Additionals he had just dismissed, he believed a few critical remarks would make obvious its unworthiness of a full reply.[25]

The possible effect of Grene's translation and remarks upon English Catholics and Catholic sympathizers in danger of being influenced by the *Provinciales* is a question to which we shall return. For all its earnestness, however, the *Answer to the Provinciall Letters* can have accomplished little in checking the general popularity in England of the work it was seeking to suppress. Produced by a small group in exile, it lacked the official support the ecclesiastical authorities were able to give the various Jesuit replies in Catholic countries, and had to contend with English Protestant fervour. Moreover, it could not hope to compete with the English version of

the *Provinciales* in circulation; for not only was the *Answer* printed
abroad, but, as the translator of a later Jesuit defence was to comment, owing to the political unrest in England at the time, 'very few
Copies of it could then be imported to ballance the Influence of that
said Mystery.'[26] Long in argument but short in wit, the *Answer* was no
match for the *Provinciales* despite Grene's efforts at presentation;
and knowledge of the work seems to have been largely confined to
those Englishmen with a serious or professional interest in religious
controversy, who, predictably, would tend to view it with disfavour.

Six years after its second English edition, we are told the *Provinciales* were 'commonly to be had at every Bookseller's shop,'[27] a
success the *Answer* could never have approached. As an extension of
the original French dispute to an English setting, and as an attempt
by the Jesuits to reply to the particular challenge of Hammond and
his associates, Grene's translation is of some importance, and it
stands as a reminder that the popularity of the *Provinciales* in England did not advance unopposed; but, as in the case of the Jesuit
replies in France, its principal significance, in spite of its closely
argued refutations, consists in its being a reluctant admission of the
extent to which its rival had already captured the mind and imagination of the English reading public. To an examination of this popularity we shall now turn.

[II] The extent to which the publication of the *Lettres provinciales* in
English assisted in strengthening the Church of England remains
somewhat speculative. The prospects for the national church suddenly improved with the Restoration, although for several reasons
the Anglican interest in the work was to continue. Moreover, as
Hammond may have sensed before his death in 1660, it became less
likely Jansenism would lead the church in France to a state of
independence and closer ties with the Church of England; for
ecclesiastical hostility and signs of royal disapproval had already
shown the direction in which the fortunes of Port Royal and Jansenism would lie. Once introduced to an English audience, however, ,
the *Provinciales* immediately exerted an appeal that reached beyond
Anglican circles, with the result that the work may be said to have
contributed in a larger sphere to the vigour of English Protestantism
as a whole in this period. Interest in the course of the dispute in
France increased rather than diminished with the accumulation of
Port Royal's troubles; for, during the decade or so following the first
English edition of the *Provinciales*, several works by Arnauld, Nicole,
and others were also translated and published in London, and it was
seldom a year passed without the appearance of at least one book
concerned with some aspect of the Port Royal affair. The majority of

these works chosen to be translated demonstrate the growing support of English Protestant opinion for the Jansenists, and the maintenance of strong anti-Jesuit feeling.

The nature of Pascal's early reputation in England, albeit in somewhat anonymous form, may thus in some important respects be estimated by the success of the *Lettres provinciales* in the context of associated publications. A more accurate conclusion may perhaps be drawn, however, from an enquiry into the available evidence as to who at that time read or possessed a copy of the *Provinciales* or allowed them to influence his thoughts, which in turn enables us to perceive which features of the work aroused the strongest reaction from English readers.

It may be presumed that, in giving the *Provinciales* the sub-title of 'The Mysterie of Jesvitisme,' those responsible for the publication were suggesting that the mind and operations of the Society of Jesus had at last been dramatically laid bare — 'mystery' in this sense meaning the professional secrets of a craft or company.[28] Of the secrets brought to light by the *Provinciales*, the two which seem to have struck the English reader most forcibly were the degree to which the Jesuits were shown to have developed their casuistry, which produced a depraved system of morality far removed from traditional Christian teachings, and their alleged unscrupulousness in achieving their ends, particularly their willingness, if necessary, to commit murder. In both instances the *Provinciales* reinforced fears dating back to the reign of Elizabeth, but the contents were especially suited to the uncertain mood of the times. The defensive outlook of the Church of England, together with the deep-rooted hostility of the Puritans towards Rome, created a heightened awareness of the doctrinal threat embodied in the Jesuits; while the unpredictability of the political scene increased the long-standing belief, real or imagined, in the danger of Catholic plots and subversion.

To Samuel Clarke (1599-1683), curate of a London church and author of *Medulla Theologiae: or The Marrow of Divinity*, the *Provinciales* were an excellent, contemporary exposure of Jesuit doctrines, verifying all earlier suspicions. In his lengthy work which appeared in 1659, concerned with 'Questions and Cases of Conscience, both Speculative and Practical,' he began by explaining why he had undertaken his task:

It hath been long and often complained of, that our English Divines, who of all others are judged the fittest, and ablest to write Cases of Conscience, in regard of their manifold experiences in this kind, have yet done so little. The Friers and Jesuites have written many large Volumes of this Subject, which yet are rather so many dunghills, then so many Gardens of sweet smelling Flowers, and tend rather to the corrup[t]ing of, then to the satisfying of troubled soules, as may be amply seen in a book lately taught to speake English, called the Mystery of Jesuitisme.[29]

In the same year, Richard Baxter (1615-91), like Clarke a leading nonconformist after the Restoration, published *A Key for Catholicks, To open the Jugling of the Jesuits*, and in it frequently made reference to 'the Jansenist Montaltus.' Dedicating his work to Richard Cromwell, he sought to make the Protector more aware of the numerous dangers to be expected from Catholic activity, since 'their doctrine corrupteth almost all Morality.' 'What need we fuller clearer proof,' he asked, 'then the Jansenian hath given us in his Mysterie of Jesuitism? and much more may be added.'[30] The Papists were as ready to murder or depose a ruler as the Jesuit casuists 'cited by the Jansenian' had stated; and 'he that would see more of their mind in this, let him read . . . the Jansenians mysterie of Jesuitism.'[31] Arguing at one point that the Jesuits 'win the Great Ones and multitude by suiting their Doctrine and Worship to the fleshly conceits and inclinations of ungodly men,' Baxter enthusiastically commended the author who had recently exposed their secrets:

Lastly, how the Jesuites have fitted their whole frame of Moral doctrine and Case Divinity to humour the unconscionable, Montaltus the Jansenist will fully shew you through the whole (fore-cited) Mysterie of Jesuitism. Those that would escape any worldly trouble or danger, the Jesuites have a help at hand for, even their doctrine of Equivocation, and Mentall reservation (which makes the Popes Dispensation with oaths and promises needless.) What accommodations they have for him that hath a mind to Murder his adversary, to calumniate another, to take Use without Usury, to forbear restoring ill-gotten goods, to commit fornication, to rob another, and many the like, you may see in their own words cited in the said Book. Yea what comfort they have for a man that loveth not God, so he will not hate him. Trust not my report, but read the Book; for its worth the reading.[32]

Baxter also made extensive use of the *Provinciales* when refuting the Catholic boast of unity in contrast to the divisions of Protestantism; and, in doing so, he showed considerable interest in the Jansenist controversy:

. . . they are many of them greater differences then are with us. I pray read over the Iansenians Mysterie of Jesuitism, and take notice of the differences between the Jesuites and them in Case-Divinity, and judge whether they be small. And let it not offend your ears if I recite some of their Differences in that

Papists own words, as he cites the Jesuites, and tells you where to find what he saith.

Three pages of detailed quotations from the fifth, sixth, and seventh letters then followed, chiefly dealing with the doctrine of probable opinions, its disastrous effect upon morality, and the numerous occasions when murder might be considered allowable, each quotation ending with a statement such as 'but the Jansenists think otherwise.' The whole volume was described as consisting of such passages, and the reader was asked to familiarize himself with it 'and then judge whether Papists or the Reformed Catholicks are more at unity among themselves.'[33] In general, the Jesuits constituted a threat to true religion wherever it was to be found:

Montaltus the Jansenian takes the Jesuites for false unworthy calumniators, for giving out that they have long had a design at Port-Royal to overthrow the Gospel, and set up Infidelity and meer Deism. But I am sure they deserve much harder words of us in England, between them, for doing so much to destroy the Christianity of many, in order to the setting up of Popery. I do not charge it all and only on the Papists. I know the Devil hath more sorts of Instruments then one: But that they have had a notable hand in this Apostasie, we have good reason to satisfie us.[34]

From Baxter's admonitions, we turn to note with some amusement that, in the more relaxed atmosphere of the Restoration, passages from the *Provinciales* could be adapted for the London stage to satirize the Puritan fondness for intricate argument instead. In his comedy *The Cheats*, written in 1662 and presented with repeated success during subsequent years, the royalist lawyer and dramatist John Wilson created the character of Scruple, a nonconformist minister easily persuaded by casuistry and ready to act from hypocritical motives. Following the Commonwealth years such a figure was a natural target for ridicule, and, drawing upon several works of literature for his play, Wilson found in the *Provinciales* particularly appropriate material for certain of Scruple's discourses. Wondering whether to accept a living of three hundred pounds a year at the price of conformity, Scruple was made to reason with himself in a soliloquy which brought together characteristic Jesuit opinions voiced in the *Provinciales:*

... —what Say the Casuists, if a man promisses —and had no intention to ingage himselfe, when he made it, he is not obligd vnless he be bound by oath or Contract for when a man Sayes Simply will doe thus [and] or thus, it shall be conceiued he meant if his mind did not Alter, for to doe otherwise were to depriue him of his liberty, but there is an oath in the case (frind Scruple) there

is an oath – Suppose there be two, – I take it our Brethren are cleare in the
point, Equiuocation (in cases of necessity) may be lawfull, Tis apia fraus, I
am Sure at worst, It is a ƥbable opinion and all ƥbable opinion are equally Safe
in them-Selfes, but are not oaths to be taken according to the meaneing of the
exactor, ƥhaps they are – but Supposs I bring a ƥbable opinion, for the
meaning of the taker, – what then – the extreames are wide – I haue found
an Expedient, (And yet not mine but our Brethrens) the Swearer is not
bound to the meaning of the prescriber, or his owne meaneing, how
then – Sweetly – to the realtie of the thing Sworne, – I thing the haire is
Split – but whoe Shall be Iudge of that, – of that here after – In the
meanetime here is 300£ a yeare, and a goodly house vpon't, – I will con-
forme, reforme, transforme, deforme, any forme – forme – forme – tis but
one Syllable and has no very ill Sound, it may be Swallowed.[35]

Almost word for word from the *Provinciales* were the excuses
given by Scruple elsewhere in favour of gluttony and simony; while
another passage adapting Jesuit arguments regarding abortion
seemed too controversial to the Master of the Revels, and was
marked for extensive revision or deletion.[36] In causing a nonconformist to reason like a Jesuit, Wilson in his play caricatured a
familiar Puritan type by skilfully creating a resemblance to that
which the Puritans abhorred; and perhaps, with the current popularity of the *Provinciales* and associated works, the source of Scruple's
casuistry did not pass unrecognized by at least some in the audience.

A more serious interest in the *Provinciales* is exemplified again by
the appearance in 1669 of *The True Idea of Jansenisme, both Historick
and Dogmatick*, by a Calvinist supporter of Port Royal, Theophilus
Gale (1628-78). This, the first original English work on the controversy, owed its production to 'a sober Curiosity' on the author's
part to inform himself and his friends more adequately. For thirty
years, the Jansenist movement had 'made so great a noise in
Europe,' and now, in all likelihood, it would 'yet prove more
diffusive.'[37] Gale had conversed with the different parties, and
strove to write as an impartial historian according to the best available sources; but, not unexpectedly, his sympathies became quite
evident. In his historical sketch, he mentioned the appearance of
'seventeen Letters to a Provincial, (which in the English Version is
stiled the Mysterie of Jesuitisme) wherein the corrupt notions, principles, and distinctions of the Jesuits, for permitting and allowing
the practice of all manner of sin, are brought to light.' 'These
Letters,' he continued, 'have much galled the Jesuits, especially since
they have been examined and censured by some of the Bishops and
Ecclesiastick Assemblies of France.'[38]

Gale's curiosity was shared by the famous Puritan divine John Owen (1616-83), Dean of Christ Church and Vice-Chancellor of Oxford under Cromwell, who contributed a preface. Chiefly wishing to expose the divisions in Roman Catholicism, Owen regarded the Jansenist controversy as having political as well as religious significance; and, though he believed few could have remained ignorant of the developments in France, he commended Gale's book as being generally helpful for an understanding of the extent and implications of the dispute.[39] Like Gale, Owen appears to have had first-hand knowledge of the *Provinciales*; for, at his death, his library included a copy of the second English edition and of the relatively scarce *Answer to the Provinciall Letters*, as well as other books relating to Jansenism.[40] Further Puritan interest may be shown if the initials 'J.M.' on the title-page of another copy of the same second English edition do indicate, as has been speculated, that the book once belonged to John Milton.[41]

In spite of the work's apparent popularity at this time, it seems the authorship of the *Lettres provinciales* still remained uncertain. In France, Pascal's name had first been attached to them in 1659; but in 1670, the English translator of *The Jesuits Morals*, believed to have been Israel Tonge, who was later notorious for his association with Titus Oates, set down some prefatory remarks to his publication which reveal a degree of confusion. Miss Ruth Clark has suitably described some of the statements that were included:

> *This book was by Perrault and had an introduction by Varet, but the translator whose ideas concerning Arnauld and Pascal were slightly muddled conjectured that the advertisement seemed to be Father Arnold's, the preface and the work itself by 'his Nephew (!) Monsieur Pascal', who was supposed to have written the* Provincial Letters *'not without his Uncle's Privity and assistance: whose head and hand could not be wanting to this work also, if his'. 'The style much differing' – indeed it did! – 'and Lewis Montalt affirming himself to be no Doctor' made the translator suspect 'a third hand to have been made use of in drawing up these Letters.'*[42]

In his belief that Arnauld and Pascal were the 'Head-contrivers' of the *Provinciales*, the translator persisted in ascribing Pascal's authorship to *The Jesuits Morals*, similar passages in his view having appeared earlier in the *Provinciales*.[43] Perplexed though he was, he nevertheless showed some awareness of the real identity of Louis de Montalte to whom the *Provinciales* may still have been sometimes assigned.

The interest evinced by Puritans and nonconformists in the *Provinciales* is partly attributable to the growing awareness of some resemblances between Puritanism and Jansenism. The importance attached by the Jansenists to moral conduct, their independent spirit, and their doctrinal emphases caused many English Protestants to assume some identity with them in spite of the Jansenists' association with Catholicism. Although after 1670 there seems to have been a lessening of direct interest in the controversy – and, in fact, during that period Port Royal enjoyed some respite – the sense of common purpose developed by English Protestants in the face of a mutual enemy continued in strength, and the *Provinciales* remained a valued book. In 1674, a *Fair Warning to take heed of Popery* 'by an Anti-Papist' made reference to it repeatedly;[44] and, in 1676, David Clarkson (1622-86) mentioned the *Provinciales* with *The Jesuits Morals* as works he had taken note of when writing his *Practical Divinity of the Papists Discovered*. Setting out to uncover the true facts about Roman Catholicism, 'how pernicious and inconsistent with the way to Salvation declared in the Scripture,' he readily accepted that 'I have herein the concurrence of some (few in comparison) of that Church, who are sensible of such Doctrine prevailing amongst them.'[45]

During these years, the Anglican interest in the *Lettres provinciales*, which had caused the work to be introduced to English readers in the first place, did not subside but rather continued in less striking fashion. Other divines besides Hammond sought to defend the national church against Catholicism, and after the Restoration their concern was deepened by the new fear that Charles II might follow his brother's conversion to Rome. It is possible Jeremy Taylor, Bishop of Down, best-known for his *Rules and Exercises of Holy Living* and *Holy Dying*, was influenced by the *Provinciales* when he wrote *A Dissuasive from Popery* (1664). A certain resemblance between the two works has been noticed, and Taylor drew attention to some examples of casuistry that had been similarly exposed in the *Provinciales*.[46] Other leading Anglicans, all at some time bishops, who attacked the Jesuits more directly were Henry Compton of London, Edward Stillingfleet of Worcester, and Gilbert Burnet of Salisbury. As will be seen shortly, Compton was directly implicated in the reissuing of the second English edition of the *Provinciales* in 1679, and the libraries of both the other two churchmen show they had some familiarity with the *Provinciales* and related works.[47]

Libraries in fact provide further records of the extent of the Anglican interest. Among those known to have possessed copies of the *Provinciales* are Richard Perrinchief (1623?-73), prebendary of Westminster, and Thomas Plume (1630-1704), archdeacon of Rochester.[48] In 1685, or shortly after, Anthony à Wood acquired a copy of the first English edition of 1657 with a number of books formerly belonging to Andrew Allam, a fellow antiquary at Oxford with a particular interest in church history.[49] Archbishop Leighton of Glasgow was considerably influenced by Jansenism, and the library of Thomas Ken, Bishop of Bath and Wells and later a leading Nonjuror, contained several books relating to Port Royal, among them an English translation of the *Provinciales*. Archbishop Tillotson owned two copies of the second English edition.[50] In Ireland, Archbishop Marsh of Armagh founded a library bearing his name in Dublin from the former collection of Bishop Stillingfleet, and contributed numerous books of his own, among them an English translation of the *Provinciales* which had earlier belonged to Michael Jephson (d. 1694), Dean of St. Patrick's.[51] Such evidence may be neither fully adequate nor representative, but it would appear the *Provinciales* were considered important by men of prominence in the Church of England, and a more extensive search would no doubt further substantiate this impression.

So far it has seemed it was principally those with religious interests, as well as lovers of the sensational, who read the *Provinciales* and other works relating to the Jansenists and their opponents. The conflict, however, was a matter of some concern to those in government, and this resulted in two of the collections of documents relating to the Jansenist controversy, published in England as sequels to the *Provinciales*, being translated by John Evelyn at official request. Although Evelyn did not, as has been sometimes said, make a translation of the *Provinciales* himself,[52] his part in circulating information about the controversy illustrates the seriousness with which men of affairs were viewing the conflict in which Pascal had become a leading figure, and its revelation of the Jesuits' unscrupulous activities.

The first volume for which Evelyn was responsible was a collection of works by Arnauld, Nicole, and miscellaneous writers, which was entitled *To Mystérion tés Anomias: Another Part of the Mystery of Jesuitism or the New Heresie of the Jesuites* — the new heresy in question being the doctrine of the Pope's infallibility, against which Arnauld had recently written in the major piece included. On January 2, 1665, Evelyn recorded in his diary that the book had been published, but without its bearing his name.[53] He chose to remain anonymous, he explained in a letter to Robert Boyle, because 'so little credit there is in these days, in doing any thing for the interest of religion!'[54] Evelyn's library contained a copy of the second English edition of the *Lettres provinciales*,[55] but the nature of the times must have made him reluctant to become actively involved in controversy, and it is curious to note how he came to undertake the translation in the first place. It appears he was commanded to translate the pieces in question by the Lord Chancellor, Clarendon, and his son, Lord Cornbury; and he received his French copy from Sir Robert Moray, a prominent figure in the government of Scotland and, like himself, an active participant in the early meetings of the Royal Society.[56] Nevertheless, Evelyn's strong feelings about the value of his work are revealed in his dedication of the book to Moray, in which he compared the weakness of his talent as translator 'with a Zeal so much the more propense, as I judged the publication might concern the World of those miserably-abus'd Persons who resign themselves to the conduct of these bold Imposters.'[57]

Copies were presented to Clarendon for inspection and given by Evelyn to Sir Henry Herbert and Thomas Barlow, Bishop of Lincoln, as well as to Lord Cornbury. The Bishop, who had received his copy through Dr. John Wilkins, wrote a warm letter of thanks for the labours that had caused the villainies of the Jesuits to be 'now not more a Mystery.'[58] It also received favourable attention at a still higher level as Evelyn recounted with some satisfaction in his diary for January 26, 1665: 'This night being at White hall, his Majestie came to me standing in the Withdrawing roome, & gave me thanks for publishing the Mysterie of Jesuitisme, which he said he had carried 2 days in his pocket, read it, & encouragd me, at which I did not a little wonder; I suppose Sir Robert Morray had given it him.'[59]

Of Charles II's relationship with Port Royal during his years of exile, more will be said later. How serious and lasting this interest had continued to be for him is difficult to tell, although, in his rather insecure position, he would have had every reason to be kept informed of all developments in France and their possible effect upon affairs in England. At any rate, Evelyn was to record in his diary a little over a year later, on March 1, 1666, that he had presented the King with a copy of a second work he had translated at Lord Cornbury's request. This was *The Pernicious Consequences of the New Heresie of the Jesuites against the King and the State*, written by Nicole; and, in the dedicatory preface to Clarendon, Evelyn listed Jesuit crimes against rulers and spoke of the general danger from Catholics to church and government before concluding with sympathy for the Jansenists.[60]

It was in the autumn of 1678 that the varieties of anti-Catholic feeling then existing in England combined and exploded with the supposed discovery of the Popish Plot. Protestant hostility towards Rome, apprehension of the growing power of France, the uncertain religious position of Charles II himself, and the likelihood of a Catholic succession to the throne, all contributed to widespread

Moſes delivers the Law.

EXOD. X X.

I.
Non ha=
=bebis

II.
Nonfacies

III.
Non aſſu=
=mes

IV.
Recordare
diei Sab=
=bathi

V.
Honora

VI.
Non occides

VII.
Non mœ.
chaberis

VIII.
Non fura=
=beris

IX.
Non loquèris
teſtimonium
mendax

X.
Non concu=
piſces do=
mum pro=
ximi tui.

Joh. 1.17. The Law was given by Moſes but Grace and
Truth came by Ieſus Chriſt.
Theſe words the Lord ſpake unto all the Aſſembly in the
mount out of the midſt of the fire with a great voice, &
he wrote them in two Tables of ſtone, &
delivered them unto me. Deut. 5.22.

PLATE 2 Frontispiece from *The Mystery of Jesuitism*
(London, 1679)

fears in the public mind upon which Titus Oates and his associates were able to play with immense success. Numerous publications violently attacking Roman Catholicism appeared, and the time clearly seemed appropriate for a re-issue of the *Lettres provinciales*. In 1679, the second English edition of 1658 was therefore reprinted by Royston, and it now carried the stamp of approval of Henry Compton, Bishop of London.

In all but a few details this production followed its predecessor, but some of its differences have significance. Instead of retaining the title in French as earlier editions had done, the work was presented simply and sensationally as *The Mystery of Jesuitism*. Moreover, in the group portrait of five prominent Jesuits which had adorned Evelyn's first volume of translations as well as the 1658 edition, the figures of Vasquez and Escobar were now described as depicting Garnett and Parsons, the most notorious of the English Jesuits. A quotation in Latin and English from the Lutheran Spalatinus was placed at the head of the engraving: 'Let Kings take notice of this, that the Popes and their followers make it their business, to lessen the Authority of Princes, and to make it as weak and contemptible as they can.' A frontispiece with suitable biblical texts showed Moses bringing down the law from Mount Sinai, in obvious contrast to the Jesuit casuistry exposed in the subsequent pages.[61]

The excitement generated by the alleged discovery of the plot began to die down with the discrediting of many of the rumours and the assumption of firm authority by the King. The fear of a Jesuit conspiracy leading to Catholic control of the country nevertheless remained strong, and was renewed with the accession of James II. The anonymous author of *The Missionarie's Arts Discovered* (1688) made use of both the *Provinciales* and the *Answer to the Provinciall Letters* when he warned of the ways of insinuation and the artifices of the Jesuits, their defence only serving to incriminate them further;[62] and in 1687, when events were becoming increasingly critical, Evelyn rather fearfully wrote: 'Came out now a Proclamation for Universal liberty of Conscience in Scotland and dispensation from all Tests & Lawes to the Contrary; as also capacitating Papists to be chosen into all Offices of Trust: &c. The Mysterie operats.'[63]

The Glorious Revolution, which led to the securing of a Protestant succession and inaugurated a long period of relative stability, was to alleviate such fears; while the eighteenth-century mind on the whole came to prefer other areas of dispute than the differences between branches of the Christian religion. The concern voiced by Evelyn and others, however, by no means vanished completely, and it seems quite likely that, when the next English edition of the *Provinciales* appeared in 1744, less sensational in form it is true, both translator and printer had partly chosen the moment because of the possibility once again of foreign, Catholic intervention, which was to materialize in the rebellion of '45.

[III] One other area of importance regarding the arrival and reception of the *Lettres provinciales* remains to be examined. There is no doubt as to the interest shown by Anglicans and nonconformists; for various reasons, the work was offered an enthusiastic welcome. What, however, was its effect upon the Catholics of Britain and Ireland? Attention has already been drawn to the alarm of the Jesuits that the *Provinciales* would greatly increase English prejudice against them, which led to Grene's translation of the reply by Nouet and Annat; but the Society could no more prevent a lively interest in Jansenist teachings from developing among British and Irish Catholics at home and abroad. For several causes, Jansenism appealed to many of these adherents to the Roman Church, and the *Provinciales* not infrequently played a part in the events and disputations that ensued. The results of an investigation into this area are such that, as well as revealing a distinct episode in the history of the *Provinciales* in England—or rather the British Isles—the details also supplement certain features of the preceding account, and enlarge our view of the whole circumstances in which this aspect of Pascal's early reputation there developed.

From the first days of the Jansenist movement, men from the British Isles are to be seen in close association with it in one form or another. Florence Conry, Archbishop of Tuam (1561-1629), shared similar views to Cornelius Jansen, his colleague at Louvain, on man's fall from grace and the means of redemption; and it was due to the efforts of Saint-Cyran, Port Royal's famous director, that Conry's major work, *Peregrinus Jerichuntinus*, was published in 1641. Its contents seem to have been approved by many other Irish living abroad, as well as being valued at Port Royal. Towards the end of his life, Jansen himself became interested in certain difficulties existing among English Catholics, while another Irishman of his opinion at Louvain was John Sinnich (c. 1603-66). The author first of a parallel study between Augustine's doctrine and that of Jansen, Sinnich travelled to Rome to uphold Jansen's teachings against the papal bull of 1642. Not unnaturally, Pascal shared in the respect for these figures at Port Royal, for, in his *Ecrits sur la grâce*, he consulted Conry's book and made extensive use of *Sanctorum Patrum de Gratia Christi et Libero Arbitrio dimicantium Trias*, one of several later writings that had appeared from Sinnich in defence of the Jansenist position.[64]

Other associations existed on a more personal level. In 1609, when Jacqueline Arnauld was attempting to reform Port Royal, an English Capuchin became director to the convent; a member of the Herbert family, Earls of Pembroke, he acted in this capacity during the following three years, giving helpful assistance. Some forty years later, Dr. John Callaghan (1605-64) found Port Royal a refuge from ecclesiastical politics in Ireland, and the developing sympathy he expressed for Jansenism earned him the hostility of the Jesuits to such an extent that 'Calaganes' became a term of Jesuit abuse against their opponents. In a less conspicuous manner, two Scotswomen were among the lay sisters at Port Royal, while for many years the gardener was an Englishman, Francis Jenkins.[65]

The existence of these connections partly explains the readiness with which Port Royal and its friends offered assistance to royalist exiles from the Civil War, many of whom were sympathetic towards Catholicism if not already Catholics; and a second chapter opened in the relationship. The objects of charity were many, ranging from Queen Henrietta Maria to a group of English Benedictine nuns. Prominent among those befriended were the families of Sir George Hamilton and his brother-in-law, Lord Muskerry; daughters of these two Irish royalists were placed in the care of the nuns at Port Royal, and the hardships of their parents and the other children were also relieved, the young Anthony Hamilton eventually becoming well-known for his *Mémoires de Grammont*. Generous as Port Royal was to all in need, the reasons for its charity are most clearly to be seen in the particular attention it gave to the exiled claimant to the throne himself.

The young Charles II was known to have inclinations towards the Roman Church, and the possibility of a conversion or at least a promise to grant greater freedom to Catholics upon his restoration much aroused Port Royal's interest. Besides wishing to exert a religious influence upon him, the community was prepared to assist him financially, and news of this support and of the apparent sympathy towards Jansenism with which Charles responded became a matter of concern to the government of Cromwell.[66] Charles continued to receive both money and literature after he had been obliged to retire from France in 1654, and it is very likely that, among certain writings that were sent to him, were copies of the *Provinciales* as they appeared.[67] No doubt he appreciated them for their brilliance and wit, as well as for whatever more serious features may then have appealed to him; and, as a result, he would seem to have retained an intelligent man's interest in the later developments of the controversy, as Evelyn's diary bears witness. Charles evidently had no objection to his illegitimate son, the Duke of Monmouth,

briefly attending a Jansenist school, and it is recorded that both he
and his brother, the future James II, believed in the authenticity of
the miracle of the holy thorn when a cure was effected upon Pascal's
niece in March 1656.[68] In an attempt to counteract the Jansenist
influence, early replies to the *Provinciales* were sent by an Irish
Jesuit, Peter Talbot, to Charles' adviser, the Duke of Ormonde; but
in these, as in other matters, it is difficult to read the King's mind
with exactness. Although a certain tendency towards Jansenism may
be detected, his commitment seems to have been partly based upon
expediency and ultimately equivocal.

The discontents of the community of exiles and their joy at the
King's restoration must have lain in Pascal's mind when he wrote of
Cromwell's constant warring and the peace that came to Christen-
dom on the usurper's death.[69] Such an involvement in the affairs of
England was later to place Port Royal's loyalty in question, and
contributed towards arousing the opposition of Louis XIV to the
community. Across the Channel, however, examples of doctrinal
agreement and personal acquaintance formed a background from
which the interest of British and Irish Catholics developed, as awareness of Jansenism and Port Royal was extended and the *Provinciales* came to be read. Grene's translation of the *Answer* of Nouet and
Annat sought quickly to refute the charges against the Jesuits and
check further spreading of the unorthodox Jansenistic teachings;
but, in spite of this and other efforts, a number of Catholics were
clearly persuaded by the Jansenist case. Moreover, although Grene
had begun by dismissing any influence from the *Provinciales* upon
the Jesuits' reputation, he subsequently admitted that the appearance of the work had greatly increased the difficulties of conversion:

*There was not very long since one, who seeing the multiplicity of Religions,
that swarm daily in England, was resolved at length to embrace the Catholique Faith. But unfortunately it happened, that the person, before the day was
come of being Reconciled, light on the Book of the Provinciall Letters; and
having read it, resolved never to become Catholique: and in effect quitted all
former good thoughts, upon this Enthymeme, If the Doctours of the Catholique Church teach such horrid Maximes, what good can I there expect for my
soul?*[70]

British Catholics found the *Lettres provinciales* especially attractive
because several of the arguments against the Jesuits seemed relevant
to their own condition. Like their fellow-countrymen, the Catholics
of Britain and Ireland tended to view foreigners with suspicion, and
the progress of a vigorous offensive against the Society drew the
keen interest of those secular clergy and laity hostile to ultramon-

tane authority, as well as of other orders jealous of Jesuit power. At the time of the Popish Plot, David Morris, a secular priest, was ready to contrast the loyalty of himself and his associates with the Jesuits' avowed beliefs as disclosed by the *Provinciales*.[71] In addition, the exposure in the *Provinciales* of the doctrines of probability and the extension of papal power, and of the whole system of Jesuit morality, agreed with those Catholics wishing to make legitimate protest against prevalent abuses, so that their Church might be placed in a more advantageous light.

Prominent among English Catholics of this nature was the prolific and argumentative Thomas White (1593-1676), one of whose several pseudonyms gave its name to Blackloism, the body of teachings for which he and others were violently condemned. White acknowledged his indebtedness to Jansen and valued the *Provinciales*, protesting against their prohibition. Writing in 1659 to vindicate himself, he praised the work while emphasizing the different spirit of his own:

Though I confess our Nation is easily affected with the modes of France, yet by no means would I have thee mistake [t]his Paper for an English Provincial Letter, such keen-edg'd tools may possibly hereafter come in fashion even among us too, and for my part I shall never blame the sharpness of the knife, if the branch it cuts off be fruitless and the season fit. But here I would have thee expect a milder, yet manly proceeding.[72]

In the same defence, White rejected the charge of causing dissensions in his Church and claimed, supported by his understanding of the *Provinciales*, that he had sought only to clarify the areas of real difference in faith for the benefit of religion in England:

. . . whatsoever falls once under the press, it little imports whether it first see light here, or in any adjacent Catholick Country: Take for proofs the French Provincial Letters; not only vulgarly known, but render'd also into our vulgar tongue; and truly if I mistake not, the publishing such truths is more expedient here then in any part of the world; nothing being more importantly conducible to the reduction of our separatists, then the discarding superfluous controversies, and contesting with them only necessary Doctrines; without engaging for the uncertain and wavering opinions of Doctors of the Faith deliver'd us by Christ and his Apostles.[73]

White and his followers were also accused of recommending the oath of unreserved allegiance to the secular power, a matter of much importance to the Catholic minority. The *Provinciales*, however, had evidently suggested an ingenious solution to this problem to another English Catholic, who, by following the example of some Jesuits, found himself on equally controversial ground, as this reproof administered by Grene attests:

One there is in the World, who beareth the name of a Divine, who assevered that one might take the Oath of Abjuration, though (as he allowed it to be) against his Conscience; and in effect made some take it. His reason was this, The Authour of the Provincial Letters, saith he, telleth us, Let. 5. that the Jesuits in China permit the Christians to commit Idolatry by a subtil invention, viz. that of enjoyning them to hide under their clothes an Image of Jesus Christ, to which they teach them by a mentall reservation to direct those publique Adorations, which they render to the Idol Cachim-Choam, and their Keum-Fucum: *Since therefore that the Jesuits permit Idolatry in China, we may permit (saith this unworthy Divine) the Oath of Abjuration here in England. Did ever man hear such a senslesse discourse? If the Jesuits do permit Idolatry in China, they ought to be punished most severely; but no man ought to inferre, that because the Jesuits commit (as this story would have it) a most hainous crime in China, therefore we may commit as horrid sins here.*[74]

Concern was frequently expressed during the later decades of the seventeenth century regarding the influence of Jansenism among the Catholics of Ireland; and, in France, the Collège des Ecossais was long suspected of training priests with a Jansenist bias. Indeed, it may be presumed that, wherever suspicions of Jansenism in Britain and Ireland were apparently well-founded, an acquaintance and some agreement with the *Provinciales* in all likelihood existed.

As an open Catholic, the interest of James II in Jansenism, deriving from his early years in France, was more explicit than that of his elder brother, and, while briefly king, he offered Antoine Arnauld a refuge in England. He reaffirmed these sympathies during his second exile, and his more orthodox consort, Mary of Modena, was alarmed to discover that their son's tutor, Dr. John Betham, favoured Jansenism and was ready to defend and make a gift of the *Provinciales*.[75] Others at the court of Saint-Germain were intrigued and amused by the work. It was reported in 1697 that the Duke of Berwick was introduced to it by reading the extracts contained in Père Gabriel Daniel's refutation, and, enjoying their wit, asked for the complete letters: 'Il en a communiqué sa bonne opinion aux autres seigneurs et aux mylords qui en ont envoyé chercher diligemment à Paris. A peine nos libraires leur en ont-ils pu fournir assez d'exemplaires et assez tôt à leur gré. Cela est vrai à la lettre.'[76] Even Nicole's Latin notes were translated into French to satisfy the court's curiosity. James, the Old Pretender, seems to have had no Jansenistic leanings in spite of being taught by Dr. Betham, but the interest in Jansenism among the group of Jacobite exiles in France continued until well into the eighteenth century.

Daniel's refutation, which had inadvertently prompted Berwick and others to discover the pleasures of the *Provinciales* themselves, had appeared in France in 1694. The most readable of the Jesuit replies, it was translated into English possibly in the same year by William Darrell (1651-1721), and, as *The Discourses of Cleander and Eudoxus upon the Provincial Letters* by 'a lover of Peace and Concord,' was first published at Cullen in 1701. It must have reached a wider audience when a new edition with the title slightly altered was printed in London in 1704; and, for this, Darrell, an English Jesuit, saw fit to add a lengthy preface of his own composition. The contents of this preface testify to the persistence of an official opposition to the *Provinciales* in England, but are also striking for their account of the lasting popularity of the work among English readers from a Jesuit perspective. As was the case with the *Answer to the Provinciall Letters*, the appearance of the *Discourses* may be said to have constituted an admission that the author of the *Provinciales* remained, in certain respects, a formidable opponent.

Darrell considered some apology necessary when introducing yet another reply to the *Provinciales*, and, in doing so, he granted that their success had been extraordinary:

A New Answer to the Provincial Letters! What? Have not these same Letters stood the shock of the whole Body of the Jesuites for above these forty Years? Have they not passed the Alpes into Italy, the Seas into England, and carried all this while, in all places, the Reputation of a Master-piece, in spight of whatever the Jesuites could say or write against them? And shall any Man, at this time of the day, assume the Confidence to attack them and their Reputation, such Prescription notwithstanding?

The reason for the appearance of this reply, however, lay in its being by the Jesuit, Father Daniel, 'a notable Man, I'll assure you, and a fair Enemy, but not apt to give Quarter.' Daniel had earlier attacked the works of Descartes, and 'the Wounds of that body of Philosophy bleed still'; and Darrell believed this success had led to an assault upon the *Lettres provinciales*. In the translator's opinion, the resulting judgment upon Pascal was generous or condemnatory where appropriate, and most ably formulated and reviewed:

He owns him Master of a great deal of Wit, a neat Expression, a polish'd Style: That Nature, Art, Life and Address, quicken, beautifie, recommend, and enforce his Satyr to admiration. This is to do Pascal Justice. But then again he pretends to observe in him, strains of Insolence against the highest

Powers, of Calumny against known Innocence, and a declar'd eagerness to run down, or turn the Mobb upon, all those who oppose a Faction condemned by the Church. This made P. Daniel proceed to study his Man, strip his Arguments of their fine Dress, search into the Grounds of his Consequences, and the Foundations of his Systems, which he thinks will appear Imaginary, in reference to the Jesuites, and real only as to the retrieving or improving the Credit of his Party. And if this be so, we must be so equitable, as to allow, P. Daniel has done Justice upon Pascal.

Like Pascal, Daniel had chosen to write in the form of a dialogue; and, since apparently the dialogues in the *Provinciales* had been widely regarded as genuine conversation, Darrell hastened to correct this impression when comparing the two books. The *Provinciales* had proceeded entirely from the mind of Pascal himself, no matter what his admirers might say; and Darrell also informs us, incidentally, that Pascal's public in England at this time consisted of women as well as men:

For whereas Monsieur Pascal tells us plainly, that he went to the Convent of the Dominicans, and the College of the Jesuites, call'd for his two good Fathers, discoursed them on such and such Heads of Grace and Morals, enter'd the Replies into his Pocket-Book on the spot; yet the truth is, that there is not a Word of Truth in all this. I am sensible how surprizing this word may be, especially to Ladies; however I am bold to say, that whatever such may have heard, from their refined Teachers, of the sincerity of Monsieur Pascal; whatever they may have observ'd he says himself of his own exactness in reporting, scrupulosity in Circumstances, niceness of Conscience in the whole matter of his Conferences with the Dominican and Jesuite; yet it is true, all this notwithstanding, that he went to neither Convent nor College, d[i]scoursed no such Dominican nor Jesuite, writ nothing in his Pocket-Book from either of their Mouths, nor went out of his Study all the while. Zeal may prompt the Shee-Wits, to cry out Calumny, Calumny on this occasion; and their little witty Masters, who have Pascal at their Fingers ends, will be apt to tell them, this is Vera Crux, and Dellacrux all over: But I must deal frankly with them, and tell them my Voucher, his Name is in the highest veneration with that sett of Zealots; and it is Monsieur Arnaud himself. . . .

I had not taken any notice of this, but that I have found some People, in other things, sharp enough, so injudiciously credulous, as to believe Pascal incapable of such a Practice. You may observe them very earnest against Equivocation, zealous for Truth, breathing nothing but Charity, nothing but the love of God. At the same time wondring how the Jesuites durst broach such Doctrine, oppose Truth, set up the fear of Hell, trample under foot the Love of God. And when you come to ask them, how they come to be so knowing in such

*Matters, they will readily reply, Monsieur Pascal took it from their own
Mouths. Let such People take notice hereafter, that Monsieur Arnaud assures
them, Pascal did no such thing; that it is but banter upon them, and a pretty
trick in their Art of Dialogue.*

Darrell shortly proceeded to sketch the career of the *Provinciales*
in England. It was more than forty years since 'a good Man made no
Conscience of turning Pascal's Letters loose in English'; copies of the
Answer translated by Grene, 'judiciously, solidly, and unanswerably
done,' had been too scarce to check their influence and that of
White's teachings, but, as he saw it, 'after the King's thrice happy
Restauration those Topicks went out of fashion.' The Popish Plot,
however, had revived controversy over the Jesuits, and, to Darrell's
dismay, the *Provinciales* were once more attracting readers while he
was writing – by which time the *Pensées* in English had also appeared:

*Thus things went happily and calmly on, till it enter'd into Doctor Israel
Tong's Head to do more than Pascal or his Translator had done, which was to
turn out of French into English, Pascal's Ware-House, call'd the Jesuites
Morals: I give it that Name, because his Learning was here furnished with
what he Retails to us in his Letters; and his Caution is such, as to conceal P.
Causin's Answer to it, and the Hangman's Hand that burnt it by Authority.
Tong's Edition was backed by Oats's Narrative; that Confirmed by Narra-
tives of all sorts, sizes and shapes, and some good Men thought it a proper time
to give the Jesuites a cast of their Office too at the Oxford Parliament, to whose
Votes you are referred, which were printed by Authority. But as that Parliament, so was this Humour too hot to hold, and I was in hopes it would have
broken out no more. But it was my mistake, and I find it is afloat again, and
Pascal is to be met withal gay and brisk in the Ale and Coffee-Houses, and
nothing wanting to make his Letters as Authentick as Fox's Martyrologe, but
to be chained to the Board's-end. I hope those concern'd in this, are not
actuated by Tong's Spirit. Be that what it will, none now can take it ill, that I
turn P. Daniel into the Ring, and so may he fare, as he deserves.*

Much of Darrell's preface consisted of an analysis of the *Lettres
provinciales* from a theological point of view, seen against the background of events in France. Anxious to discredit Pascal wherever he
could, he drew attention not only to what he considered his lack of
truth and of training in divinity, but also, for good measure, his lack
of memory, generally believed instead to have been prodigious:
'The Instance . . . is, that in the 18th Letter he asserts the Jansenists
ever held the Opinion of the Thomists concerning Grace. Now, poor
Man, he had forgot how he had redicul'd that in his 2d Letter, and

called it Bizarre, and what not.' 'The Gentlemen of Port Royal' had
dissociated themselves from the work, which, they said, relied too
much upon second-hand information, and it had met with condemnation at Rome and in France and the Netherlands; for, 'after the fit
of Laughter was once over, People began to reflect, that if care were
not taken, it might do mischief.' Perhaps it was destined to meet an
unfortunate end, for the letters had been issued over a period that
could be estimated to make them 'an Enfant de treiz mois, and such
are apt to be unlucky ones'; and, with a description of the burning of
the book by the common hangman in Paris, Darrell concluded his
attack.[77]

Although more calculated to attract readers than previous replies,
this presentation by Daniel and Darrell of Pascal's various faults and
errors could not be expected to alter significantly English Protestant
opinion of the *Provinciales*, if at all; and, though the *Discourses*
perhaps fortified some of the English Catholic minority, their effect
would seem to have been limited in those circles as well. About five
years after the appearance of the *Discourses* in London, we hear of a
member of the secular clergy in the north being accused, among
other offences, of expounding the *Lettres provinciales*;[78] and it was
through reading the *Provinciales* that Richard Short, a Catholic
physician in London, was led to open correspondence in 1706 with
Pasquier Quesnel, who had succeeded Arnauld as head of the Jansenist movement. It was one of Quesnel's hopes that Nicole's notes to
the *Provinciales* might also be translated into English; but Short's
interest caused him instead to arrange for the translation of his
mentor's *Réflexions morales* upon the gospels.[79] Such examples of a
continuing sympathy towards Jansenism involving an appreciation
of the *Provinciales* no doubt represent many more.

The Jesuits also turned their attention more spectacularly at this
time to the English College at Douai, which was repeatedly charged
with Jansenism in a violent dispute. The details need not concern us,
but, when by 1715 the Jesuits' major offensive had failed, as far as
England was concerned there was a weakening of the particular
conflict that had featured the translation and publication of the
Provinciales. Some English Catholics might remain favourably disposed towards Jansenism; but the more moderate views developing
in the eighteenth century created a different state of affairs from the
earlier period, when Jansenists and their teachings had been pursued so ceaselessly. Jesuit influence in England began to decline
after the Revolution of 1688, and the effect of the *Provinciales* upon
Catholic opinion as well as Protestant may be regarded as one of the
reasons.

As we survey the entire response given by the English reading public to the *Lettres provinciales* in the years following their arrival, we are led to conclude that the immediate success which attended their appearance in 1657 continued without any notable reverse, and that appreciation resulted more from their anti-Jesuit content that any other factor. Though written for a controversy between groups within Catholicism, the work was exploited by both Anglicans and nonconformists as a cogent argument against the Roman Catholic Church itself and especially the religious and political activities of the Jesuits. The *Provinciales* played an important part in developing an awareness of resemblance between English Protestantism as a whole and the Jansenist movement, and their popularity through various causes existed conspicuously among parties extending from the Puritans to the court of Charles ii; but, as an instrument in hastening closer relations between the Churches of England and France, they had hardly any effect in view of the project's temporary discontinuation.

The problem of Pascal's Catholicism was recognized but never explained with complete satisfaction by his English admirers, and with Hammond we see the first of numerous attempts to conceal or omit aspects of the author and his writings which were considered unsuitably to favour Rome. As sympathy for Jansenism increased, this dilemma was partly resolved by regarding Pascal and his associates, as Gale did, as more serious Papists whose opinions were welcome to Protestants. As far as English Catholics were concerned, the official opposition to the *Provinciales* seems only to have been partly effective, and the work not infrequently assisted in persuasion towards Jansenism. Other aspects of the accumulated hatred for the Jesuits are no doubt more important; but the enthusiastic reception given the *Provinciales* by Protestants and some Catholics in the British Isles was surely one cause of the eventual curtailment of the Society's general activities there, and, on a wider scene, made a small contribution towards its later downfall. A modern Catholic apologist has seen the doctrine of equivocation related in the *Provinciales* as having particularly affected the Jesuits' English reputation.[80]

The literary merit of the *Provinciales* appears to have been noticed far less among English readers than among the French, and it is not until the time of Darrell's preface to *The Discourses of Cleander and Eudoxe* that we hear of a ready appreciation being given to such qualities. During the eighteenth century, the work became a permanent part of the library of foreign classics with which every educated Englishman was likely to be familiar. Their initial success, however, had firmly established the *Provinciales* as part of the national arsenal against Catholicism, and in that capacity also they were to endure; for they continued to be brought into combat until well into the nineteenth century whenever English Protestants believed themselves once more threatened by a resurgence in the power of Rome.[81] Indeed, they have probably still not exhausted their usefulness in this respect among certain extreme groups of opinion.

CHAPTER TWO

The Ingenious Monsieur Pascal

[I] The circumstances surrounding the interest of John Evelyn in the Port Royal affair have shown how early awareness of Pascal in England, deriving largely from the translation of the *Lettres provinciales*, was not confined to men engaged in purely religious controversies but was shared by those occupying positions of authority in the state. Religious and political issues at the time were closely joined, and, though Rome was hated for its doctrines and organizational strength, it was as much feared for the constant menace of foreign interference that any reintroduction of its power implied. It was therefore natural that, whatever the shades of intellectual disposition among them, the majority of the first English readers of the *Provinciales* took notice of Pascal as a writer of whom they could wholeheartedly approve.

Before long, however, the nature of Pascal's reputation in England began to undergo a significant change. Appreciation of him as the brilliant exposer of the Jesuits had been permanently established; but, in the years following his death in 1662, there developed among certain educated men a more complete understanding of his various accomplishments and writings, and of the direction and ultimate quality of his work and thought. Here again, Evelyn provides a useful link between the two concentrations of opinion. Like many of his leading contemporaries, he was a participant in several interlocking circles, each of which was occupied with some particular interest or business. The membership of these circles did not vary greatly; broadly speaking, in each of them certain matters were discussed without excluding the relationship of the men or the issues concerned with the larger world of thought and general affairs. One of these circles with which, it will be remembered, Evelyn and some of his acquaintances were associated, was the Royal Society.

It is well-known that the Royal Society had its beginnings in the periodic meetings of a group of men at Oxford during the years of the Commonwealth. Owing much to the teachings of Bacon and to the impulse to seek refuge from the uncertainties and disruptive passions of the age, these meetings were conceived in some antipathy to the influence of religion, and especially religious controversy, upon the pursuit of knowledge. This spirit was carried forward when many of the group moved to London, and was given more permanent form when the Society received its charter from Charles II. It was in such an atmosphere, which gradually extended from the confines of the Society until it affected most educated men, that the new evaluation of Pascal first occurred. Members of the Society knew the *Provinciales*, and many must have responded to the letters in a manner similar to Evelyn's; their desire to protect the experimental nature of their thought and activities against unsuitable religious interference doubtless added a new feature to their fundamental dislike of Catholicism. The Society as a whole rapidly demonstrated where it considered its true interests lay, and the importance it attached to Pascal's other writings and achievements is in some ways symbolic of its commitment to the new learning.

As news of Pascal's discoveries in mathematics and physics began to reach England, men engaged in such areas of research realized their importance and made his conclusions the basis for further problems and experiments. The early transactions of the Royal Society frequently reveal attention being paid to matters to which Pascal had contributed, and, with few exceptions, English *virtuosi* responded with admiration for him and showed an anxiety to be kept informed of his findings. More central to this particular study, however, is the steady development, by various means, of an acquaintance by men of this circle with the Pascal of the *Pensées*. Although for several years the *Pensées* were available only in French, the reader able to comprehend the originality of the work and the precise method of reasoning employed by the author was likely to recognize in it, for all its unfinished state, a discussion of matters of intellectual and religious belief carried through in a peculiarly congenial and forceful manner. Moreover, the literary style of the *Pensées* possessed great facility of expression, which no doubt increased the work's attraction to a group much concerned with exactness and simplicity in language.

With the first English edition of the *Pensées* still in the future, we shall follow the emergence of Pascal as a reasoning thinker upon religious and moral subjects onto the English scene. It will be shown how John Locke became familiar with this aspect of Pascal during a period of residence in France, with the result that he entered reflections upon certain themes from the *Pensées* in his journal and later included them in expanded form in *An Essay Concerning Human*

Understanding. Copies of the *Pensées* were also making their way across the Channel. It seems very probable that Samuel Pepys was not only among the first English readers but also the private translator of a certain passage giving Pascal's views upon human ability and the reasoning process. A similar interest in the same views and their merits is displayed in the correspondence of Sir William Petty and Sir Robert Southwell. In tracing the initial stages of this most important side to Pascal's reputation, the beginning of a trend may be discerned which would lead to his attaining an influential place in English thought while his vision was suited to the age; and it is not wholly surprising that, when Joseph Walker undertook the first English translation of the *Pensées* which was to appear in 1688, he received assurance that his labours would be 'well accepted.'

[II] In all likelihood, the first Englishman to learn of Pascal's particular gifts in mathematics and physics was Thomas Hobbes. The Pascal family had settled in Paris in 1631, and, to further his son's remarkable talents, Etienne Pascal had introduced him to the *académie libre* of Père Mersenne. Members of this circle gathered weekly to discuss new philosophical and scientific theories with bold curiosity, and it was while visiting Paris during the winter of 1636-37 as tutor to the third Earl of Devonshire that Hobbes first attended their meetings. The precocious boy of thirteen no doubt attracted his attention, and, after Hobbes rejoined the group in 1640 as an exile, he and Pascal would have been informed of each other's successive discoveries. Following Pascal's publication of an account of his experiments on the vacuum, entitled *Expériences nouvelles touchant le vuide* (1647), Hobbes wrote to Mersenne regarding the dispute that had arisen between Pascal and the Jesuit, Noël;[1] while, in 1658, Pascal recalled that Hobbes had produced a mistaken theory with respect to the parabola about fifteen years previously.[2] The evolution of Pascal's thought may have been partly indebted to Hobbes for certain insights relating to the scale of the universe and man's insignificance; and there is a similarity too between their conceptions of society, their fear of anarchy, and respect for authority.[3] Both *De Cive* and *De Corpore Politico* would have been available to Pascal to supplement any recollections of Hobbes' views; but their paths divided, for Pascal came to reject secular conclusions as were offered by the Englishman, whereas Hobbes, increasingly contentious, was to attack Robert Boyle for his acceptance of Pascal's findings on air pressure. We may assume that Hobbes knew of the *Lettres provinciales*, since his Catholic friend Thomas White would surely have referred to them at some stage during their many arguments; and White, who had an interest in mathematics, probably both followed Pascal's work and came to Pascal's attention as the author of a treatise on geometry.[4]

It is odd that Isaac Barrow did not mention Pascal in a letter from Paris in February 1656. Several other figures in French mathematics were named, notably Pascal's colleague, Roberval; and Barrow's sympathy with the Jansenists might have led him to remark upon the *Provinciales,* which began to appear during his stay.[5] It may be, however, that it was not until he presented his competition on the properties of the cycloid – the line traced by a point on the perimeter of a wheel moving in a straight direction upon a plane surface – that Pascal became generally known to English mathematicians. For a brief account of the competition and its aftermath, we may turn to a letter of Henry Oldenburg, written while in France in April 1659:

Icy à Paris on rencontre beaumonde de scavans dans les mathematiques et la belle philosophie. Un certain gentilhomme nommé Pascal ayant propose à tous les mathematiciens des certaines problemes touchant la Cycloide ou Roulette, et demandé une methode demonstrative de mesurer les centres de gravité des solides de la Cycloide, dite Trochoide, et de leur parties, tant autour de la base que autour de l'Axe, et deposé un prix de 60. pistoles entre les mains d'un autre gentilhomme pour l'inventeur (pourveu qu'il en envoyat sa demonstration entre les mois de juin et d'octobre), a gagné le prix luy mesme, personne n'ayant reussy, quoy que plusieurs y ayent pretendu. Cependant un jeun homme Anglois en cherchant la resolution de ces problemes a trouve la proportion entre une ligne courbe et droite, en ce qu'il a demonstré Trochoidem ad summum axem est quadruplam.[6]

The events which the future secretary of the Royal Society reported became famous at the time, principally because of the intense objections of John Wallis, the noted professor of geometry at Oxford, to the final award. Pascal had issued his anonymous challenge to the mathematicians of Europe in June 1658, and copies were sent to Wallis and Christopher Wren by Sir Kenelm Digby, who was close to scientific circles in Paris.[7] Without apparently seeking the prize, Wren, Oldenburg's 'jeun homme Anglois,' had proceeded to make a connected discovery which he communicated to Pascal's agent, Pierre de Carcavy, afterwards receiving a reply from Pascal himself.[8] In his *Histoire de la roulette*, Pascal was to praise Wren highly for his achievement;[9] but in contrast his relationship with Wallis was marked by misunderstanding and bitterness.

Wallis had received his copy of Pascal's challenge on August 10, and, since time was limited, immediately set to work, returning an answer which he considered to be essentially accurate nine days later, the date certified by an Oxford attorney. Protesting the irregular mail, he reserved to himself the right to make corrections, and, on September 3, wrote to Carcavy again informing him of a number of minor errors. This was followed by yet another letter of a similar kind; but, when Carcavy and Roberval met in October to adjudicate the papers received, they decided Wallis' original reply must stand, and that neither he nor the other contestant, the Jesuit Lalouère, were eligible for the prize.[10] This strict interpretation of the terms regarding the arrival of solutions in a completed state reaffirmed the unalterable deadline of October 1, even though, as Pascal had said, the date when solutions were sent was attested by officials in distant towns 'du fond de la Moscovie, de la Tartarie, de la Cochinchine ou du Japon.' Such a decision, however, was construed by Wallis both as a personal affront and as an insult to English mathematicians in general. He had suspected Pascal's authorship of the competition, and, when he published a tract upon the cycloid the following year, he proceeded to list his grievances in detail; he also charged Pascal – 'lupus in fabula' – with plagiarizing the work submitted to him, when the Frenchman had rapidly produced his own solution.[11]

Interest in the controversy spread, and, after Pascal's calculations had appeared in more comprehensive form as the *Lettres de A. Dettonville*, Carcavy sent copies to Wren, Hobbes, and Seth Ward, as well as to Wallis, by way of Christiaan Huygens.[12] To include Hobbes showed some cunning since both he and Wallis were already fierce enemies. In March 1660, Huygens, who seems often to have acted as an intermediary between the parties, reported on Wallis' tract *De Cycloide* to Carcavy, allowing that 'ce Monsieur Wallis tesmoigne certes d'avoir l'esprit prompt et il y a du plaisir a veoir comme il tasche a toute force de maintenir l'honneur de sa nation'; but, in his reply, Carcavy no doubt expressed both Pascal's opinion and his own when he totally rejected Wallis' accusations. The motives imputed to the competition committee were figments of the imagination, while Pascal's own solutions to problems in this area were demonstrably prior to those of other mathematicians in significant details. 'Il faut auoir bien peu de sincerité,' he commented, 'pour faire paroistre aux yeux de tout le monde des bagatelles et des bassesses de cette nature, pour moy Je ne scaurois conceuoir les raisons qu'il ont porté a cela.' Wallis in turn denounced Pascal, Carcavy, and Roberval afresh, and appealed to Lord Brouncker, the Royal Society's first president, as a witness to his claims. He refused to be placated, and ever afterwards bore a violent animosity towards Frenchmen.[13]

Although the conditions under which seventeenth-century mathematicians tried simultaneously to communicate with each other and yet preserve recognition for original proofs naturally fostered ill-feeling, it is hard to exonerate either disputant entirely.

Wallis' passion for argument and his known readiness to appropriate other men's discoveries detract from the merits of his case; and Pascal's conduct in arranging the competition and the manner in which he publicized his own solution are equally open to criticism. Whatever prejudices towards Pascal Wallis may have aroused among English mathematicians at the time, it was nonetheless sure to happen that Pascal's valuable work upon the cycloid and other problems would be rapidly utilized and incorporated into ongoing research. Propositions resolved in the *Lettres de A. Dettonville* became well-known, directly or indirectly, to Barrow, Newton, and the Scotsman, James Gregory; and, in a letter to his fellow-mathematician John Pell, then a guest of Lord Brereton, John Collins wrote: 'My Lord may be pleased to have and keep Dettonville, and the second part of Galilaeus, if they are liked.'[14] Collins has been called the English Mersenne for his zeal in spreading news to others and stimulating them in their enquiries, and when Pascal's *Traité du triangle arithmétique*, developing and applying the theory of binomial coefficients, appeared posthumously in 1665, he soon informed Wallis; a few years later, having given his own copy to Edward Bernard, the Oxford astronomer, he requested Francis Vernon, then secretary to the British ambassador to France, to purchase him a second.[15] The Earl of Essex was responsible for bringing a copy from Paris to Oldenburg.[16] When Collins considered calculations submitted to him to be too similar to those set down in Pascal's *Traité* to bear publication, he would recommend a study of the book for enlightenment. 'I could have wished yourself had been chancellor of [his] performances,' he wrote to Thomas Strode of Somerset, and forthwith lent him an available copy of the work itself.[17]

While in France, Oldenburg may well have seen Pascal's calculating machine, and, in 1665, he wrote to Robert Boyle that Wren had been shown it during a visit to Paris.[18] The high estimation of Pascal held by both Oldenburg and Collins led to their enquiring after any further manuscripts on conics that Pascal might have left;[19] and Vernon offered some encouragement to Collins when he sent a reply in 1672:

That Pascal Conics, which Des Cartes you say mentions as extant, is not so: I have spoken with a bookseller in Paris, M. de Priz, who hath printed all Pascal's other pieces; he tells me, that he hath had the manuscript in his hand, and was once undertaking to print it, when Pascal died; but that effectually it never was printed: and he saith the original is now in Auvergne with his brothers, who, he saith, have thoughts this summer of coming and settling themselves here at Paris, and that then possibly he may get the copy and print it.[20]

Such papers, Collins later wrote to Oldenburg, would afford a 'variety of good new and usefull Speculation';[21] but there must have been practical limits to their interest, for, when writing to a friend two years afterwards about the publishing difficulties in France which condemned work by Pascal and others to obscurity, Collins mentioned, 'they have offered to send over hither, on condition of getting the same printed, but we have refused'—no doubt because, as he said, 'Mathematical learning will not here go off without a dowry.'[22] What remaining manuscripts of this kind by Pascal there were seem to have been fragmentary, and many were subsequently lost; but the degree of persistence with which they were sought by English scientists and mathematicians bears witness to the value attached to any research believed to have come from Pascal's resourceful mind.

During the same years, keen interest was also being aroused by reports of Pascal's physical experiments. In 1646, he had begun research upon the phenomenon described by the Italian, Torricelli, in which a tube of mercury was inverted into a bowl already full of the same substance. The puzzling result was that, although some mercury ran down into the bowl, a column of it remained at a certain height in the tube, posing the question of what the void at the top of the tube consisted. In a notable demonstration carried out under his direction in 1648, Pascal showed that the mercury in a Torricellian tube or barometer was subject to the effect of atmospheric pressure.[23] Within a few years similar enquiries were being conducted at Oxford, and it was then that the details of Pascal's discoveries would have become known to Robert Boyle, who subsequently devoted a considerable part of his energies to investigating air and water pressure and the vacuum. In 1660, Boyle published his *New Experiments Physico-Mechanical, touching The Spring of Air, and its Effects*; and, when discussing air compression, he proceeded to describe and comment upon this, perhaps the best-known, of Pascal's observations in the following manner:

For that noble experimenter, Monsieur Pascal (the son) had the commendable curiosity to cause the Torricellian experiment to be tried at the foot, about the middle, and at the top of that high mountain (in Auvergne, if I mistake not) commonly called Le Puy de Domme; whereby it was found, that the mercury in the tube fell down lower, about three inches, at the top of the mountain, than at the bottom. And a learned man awhile since informed me, that a great Virtuoso, friend to us both, hath, with not unlike success, tried the same experiment in the lower and upper parts of a mountain in the west of England. Of which the reason seems manifestly enough to be this, that upon the tops of high mountains, the air, which bears against the restagnant

*quicksilver, is less pressed by the less ponderous incumbent air; and conse-
quently is not able totally to hinder the descent of so tall and heavy a cylinder of
quicksilver, as at the bottom of such mountains did but maintain an aequilibrium with the incumbent atmosphere.*[24]

Boyle's support of Pascal's findings led to an attack from the more
traditionally minded Francis Line (1595-1675), an English Jesuit,
who believed an invisible membrane prevented the mercury from
rising beyond a certain height in the tube. In *A Defence of the Doctrine
Touching the Spring and Weight of the Air* (1662), Boyle rejected Line's
arguments by proofs from a new experiment he had devised, which
led to the formulation of the law, which bears his name, on the
numerical relation between pressure and volume; and he further
commended the discoveries made at the Puy de Dôme, which had
been recently confirmed by 'that known Virtuoso Mr. J. Ball' at a
mountain in Devonshire, and by 'that ingenious gentleman Mr.
Rich. Townley' in Lancashire. Boyle himself, 'for want of hills high
enough,' had attempted the experiment with a tube filled with water
on the roof of Westminster Abbey, the tube afterwards being low-
ered onto the pavement inside. Research was hindered by accidents
to the equipment, but Boyle considered sufficient evidence had
been gathered to support Pascal's deductions.[25] Another critic was
Hobbes, who believed that 'interspersed particles' regulated the
mercury's height, and that, whereas an experiment of Pascal's had
shown that a lightly inflated bladder would expand when atmospheric pressure diminished, such swelling was explicable by the
'vehement agitation of the ambient air.' Such theories Boyle demonstrably refuted.[26]

Similar work was meanwhile being carried out by Henry Power,
physician and naturalist, who, in 1664, brought his observations
together in his *Experimental Philosophy*. Describing his enquiries into
the properties of mercury, Power had made use of 'an ingenious
Experiment borrowed from the Mechanical Wit of Doctor Pascal' to
show that, in a barometer, 'the deserted part of the Tube, is not filled
up with any Hydrargyral emanations.' The rival hypothesis had, he
believed, been sufficiently disproved by Pascal's account of having
substituted water during his research, first with a forty-six foot pipe
and then with a glass syringe; and he later gave the opinion that the
former test was 'very creditable to those that want Instruments to try
it.' As early as 1653, Power had repeated the experiment of the Puy
de Dôme near his home at Halifax, and noted that the resulting
discovery might be useful for ascertaining the height of mountains,
even 'the height of the Atmosphaere it self.' His willingness to

investigate these matters indeed extended to the most laborious procedures:

We tried the Pascalian-Experiment in a Tin-Tube of 33. *foot long, made of several sheets of Tin, and closely soddered up with Peuter: To the upper end whereof we fastned a long Glass-Tube, open at both ends; then, having soddered up the lower end, we reared the Tube to a Turret at Townley-Hall, and fill'd it with water; then closing the top of the Glass-Pipe, and immersing the other end of the Tin-Tube into a cistern of water a foot deep, we opened the lower end, and perceived the water to fall out of the Glass-Tube into the Tin, but how far we could not tell, onely we conjectured to be about the proportion given by Doctor Pascal; viz. that a Cylinder of water stood in a Tube about* 32. *foot high: but presently our Glass-tube, at the juncture to the Tin, began to leak, and let in Ayr; so we could make no further Process in the Experiment: onely one thing we observed in filling of the Tube, that after the water which we tunnelled in had gone down a pretty way into the Tube, part of it (by the rebounding Ayr) was violently forced up again, and shot out at the upper end of our Glass-tube two or three foot high into the open Ayr: Which Experiment may be a caution to Pump-makers, & all Artificers that deal in Water-works, that they attempt not to draw water higher than* 33. *foot (its Standard-Altitude) lest they lose both their credit, cost, and pains in so unsuccessful a design.*[27]

Both Boyle and Power would seem to have known of Pascal's physical experiments largely through reports or such secondary sources as the writings of Gassendi and Pecquet. In 1663, however, such information was considerably increased by the appearance of the *Traitez de l'équilibre des liqueurs et de la pesanteur de la masse de l'air*, the most systematic account of Pascal's various scientific observations, brought together and published as such for the first time by his brother-in-law, Florin Perier. Perier, in fact, appended to his edition a summary of the contents of Boyle's *New Experiments Physico-Mechanical*, to show their relationship to Pascal's discoveries and 'pour confirmer encore davantage le principe qu'on y a estably de la pesanteur de la masse de l'Air.'[28] Huygens arranged to send a copy to Sir Robert Moray, but, in a letter of thanks on its arrival, Moray told him that 'nous auons fait la pluspart des experiences dont il parle.'[29] This was a reference particularly to the activity of Boyle, who, 'upon perusal of Monsieur Pascal's small French book, which was put into my hands,' had undertaken at the Royal Society's command to determine the validity of its author's demonstrations. In his characteristic manner, Boyle tried to perform the experiments described therein himself, and presented his findings to the

Society in May 1664, two years later publishing them under the title of *Hydrostatical Paradoxes, made out by New Experiments, For the most part Physical and Easy.*

Much as Boyle might admire Pascal, his devotion to scientific truth caused *Hydrostatical Paradoxes* to consist mostly of corrections to Pascal's work derived from personal investigation. He noted that the 'small French book' was composed of two separate treatises, and, in his opinion, the second of these, on atmospheric pressure, dealt with an area of research which had been already satisfactorily examined. He had recently communicated the news of Pascal's invention of a pair of bellows without vent for measuring such pressure. The former section, however, which Boyle described as 'The Treatise of the Aequilibrium of Liquors,' set down conclusions which seemed essentially without fault, but which appeared to be partly deduced from experiments which, to him, were questionable. He early summarized his reasons why, 'notwithstanding that I like most of Monsieur Pascal's assertions,' he declined to follow his methods of proving them:

First, Because though the experiments he mentions be delivered in such a manner, as is usual in mentioning matters of fact; yet I remember not, that he expresly says, that he actually tried them, and therefore he might possibly have set them down, as things, that must *happen, upon a just confidence, that he was not mistaken in his ratiocinations. And of the reasonableness of this doubt of mine, I shall ere long have occasion to give an instance.*

Secondly, Whether or no Monsieur Pascal ever made these experiments himself, he does not seem to have been very desirous, that others should make them after him. For he supposes the phaenomena he builds upon to be produced fifteen or twenty foot under water. And one of them requires, that a man should sit there with the end of a tube leaning upon his thigh; but he neither teaches us, how a man shall be enabled to continue under water, nor how in a great cistern full of water, twenty foot deep, the experimenter shall be able to discern the alterations, that happen to mercury, and other bodies at the bottom.

And thirdly, These experiments require not only tubes twenty foot long, and a great vessel of, at least, as many feet in depth, which will not in this country be easily procured; but they require brass cylinders, or plugs, made with an exactness, that, though easily supposed by a mathematician, will scarce be found obtainable from a tradesman. [30]

It is generally conceded, in support of Boyle's suspicion, that certain of Pascal's experiments remained purely hypothetical, and that their inclusion was merely an attempt to fortify arguments resting upon a selection of demonstrable proofs. A distinction be-

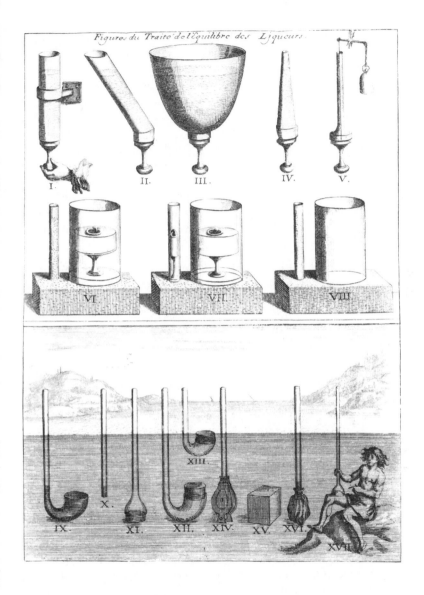

Figures du Traité de l'équilibre des Liqueurs.

PLATE 3 'Figures du traité de l'équilibre des liqueurs,' from Pascal's *Traitez de l'équilibre des liqueurs et de la pesanteur de la masse de l'air* (Paris, 1664). Figure XVII portrays one of the experiments principally questioned by Robert Boyle in *Hydrostatical Paradoxes*.

tween actual and imagined experiments was never clearly drawn, however, and Power's experience with a thirty-three foot tube must have been typical of several efforts to repeat procedures described by Pascal which called for unusually large and exact apparatus. To Boyle, such methods seemed 'more ingenious than practicable,' and he applied himself to discovering 'a far more expeditious way to make out, not only most of the conclusions, wherein we agree, but others, that he mentions not.' He related the improvements he had made in the conduct of a number of experiments, invariably in the direction of simplification and greater efficiency;[31] and, although he thus contributed to a greater understanding and some further development of Pascal's discoveries, he did not hesitate to refute anything which, from his own observation, he found to be untrue. For instance:

The ingenious Monsieur Pascal would persuade his readers, that if into a glass vessel, with luke-warm water in it, you cast a fly; and, by a rammer, forcibly press that water, you shall not be able to kill, or hurt the fly. Which, says he, will live as well, and walk up and down as lively, in lukewarm water, as in the air. But, upon trial with a strong fly, the animal was (as we expected) presently drowned, and so made moveless, by the lukewarm water.

Boyle therefore substituted another experiment, which was not only more likely to succeed, but enabled him to measure the force to which 'the included animal' had been exposed. Tadpoles were used instead of a fly, and it was found that these creatures easily survived the equivalent weight of three hundred feet of water upon them, since the water's pressure was exerted equally in all directions; and, from this, he concluded a diver should be able to operate at such a depth unharmed.[32]

'Experiments, that are but speculatively true,' Boyle wrote, 'should be proposed as such, and may oftentimes fail in practice.' Moreover, they were liable to bring the new philosophy into disrepute, for, if any research were founded upon an almost impossible experiment, Boyle feared that 'most men would rather reject the experiment as a chimerical thing, than receive for its sake a doctrine that appears to them very extravagant.'[33] Although Boyle himself was sometimes ready to accept other men's findings without such a rigorous check, the comparative insistence upon accuracy and straightforward intelligibility which he exhibited in *Hydrostatical Paradoxes* had the effect of rendering Pascal's work more useful to English scientists, while advocating recognition of the many important discoveries Pascal had undoubtedly made. The progress of research increasingly advanced or qualified the conclusions Pascal had reached, but his achievements in physics continued to be regarded as having lasting value;[34] and it may be claimed that, though some of his investigations remained open to improvement, Pascal played a significant part in familiarizing Englishmen with certain fundamental aspects of scientific procedure. In fact, the mathematician and astronomer John Keill, lecturing upon experimental philosophy at Oxford at the beginning of the next century, singled out Torricelli and Pascal for having carried forward the practice of the scientific method in the years between Galileo's discoveries and the founding of the societies of London and Paris.[35]

Boyle retained his interest in these areas of Pascal's research, for among a collection of papers awaiting publication at his death in 1691 was an account of an experiment similar to that of the Puy de Dôme carried out at Salisbury cathedral in 1684, and also an extract from the *Traitez*.[36] Indeed, given the nature of Boyle's own experiments and his general character, it cannot have seemed inappropriate to contemporaries for his name and Pascal's to have been linked together during his lifetime. The writings of most English scientists and mathematicians of this period are one in showing respect for Pascal's many abilities, national considerations notwithstanding; and Lord Brouncker certainly voiced an opinion widespread among the *virtuosi* when he commented upon a mechanical device which Pascal had left in a preliminary state, 'I canot doubt but that Monsr Pascal would [have] brought it to perfection.'[37]

[III] The association of John Locke with the Royal Society, first on an unofficial and later on an official basis, lasted through almost the whole of his adult life; but, although on terms of close friendship with a number of leading members, notably Boyle and Lord Ashley, his interest in the Society's affairs was somewhat spasmodic and never of a very active kind. It is clear, nonetheless, that Locke's development as a thinker was very greatly influenced by his intimacy with that group of men in England who shared a devotion to the new learning; and it was this circle of opinion that forever shaped the broad lines of his intellectual growth and provided him with the background against which his enquiries were pursued. Between 1675 and 1679, however, he travelled extensively in France, and this experience also proved highly formative in that it enlarged and refined many of his ideas upon subjects of a philosophical nature through the familiarity he gained with contemporary French thinking. One of the French writers to whom he was most attracted was Pascal, whose *Pensées* had appeared publicly for the first time in 1670 in the so-called Port Royal edition; and a study of Locke's reading in

France throws light upon the circumstances in which this more complete view of Pascal became permanently known to him, and provides a leading illustration of how an Englishman with his interests and predisposition might grow into an appreciation of the *Pensées* from an earlier knowledge of the Pascal of Jansenism and scientific experiment.

It was apparently for reasons of health that Locke left England for Montpellier in France in November 1675, although it is possible that Ashley, by then Earl of Shaftesbury, thoughtfully sent him abroad to avoid suspicion during the secret negotiations between the Whigs and the French. One of his notebooks reveals some knowledge of Pascal's discoveries in physics before he travelled to France; and he could hardly have remained ignorant of the fame of the *Lettres provinciales*, especially since he was to display a marked aversion to the Jesuits. A brief visit to Paris in the autumn of 1672 may well have given him a greater awareness of French intellectual activity; but there is little doubt that it was during his second, three-and-a-half year stay in France, and particularly while he was living at Montpellier, that Locke first read widely among the leading French writers of the time, covering practically all fields but the purely literary. Throughout this stay he kept a journal which is our principal source for tracing the development of his interest in Pascal, perhaps shown most clearly and simply in the records he left of his reading and his purchases.

On March 24, 1677, Locke noted in his journal that he had left certain books with his companion, George Walls, among them 'Sur les Panses de Pascal' – the *Discours sur les Pensées de M. Pascal* by Jean Filleau de la Chaise, which had been published in 1672. It is practically certain, though, that Locke had also read or come to know of the *Pensées* themselves by then, for in entries dated July 1676, and February 1677, he appears to borrow some striking phrases from that work, about which more will be said later. At any rate, when, in April 1677, he was recording a list of 'things sent home' from Bordeaux, he included the 'Pensées de Pascal.' Between June 1677, and May 1679, he was mainly in Paris, and it was probably there that he purchased a copy of the *Lettres provinciales* and another of the *Pensées*, both of which he noted on June 30, 1678, as having been packed away in certain numbered boxes. Finally, in early July 1678, he jotted down that he had purchased a copy of the *Discours* by Filleau de la Chaise, which seems to have been sent with some other books to England by way of Dieppe the following year.[38]

The lists Locke subsequently compiled of the contents of his library in England disclose that these books became lasting features of his collection, and provide us with further details concerning them. His library included two copies of the *Pensées* (Lyon, 1675, and Paris, 1678), one of the *Lettres provinciales* (Cologne, 1669), and one of the *Discours* by Filleau de la Chaise (Paris, 1672), all of which would likely be the purchases he recorded while in France; and, towards the end of his life, he also possessed the *Suite des Caractères de Théophraste et des Pensées de Pascal* by Pierre Jacques Brillon (Amsterdam, 1698). Less inclined towards mathematics, Locke owned the *Traité du triangle arithmétique,* perhaps at the instigation of Nicolas Thoynard; and, in 1693, the Earl of Pembroke recommended to him Pascal's writings on geometry as the 'best booke to begin with' in attempting to understand the Newtonian system. For some reason, Locke's copy of the *Provinciales* bore, like a few of his other books, an obscure sign at the end of the text suggesting it may have been singled out for special attention at some time.[39]

The reference to Thoynard may serve to mention that Locke not only became more familiar with Pascal's writings while in France, but also developed an acquaintance with the circles in which Pascal had moved. While in Paris he formed a close association with Thoynard, a noted linguist and scientist, and remained in frequent correspondence with him afterwards. Thoynard himself had learned mathematics from Roberval, and carried out experiments on atmospheric pressure in the cathedral at Orléans with Pascal's nephew, Etienne Perier; and, when the two friends exchanged models of calculating machines, he pointed out to Locke the degree to which Perier had perfected his uncle's original invention.[40] When news of Perier's death reached Locke in 1680, he expressed his regret to Thoynard and described Perier as 'ex sanguine Pascalis desideratissimi, cujus ego memoriam veneror.'[41] In April 1679, Locke in Paris conversed with François Bernier, the famous traveller and a disciple of Gassendi, upon Pascal's physical discoveries, and, in his journal at that time, he briefly described the mathematician Le Pailleur as 'mentiond in the preface of Mr. Pascal's Hydrostaticks.'[42] Locke's interest also extended in the direction of Port Royal. He had known of Nicole as early as his notebook of 1664 – 66, and purchased several leading works by both Nicole and Arnauld during his second visit to France. His habits of thought were assisted by the *Logique de Port-Royal*; and, also while in France, he translated three of Nicole's *Essais de morale*, which, having decided to leave in manuscript, he dedicated to the Countess of Shaftesbury. One of these, seeking to prove the existence of God, seems particularly to have remained in Locke's mind.[43] It is indeed probable that certain arguments of Pascal's that Locke found in the *Pensées* may equally have been trasmitted to him by way of Nicole.

The same journal which allows us to follow the growth of Locke's knowledge of Pascal also provides us with an opportunity to perceive the early effects of Pascal's thought upon Locke's intellectual development. Professor Gabriel Bonno, to whose study I am indebted at this point, has shown that, while Locke was in France, his ideas concerning man's ability to reason and his capacity for knowledge received an important stimulus from reading the *Essais* of Montaigne, the *Pensées* of Pascal, the *Caractères* of La Bruyère, and the *Maximes* of La Rochefoucauld; and the *Pensées* may certainly be considered to have had as great an influence upon Locke's thinking as any other one of these works. The exact date when Locke read the *Pensées* is not clear, but Bonno has drawn attention to what he believes to be striking analogies to themes in the *Pensées* which began to appear in occasional passages in the journal as early as July 1676; and he has further shown how two of such themes especially were later given more developed expression in a style more Locke's own in the *Essay Concerning Human Understanding*.[44]

Locke's journal consists mostly of the record he kept of his travels in France, but here and there are certain entries where he set down his expanding thoughts on several subjects; and, taken together, these passages may be seen as, in effect, an early draft of the *Essay*. On July 29, 1676, Locke wrote in this manner some brief reflections upon the problems of belief in God and the immortality of the soul, which supply the first indication that he may have already become acquainted with the *Pensées*. In an attempt to establish the grounds for belief he gave two justifications, and both of these show he had already been struck by Pascal's famous argument of the wager.

Locke began by writing:

I shall only adde that if perhaps the proofs . . . author which I thinke are very clear and cogent are not yet perfect demonstrations and that after all there will remain some doubts and difficultys unresolvd, it is not reasonable for any one to reject the doctrine of a deity, and the immortality of the soule, because he can raise some objections against it, till he hath established some other hypothesis upon surer foundations made out by clearer evidence and deduction of reason, and wherein there are not to be found any such difficultys as he pretends frights him from the imbraceing of this. If he doth otherwise tis to be suspected that there is some secret and strong bias that inclines him the other way, and it must needs be some great irregularity that must force a man against his reason, which always follows the more probable side, and makes him in the great concernment of religion and happynesse take a course quite contrary and proceed by other measures then he doth in all his other perswasions and the ordinary affairs of his life. [45]

From a marginal note, the author referred to may be identified as Nicole; but the argument corresponds exactly to the position taken by Pascal in two passages of the *Pensées* concerning certainty and free-thinking.[46] Locke's second argument to justify his views is, however, even more convincing an example of Pascal's influence than the first. At greater length, he proceeded to discuss the manner in which a thoughtful man would choose against the standpoint of an atheist, even though the atheist might perhaps seem more likely to be right; for, if there is any chance of eternal happiness, it must surely be preferable to perpetual unconsciousness, which the atheist claims is more probable, or to the unending misery which awaits the atheist if his opinions happen to be false. Comparing this entry in Locke's journal with its counterpart in the *Pensées*, Bonno has stated his strong belief that Locke was writing under the influence of Pascal's wager; for, though the essential argument is traditional, Locke's very expressions recall the language of the gambling table Pascal had used to catch the imagination of his free-thinking friends. 'Pesons le gain et la perte,' Pascal had set down, 'en prenant choix que Dieu est. Estimons ces deux cas: si vous gagnez, vous gagnez tout; si vous perdez, vous ne perdez rien. Gagnez donc qu'il est sans hésiter.' Locke in turn wrote that when 'annihilation or which is noething better eternall Insensibility'–the best an atheist can hope for if he is right–is 'put in the ballance with everlasting happynesse,' it would 'make a man very wary how he imbraces an opinion where there is such unequall ods and where the consequences are of such moment and soe infinitely different.'[47]

The argument of the wager obviously retained its appeal to Locke, for, when the *Essay* appeared in 1690, the following remarks amplified the earlier passage in his journal and expressed its ideas more clearly:

The rewards and punishments of another life, which the Almighty has established, as the enforcements of his law, are of weight enough to determine the choice, against whatever pleasure or pain this life can show, when the eternal state is considered but in its bare possibility, which nobody can make any doubt of. He that will allow exquisite and endless happiness to be but the possible consequence of a good life here, and the contrary state the possible reward of a bad one, must own himself to judge very much amiss if he does not conclude, –That a virtuous life, with the certain expectation of everlasting bliss, which may come, is to be preferred to a vicious one, with the fear of that dreadful state of misery, which it is very possible may overtake the guilty; or, at best, the terrible uncertain hope of annihilation. This is evidently so, though the virtuous life here had nothing but pain, and the vicious continual pleasure: which yet is, for the most part, quite otherwise, and wicked men have not much the odds to brag of, even in their present possession; nay, all things rightly considered, have, I think, even the worse part here. But when infinite happiness is put into one scale, against infinite misery in the other; if the worst that comes to the pious man, if he mistakes, be the best that the wicked man can attain to, if he be in the right, who can without madness run the venture? Who in his wits would choose to come within a possibility of infinite misery; which if ⋅ he miss, there is yet nothing to be got by that hazard? Whereas, on the other side, the sober man ventures nothing against infinite happiness to be got, if his expectation comes not to pass. If the good man be in the right, he is eternally happy; if he mistakes, he is not miserable, he feels nothing. On the other side, if the wicked man be in the right, he is not happy; if he mistakes, he is infinitely miserable. Must it not be a most manifest wrong judgement that does not presently see to which side, in this case, the preference is to be given?[48]

The second principal theme which Locke drew from Pascal was that of the insignificance of man in the universe. On February 8, 1677, over thirty pages in his journal were devoted to a number of reflections upon the limits of human reason; and here also Locke made use of two arguments which had surely been taken from the *Pensées*:

Our mindes are not made as large as truth nor suited to the whole extent of things amongst those that come within its ken it meets with a great many too big for its graspe, and there are not a few that it is faine to give up as incomprehensible. It findes it self lost in the vast extent of space, and the least particle of matter puzzles it with an inconceivable divisibility. . . .
For what need have we to complaine of our ignorance in the more generall and forain parts of nature when all our businesse lies at hand why should we bemoane our want of knowledg in the particular apartments of the universe when our portion lies only here in this little spot of earth, where we and all our concernments are shut up.[49]

Bonno has again noted the manner in which Locke's thoughts clearly allude to the earlier expressions of Pascal. The vivid and concise language departs from his usual style of writing in the journal; and his description of the world as something very small, a place of captivity, seems to echo Pascal's reflections on man's cosmic unimportance.[50] His treatment, too, of the distance between the two infinities—the 'vast extent of space' and the 'least particle of matter'—is reminiscent of Pascal's handling of the same subject. Turning once more to the *Essay*, we find these sentences have likewise been expanded and elaborated, but their 'accents pascaliens' remain unmistakable:

When we consider the vast distance of the known and visible parts of the world, and the reasons we have to think that what lies within our ken is but a small part of the universe, we shall then discover a huge abyss of ignorance. What are the particular fabrics of the great masses of matter which make up the whole stupendous frame of corporeal beings; how far they are extended; what is their motion, and how continued or communicated; and what influence they have one upon another, are contemplations that at first glimpse our thoughts lose themselves in. If we narrow our contemplations and confine our thoughts to this little canton—I mean this system of our sun, and the grosser masses of matter that visibly move about it, What several sorts of vegetables, animals, and intellectual corporeal beings, infinitely different from those of our little spot of earth, may there be in the other planets, to the knowledge of which, even of their outward figures and parts, we can no way attain whilst we are confined to this earth; there being no natural means, either by sensation or reflection, to convey their certain ideas into our minds? They are out of the reach of those inlets of all our knowledge: and what sorts of furniture and inhabitants those mansions contain in them we cannot so much as guess, much less have clear and distinct ideas of them.[51]

Bonno has pointed out a particularly striking proof here of the closeness with which Locke followed Pascal. It is difficult to believe the use of the same word 'canton' by the two authors is only a coincidence, for in the special sense of a corner or a minute piece of territory the term in English is extremely rare. Locke's phrase, in fact, is the only representative of this particular usage given in the *Oxford English Dictionary*.[52] Other passages in the *Essay* imply that Pascal's influence may have affected other areas of Locke's thinking, such as when he declined to investigate the idea of a perfect being as a proof of the existence of God, and when he remarked upon the inability of the human mind to come to a true knowledge of the substance of things—for, since everything is inter-related, only a general knowledge is possible.[53] Perhaps, when Locke wrote '[the understanding's] searches after truth are a sort of hawking and hunting, wherein the very pursuit makes a great part of the pleasure,' he was recalling a thought of Pascal's;[54] and his apology for the *Essay's* length – 'to confess the truth, I am now too lazy, or too busy, to make it shorter' – may be the first English expression of a phrase popularized by the *Provinciales* which many after him found attractive.[55] Lastly, both in the *Essay* and when he stated his personal attitudes elsewhere, Locke no less resembled Pascal in acknowledging that, in matters of religion, revelation understood through faith might supplement and complete a belief acquired through reason.[56]

In addition to these examples which, by direct or suggestive similarity, reveal Locke's indebtedness to the *Pensées*, there appeared also in the second edition of the *Essay* (1694) an interesting reference to Pascal of a biographical nature. Into a chapter upon the powers and defects of the memory Locke inserted the following story he had heard about the famous Frenchman, which served to illustrate both human abilities and limitations. The account of Pascal's life by his sister, Mme. Perier, widely circulated as a preface to the *Pensées* after 1684, had stated that Pascal had never forgotten anything he wished to remember; but, if he did not confuse this report, it is possible Locke had at some time read Nicole's eulogy of Pascal and was recalling the claims for Pascal's ability of total recollection made there:

There is another defect which we may conceive to be in the memory of man in general; — compared with some superior created intellectual beings, which in this faculty may so far excel man, that they may have constantly *in view the whole scene of all their former actions, wherein no one of the thoughts they have ever had may slip out of their sight. The omniscience of God, who knows all things, past, present, and to come, and to whom the thoughts of men's hearts always lie open, may satisfy us of the possibility of this. For who can doubt but God may communicate to those glorious spirits, his immediate attendants, any of his perfections; in what proportions he pleases, as far as created finite beings can be capable? It is reported of that prodigy of parts, Monsieur Pascal, that till the decay of his health had impaired his memory, he forgot nothing of what he had done, read, or thought, in any part of his rational age. This is a privilege so little known to most men, that it seems almost incredible to those who, after the ordinary way, measure all others by themselves; but yet, when considered, may help us to enlarge our thoughts towards greater perfections of it, in superior ranks of spirits. For this of Monsieur Pascal was still with the narrowness that human minds are confined to here, — of having great variety of ideas only by succession, not all at once. Whereas the several degrees of angels may probably have larger views; and some of them be endowed with capacities able to retain together, and constantly set before them, as in one picture, all their past knowledge at once. This, we may conceive, would be no small advantage to the knowledge of a thinking man, — if all his past thoughts and reasonings could be* always *present to him. And therefore we may suppose it one of those ways, wherein the knowledge of separate spirits may exceedingly surpass ours.*[57]

It would be a mistake to place too great an emphasis upon Locke's experiences in France, since there is an essential continuity about his intellectual development and the *Essay* drew upon his reflections under various circumstances over several decades. Nevertheless, his discovery of the Pascal of the *Pensées* among the leading French writers of the day was an important one—important for its effect upon the enquiries Locke was pursuing himself, and important with regard to the manner in which this aspect of Pascal came to be introduced to the English reading public.

As Bonno has said of the resemblance between passages in the *Pensées* and their counterparts in the journal, 'ces analogies ne semblent pas fortuites'; and clearly, while Locke was in France, he was influenced by the *Pensées* not merely to the extent of being impressed by Pascal's argument of the wager and his description of the insignificance of man, but also in being led to approximate his own style and method of thinking to that characterized by those sections of the *Pensées*. Locke was, of course, receptive to many currents of new opinion, but much of the *Essay* may further be claimed to bear some resemblance to the general thought of Pascal, both in what it discusses and in what it declines to pursue; and it would seem to have been chiefly with respect to Locke's orderly mind, proceeding by way of definitions, that Voltaire later described him as 'le Pascal des Anglais.'[58]

The impact of Locke's *Essay* upon English intellectual life was profound, and it was certainly one of the most widely read and acknowledged works during the following century. The generation after Locke's had ready access to both the *Essay* and the *Pensées*, and it forms a tribute to each of the two authors that Francis Atterbury, later Bishop of Rochester, chose to crown an argument he was presenting by linking their names and their words together. In 1706, Atterbury had preached a masterly sermon at the funeral at St. Paul's of Thomas Bennet, the London bookseller; but he afterwards felt obliged to answer certain charges of novelty of doctrine with regard to the connections he had drawn between morals and belief in the soul's immortality. In his defence, he proceeded to support his opinions by reference to numerous authors, ancient and modern, English and foreign, all 'commonly to be met with'; but he eventually preferred to let his case rest with two figures in high contemporary repute:

Need I urge any further Authorities? perhaps the Names of Mr. Locke, and Mons. Paschal, may be of greater weight with some Men than most of those I have mentioned; and therefore a few Lines, taken from either of their Writings, shall close these Citations.

Locke's Hum. Underst. Book xi [sic]. Ch. 21. Sect. 35. 1. Ed. If Men in this Life only have hope, if in this Life only they can enjoy, 'tis not strange, nor unreasonable, they should seek their Happiness, by avoiding all things that displease them here, and by preferring all that delight them; wherein it will be no wonder to find Variety and Difference; for if there be no Prospect beyond the Grave, the Inference is certainly right, Let us eat and drink, *let us enjoy what we delight in,* for to-morrow we die.

Paschal, according to his way, hath rather hinted, than fully expressed the same thought. However, those who are acquainted with his manner of writing, will easily learn his opinion from what follows: 'Tis certain that either the Soul is mortal, or immortal. And the Rules of Morality will be entirely different according to the one, or the other of these Suppositions. Nevertheless the Philosophers treat of Morals without any regard to this Distinction. What a Degree of Blindness was this? All our Actions, and all our Thoughts ought to be conducted after so different a manner, according as there is, or is not an eternal Happiness to be hoped for, that it is impossible wisely to take a single Step in Life, without regulating it by this View—'tis our great Interest, and our chief Duty, to satisfy ourselves on this Head, upon which our whole Conduct depends.[59]

Such identification with Locke no doubt served to increase the standing of Pascal with some of Atterbury's readers, and Locke also perhaps gained by the association in certain quarters. In light of its recognized importance, the *Essay*, with its affinity to certain features of the *Pensées*, must also at an earlier date have assisted in preparing English readers for the *Pensées* themselves when they began to appear in translation. The argument of the wager and the theme of man's insignificance seem to have become well-known to educated men at about this time, in some measure owing to their growing familiarity with the thought of the *Pensées* in French or English, but reinforced, no doubt, by Locke's presentation of them in his *Essay*. Moreover, it seems that the extraordinary memory of Pascal soon became one of the few facts about the Frenchman that were general knowledge; and, although Mme. Perier's life of Pascal, translated into English, told this and other tales of interest, the spreading of this particular information about him must have been assisted by the reference in the *Essay*. Locke's discovery of the *Pensées* thus had an effect that was far greater than merely personal. His stay in France made him aware within contemporary limitations of the complete Pascal, but also played an important part in bringing certain features of the Pascal of the *Pensées* towards acceptance by an English audience.

[IV] It is, perhaps, a little surprising that the *Pensées* were not published in an English version until eighteen years after they had appeared with success in France; but English interest in Port Royal was not as consistently active during that time as previously, and the work could hardly be seen as yet another supplement to the *Lettres provinciales*. The *Pensées* lent themselves neither to current religious polemics nor to the furtherance of ecclesiastical policies as the *Provinciales* had done, and they did not specifically make a contribution to science. As a result, appreciation in England of this aspect of Pascal's achievements was very restricted at first, and the *Pensées* only enjoyed some reputation among those who were in touch with French thought or otherwise involved in the intellectual currents of their age.

Locke had discovered the *Pensées* while in France, but there are several examples of the book making its way to England during the years immediately following its publication in 1670. Possibly the first copy to arrive was that sent to Sir Joseph Williamson, a Fellow of the Royal Society and at one time Secretary of State, who, as one of the founders of the *London Gazette*, had standing arrangements to be kept informed of news and new publications in France. Francis Vernon, who also assisted John Collins from his position at the embassy in Paris, dispatched the *Pensées* to Williamson in January 1671, in the hands of the Earl of Northumberland's steward, and commented in an accompanying letter: 'Monsieur Pascal's booke about religion wch is only a designe of a great work he intended to finish upon that subject, butt because of the Eminency of the author they have published it imperfect as it is and all ye court, Madame Montespan, Valiere, the King, Marechal Turenne all buy it, there are 500 sould since St Stephen's day and Desprez is going to print another edition.'[60]

In his diary for February 1675, the scientist Robert Hooke recorded purchasing the 'Pensées de Paschall' from the Royal Society's printer at the price of two shillings. He returned it ten days later, perhaps because he was unprepared for its character; but, at his death in 1703, his library contained a copy of the *Pensées* published at Rouen in 1675.[61] On Barrow's death in 1677, Newton compiled a catalogue of his books, in which both the *Pensées* and the *Lettres provinciales* were listed; it may well be that Newton glanced through them.[62] Other men knew the *Pensées* by way of their religious interests; it was among the works relating to Jansenism in the library of Archbishop Leighton, and Bishops Stillingfleet and Burnet owned copies published in Paris in 1671 and 1684 respectively.[63]

It is appealing to imagine that Sir Thomas Browne read the *Pensées* before his death in 1682. There is evidence to suggest he did, for, when the combined library of Browne and his son was sold, copies of the *Pensées* (1670) and the *Discours* by Filleau de la Chaise (1672) were among the several books of French literature and philosophy.[64] Though not a member of the Royal Society, Browne was well-informed of new scientific experiments, and those described by Henry Power in *Experimental Philosophy* caused him to revise his own *Pseudodoxia Epidemica*. Browne's most productive years as a writer were past when the *Pensées* first appeared, but his many similarities to Pascal have inevitably provoked comparison. In a transitional age, both men found science absorbing and attempted to define its relationship to Christian belief in prose which, for different reasons, has been much admired. The scope of Browne's vision of man and his world resembled that of Pascal, and both men took pleasure in seeking to extract meaning from what was symbolic or obscure. Browne, however, never abandoned his scientific interests as Pascal seems progressively to have done, and, though placing the greatest importance on certain matters of the spirit, resisted the mystical and ascetic tendencies which came to characterize Pascal at Port Royal. Lacking both Pascal's powers of logical thought and his fears of death, he might hold to the concept of a God known ultimately through faith, but was not alarmed by the 'Battle of Lepanto' between faith and reason being continually fought in his mind without a conclusive outcome. Like many Englishmen of his generation, the discoveries of science for Browne served to illuminate the designs of the deity instead of creating a demand for the redefinition of belief. As a book with a European reputation, *Religio Medici* may have been known to Pascal; but its intention, in contrast to the *Pensées*, was not to encourage free-thinkers towards acquiring Christian convictions, but rather to represent a religious mood in which man, 'that great and true Amphibium,' might satisfactorily pursue his various interests.[65]

One section of the *Pensées* at least, that part of the thirty-first chapter of the Port Royal edition concerning the difference between 'l'esprit de géométrie' and 'l'esprit de finesse,' came to be studied closely by certain prominent members of the Royal Society, and it is probable that these included Samuel Pepys. Pepys did not mention Pascal in his diary, but his library contained many French books, either in the original language or in translation, and among them were the *Lettres provinciales* in the Cologne edition of 1669. It is not known if he ever possessed a copy of the *Pensées*, but, among his miscellaneous papers dating mostly from 1684 or 1685, were left some handwritten pages entitled 'A Chapter touching the Diversity of Wit. A translation. Mr. Paschall's Thoughts. 31 Chapter.'

Unfortunately, it does not seem possible to attribute this fragment of translation to Pepys with complete certainty. The handwriting and other features of the manuscript indicate that the contents were probably dictated to a clerk, as were a number of similar documents left by Pepys; but, as Ladborough has said in his brief study, 'that the fragment from the *Pensées* was actually translated by him, it is impossible to determine, tempting though it is to say so. All we can assert is that it is not unlikely.' This opinion that Pepys might well have been the translator is based principally upon the intelligence and style of the translation; moreover, the passage chosen to be translated dealt with a subject that would especially have attracted him—the difference between two sorts of mental ability which reasoned from either very few or a great number of principles, or, in the words of the fragment itself, 'between a witt adapted for geometry and a witt disposed unto Reaches and Sagacitye.' Pepys also moved in circles becoming familiar with the Pascal of the *Pensées*; besides, his wife was French, and he himself was proficient in the language.

In all likelihood, these few pages also have the distinction of being the first recorded translation of any part of the *Pensées* into English; and the first English translation of the entire *Pensées*, which was to appear in 1688, contains sufficient individuality in this passage to rule out any conjecture that Pepys may have obtained an intended part of that book. Although the available facts serve to indicate that the *Pensées* were known to Pepys and that he considered certain of Pascal's reflections as important enough to turn into English, the mere existence of such a translation before the work came to be widely available is a sign of the steady growth in England of interest in Pascal as a thinker.[66]

The same section called forth a hearty correspondence at this time between Sir William Petty, the statistician, and his friend and cousin by marriage, Sir Robert Southwell, both men being members of the Royal Society and Southwell later its president. It appears the exchange originated with Southwell, for, on September 8, 1685, Petty wrote: 'I thank you for Mons' Paschall's Thoughts. The Author and the Subject invited me to read them over and over, but I except against most of his expressions, so as I could not draw any clear noĉon or science out of it.'

Southwell, in reply, hastened to inform him that Pascal's views had proved acceptable to at least one of their fellow-members: 'As to Mr. Paschall's paper, I will sett Sir John Louther uppon you, who admires it. If there be noe foundation of Truth in his position, then all the fine Stroakes upon the diversity of Witts are quite besydes the marke; but because Sir John Louther is not a single man that is deluded with this fancy, I wish you would generally bestowe one halfe sheete to undeceive Them.'

This aroused a spirited rejoinder from Petty: "As to Mons' Paschall's paper, let it alone till you come to Towne and then I will roast Sir John Lowther and your self both upon one Spitt.'[67] However, on September 21, he set down his objections for Southwell at some length, and, since they were specifically concerned with that part of the thirty-first chapter, this must, in fact, have constituted the 'paper' that Southwell had sent. In his argument, as summarized by Petty elsewhere, Pascal had attempted to distinguish between the two methods of reasoning, their characteristics being 'a witt strong in a narrow compass,' and 'a witt much extended but of little force.' Although recognizing the value of the former, Petty, as a man of the world, saw advantages in the latter's ability 'with a single glance of the eye to survey all business at once';[68] and, writing to Southwell, he criticized the propositions of Pascal, 'whose name I honour,' for lack of clarity, affirming too that a combination of both methods of reasoning might produce better results than either applied exclusively. Petty sought to test his opinion by examples from among the ancients – Archimedes, Aristotle, Hippocrates, Homer, Julius Caesar, Cicero, Varro, and Tacitus – and the moderns – Molière, Suarez, Galileo, Sir Thomas More, Bacon, Donne, Hobbes, and Descartes; and, from these, he deduced that 'the good parts of men' consisted of:

(1) *Good Sences,*
(2) *Tenacious memory of figures, colors, sounds, names &c,*
(3) *A quickness in finding out, matching and compareing, as alsoe in adding and substracting the* sensata *layd up in the memory,*
(4) *A good method of thinking,*
(5) *The true use of words,*
(6) *Good organs of speech and voice,*
(7) *Strength, Agility, and Health of Body and of all its parts.*

Out of these 'Ingredients,' resembling the colours on an artist's palette, Petty claimed he could make 'an Archimedes, an Homer, a Julius Caesar, a Cicero, a chess-player, a musitian, a Painter, a dancer of the Ropes, a couragious Spark, a fighting fool, a Metaphysicall Swarez &c'; and he ended by stating his disbelief in how, according to Pascal's strict definitions, 'all the above mentioned species of Transcendentall Men can be produced.'[69]

Perhaps some memory of the *Provinciales* prompted Petty to include the Jesuit Suarez in this assorted company. Apparently before receiving these remarks, Southwell had lightly ridiculed Petty's announcement that he and Lowther would meet their fate at his hands together, 'and this for believing too easily the most celebrated and mathematical Thinker of France.' A few days later, however, he admitted he was much in agreement with Petty's criticisms:

But I must take notice and thankfully acknowledge what you sett forth on Mr Paschall's Thoughts. I am convinced that his Path is narrow and incompe-

tent. That he lays down for a Generall Definition of Witt, That which in Truth is but a fine description of two particular Characters; and I confesse alsoe that he makes those things opposite which are promiscuous. For when I think of Judge Hale, Sir W.P., and a few others, I see how Geometry and sagacity consist, and how unnaturall it is to divide them. Soe that he did rather consider Severall of his friends, some that were wholly plunged in Mathematicks without meddling with the World, Others that were all World, Sagacity, and noe Mathematicks; and thereupon pronounced them as Jew and Samaritan, and that they were each of them incapable of mixing in the Business of the other.

Noe, Cozin, your Painter's Pallet is a more generous offspring of Colours and Ingredients to build up Heros of every sort. The various fountains you assigne afford all that is necessary, and I am even charm'd with considering how I am buoy'd up aloft from the Errour I was in.[70]

The mutual curiosity of Southwell and Petty towards these views of Pascal partly arose from their anxiety over the education of their sons, a matter on which they were frequently consulting each other. As Southwell wrote, 'the subjects of this Nature doe the more excite and entertaine me because of carving (as it is your Phrase) a figure uppon our Neddy.' Petty had considered Pascal too narrow and theoretical a guide for developing the men of parts he and Southwell both wished their sons to be; but, wondering whether he had been too idealistic himself, he humorously commented that 'in consequence of what I said to Monsr Paschall's paper, you would have mee do by deare Neddye's head as my Lady Duches of Ormond did to the round tower in Kilkenny'—in other words, change all but the most basic structure. The young Edward Southwell had, nonetheless, begun to experience the effects of Petty's analysis, for his father next wrote: ' . . . after your further enlargements of Monsr Paschall's materials of Ability, I have done my best to drive in those 7 spikes into our young man's Scull which you have already Assigned, and am convincd those 7 Ingredients made up the 7 wise men of Greece.'[71] Other topics intervened, but, in the following year, Petty was to recall his estimation of 'the great Pascall' when giving Southwell his ideas upon 'the faculty of Imitacon,' also 'mimicks and Ridicule.'[72]

The emphasis placed upon this single, relatively inconspicuous section from the *Pensées*, drawn from the final chapter composed of Pascal's miscellaneous thoughts, suggests it may have circulated separately in some form among a group of acquaintances in the Royal Society, or at least have been marked within the book as being especially noteworthy. We might hazard to say that the translated fragment found among Pepys' papers existed in more than one copy, and that it was one of these which within a short time came to be known to Southwell, Lowther, and probably others, as well as being summarized and commented upon by Petty. If so, it is intriguing to speculate how and with whom the interest within the Society might have originated.

Once attention had been directed towards these particular propositions of Pascal, it is not difficult to see why they should have been recognized as broadly pertinent. During the Society's early years, much importance was attached to evaluating those mental habits and characteristics that made a man best fitted for the pursuit of the new learning; and Pascal's reflections describing features of the deductive method compared to other kinds of reasoning would have been considered relevant to a number of discussions. In seeking to ascertain the true nature of the physical world, the English *virtuosi* were aware of the extent to which they should rely upon an approach of objectivity, supported by experimentation; and, by and large, Pascal's own record made him an acceptable mentor in their efforts. At the same time, they were cultivated men who had not forgotten that worthwhile knowledge might also be reached through broad experience, and who were willing to believe that the most admirable, 'Transcendentall' type of man should hold several aptitudes in harmony. Pascal's discussion of the rival merits of 'l'esprit de géométrie' and 'l'esprit de finesse' demonstrated that he, too, had been conscious of the benefits and deficiencies of the 'witt adapted for geometry,' and, although his definitions might seem arguable, they were still generally provocative. His distinction as a mathematician and physicist conferred an authority upon his opinions among others desirous of attaining a scientific mind; but, whereas it might have been shown that, in his physical experiments, Pascal had occasionally deduced too much, his sometimes wide-ranging approach to science, grounded upon the empirical method of analysis, would later commend itself in the examination of religious truths when the remainder of the *Pensées* came to be more widely known.

On the eve of the appearance of Joseph Walker's translation of the *Pensées*, one is struck by the unique nature of Pascal's reputation in England at this stage. In future years, his work as either a religious polemicist, a scientist and mathematician, or a moralist and thinker might receive special prominence; but, during the late seventeenth century, equal importance was accorded to the entire range of his achievements, which were also seen as vitally inter-connected. In the libraries of such members of the Royal Society as John Ray, Sir Kenelm Digby and Robert Hooke, *The Mystery of Jesuitisme* in one or other of its forms lay on the shelves with books of science and, in Hooke's case, the *Pensées*;[73] and perhaps more markedly indicative is a letter from Oldenburg to Boyle in 1664, which announced the arrival of a packet of books containing both Nicole's *Les pernicieuses conséquences de la nouvelle hérésie des jésuites* (soon to be translated by Evelyn) and an attempted refutation of Pascal's discoveries of atmospheric pressure.[74] Catholicism, Jansenism, scientific experimentation, and happenings in France were all concerns of the day which evoked from active, intelligent men a response or reaction; and the contributions of Pascal to all these areas of interest during these early years had a freshness and a relevance which later periods were able neither to retrieve nor duplicate in such an invigorating totality. Among Pascal's major available writings, the *Pensées* would seem to have been perhaps the least known until their publication in English in 1688. Intellectual unrest, however, had been causing opinion to incline in the direction of his manner of religious enquiry, and, after the selective appreciation given to the work by a few men for special reasons, there began for the *Pensées* a period of relative ascendancy over the other accomplishments of their author.

CHAPTER THREE

The Greatest Genius
on the Greatest Subject

[I] No study of Pascal can proceed far without of necessity contrasting and evaluating the several versions of the *Pensées*. An appraisal of the text of the Port Royal edition will shortly make plain that the *Pensées*, as read by Englishmen of the eighteenth century, differed substantially from those versions which modern scholarship has made available. Most of the problems that have caused this confusion are rooted in the work's unusual origins, which, from the very beginning, have provided ground for discussion. After Pascal's death, a great number of notes were found among his possessions, written on scraps of paper that had been pinned together and tied in bundles. Much of this material dated from 1657 and 1658, when he had considered writing a work of Christian apologetics in an effort to convert his sceptical friends; but, under the impression that these notes consisted of a collection of random thoughts, arranged in no particular order, an informal committee representing Pascal's family, his friend the Duc de Roannez, and certain members of Port Royal was established to prepare these literary remains for publication. In 1670, this committee produced a somewhat non-controversial selection from the notes and gave them the title of *Pensées de M. Pascal sur la religion et sur quelques autres sujets*; and, becoming known as the *Edition de Port-Royal*, this selection, with slight variations, constituted the *Pensées* as they were known to the world for over one hundred years.

The volume aroused much interest and was reprinted several times; but, compared to the *Lettres provinciales*, knowledge of the *Pensées* remained largely confined to France and Holland and spread only slowly among readers elsewhere. The first translation, into Dutch, was published in 1686, appealing to an audience with both Jansenist and Huguenot sympathies that had already become acquainted with editions in French printed in Amsterdam. A new chapter in the history of Pascal's reputation in England, however, begins with the appearance two years later of the first English translation. Entitled *Monsieur Pascall's Thoughts, Meditations, and Prayers, Touching Matters Moral and Divine, As they were found in his Papers after his Death*, the work was 'done into English' by Joseph Walker. Presented to the public in the same volume were three shorter works, also translated by Walker, each of which bore some relation to the *Pensées*— a *Discourse upon Monsieur Pascall's Thoughts*, 'wherein is shewn what was his Design,' another *On the Proofs of the Truth of the Books of Moses*, and a treatise 'wherein is made appear that there are Demonstrations of a different Nature, but as certain as those of Geometry, and that such may be given of the Christian Religion,' all by Filleau de la Chaise.[1] The venture had been undertaken by Jacob Tonson, a rising figure in the London printing and publishing profession; and the inclusion of Mme. Perier's life of Pascal with the supplements implies that Walker made his translation from one of the similar French editions published since 1684.

Walker himself is something of an enigma, and the few attempts to determine his identity have not met with much success; but, since he has some degree of importance in the story of the *Pensées* in England, it may be worth trying to trace him as far as possible. It is plain that, over a period of about twelve years, he earned part of his livelihood, at any rate, by translating the works of French authors, of which Pascal's *Pensées* appears to have been the last. He is also known to have produced *An Answer To the Bishop of Condom's Book* in 1676, a reply by the Huguenot Marc Antoine de la Bastide to Bossuet's *Exposition de l'église catholique sur les matières de controverse*:[2] *News for the Curious; A Treatise of Telescopes* (a miscellany from several authors), and *The History of the Eucharist*, a lengthy work by another Huguenot, Matthieu de Larroque, both in 1684:[3] and, in 1685, *Caesarion, or Historical, Political, and Moral Discourses*, an entertainment 'very Pleasant and Useful for all Orders of Men whatsoever' by César Vischard de Saint Réal.[4] The variety and quality of these efforts make it likely that, whatever his previous career, Walker had become a hack writer, taking work where he could find it.

Until further evidence is forthcoming, it would seem that all else discoverable about Walker is provided by the dedicatory epistles and other incidental details contained in these works, in which he consistently strove to present himself in a favourable light. What emerges with some clarity is that he was a man of staunch Protestant, no doubt Anglican, convictions, and that, though probably English, had a certain familiarity or associations with Ireland. From his epistle preceding the *Pensées*, we learn that he lived at one time in a sea port from which the crossing to the south of Ireland could be made;[5] and his *Answer To the Bishop of Condom's Book* was largely designed for the Irish reader. Published in Dublin and dedicated to its archbishop, Walker spoke in it of 'how blind Tradition and custome in matters of Religion, have inthralled the minds of most of the Natives of Ireland'; and, since this had caused them to be 'the more unfit in all respects for the service of their Prince,' he had been moved 'to expose the following Treatise unto publick view in that Kingdom.' He recalled Bishop Jewel's success in the previous century against the 'Roman Champions,' which had revealed again 'the excellent nature of Truth';[6] but, in *The History of the Eucharist*, he defined his religious sympathies still more emphatically. He condemned the persecution of French Protestants during recent years, and charged Arnauld and others with being 'Ambodexters of the times,' who, in their 'polite and disguised Writings . . . in vain rack their Invention to please two Masters at once, halting betwixt God and Baal, their Duty and Obedience unto their King, and Allegiance to the Bishop of Rome.' He expressed the hope that 'the sinister Councils of a Plotting Jesuitical Faction will not always prevail, to the Ruine of so many faithful good Subjects, and of so flourishing a Kingdom.'[7]

Such sentiments were linked in spirit to those which greeted the *Lettres provinciales* in England, but Walker had apparently picked up elements of a broader education, demonstrated both by the nature of the works he translated and by his references in the *Pensées* to George Herbert, John Donne, and the first Earl of Manchester—which further suggest an Anglican loyalty;[8] however, the standard of his translation shows he had no conspicuous literary accomplishments himself, and that his knowledge of French might fail at times to achieve a desirable fluency. The Archbishop of Dublin must nonetheless have thought well of *An Answer To the Bishop of Condom's Book*, for, eight years later, Walker wrote that it was through his liberality that he was now dedicating *The History of the Eucharist* to Sir Hugh Wyndham, a judge who, under the Commonwealth, had spoken with some vehemence against clergy who restricted those taking that sacrament.[9] One introduction apparently led to another, since in *Caesarion*, dedicated to Sir Edward Wyndham, Walker thanked 'the Antient, Loyal, and Flourishing Familys of the Wyndhams & Hungerfords in general' and Sir Edward in particular for granting many favours to him.[10] Gratitude for favours was also the motive for dedicating *News for the Curious* to Sir William Portman, a member of the Royal Society and a staunch Tory;[11] and, as both Portman and Sir Hugh Wyndham were prominent men of affairs in Somerset, we may conjecture the sea port of Walker's sometime residence was possibly Bristol.

The dedication Walker wrote to Sir John Hewet, which introduced the two discourses and treatise accompanying the *Pensées*, is particularly informative. Hewet, the third baronet, had succeeded his father in 1684, and the royalist family had evidently treated Walker with some partiality, for which he owned 'great Obligations':

It is not yet twice Seven years since my Honour'd Friend, your good Father, of his own Inclination, was the Instrumental Cause of settling me in a Publick Imployment in His Majesties Service, where amongst many other Pleasures and Benefits I enjoy'd, I design'd to Translate the History of the Eucharist into English, and in order thereunto, I had writ and perfected near one Fourth part of it. But that Work and Subject was of too great Weight and Purity to be handled by a Publican, therefore God (who sees not as Man sees) was pleas'd to call me from the Receipt of Custom.

It thus seems likely that, in about 1675, Walker had been appointed a customs collector through the intervention of Hewet's father, but that he resigned or was dismissed a few years later. Although he might explain this as the working of a divine plan, he must have lost a large measure of security, and, for whatever reason he had selected *The History of the Eucharist* to translate beforehand, its commercial aspects must then have seemed of greatest importance. Having lost the part he had already completed, 'I was struck with such a damp, that I had Thoughts of wholly quitting my Design'; but, in the belief that 'God was not pleas'd any part of the Old Materials should serve in the Building . . . I set my self a work *De novo*, and with Gods Blessing and Assistance, accomplish'd my desire.'

Many of Walker's other thoughts dwelt on the subjects of death and eternity, and clearly indicate that, by the time he translated the *Pensées*, he believed he was nearing the end of his life. 'I have liv'd a good while in the World,' he wrote, 'and have concern'd my self but with few Persons, nor Businesses, nor do I much desire it; I desire as Dr. Donn did, to swim like a Fish, quietly to my Long Home.' As a token of thanks for the favours he had received from both Hewet and his father at their Huntingdonshire seat and in Cambridge and London, he wished to dedicate this 'Detachment from Monsieur Pascall's Book' to his protector, 'being assured Sir John Hewet and his Friends in and about Cambridge, &c. know very well how to Exercise and Improve it to the best advantage.' Walker concluded with a remark, arising, perhaps, from his recent interest in astronomy, that a 'Concurrence of certain Planets' he had just observed promised good fortune in the coming year to 'some Illustrious Families.'[12]

Possibly Hewet already knew of the writings of Pascal from

friends at Cambridge, but it is more likely that Walker was only trying to make what he called a 'slender Retaliation' for kindnesses received. A closer relationship is visible, however, between the translation of the *Pensées* themselves and the dedication preceding, the epistle providing us with our most intriguing knowledge of Walker; for it is addressed to none other than Robert Boyle, informs us that Walker was acquainted with Boyle's elder brother, the statesman and dramatist Earl of Orrery, and places his earlier connection with the Archbishop of Dublin on a new footing since that prelate happened to be Michael Boyle, another member of the family.

There is no definite trace among Boyle's writings of a familiarity with the Pascal of the *Pensées* and the *Lettres provinciales*, although, as has been noted, Evelyn wrote to him regarding his translation of one of the supplements to the latter. Seeing the circles in which Boyle moved and his general respect for Pascal's achievements in physics, he would very probably have heard of the *Pensées* and have perhaps read and talked about them. Whether or not this was the case, it is evident from Walker's dedication, hopes of favour aside, that one reason why the translator chose to address himself to the famous scientist was because he was aware that Boyle, like Pascal, was deeply interested in the harmonization of religious belief with the methods and conclusions of rationalist philosophy. It must have seemed eminently suitable to contemporary bystanders that the first appearance of the *Pensées* in English should have been offered to a man as widely known for his piety as for his scientific discoveries, and who, in *The Christian Virtuoso* (1690) and by the lectures he established in his will, would attempt to defend the ways in which the Christian faith might benefit from what he regarded as the proper use of the new learning.

Walker's epistle to Boyle is an important document in several respects in the study of Pascal's developing reputation in England. It hints at the extent to which the *Pensées* were known before the first translation was made, and it interestingly contains a few critical observations on the text. Its chief significance, however, lies in the degree to which Walker drew comparisons between Boyle and Pascal, seeing similarities at almost every turning of their lives. Much as both men gained by being measured against each other's virtues, the flattery was ultimately intended, of course, to enhance Boyle; and it would be scarcely an exaggeration to suggest that, rather than appearing as an individual in his own right, the Pascal of the *Pensées* was first presented to the English reading public as a French Robert Boyle—as it were his counterpart across the Channel in the devotion he gave to both science and religion, and one who, in spite of his

Catholic faith, might conceivably have been among the early members of the Royal Society.

When Walker wrote his dedication to Sir John Hewet, he spoke of drawing out 'a Detachment from Monsieur Pascall's Book, (for which the Generous Mr. Boyle will excuse me)'; but, from the epistle preceding the *Pensées*, it does not seem he had any direct acquaintance with Boyle. In the opening sentences he explained that Boyle's brother, the Earl of Orrery, when once taking ship for Ireland, had requested him to translate a certain treatise—apparently a piece by the Baron de Lisola, a diplomat in the imperial service, whose denunciations of French power and ambitions Orrery might have thought useful for a pamphlet he had in mind. The Earl expressed satisfaction at the result, and, as Walker commented, 'the Approbation of so great a Judge, incouraged me to set on farther Attempts of that kind.' The eventual outcome was his translation of the *Pensées*, which he was assured would have a favourable reception, and for which he considered Boyle would be an exceedingly appropriate patron:

> . . . *hearing by a Judicious Person, that Monsieur Pascall's Works would be well accepted, I got one of the Books, and have used my Endeavours about it, and observing a Parity there is (in some things) betwixt your Honour and our Author, I thought I could not commit the so much Admir'd and Esteem'd Monsieur Pascall and his Precious Remains, into safer and better Hands than the Famous Master Boyle's, nor recommend him to Travel the Kings Dominions, under a better or safer Conduct, than that of your Honours Favourable Approbation and Acceptance.*

In attempting to reconstruct the course of Walker's career and the nature of his personality, we have necessarily proceeded as much by way of inferences as of the few certain facts. In consequence, it is surely allowable to surmise that the 'Judicious Person' who 'so much Admir'd and Esteem'd Monsieur Pascall and his Precious Remains' was none other than Jacob Tonson, since it is altogether most likely that the translation was undertaken at his initiative. Aware, no doubt, of the importance attached to Pascal's scientific writings, and not forgetful of the success of *The Mystery of Jesuitisme*, Tonson must have concluded that the publication of the *Pensées* in English would be a worthwhile proposition; and, casting around for a suitable translator, found in Walker enough to recommend him for the task. Having previously 'done into English' French works of religion, science, and literature, Walker might be assumed to have had experience he could usefully apply to the themes and expressions of the *Pensées*, and his slight connections with the Boyle family would also have fitted Tonson's purpose. Naturally the publisher hoped the name of Pascal would attract many potential readers, but he probably had in mind above all the interest of the *virtuosi* in Pascal's thought which had possibly suggested the venture to him in the first place.

To attach by some means the name of Boyle to the book would have the effect of drawing upon that interest in Pascal already existing among members of the Royal Society, and also render Pascal's thoughts acceptable to a numerous audience for whom Boyle symbolized rectitude in religion as well as accomplishment in science. The sentiments in Walker's dedication should therefore be seen not merely as humble expressions of goodwill, but as complying with Tonson's calculations as a business man. With both ends in view, Walker accordingly proceeded to develop his leading theme of the resemblances between Pascal and Boyle, comparing one leading characteristic after another, and finally emphasizing the extent of their influence as moral forces:

Monsieur Pascall was Nobly Descended, and a great lover of Vertue and Learning from his Infancy, Every body knows, Sir, you Eminently enjoy these Advantages.

He was call'd a Christian Philosopher, and Mathematician; who knows not but your Honour deserves these Epithets, by the many Learned and Profound Treatises you have Compos'd. He made all his Works, and Actions of his Life, tend to the Temporal and Eternal good of Men: You have Employ'd your whole Life and Estate in Laborious Studying the abstrusest Recesses of Nature, for the Glory of God, of Religion, and the good of Mankind. as appears by your Excellent Treatise of the Stile of the Holy Scritures, &c.

Monsieur Pascall was Eminently Charitable, Pious, and Exemplary in his Morals, hating and reproving Vice in himself and others, wherein he surpast most of the Clergy: These things, Sir, cannot be deny'd you to such a Degree; that for disapproving Vice, you acquir'd the Title of Lay-Bishop; for those truly deserve double Honour who throughly Reform themselves, and do sincerely reprove Sin and Vice impartially in all sorts of Persons whatsoever. The Prophets, Christ, the Apostles, and all Good Men have done so. Those who are indifferent in this regard, and that manage themselves and Interests with a kind of human Policy, thinking thereby to scape in a whole Skin; let such tremble, for a Monsieur Pascall and a Master Boyle will Rise up in Judgment and condemn them; such doings will not turn to Account in the End, as appears by our Next Neighbours sad Experience.

I observe, and could Instance other particular Strains in Monsieur Pascall's and your Honours Works, and Life, which the World would be

Proud to know; but I hold my Hand, and referr so weighty a Work to be perform'd by your Panegyrists.

Like other translators of Pascal before and after him, Walker had to decide how to portray Pascal's piety and estimable character to the English public while admitting that Pascal himself had been a Catholic. In *The History of the Eucharist* he had charged Arnauld with being an 'Ambodexter,' but Walker was now ready to present Pascal decisively as one whose life and writings demanded firm approval, although he had been a Papist:

It is very seldom such Vertues as were in him, are found in those of the Communion wherein he Liv'd: But when I consider and compare his Writings and Life, with a Lord Treasurer Manchester, a Master Herbert, and many other Worthies that have liv'd and shin'd in the English Climate, I will not presume, but shall leave it to the Learned World to judge the apparent differences may be discern'd.

It is true Monsieur Pascall is Dead, but his great Purity of Life and Zeal, according to what he could discern through the Mists of Superstition, and part of his Remains in this Treatise: and you Illustrious, Sir, in the Numerous Issue you have enrich'd the World with: I say the Pious and Learned Master Boyle, and Monsieur Pascall, in their Excellent Works, do yet, and Will for ever Live and Shine, and speak aloud in the Temple of Fame, and will be rever'd in the Memory of Good Men, and thereby have acquir'd a Name better than of Sons and Daughters.

Most of Walker's remaining remarks were full of praise for the distinguished reputation of Boyle alone as a scientist, and in particular for his having found how salt water might be made drinkable, a great blessing to seamen. In successive classical allusions, he described the satisfaction of Boyle's 'Illustrious Relations' at the honours he enjoyed, and compared the extent of Boyle's discoveries to the conquests of Alexander the Great. Ultimate commendation, however, was reserved for the manner in which Boyle had devoted himself to an upright life, informed by the new learning yet respectful of the dictates of God: 'Some boast of their Atchievements in Wars by Land, others of their Successes by Sea, it is only the Vertuous Man that feels true Content and Pleasure in controlling his own unruly Passions, by bringing them in Subjection to the Rules of Right Reason, and of the Will of God.'

In view of the numerous deviations from the text and mistranslations that abound in Walker's version of the *Pensées*, it is a relief to find him offering excuses for the quality of his work. According to him, it lacked 'the Advantages of Art and Elegancy it requir'd and deserves'; but, 'the Will must pass for the Deed; much Silver cannot be expected out of a Lead Mine.' He had tried to keep to the author's sense as much as possible, but readily believed others would be able to improve the standard of his performance. He must take credit, however, though perhaps at another's instigation, for suspecting the existence of discrepancies between the text of the *Pensées* and their history as given by Mme. Perier, and the preface and advertisement to the Port Royal edition, which he also translated and included. From these he knew that the *Pensées* had been found in an unfinished and apparently disorderly state; and his resulting belief that the editors' treatment might have affected the nature of their production led him to come forward with a warning to the reader:

I know it is a common Practice to Expose Pieces as the Real Product of a Cowper, a Carrachio, a Vandike, &c. and to impose on Men Spurious Brats for Legitimate Children, because they may have some Features of their Parents.

I dare not assure the World that the Account here given us of Monsieur Pascall's Life and Works, are a Lively and Perfect Representation of him; on the contrary, having seriously consider'd the Solidity and Design of his Book, in most parts of it, I am rather apt to believe, there are many Strokes and Alterations made by other Hands, through that which some call pia fraus, *that were never intended by him, had he liv'd to have seen his own Works finish'd.*[13]

Walker's translation must have met with only moderate success, for Tonson did not reprint it, and it soon yielded in popularity to the translation by Basil Kennett which went through several editions in the eighteenth century. The dedication Walker wrote should by no means be ignored, however, since it served to introduce the first appearance of the *Pensées* in English, and cannot have failed to affect the growth of Pascal's reputation in certain directions. By bringing the *Pensées* to English readers under the protection of the name of Robert Boyle, Walker, the one-time customs collector, with his Anglican sympathies and knowledge of French, a man of no outstanding abilities and dependent upon publishers or families like the Boyles for patronage, with some degree of skill clothed Pascal in Boyle's virtues as well as his own. In this manner, he enhanced the distinction of each of them, as notable representatives of the new learning and experimental philosophy, and as men of deep piety who had sought a fuller understanding of the Christian faith.

But if the first translation of the *Pensées* initiated a new era in the English view of Pascal, it also may be seen as announcing the end of one too. Although the *Pensées* were relatively unknown before they appeared in English, during that early period they had taken their place among the other achievements of Pascal, all of which were regarded in their various ways as somewhat comparable in value and importance. In many respects, for all its flattery, Walker's dedication to Boyle summarized this early, native form of appreciation and preserved it for posterity. Scientific discovery was moving forward, and the *Lettres provinciales*, brilliant though they were considered still to be, were enjoying a more settled popularity except on occasions when anti-Catholic feeling flared again. The publication of Locke's *Essay* in 1690, and the steady effect of a new philosophy based on reason upon all areas of English intellectual life moreover were creating an atmosphere of thought in which the *Pensées* were recognized as being often remarkably apposite. When Kennett offered his translation of the *Pensées* to the public in 1704, his interest was entirely centred upon the work itself, and its religious and philosophical implications. It is one of the merits of Walker's edition to have captured the broader prospect of Pascal as he emerged onto the English scene, and to have recorded it both before any one aspect of his reputation came to be seen as important or relevant at the expense of the others, and before a composite view of his genius was freshly derived from foreign sources. Although adulatory, uncritical, and only briefly sketching the outlines of Pascal's career, Walker was able to present the author of the *Pensées* more totally than later commentators were often inclined to do, and the resulting portrait comes down to us as an engaging primitive.

[II]   Although the success of Walker's version of the *Pensées* would seem to have been limited and another translation was not published for sixteen years, English references to the *Pensées* and their author began to appear increasingly during the intervening period in a manner foretelling the greater popularity of the early eighteenth century. The work itself was becoming better known, and other French books of the time, in original or translated form, were bringing aspects of Pascal's thought to the English public's attention. French editions of the *Pensées* were likewise steadily arriving in England over these years; Thomas Bennet, for instance, one of London's leading theological booksellers, imported copies by way of Holland in 1701 and 1702.[14] The growth of English familiarity with the *Pensées* was assisted most of all, however, by the publication in 1704 of the translation by Basil Kennett which was to reach a far more extensive audience than Walker's had done, appearing a further five times during the next half-century. Kennett's characterization of Pascal in his introductory preface should, indeed, be counted as one of the strongest forces guiding Pascal's reputation in England during the succeeding age.

In contrast to the little that is known of Walker, details of Kennett's life and career are available in abundance. He was born on October 21, 1674, the second son of parents who came from merchant families. His father, whose Christian name he took, had received Holy Orders a few years previously, and at the time was Vicar of Postling, in Kent; two years later he was presented to the rectory of Dymchurch, which he was allowed to hold in plurality with his former position. After having been educated at Bicester, where his elder brother White, later Bishop of Peterborough, was curate and assistant schoolmaster, Basil Kennett proceeded to St. Edmund Hall, Oxford, of which his brother had by then become vice-principal. In 1690, he was elected a scholar of Corpus Christi College, and eventually became a fellow and tutor in 1697. His amiability and learning won him general liking and respect, but such qualities were often shown to be accompanied by little aptitude for the practical management of his affairs.

Kennett's university career was temporarily interrupted when, in 1706, he was appointed chaplain to the English trading factory at Leghorn, his letters of commission being forwarded from the Secretary of State's office by Joseph Addison who had known him at Oxford. On arriving at his post, the scholarly cleric met with considerable hostility from Italians and the Inquisition, and we are told that 'he was forced to confine himself in his Chamber, and to have an armed Guard at the Stair's Foot; and when, in some Evenings, he walk'd out for Air, he walk'd between two English Merchants, who with their Swords drawn resolv'd and declar'd, that no Body should dare seize him at their Peril.'[15] In spite of this harassment and his own frequent ill-health, Kennett remained in Leghorn with the determined support of his government for close to seven years, and afterwards made a leisurely journey back to England through Italy and France, visiting French scholars and buying books, sculpture, and curiosities. The expenses he incurred greatly alarmed White Kennett, who wrote to a friend that his brother had already drawn bills upon him for at least three hundred pounds, 'and I expect more daily. There is something unaccountable in it: at the least a neglect and contempt of the world, as if he was not to live in it.'[16]

With the Bishop's assistance, Kennett received certain ecclesiastical appointments on his return; but Oxford was his home, and, taking up residence there again, he was created D.D. and elected President of his college shortly before he died on January 3, 1715, being buried in the chapel. His failure to manage his finances during his life resulted in his having left substantial legacies of money and books to Corpus Christi while still in a state of debt, a situation which his brother again had to resolve. White Kennett retained a warm affection for him, however, and, in 1721, suggested to his own son that he might prepare a life of his uncle, a project which unfortunately seems never to have been brought to completion.

Kennett's leading work as an author was *Romae Antiquae Notitia, or the Antiquities of Rome* (1696), which passed through many editions and included two prefatory essays on Roman learning and education. Other original writings were *The Lives and Characters of the Ancient Grecian Poets* (1697), an exposition of the Apostles' creed (1705), and a paraphrase of the Psalms into verse (1706). Although admired as a man of learning and a poet, Kennett's chief significance for us naturally lies in his activity as a translator, which reveals his proficiency as a linguist. Apart from an interest in works of law and politics by Pufendorf and Balzac, he seems to have been mostly drawn towards producing English versions of books either of a literary or a religious nature. As well as the *Pensées*, he was responsible for translating works of Christian instruction by Bishop Godeau and Jean La Placette, and in 1716 there posthumously appeared his edition in English of Rapin's collected criticism. No doubt some of these were undertaken at the suggestion of publishers, and it may have been Tonson who recognized in Kennett a suitable translator for a second, more polished English edition of the *Pensées*. There is some evidence of previous communication between the two men, and Tonson's name appeared with those of two other publishing businesses on the title-page of the *Pensées* in 1704. If so, his selection on this occasion met with greater success; for Kennett's learning and his preference for the fields of literature and religion, in both of which Pascal was increasingly regarded as a figure of consequence, resulted in a translation which treated the arguments of the *Pensées* with sympathy and whose literary merit, compared to the work of Walker, was marked by relative distinction.

For some reason, by his choice or the publishers' omission, Kennett's name was nowhere set upon his work, and also absent were the two discourses and treatise which Walker had included. From an examination of the text, it would appear that Kennett made his translation from one of the early editions published in France between 1670 and 1677, excepting the first; for the thirty-nine *pensées* which were added to the existing collection in 1678, one of which had previously appeared only in the first edition, have not found a place in his version. Kennett was, however, familiar with the supplementary pieces by Filleau de la Chaise through later French editions, and excluded them because, in his opinion, they were not sufficiently worthy to stand alongside the *Pensées* themselves. The discourses, he said, 'would have pass'd with Reputation, had they not the Disadvantage of appearing with M. Pascal's Compositions.' The certificates of approval from French bishops and clergy which were features of the Port Royal edition were also set aside, since, 'as they are not here needful, so in some respect, they might have seem'd prejudicial'; and neither did Mme. Perier's life of her brother form part of the volume. Pascal's *Pensées* were thus reintroduced to the English public without most of the accompanying or expository writings with an almost traditional association, and without a dedication from the translator to some appropriate personage, but with only an anonymous translator's preface to the reader in addition to the editing committee's preface and advertisement.

Having assumed that 'the Name of Monsieur Pascal is dear to All who have the Happiness to be affected with what is either profound in Knowledge, or exact in Wit,' Kennett politely sought in his own preface to justify the appearance of the translation he had made. There were, he believed, 'still many Persons of Learning and Judgment, who continued Strangers to the Language of the Original, either as neglecting so easie a Conquest, or as despising an Attainment, which is now become rather Vulgar, than fashionable.' Pascal's friends on the editing committee had described the background to the *Pensées* and had fittingly represented their content, but the translator wished still, at the risk of being superfluous, to 'premise some recommendations of his Author.' From the outset, Kennett displayed the highest regard for Pascal, and even the defects arising from the original fragmented condition of the *Pensées* were discounted by him as a positive advantage: 'In the main Attempt we are shewn what the Greatest Genius could do on the Greatest Subject: For tho' the Draught is far from being finish'd, yet it consists entirely of Master-strokes, and therefore may the more easily be dispens'd with for the want of Colouring and Shade.'

Kennett was, however, still faced with the difficulties that Walker had experienced earlier, of explaining Pascal's Catholicism to English Protestant readers while attempting to reconcile certain inconsistencies in the work itself. He chose to see these problems more specifically in relation to each other than Walker had done, and allowed his admiration for Pascal to lead him boldly towards a drastic solution; and, in doing so, he indicated that he also knew Pascal, if only by repute, as the author of the *Lettres provinciales*:

How much soever the Performance may have suffer'd for want of those Advantages which were peculiar to the Author, yet it is here presented entire, excepting some Lines which directly favour'd the distinguishing Doctrines of those of the Roman Communion. If that excellent Person thought fit to pay this Submission to the Authority of his own Church, we cannot be injurious to Him, in expressing the like Veneration for Ours. But considering the great liberty with which these Fragments were put together, it is not wholly improbable that M. Pascal's Friends might officiously insert some Marks of this kind, to prove him (in their Notion,) a Good Catholic, and to shelter his Memory from the Odium of some, whom in another admirable Book, (Lettres aux Provinciaux,) he had proved not to be very Good Christians. Yet, as to any such Passages, it is not so generous to dispute the manner of their coming in, as to be satisfied with the power of leaving them out.

The main substance of Kennett's preface lay in his consideration of 'some of the principal Parts' of the *Pensées*, being those aspects of Pascal's apologetic which he had found of greatest interest to the current state of religion and philosophy. Intellectually drawn towards Pascal, he briefly summarized and reviewed several of the most striking points the Frenchman had made, and to some extent he was probably reflecting the comment around him when he referred first to Pascal's discussion of the rival claims of faith and reason and his argument of the wager:

The most rational and most pathetical Addresses to the Sceptics demonstrate, that were the utmost latitude indulg'd to these Men, 'til they should be lost in their Privilege of free-thinking, they could not otherwise recover and come to themselves, but by setling upon the Foundations of Faith, which is as Natural a Cure for the wandrings of Reason, as Reason itself is for the Extravagancies of Imagination: and that the only Cause why so many have miscarried in this Adventure, has been their want of Strength to go thro' the Course, and to ride out that Storm which Vice, or Rashness, had brought upon their Faculties. It will be observ'd, that in one Essay against this Spirit of Indifference, the Author has proceeded upon the Supposition of his Adversaries, and has evinced, that if Reason, (as is pretended,) were doubtful in the Case, yet Prudence ought to incline to the safer side. But it should likewise be observ'd, that a peculiar Advertisement is prefix'd to that Chapter, and that this was a way of arguing which Monsieur Pascal, or his Friends, confess'd to stand in need of an Apology.

Pascal's qualities of learning, insight, and piety and his talent for exposition had led him to treat comprehensively the more abstract areas of enquiry and belief with lucidity; and Kennett especially commended Pascal's examination of prophecies and miracles which he regarded as strengthening one of the chief defences of the Christian religion:

The Metaphysical Speculations seem most refined and accomplish'd, not only for their surprizing Novelty, and for the engaging manner in which they are deliver'd, but chiefly on account of those more Sublime Views in which they terminate and conspire. For 'tis absurd to condemn the jejuneness of the Antients in this Science, if our Reasonings be as Heathenish as their Language was Barbarous; and if instead of the dry truncs of their Terms and Distinctions, (which, being rightly transplanted, we might improve into useful Fruit,) we cultivate an unprofitable Elegance, and under all the verdure of Expression betray a Barrenness of Thought. Which is yet the Case of these abstracted Doctrines, when rais'd upon Principles merely human; upon that Wisedom which is earthly, and cometh of the Earth, but is not water'd from above, or, mingled with the Fountains of Truth. Whereas, therefore, some professing this retired Knowledge have much impair'd the credit of their Labours, by seeming to derogate from that of the Holy Scripture; Monsieur Pascal, by his accurate Knowledge of its Harmony and Agreement, his peculiar discernment of Prophecies and Miracles, and his singular Art of illustrating and comparing different Texts, has made it appear Venerable, even to such as are not wont to read it with his sincerity of Intention, and his truly Christian Heart.

The *Pensées* were particularly valuable in such matters, but to Kennett they were also full of a variety of excellent reflections which revealed the broad extent of Pascal's genius applied to religious understanding. His gift for mathematics, his recognition of the infinite distance between the attributes of God and man, the superiority of his powers of expression as well as reasoning to those of the writers of antiquity, were some of the features of the work to which the translator, a classical scholar, sought with warmth to draw the reader's attention:

How useful are those curious Enquiries concerning the Extent, and Divisibility of Matter, and the powers of Numbers, (of which the Author had so vast a Comprehension,) in rendring the Mysteries of Nature subservient to those of Faith; in abasing the Pride of our Understanding, and in ascribing Glory to Him who alone is truly Infinite, and who while He has given us Ability to make and compare, these seeming Infinities, does yet present us with something, even in these, which is much more unfathomable to our Perfections, than incommensurate to His own? How may the Reflexions upon Mankind, so sprightly and vigorous, so penetrating, and sensible, invite us to observe, that the Sentence which the Wisest of Men, so long since pronounced on Mortal Vanity, has been most strongly confirm'd by those who have made the nearest approaches to his Wisedom; and that, as He resolv'd the whole matter, (all that was Good, or Great in Life,) into the fearing GOD and keeping His Commandments; so these have centred all their Contemplations in Religious Belief and Practice, as the only things which can restore the Credit of our Nature, and reconcile us to our own Good Opinion? How do the Thoughts upon Death exalt the Consolations of Phylosophy into the Hope and Assurance of Religion? Did Aemylius, or Cato, or Tully, deliver themselves with so composed Gravity, and yet so tender Affection, on the Loss of their Children, as M. Pascal has done, on that of his Father? Or, was he not, indeed, an early Proficient in that better School, and Discipline, which alone could make him wiser than the Antients, and give him more Understanding than those Teachers, and Examples? Lastly, does he not, in the Chapter of Miscellaneous Thoughts, discover the same true relish of what is just and natural, in Style, and Behaviour, as before of what is deep and solid in Reason? and does not the Prayer annex'd, by evincing that this Great and Universal Capacity was animated by a true Spirit of Humility and Devotion, seem equally proper, to complete his Character, and his Works?[17]

Such repeated instances of Kennett's lively interest in Pascal surely exceed what might be expected from a writer occupying himself purely on the basis of a publisher's commission. At one point he wrote 'the Translator having been almost insensibly engaged in this delightful Task, was afterwards induced to communicate the Satisfaction'; and it must have been conspicuous from his preface that he genuinely wanted his readers to share in his enjoyable discovery of the *Pensées* and their author. His respect for Pascal's numerous talents and Christian virtues was there for all to see; and the sympathies which decided him to omit those lines upholding Catholic doctrines and the certifying statements by French bishops and clergy would have been welcomed by a great many of his readers, who would have also found good cause for thus assimilating the thoughts of the *Pensées* so exclusively upon Protestant terms. Kennett's admiration for Pascal accordingly led him to produce a version of the *Pensées* that was ensured with the maximum of acceptability.

Kennett himself gave further expression to his approval of Pascal's religious views when he drew upon his intimate knowledge of the *Pensées* in the sermons he preached to the small community of British merchants at Leghorn. On the first occasion he celebrated holy communion there, he included in his address an illustration from Pascal:

The Pious and Ingenious Mr. Pascal, seeing two Persons, who came from a solemn Act of the Religion of his Country, the one full of Joy, the other with visible Marks of Trouble and Fear, said each of 'em was so far defective, as he had not the Temper of the other, and that these two Men put together would make One good one. I believe the ground of this fine Observation, may be most fitly and eminently applied to the Blessed Eucharist, and, in Proportion, to all other Exercises of Christian Piety, in as much as a Temper compos'd of Joy and Fear, mutually check'd and restrain'd, is the very Spirit of Devotion.[18]

A later sermon on the text, 'That we being deliver'd out of the Hands of our Enemies, might serve Him without Fear' (Luke 1:74), which was preached 'before the Admiral, and Commanders of Her Majesty's Fleet in the Streights,' led Kennett to pay tribute again to Pascal as a master in the proper interpretation of biblical prophecy. He had sought to examine the words of his text as they might have been earliest understood, and drew his conclusions together by saying:

This is suitable to the Observation of that great Genius Mr. Pascal, than whom none perhaps had ever a clearer Discernment, and Apprehension of the Holy Scriptures, or with a more accurate Judgment evinc'd their Authority, and distinguish'd their Excellencies and Beauties. A Messiah was promis'd, says he, who should rescue Men from their Enemies; a Messiah is come, but to rescue Men from no other Enemies than their Sins. When David says, that the Messiah shall deliver the People from their Enemies, this by a carnal Expositor may be applied to the Egyptians, (or to the Babylonians, and other Nations,) And then I confess, I am at a loss to shew him, how the Prophecy has been fulfilled. Yet it may likewise be applied to Men's Iniquities, or Offences, since these, and not the Egyptians, (or any of those Nations,) are to be look'd upon as their real Enemies. But if in other Places he declares, as he does, (together with Isaiah, Daniel, &c.) that the Messiah shall deliver his People from their Sins, the Ambiguity is taken off, and the double Sense of Enemies reduc'd to the single Meaning of Iniquities. For if these latter were chiefly in his Thought, he might well express them by borrowing the Name of the former: but if his Mind was bent upon the former, it was impossible he should signifie them under the Appellation of the latter.[19]

Kennett's version of the *Pensées* did not alone determine the course of Pascal's English reputation during the ensuing fifty years; other influences were present, and, to some degree, Kennett himself was doubtless combining and transmitting a number of existing opinions of Pascal rather than consciously trying to inaugurate a new trend in appreciation. In this regard, his translation may perhaps be seen as the final major contribution of Restoration Oxford towards creating an awareness in England of Pascal and his several achievements. Hammond, Boyle, Wallis, Wren, and Locke, to name only a few, were all men with close associations with that university, and Kennett's attitudes towards Pascal as a writer, mathematician, and thinker would have been largely formed in his academic environment. In other ways, this interest in Pascal at Oxford would continue into the future.

Kennett's personal attraction towards Pascal is an outstanding preliminary to any discussion of his translation's popularity, but the chief cause of the particular influence his version gained lies in the work itself having been well suited to the developing mood of the time. Pascal was valued as a thinker by those who already knew the *Pensées*; but, whereas Walker had been mainly concerned with tracing similarities between Pascal and Boyle, Kennett's portrait was drawn directly out of the *Pensées* themselves which he regarded pre-eminently as a work on religion, the greatest of subjects, that had proceeded from an acknowledged genius of recent times. By the same token, it was Kennett who, at a relatively early date, the most eloquently presented a summation of Pascal's thoughts to the English public, and praised him as a supremely worthy example of the philosophical mind joined to a Christian disposition. The movement of intellectual currents would have led the reader of 1704 to find this approach to the *Pensées* even more rewarding and readily understandable than would the reader of 1688; and it was perhaps Kennett's greatest service eventually to have made his conception of Pascal's significance available to an audience which was increasingly predisposed to appreciate the *Pensées* for reasons of the same kind.

Although further editions of his translation did not begin to be published with frequency until 1727, the first edition for a while remained generally available;[20] and, during that period, Kennett's remarks would certainly have guided his readers towards the formation of their own views of Pascal amid a climate of opinion that was, for the most part, inclined to see reason as the potential ally of religion. Appreciated in the past as a protagonist against the evils of Catholicism or as a scientist and mathematician, these and other themes were to continue to have their place in the regard with which Pascal was held; but, in the future composition of his reputation, such emphases were increasingly seen as secondary to the celebration of Pascal as an exemplary opponent of both the emotionalism that had accompanied seventeenth-century religion and the excessive scepticism being generated by the rationalist philosophy. For as long as a balance between the claims of faith and reason was earnestly desired by many leaders of English thought of several persuasions, it was natural the solutions reached by Pascal through careful, clearly stated argument should have exerted an immense appeal, and that his fame as author of the *Pensées* would overtake his other distinctions. By defining Pascal's qualities in this regard and encouraging English opinion to approach them with understanding and pleasure, Kennett rendered the *Pensées* more acceptable to a greater number of readers. He also assisted the work towards achieving considerable popularity and respect while that balance which Pascal represented remained a standard for aspiration.

[III] Before we proceed to examine the text of the *Pensées* as it was known to Englishmen of the eighteenth century, one other feature of Pascal's enlarging reputation demands to be taken into account. Each of his leading achievements had received admiration in turn, but, while Kennett was increasing English familiarity with Pascal as a religious thinker, a growing interest was beginning to be shown in the details of his life. The versatile brilliance of Pascal inevitably stimulated further enquiry, and opportunities readily existed for this demand to be satisfied. Kennett's description of him as 'the Greatest Genius' to some extent reflected the new understanding of Pascal's career in its totality which was developing at that time, and which was coming to see the *Pensées* essentially as the final literary bequest of an extraordinarily gifted, perspicacious, and quite unusual man.

For some years after the *Lettres provinciales* had appeared their authorship had remained speculative, and, although some mathematicians and scientists had had direct access to Pascal and his circle, it was probably not until Walker prefixed Mme. Perier's biography of her brother to his translation of the *Pensées* that the facts of Pascal's life began to be at all widely known in England. The preface of the committee which edited the Port Royal edition had sketched Pascal's career and character in outline, but such information was greatly extended by Mme. Perier, who, in an appealing manner, provided numerous stories of her brother's talents and scientific aptitude while emphasizing the fervour of his eventual attachment to religion.[21] Her biography was not included by Kennett in his translation, however, and it was not available again in English until 1723. Knowledge of this source for Pascal's life in its complete form was therefore largely confined during those years to readers of the *Pensées* in French, readers of Kennett's version only being given the few general details about the author in the editing committee's preface.

It is altogether more likely that the English view of Pascal's life came principally from the great dictionaries being produced by French writers, which were having a profound effect upon the course of English thought and letters. In 1694, the *Grand dictionnaire historique* of Louis Moréri was translated into English, carrying a short article on Pascal that had been summarized from the preface to the *Traitez de l'équilibre des liqueurs* and that of the editorial committee to the *Pensées*. As might be expected, this outline was mainly restricted to Pascal's youthful discoveries in mathematics, his experiments on the vacuum, and the religious convictions that had made 'Posterity to regret the want of that Work he design'd against Atheists, of which there are but some few fragments.'[22] When a second English edition of this dictionary was published in 1701 under the supervision of Jeremy Collier, the earlier entry had been fundamentally retained but its length was now doubled by the addition of two anecdotes which might further arouse a reader's interest. After a fleeting reference identifying Pascal as author of the *Lettres provinciales*, one of these anecdotes portrayed him as the advocate of loyalty to the royal power, having said that 'the Government is not only a Resemblance, but, in some measure, a Participation of the Power of God, which cannot be oppos'd by the Subject without a plain Resistance of the Divine Providence and Oeconomy.' The other, in particular, was to become very well-known during the following century:

It will not be amiss to observe his first Progress in Mathematicks, which considering his Age and Performance, was altogether extraordinary; for being but Twelve Years old, he desir'd to be instructed in this Science by his Father, who conceiving it might prove prejudicial to his Learning the Languages, refus'd to gratifie his Curiosity; however, M. Paschal importuned his Father so long, till he got a general Definition of Geometry, namely, That it teaches the Proportion that Lines and Circles have to each other: Upon this Notion of the Matter, young Paschal went to work, at his Play-hours, and made himself first Definitions and Axioms; and then proceeding to Demonstration, struck out the first two and thirty Propositions of Euclid, and being surpriz'd at it by his Father, he demonstrated his last Proposition, and upon further Questions, went backward in his Demonstrations, till he had run 'em up to his first Principles of Definitions and Axioms.[23]

Since these anecdotes were drawn not only from the life by Mme. Perier but from the *Dictionnaire historique et critique* of Pierre Bayle, they may also serve to introduce that powerful force which would strongly affect future English assessment of Pascal. Written while Bayle was an exile in Holland, the *Dictionnaire* first appeared in 1697 and examined a great many leading figures in the worlds of theology, philosophy, and literature. A leading forerunner of later encyclopaedias, it quickly became indispensable as a provocative work of reference, and, in expanding form, sought to induce a sceptical and detached approach towards themes traditionally embroiled in controversy.

During his lifetime, Bayle had a close personal relationship with the third Earl of Shaftesbury and with the deist John Toland, and his works opposing dogmatism in any form were also known to Locke, Mandeville, and some other English writers of a liberal persuasion. As founder and editor of the *Nouvelles de la république des lettres*, one of the earliest literary periodicals, he was conversant to a remarkable degree with English life and letters, which gave his works a particular attraction to Englishmen; and, from the late seventeenth century onwards, those who interested themselves in French thought were almost inevitably brought to an acquaintance with his writings and ultimately with the *Dictionnaire*. His reputation was such that, when English noblemen heard of the *Dictionnaire's* forthcoming appearance, they clamoured for the privilege of having the work dedicated to them, and English printers began to think of arranging for its translation. In consequence, the *Dictionnaire* soon came to be represented in the libraries of practically all intellectually-minded Englishmen able to afford it; and, although the work's circulation tended therefore to be limited, it has been said 'the imposing share of Bayle in the development of ideas in England is not that of a foreigner, but rather that of an adopted son.'[24]

Pascal was among those figures whom Bayle selected for inclusion in his *Dictionnaire*; and, after having no doubt gained some notice out of the first two editions in French published in Rotterdam, the article was first presented in English when a translation of the *Dictionnaire* was made by a French refugee in London in 1709. Another translation appearing in 1710 circulated more extensively, and must have given a great many readers restricted to English their primary account of Pascal's life as Bayle saw it.

After telling the details of Pascal's birth at Clermont in Auvergne, on June 19, 1623, Bayle drew attention to his subject's early relationship with his father, 'who had an extraordinary Tenderness for this Child, his only Son.' The elder Pascal was a scholar, 'an able Mathematician,' his son's first and only schoolmaster: and, although he held high office in Auvergne, his concern for his son led him to relinquish it and move to Paris in 1631, 'that he might the more usefully spend his time in the Instruction of his Son, who from his Infancy gave Proofs of a Wit far above what is common; for he desired to know the Reason of every thing . . . and when he studied to know any thing, he would never leave it till he had found out something that could give him Satisfaction.' Bayle noted that the character of the young Pascal's mind might well have led him into libertinism, but, on the contrary, he 'distinguish'd exactly all his Life-time the Laws of Faith from those of Reason.'

In fact, although Pascal made remarkable progress in mathematics and 'had taken a great deal of Pains in Experiments of the new Philosophy,' before he was twenty-four he 'forsook that Study' and made a 'holy Resolution' to 'apply himself only to that one thing which JESUS CHRIST calls necessary.' During the fifteen years which remained, as he died when he was only thirty-nine, he suffered patiently from long and frequent diseases, and devoted much of his time to 'a Work against the Atheists, and against all those who do not admit the Truths of the Gospel.' He did not live to complete this, but, 'what was found, concerning that Subject, among his Papers, was made publick, and was admir'd.' Bayle, in his summary of these last years, presented Pascal as a man of genius who had already begun to be viewed as particularly admirable for his extraordinary piety, humility, and Christian devotion, maintained even during periods of painful illness. The *Lettres provinciales* 'have been, and are still esteem'd a Master-piece'; and, finally, 'I had almost forgot to tell you, that it was from him that the Jansenists learn'd to denote themselves by *on*.'

The *Dictionnaire* is famous, however, for presenting in its voluminous footnotes all facts and opinions which Bayle deemed relevant to his subjects, in a fashion which often invited a reappraisal of their specific claims to importance. The article on Pascal was no exception. Here, where the supporting details to the text were set down in the form of long quotations from Mme. Perier's biography and other sources, the persistent reader might discover certain observations by Bayle himself which could throw the entire organization and content of the article into a new perspective for him. To take a leading example, after a very full description of Pascal's upbringing and his major discoveries, the *Dictionnaire* proceeded to an account in Mme. Perier's words of Pascal's repeated illnesses and his accompanying state of mind:

To this ardent Charity he join'd, during his Sickness, an admirable Patience, which edified and surpriz'd all Persons that were about him; and he said to those who declar'd they were troubled to see him in such a condition, that, for his own part, he was no wise troubled, and that he was even afraid of being cur'd; and when he was ask'd the reason, he answer'd, Because I know the dangers of Health, and the advantages of Sickness. He said yet, in the height of his Pain, when some were griev'd to see him endure it, Be not troubl'd for me, Sickness is the natural State of Christians, because they should always be in a Suffering condition, depriv'd of all good things, and of all the Pleasures of Sense, free from Passions, without Ambition and Avarice, and in a continual expectation of Death. Is it not thus that Christians ought to pass their Lives? And is it not a happiness, when they are by necessity in such a condition in which they ought to be, and when they have nothing else to do but to submit humbly and peaceably? Wherefore I only desire to pray to God, that he would grant me his Grace. This was the Temper with which he endur'd all his Pains.

Bayle commented upon such behaviour by quoting some earlier remarks of his own which placed in slight question its appropriateness in a man of such distinguished abilities:

The Author of the News from the Republick of Learning, *hath made some Reflections upon this, and upon the advantage that may be drawn from the extraordinary Devotion of so excellent a Mathematician, and so great a Philosopher. It serves, says he, to refute the Libertines, They cannot now tell us, that none but little Wits have any Piety. It cannot be deny'd, but it is rare to see a great Devotion in Persons who have once tasted of Mathematical Studies, and made an extraordinary progress in those Sciences.*

He continued by casting doubt upon the wisdom of some of Pascal's ascetic practices, which, as will be seen, would increasingly come to be regarded by several Englishmen with varying degrees of suspicion:

There were in the Conduct of Mr. Pascal some other things, which are no less singular than his Maxims about Health. 'The Conversations in which he was often engag'd, altho' they were wholly about Charity, yet they sometimes made him afraid, lest he should fall into danger by them; but since he could not in Conscience refuse the Relief which some Persons demanded of him, he found out a Remedy for this. He took, upon occasion, an Iron Girdle full of Points, and put it round about his naked Flesh, and when any vain Thought came into his Mind, or he took some pleasure in the place where he was, or any such like thing happen'd, he gave himself some Blows with his Elbow, to redouble the violence of the prickings; and thus he made himself remember his Duty.' He had always in his Mind these two great Maxims, of renouncing all Pleasure and all Superfluity; and he practis'd them in the worst of his Illness, with a continual watchfulness over his Senses, refusing them absolutely every thing that was agreeable to them.

A persevering reader might learn of further instances of Pascal having 'embrac'd a kind of Life, abstracted from the World,' of maxims 'which doubtless appear very strange to worldly People,' and that Pascal had also had an excellent memory; and he would be offered the arguments proposed by the wager and contained in the *Lettres provinciales* side by side with leading efforts to refute them.

Quite possibly, he would find himself agreeing in the end with Bayle's conclusion that Pascal had not been merely a prodigy, but a 'Paradoxical Individuum of Human kind.'[25]

While the readers of Bayle were thus being invited to pursue the footnotes and to be their own judge of Pascal from a number of suggestive impressions, signs of an increased English knowledge of the life and character of Pascal became conspicuous within a broader phenomenon of the intellectual life of the time. A notable feature of English literature in the eighteenth century was the growth of the art of biography, and, in these circumstances, the life of Pascal, in whole or in part, was found for various reasons to be sufficiently unique to bear telling repeatedly. Locke's *Essay* was already acquainting its readers with Pascal's powers of memory, but some other early instances of this new trend in Pascal's English reputation showed a greater fascination with the price that had been paid by genius than with its actual attributes. In 1705, Jeremy Collier made use of Pascal as an illustration of the harm that might be caused by accelerating a child's education:

Now, some Children are too pressing, and high-mettled, and have more Will than Strength for Drudging. This seems to have been Monsieur Paschal's Case. The Ardour of his Genius made him over-drive; his Spirits were exhausted by Thought, and his Studies prey'd upon his Constitution. There are other Instances of young People that have miscarried this way, and kill'd themselves in their too eager Pursuits after Learning. As if 'twere honourable to fall a Sacrifice to Sense, and die for Love of the Muses! And tho' Life is often lavish'd away to worse Purposes, yet 'tis not good to strain too much, and set Nature upon the Tenters. A man may be too covetous of Understanding, and a Miser in his Head as well as in his Pocket.[26]

Of a more memorable kind were the remarks upon this theme placed by Eustace Budgell in an essay in the *Spectator* (No. 116, July 13, 1711), which took issue with a quotation from the *Pensées* in light of Pascal's premature death. Budgell, who was also the biographer of the Boyle family, had given an account of Sir Roger de Coverley hunting the hare, and concluded by recalling Pascal's opinion of such pastimes:

As we were returning home, I remember'd that Monsieur Paschal, in his most excellent Discourse on the Misery of Man, tells us, That all our Endeavours after Greatness, proceed from nothing but a Desire of being surrounded by a Multitude of Persons and Affairs, that may hinder us from looking into our selves, which is a View we cannot bear. He afterwards goes on to shew that our Love of Sports comes from the same Reason, and is particularly severe upon HUNTING. What, says he, unless it be to drown Thought, can make Men throw away so much Time and Pains upon a silly Animal, which they might buy cheaper in the Market?

Budgell, however, could see another, more commendable purpose in hunting, which was for the exercise it affords, contributing to the preservation of physical well-being:

Had that incomparable Person whom I last quoted been a little more indulgent to himself in this Point, the World might probably have enjoyed him much longer; whereas, thro' too great an Application to his Studies in his Youth, he contracted that ill Habit of Body, which, after a tedious Sickness, carried him off in the fortieth Year of his Age; and the whole History we have of his Life till that Time, is but one continued Account of the Behaviour of a noble Soul struggling under innumerable Pains and Distempers.

Hence, the author announced his intention of hunting twice a week during his stay with Sir Roger, and would recommend such exercise in moderation to all his country friends 'as the best Kind of Physick for mending a bad Constitution, and preserving a good one.'[27]

The stories of Pascal's youthful feats were sufficiently famous for Pope and his friends to parody them in the *Memoirs of the Extraordinary Life, Works, and Discoveries of Martinus Scriblerus*. Although not published until 1741, the *Memoirs* were written by Pope, Swift, Arbuthnot, and other members of the Scriblerus Club in the years following Pope's becoming a member of the Club in 1713. In their satire on the world of learning and many of the leading theories of the day, they made fun of a well-known episode in the life of Pascal when describing their hero's early disposition to mathematics. This was discovered 'by his drawing parallel lines on his bread and butter, and intersecting them at equal Angles, so as to form the whole Superficies into squares.'[28]

Another instance of familiarity with Pascal's life occurred when his opinions upon loyalty and rebellion as presented by Mme. Perier were directly quoted by Bishop Berkeley in his discourse *Passive Obedience or The Christian Doctrine of not Resisting the Supreme Power* ... (1712). Having emphasized in the pursuit of his theme that, as men, our actions should not be directed 'by any emotions in our blood and spirits, but by the dictates of sober and impartial reason,' he went on to say:

And if there be any who find they have a less abhorrence of rebellion than of other villainies, all that can be inferred from it is that this part of their duty was not so much reflected on, or so early and frequently inculcated into their hearts, as it ought to have been; since without question there are other men who have as thorough an aversion for that as for any other crime.

Wishing to strengthen his argument, Berkeley then placed an authoritative reference in a footnote:

'Il disait ordinairement qu'il avait un aussi grand éloignement pour ce péché-là que pour assassiner le monde, ou pour voler sur les grands chemins, et qu'enfin il n'y avait rien qui fût plus contraire à son naturel.' He (Mr. Pascal) used to say he had as great an abhorrence of rebellion as of murder, or robbing on the way, and that there was nothing more shocking to his nature. —Vie de M. Pascal, p.44.[29]

When Mme. Perier's life of Pascal next appeared in English, it was presented in a new form entitled *The Lives of Picus and Pascal, Faithfully Collected from the most Authentick Accounts of them.* The work of the otherwise obscure Edward Jesup, this parallel biography of Pico della Mirandola and Pascal was published in 1723 and again in 1730, its title-page then bearing a short advertisement for the second edition of Kennett's translation of the *Pensées*.[30] In effect, Jesup had placed side by side Sir Thomas More's *Life of John Picus, Earl of Mirandula* (1510?) and the life by Mme. Perier, both in contemporary English, and then added six pages of comparisons between 'those two Christian Worthies.' Taken as a whole, *The Lives of Picus and Pascal* is an example of the new appeal discovered in Plutarch's method of presenting parallel lives together, and the result in this case has been described as 'two simple and attractive saints' lives, in subject, style, and treatment.'[31]

Jesup's version of Mme. Perier's life of her brother takes its place with the repeated appearance of the same work in French editions of the *Pensées*, the translation by Walker, and the account given by Bayle in both French and English editions of his *Dictionnaire*, as a leading source from which English readers might discover in some detail the facts regarding Pascal's life and personality. *The Lives of Picus and Pascal* also contained some interesting opinions regarding Pascal at the time of its publication, to be found chiefly in the concluding comparison by Jesup, and in the preface by William Bond (d. 1735), a second-rate dramatist and miscellaneous writer, who unblushingly conceded his thorough plagiarization of Bayle.

In his fulsome dedication to the Duke of Grafton, Jesup regretted his incapability of presenting an original work to his patron; but, instead, he had collected 'the Life of that Great Genius Monsieur Pascal, whose unlimited Capacity all the Polite World have confess'd.' Nothing, he believed, could better assist in immortalizing the memory of 'the Illustrious Pascal' in England than the equally illustrious Duke's support, which he saw as 'an Obligation, which reaches beyond the Grave, it is what may be properly call'd Doing

Honour to the Dead.'[32] The dedication was immediately followed by Bond's preface, which began by relating in somewhat protracted fashion his feelings on being asked to undertake such an assignment:

My Friend the Author of this little Book, has been pleased to single me out for the Task of Writing such an Introductory Preface to the ensuing Life of Monsieur Pascal: I told him that the Life of a Genius so universally celebrated, whom so many distinguish'd Doctors of the Sorbonne, Arch-deacons, Bishops, and Arch-bishops, had exerted their Eloquence in Applauding; that the Life of such a Person written by his own Sister, who was as nearly allied to him in Genius, as she was in Blood, and translated, as it appears to me to be, into a plain, easy, and familiar Style, (which is surely the best Style that a Biographer can make Use of,) could not fail to please, but must necessarily carry along with it its own Recommendation.

But Jesup had repeated his request, and Bond decided that 'as there is so much due to our Friendship, I could not persist in my Refusal.' Still voicing his reluctance, he resolved 'with so much seeming Boldness' to summon 'the learned Monsieur Bayle (whom, because he was one of the most learned Men of his time, it is therefore no wonder to find one of Monsieur Pascal's greatest Admirers)' to his assistance.[33] In fact, Bond's piece came to depend very heavily on the quotation consisting of 'A small Extract out of the News from the Republick of Letters, written by Mr. Bayle, for the Month of December 1684. pag. 531'; and his familiarity with it is not surprising, in view of the lasting influence Bayle's periodical had exerted upon English journals. Mainly describing the heights to which piety and asceticism had been carried by 'One of the profoundest Geometricians, by One of the most subtile Metaphysicians, and by One of the most solid and penetrating Genii, that ever yet existed on this Earth,' the passage, which must already have been quite well-known, opened with two sentences which would also be used by the publishers of the second English edition of the *Pensées* to advertise Jesup's book: 'An Hundred Volumes of Sermons are not worth so much as this single Life, and are far less capable of disarming Men of Impiety. The extraordinary Humility and Devotion of Monsieur Pascal, gives a more sensible Mortification to the Libertines of the Age, than if one was to let lose upon them a dozen of Missionaries.'[34]

In more ways than one, Bond expressed himself as being at a loss for words after Bayle's preceding remarks:

All I can add after this, is, that if ever any Book could be said to be well recommended, this little one is certainly so: For I may with Truth alledge, in

Imitation of what Mr. Bayle so beautifully says of Pascal's Life, that a hundred recommendatory Prefaces from different Hands, would not be worth so much as this single Extract, or more capable of exciting the Curiosity of Readers to peruse it, or fixing in them a more favourable Opinion of it when they had perused it.

But his indebtedness was not yet complete, for he brought his preface to a conclusion by referring once again to Bayle's writings on Pascal:

I know nothing that I could have added to it, that could have been further grateful to the Reader, if I had not met with an excellent Latin Epitaph which follows it, that is fix'd on Monsieur Pascal's Monument, at the Parish-Church of St. Stephen of the Mount, and translated into English by a very ingenious Gentleman, Mr. Sewell. I shall detain the Readers no longer from a Life that is so highly recommended to them by so great an Authority, both for their Entertainment and Instruction, and so bid them heartily Farewel. [35]

In all probability, the 'very ingenious Gentleman' was George Sewell (d. 1726), an unsuccessful physician, who was forced to augment his living by writing a number of pamphlets, plays, translations, and poems, none of which were of much consequence. By any standard, his verse translation of Pascal's epitaph was somewhat free, as may be seen by comparing it to the original Latin version with which it appeared as a postscript to Bond's preface:

> *If fair Religion does not Die,*
> HE *lives for ever in the Sky.*
> *The pious Tenant of this Stone,*
> *To married Pleasures lived unknown;*
> *In* FAITH *sincere, in* VIRTUE *bright;*
> *In* LEARNING *fam'd, in* WIT *polite;*
> *In Birth* ILLUSTRIOUS *as in Mind,*
> *A* SCHOLAR *not of Schoolman-kind.*
> LOVER *of Equity and Right,*
> *A* CHAMPION *in Truth's Cause to Fight;*
> *The* PATRON *of a single State,*
> *A* FOE *with honest pious Hate,*
> *To all, who dar'd, by Gloss or Wile,*
> *The Christian Morals to defile.*
> *All* PREACHERS *own his Eloquence,*
> WRITERS POLITE, *his polish'd Sense;*
> MATHEMATICIANS *with amaze,*
> *On his profounder Genius gaze;*
> PHILOSOPHERS *him Sage define,*

And DOCTORS *praise the deep Divine,*
His stricter Life the PIOUS *bless,*
Him all admire, and all confess,
That, from his Childhood, to his Fall,
He lived unknown, and known to all.
   Reader, why further should we run?
The PASCAL, *who is lost and gone,*
Great LEWIS DE MONTALT *he was:*
Alas! —enough is said —alas! —
Tears choak my Words—and I am Dumb;
But thou, who offerest, at his Tomb,
A Godly Prayer; all Good to Thee,
Living and Dead for ever be.[36]

Slight though it is, the final 'Comparison between Picus and Monsieur Pascal' was the most original piece of writing in the volume. Jesup began by claiming that 'all the Parallels of Plutarch seem Lame in Respect to that which runs between the two Christian Heroes, I build my Comparison upon,' and next described the principal characteristics and achievements of the two men in a manner that drew attention to their similarities: 'Picus indeed had the Advantage of Pascal in his Birth, yet Pascal was of an ancient Family, and Born to a plentiful Fortune; so that neither of them wanted the Means of indulging that Turn in Nature, which they had to Knowledge. They both promised great Things as soon as they came to the Use of Reason, and were very early Authors.'

Their youthful precocity, their powers of memory, their refusal of matrimony, and their admirable piety were mentioned in turn, and, although at one point the Frenchman appeared to be more meritorious than the Italian, the balance was quickly rectified:

Indeed the Vanity and Vices of Picus, when very Young, did not appear in Pascal; but he was so far sunk in Disquisitions, purely Humane, that he had very little Regard to the practical Part of Religion till his twenty-fourth Year, in which, by an Application to Books, he was convinced of the Necessity of being a Practical as well as a Speculative Christian; and, from that Time, reduced his Speculations to Practice, and became as Conspicuous for Devotion, as he had been before for Learning, and gave no further Application to Humane Studies, but retired, like Picus, after his Disgrace in Rome, and pass'd the rest of his Days in a pious Solitude.

After commenting that 'the Schools' played little or no part in the education of Picus and Pascal, and, later, that 'they never concerned themselves with the Questions and Intricacies of the Schools, after they became the Votaries of Jesus Christ,' Jesup went on to remark, 'they were both Disciples of St. Thomas, and preferred his System to all others.' No doubt what he had in mind was that both Picus and Pascal had looked upon reason as informing faith as conceived by St. Thomas Aquinas, without their having embraced some other characteristics of scholasticism which were being rejected by the new scientific philosophy. He proceeded to emphasize the retiring disposition and ascetic tendencies of both men and found that, in these respects, one might have followed in the footsteps of the other, Pascal having lived 'as if the Life of Picus had been his Law'; and it was upon this note that Jesup haltingly brought his comparison to a finish:

They seemed equally laborious, and possessed of an equal Courage and Resolution in the Reformation of Manners. Pascal, indeed, is charged, by some, with Prejudice and Insincerity in some Steps he took in that Way, and is vindicated by others; but whether he received a Prejudice in Education, or otherwise, that occasioned Mistakes, in his Party-Labours, I am unable to determine; but as it is not an Article of my Duty to be of a Party, in Things above my Knowledge, I hope it will not be required, that I either censure or approve his Works in that Way; but, to close my Parallel, I think I may securely (and hope, without Offence) say, that the two great Men, I run it between, were so disposed, as if the Soul of Picus had informed the Body of Pascal.[37]

It is another indication of the demand for the life of Pascal that, when a new translation of the *Lettres provinciales* was published in 1744, Mme. Perier's short biographical study was printed as an introduction to that work as well. As a result of the growing attention paid to his career and personality, Pascal began to emerge as an historical figure of some genuine importance to his English audience, being distinguished alike for his extraordinary mental and literary gifts, and for the singular manner in which he had expressed his piety; and, to a very considerable extent, his general reputation in England came to rest upon the legend of his life and the attribution to him of universal genius. It also becomes increasingly clear that the interpretation of Pascal's available writings and recorded discoveries by English readers would often proceed by way of some previous knowledge they had gained of the life and character of the man himself. A notable influence of this kind was exerted by Budgell's observations in the *Spectator*, which, as well as being widely read in that journal, were placed in an abbreviated form upon the title-page of the second edition of Kennett's translation of the *Pensées*, initiating a practice which would be continued in all subse-

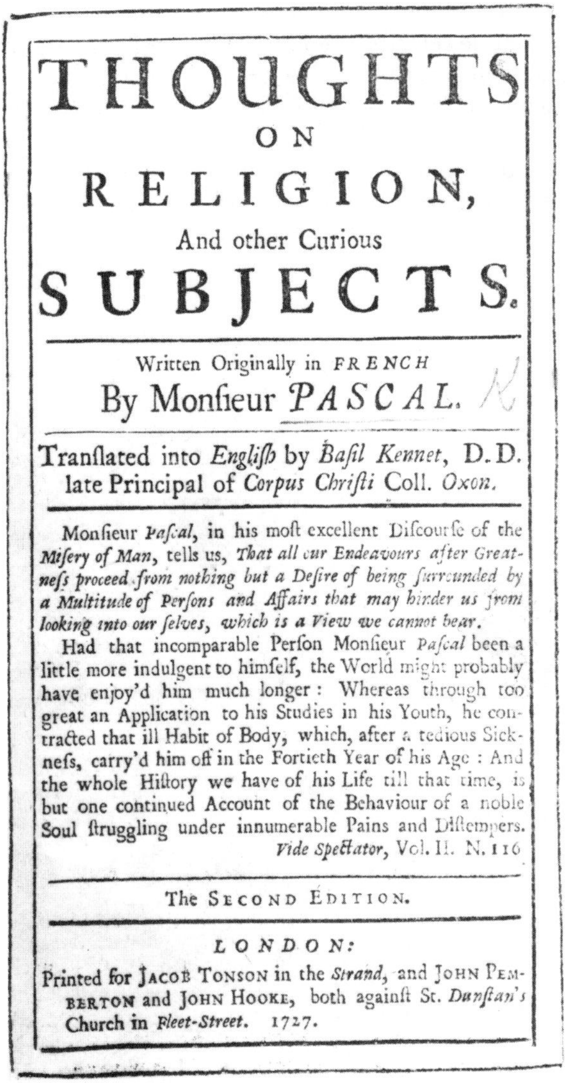

THOUGHTS

ON

RELIGION,

And other Curious

SUBJECTS.

Written Originally in *FRENCH*
By Monſieur *PASCAL.*

Tranſlated into *Engliſh* by *Baſil Kennet*, D.D.
late Principal of *Corpus Chriſti* Coll. *Oxon.*

Monſieur *Paſcal*, in his moſt excellent Diſcourſe of the *Miſery of Man*, tells us, *That all our Endeavours after Greatneſs proceed from nothing but a Deſire of being ſurrounded by a Multitude of Perſons and Affairs that may hinder us from looking into our ſelves, which is a View we cannot bear.*
Had that incomparable Perſon Monſieur *Paſcal* been a little more indulgent to himſelf, the World might probably have enjoy'd him much longer : Whereas through too great an Application to his Studies in his Youth, he contraſted that ill Habit of Body, which, after a tedious Sickneſs, carry'd him off in the Fortieth Year of his Age : And the whole Hiſtory we have of his Life till that time, is but one continued Account of the Behaviour of a noble Soul ſtruggling under innumerable Pains and Diſtempers.
Vide Spectator, Vol. II. N. 116

The SECOND EDITION.

LONDON:
Printed for JACOB TONSON in the *Strand*, and JOHN PEMBERTON and JOHN HOOKE, both againſt St. *Dunſtan's* Church in *Fleet-Street.* 1727.

PLATE 4 Title-page of the second edition of Basil Kennett's translation of Pascal's *Pensées* (London, 1727)

quent English editions of the eighteenth century. Pascal was thus from time to time reintroduced by way of the *Spectator*; but, though the intention must first have been to draw prospective readers to him by means of their acquaintance with that most successful of periodicals, the sample statement linked with the description of Pascal's maladies to which it was restricted would eventually contribute towards an assessment of his work by many in a less attractive light.

CHAPTER FOUR

Plac'd on this Isthmus

[I] The years following the appearance of Kennett's translation of the *Pensées* witnessed the rise of the greatest general popularity Pascal would enjoy in England during the eighteenth century. By various means, English opinion had come to realize his several major accomplishments, and knowledge of him was spreading to other parts of the British Isles and into the colonies in North America. After 1704, however, Pascal's reputation derived chiefly from the *Pensées*, with his life being seen as an integral part of his work. Kennett's Protestant sympathies had conferred a respectability upon the *Pensées*, and his supposition was correct that Pascal's thought might be found relevant to current preoccupations; for the manner of its reception briefly accorded the author a position of some eminence which would not be equalled until the present day.

It is crucial that any attempt to understand and analyse the effect of the *Pensées* upon eighteenth-century England should begin by recognizing the special contents and character of the *Edition de Port-Royal*; and, in the process, we must be prepared to discard the image of Pascal made familiar to the twentieth century and set in its place a figure much attenuated and even distorted in those features which now arouse most admiration. The reputation of Pascal today is more than ever established upon the *Pensées*, which assiduous scholarship has revealed to be a document extraordinarily original, moving, and profound. Few writers have described so compellingly the middle position that man occupies half-way between God and the animals, and the perils confronting him if he tries to transcend his state. Man can only reconcile himself happily to the facts of his existence by accepting his limitations and acknowledging that his final act, as a rational being, should be to recognize the inadequacy of his powers of reason and proceed thenceforward by faith. In his awareness of man's paradoxical nature and his choice of arguments for a life of purpose and hope under all circumstances, the Pascal of the *Pensées* seems peculiarly contemporary, and his definition of the Christian religion ultimately on grounds of experience has placed him as a forerunner of Kierkegaard and modern existentialist thought. The *Pensées* as known to the eighteenth century produced far less of this striking impression; and, viewed from today's perspective, it might be considered remarkable that they exercised the appeal they did. We must therefore of necessity seek to define their earlier representation, since only after acquaintance with its emphases and deficiencies can we trace with any accuracy the nature of the work's influence upon English thought and opinion.

The origins of the *Pensées* have already been described, and we have noted how, as soon as the decision was taken to publish the manuscript, the arrangement of the text became of vital concern. The editing committee representing Pascal's family and friends which met soon after his death faced the same fundamental problem that has baffled generations of scholars since—how to set the fragments in that order resembling most closely the author's assumed intentions. The committee's members considered some guide existed in a survey of his project to convince free-thinkers of the truth of Christianity, which Pascal himself had delivered at Port Royal a few years earlier; but, as they were to say, their final conclusion was that the material might best be arranged according to each topic instead, and without reference to its state when found. Their distrust of Pascal's boldness in adopting or contemplating unorthodox points of view was accentuated by the community's current misfortunes, and prudence determined that only those thoughts of Pascal unlikely to give offence in any quarter should be seen in print. A good half of the fragments were therefore omitted, the dimensions of Pascal's project were cut back, and much that was most arresting about his thought caused to disappear. As a further safeguard, a limited edition of the resulting version of the *Pensées* was submitted to the ecclesiastical authorities in 1669, and only after their approval was the accepted first edition placed on sale in January 1670. Its success during the following years encouraged the publisher, Guillaume Desprez, to seek permission to produce a slightly expanded version that might contain as well Mme. Perier's life of Pascal and the essays by Filleau de la Chaise. Port Royal's circumstances became more relaxed, and, in 1678, thirty-nine new fragments were accordingly added, creating the form in which the *Edition de Port-Royal* finally remained.[1]

The eighteenth century in France witnessed a prolonged rationalist attack upon Pascal which culminated with the publication in 1776 of a new version of the *Pensées* by the Marquis de Condorcet. Like the Port Royal edition, this constituted a selection from the fragments left by Pascal, but Condorcet's main intent was deliberately to upset Port Royal's order of presentation and by this means and some omissions to portray Pascal as a man of reason, a scientist of genius, and a sceptic, who had tragically lost his direction. Retitling the work *Pensées sur l'homme*, Condorcet's whole approach was in the spirit of announcing a literary discovery. He had seen the original manuscript and now proclaimed that, after one hundred years of deception, readers of the new *Pensées* might at last perceive how Pascal had been the enemy of humanity and a desperate, unbalanced man from the time his powers had begun to fail.[2]

In 1779, the Abbé Bossut produced the first collected edition of Pascal's works, but added only twenty-eight new fragments to Port Royal's selection.[3] Some other versions followed, but it was not until 1842 that the modern history of the *Pensées* begins when the philosopher, Victor Cousin, appealed for a complete investigation of the original manuscript and the establishment of an authentic text free from the shortcomings of all previous versions.[4] His call was heeded, and two years later Prosper Faugère produced the first edition to be regarded as approximately correct by modern standards;[5] but, as the task proceeded, opinions came to divide radically upon the method of organizing the fragments. Port Royal had fortunately recorded the order in which they had been found, but, in the view of several leading scholars, notably Léon Brunschvicg, the manuscript had been left in no precise scheme and should be arranged to make the greatest sense possible.[6] Others, in particular Louis Lafuma, attempted instead to classify the *pensées* by reference to their state on discovery, or turned to the evidence provided by the outline Pascal himself had once given.[7] Full agreement may never be achieved and several reputable versions of the text combine to create the current estimation of its author; but, of all the recent editions, that by Lafuma may be claimed as the most scholarly and, in all probability, the closest to the arrangement Pascal envisaged.

In spite of the new structure imposed by Condorcet and Bossut in turn, the selection made by Pascal's literary executors therefore remained essentially unchanged until well into the nineteenth century; and, throughout practically the entire period with which this study is concerned, the only version of the *Pensées* known in England except to the very few who took notice of the editions of Condorcet and Bossut was that presented by Port Royal. Not only was this the edition most widely available in French, but Walker, Kennett, and later Chevalier made their translations from the *Edition de Port-Royal*, and John Wesley his adaptation for his *Christian Library*. No alternative French version was produced in English until 1825. It is therefore beyond question that, since the *Pensées* in England were known so exclusively in the Port Royal edition during these years, all matters of English knowledge, appreciation, and disapproval of the Pascal of the *Pensées* must be discussed in its light.

An eighteenth-century Englishman opening a copy of the *Pensées*, most probably in Kennett's translation, would find the work consisted of thirty-one chapters of unequal length; and, perhaps curious as to its compilation, he might choose to look first at the preface submitted by the editing committee. There he would discover Port Royal's reasons for offering its chosen arrangement of Pascal's literary remains, enjoining him nevertheless to use his own judgement to conceive how the fragments 'stand related, according to the Original Idea of the Author.' Turning the pages, he might then notice a certain sequence in the earlier chapter headings: 'Against an Atheistical Indifference' (i); 'Marks of the True Religion' (ii); 'The True Religion proved by the Contrarieties which are discoverable in Man, and by the Doctrines of Original Sin' (iii); 'The Submission and Use of Reason' (v); and 'Faith without Reasoning' (vi). Pascal's wager was set forth in chapter vii, entitled 'That there is more advantage in believing than in disbelieving the Doctrines of Christianity'; however, the editors claimed in a short statement that Pascal had made his contention only for purposes of argument, not as a representation of his genuine belief.

A new section was announced in chapter viii, 'The Pourtraict of a Man who has wearied himself with searching after God by his bare Reason, and who begins to read the Scriptures.' Man's state of corruption was briefly described, and then chapters x through xx, in some respects the core of the book, discussed those grounds for the acceptance of Christianity to be derived from the Bible. The chapters following recalled some earlier themes, that on 'The strange Contrarieties discoverable in Human Nature, with regard to Truth, and Happiness, and many other things' (xxi) initiating separate evaluations of man's greatness, his vanity, his weakness, and his misery. The last part of the small volume consisted of some of Pascal's more heterogeneous reflections grouped together: 'Thoughts upon Miracles' (xxvii); 'Christian Thoughts' (xxviii); 'Thoughts upon Death' (xxix); 'Moral Thoughts' (xxx); and 'Miscellaneous Thoughts' (xxxi). Port Royal ended its selection with a postscript, 'A Prayer of Monsieur Pascal, Composed in Sickness.'[8]

The modern reader might conclude from this that the Port Royal edition contained most salient features of the *Pensées* of today, albeit in a somewhat haphazard order. A more thorough examination, however, would clearly reveal that Port Royal's whole organization of its text was designed to produce a very different impression from the work that is now available. Presentday opinion has come to hold in highest esteem Pascal's evaluation of man's perplexity in his search for salvation, but the emphasis in the Port Royal edition lay heavily upon dogmatic proofs for the validity of the Christian religion itself. Lafuma has divided the *Pensées* into two principal sections, the first treating man's condition and placing the intelligent reader in a frame of mind conducive to receiving the Christian faith, and the second marshalling arguments from history and doctrine for its truth. In the Port Royal edition this sequence is disrupted, the first two-thirds, within itself not altogether logically arranged, being composed of relatively innocuous evidence in support of Christianity. Only towards the end, where its impact would be lessened, was Pascal's analysis of man, hinted at in chapter III, allowed some elaboration. The resulting version was to foster the long-lasting impression that the *Pensées* were primarily a work of piety, defending unexceptionable Christian beliefs, and especially suitable for religious instruction or devotional purposes.

Port Royal's design was further implemented in all manners of detail. Since its leaders believed the tenets of the Christian faith might be satisfactorily explained by reason alone, many of Pascal's flights towards mysticism were eliminated and rational argument took precedence over what the heart could offer. As Port Royal favoured the Cartesian philosophy, examples of the author's hostility to Descartes were avoided; and, though Pascal had been willing to grant the value of the sceptical approach at every stage but the last in his apologetic, Port Royal considered this in dubious taste and rendered his interest in the Stoics and Montaigne less conspicuous. In general, any opinion regarding man's nature and the foundations of Christian belief which seemed to depart from a narrow orthodoxy was suppressed. Where Pascal had pointed out man's capacity for greatness, Port Royal stressed human depravity. Those *pensées* which challenged the justice of the existing political and social order were omitted, and, whenever Pascal's Jansenistic opinions on grace recalled the contents of the *Lettres provinciales*, they were expunged. Many other fragments were omitted, apparently either because Port Royal considered them incomplete or repetitive, or because they seemed to lack sufficient knowledge of theology.[9]

That minority of the total number of fragments which finally passed Port Royal's rigid tests of selection display additional signs of meddlesome interference. Numerous words were changed to tone down Pascal's intended meanings, whole sentences were inserted on occasion to steer the direction of his thought onto safer ground, and one brand-new *pensée* was even composed to further acceptability. Inevitably the stylistic devices which invigorate so many of Pascal's expressions suffered as a result, especially when Port Royal chose to substitute its preferred neo-classical forms. The personal anxiety with which Pascal had infused his manuscript was ruthlessly extracted – the phrase 'le silence éternel de ces espaces infinis m'effraie' being omitted among others;[10] and, instead of the work which holds the modern reader by its anguished and realistic questioning, Port Royal handed the world a committee's safe answers to a number of barely stated, largely conventional religious enquiries.

Such a state of affairs was hardly helped for the eighteenth-century English readers by the translations of Walker and Kennett. That by Walker was sometimes grossly inaccurate and uncouth, showing signs of haste as well as lack of subtlety;[11] and, though Kennett's work undoubtedly owed something of its popularity and hence its influence by contrast with Walker's earlier and more inelegant form of writing, his translation carried the stylistic 'improvements' of Port Royal a stage further. Perhaps the delights of his task had caused Kennett to lay restraints aside, for, in his concern for his prose, he was especially fond of adding superfluous words and expressions simply to create a more stately, grandiloquent effect. None were more keenly conscious of these flourishes of imagination than his knowledgeable readers, and their criticisms are as much to the point as ever. In 1734, Lord Forbes of Pitsligo, who knew the *Pensées* well in both French and English, observed that 'Mr. Kennet has taken a good deal of liberty generally in his Translation,' though later conceding that at times the result was felicitous.[12] Seven years later, the translator of the twenty-fifth chapter, 'Sur les Pensées de M. Pascal,' of Voltaire's *Lettres philosophiques*, known only by his initials 'R.E.M.,' advised his readers to turn to the 'beautiful translation' by 'the learned Dr. Kennett' for their further information; but such compliments did not prevent him from taking issue with Kennett several times. For Kennett to have translated 'l'homme sans lumiere' as 'a man without comfort' 'does not answer the author's idea'; and, by believing 'Cela ne vaut rien' to mean 'Let this pass for nothing,' 'Dr. Kennet supposes Paschal to countenance a thing for which he declares an abhorrence.' Perhaps most reprehensible of all was the 'very diffuse way' in which Kennett had handled 'S'il n'y avoit qu'une religion, Dieu seroit trop manifeste.' By rendering this 'Were there but one religion in the world, the discoveries of the divine nature might seem too free and open, and with too little distinction,' the critic considered that 'the learned Doctor's paraphrastical version is liable to the same objections, which M. de Voltaire has made to the original' – in other words that its meaning had been made all too clear.[13]

In 1803, it was partly a reaction to the faults of Walker's and Kennett's workmanship that prompted Thomas Chevalier to undertake a translation of his own. From the distance of a century their inadequacies seemed glaring:

For the former, though very literal, is defective and obscure, and the latter, though more polished, is too diffuse, and not sufficiently close to the original. Indeed it may with truth be observed, that there is not a single page of Dr. Kennett's Translation, in which the genuine language and stile of Pascal can be found. The stile of Pascal is close and aphoristic, but yet animated and striking: Dr. Kennett's translation is turgid, pompous, and full of bombast. To give only one specimen – At the close of Section XXI. *Pascal says,* 'What a Chimaera then is man! What a novelty! What a Chaos! What a subject of contradiction! A judge of every thing, and yet a feeble worm of the earth! The depositary of truth; and yet a mere heap of uncertainty! The glory and the outcast of the universe! If he boasts, I humble him. If he humbles himself, I boast of him; and always contradict him, till he is brought to comprehend that he is an incomprehensible monster.' *This passage Dr. Kennett amplifies into the following paragraph.* 'What a chimaera is man! What a surprising novelty! What a confused Chaos! What a subject of contradiction! A profess'd Judge of all things, and yet a feeble worm of the earth! The great depositary and guardian of truth, and yet a meer huddle of uncertainty. The glory and the scandal of the universe! If he is too aspiring and lofty, we can lower and humble him; if too mean and little, we can raise and swell him. To conclude, we can bait him with repugnancies and contradictions, till at last he apprehends himself to be a monster even beyond apprehension.' – *Circumlocutions equally absurd in themselves, and equally distant from the original may be found in almost every page.*[14]

Although its failings were recognized, Kennett's translation nevertheless remained for a century practically without a rival, and, with its spelling and some of its expressions periodically modified, became for that age the standard English version of the *Pensées*. In 1727, a second edition was published bearing his name for the first time, followed in 1731 by a third and ten years later by a fourth. The last was reprinted in 1749, and two years afterwards an edition was published in Edinburgh. To some degree, indeed, the fortunes of Pascal in eighteenth-century England may be traced in accordance with the frequency with which Kennett's translation was issued. No English version of the *Pensées*, except for Wesley's adaptation, was published after 1751 until that by Chevalier in 1803, but Kennett's work by no means subsequently vanished. Beginning in 1825 it reappeared from time to time throughout the nineteenth century, although increasingly relegated from its former position by new translations drawing upon the results of French scholarship; and its final bow to the public was possibly made in 1893 when it was presented as one of Sir John Lubbock's 'Hundred Best Books.'

No one has described the shortcomings of the *Edition de Port-Royal* more vividly than Cousin, who charged Pascal's executors with having inflicted a gross misrepresentation on a national and universal genius. Ever afterwards, the Port Royal edition has been castigated as a bad edition; but, although we are bound from today's perspective to think likewise, we must realize that the eighteenth-century reader in France, England, and elsewhere, had practically no alternative but to accept the text as Port Royal had provided it for him. The editorial committee's remarks might make an Englishman wonder to what extent the manuscript had received alteration, although if reading Kennett's version he would probably lend his approval to the translator's omission of passages upholding Catholic doctrines; but the most determined reader could only compare the slight differences that existed between Walker's and Kennett's translations and among the various examples of the *Edition de Port-Royal*, and follow the committee's admonition to use his own judgement. However much his appearance might be forcibly recast by Condorcet and Bossut, the Pascal of the *Pensées* to the eighteenth century was primarily the Pascal released by Port Royal, often being associated with the community's other writings; and, although the original scheme of the author's thoughts might still arouse the reader's curiosity, he was compelled eventually to define his opinions on the basis of that arrangement of the manuscript Port Royal had given him in the light of what might be discovered about Pascal elsewhere.

Such a conclusion naturally has important repercussions upon this study. To begin with, since most of Pascal's characteristic thoughts are in some general way represented in the Port Royal edition, or through apparent ignorance of that edition's peculiarities, the eighteenth century has sometimes been credited with more knowledge of the *Pensées* than it deserves. We must therefore seek to avoid this common pitfall and dismiss such claims when fragments not made public until the nineteenth century are involved, seeing the *Pensées* in England as only being known at any one time from the fragments then available in their contemporary version. The text of Port Royal's selection bore many touches, most of them prejudicial, which we can today recognize as the hand of the editing committee or of one of the translators, not of Pascal himself; but, as the eighteenth century had no ready means of challenging the authenticity of the text it possessed, these interpolations and changes – and the philosophy they produced – must surely enter into this analysis of Pascal's English reputation as much as if he had, in fact, originally thus written them.[15]

In consequence, we must firmly attempt to see the Pascal of the *Pensées* principally as a rather narrow devotional writer, whose anthology of remarks upon various other subjects was cast as a pendant to his major theme. We are dealing here not with the *Pensées* of today, but with the eighteenth-century's *Pensées sur la religion*. Port Royal's selection could hardly have been entitled otherwise, and, when Kennett described its contents as being mainly a treatment of 'the Greatest Subject,' he did so with accuracy. Indeed, Kennett's translation was particularly subject to the deficiencies in Port Royal's approach to the manuscript since it was taken from an edition that had appeared prior to the slight enlargement of 1678. Although many of Pascal's leading characteristics as a thinker remained plainly visible, the editing committee nonetheless stamped its impression upon them; and it is the story of the divergence of English opinions upon the merits of this Pascal sent forth by Port Royal that will henceforth largely dominate our attention.

[II] Until the closing years of the seventeenth century, knowledge of the *Pensées* in England was clearly restricted to the few who had noticed the work on account of their characteristic philosophical or religious interests. As, however, more educated Englishmen developed an acquaintance with its contents through French editions, the translations of Walker and Kennett, or from authors who drew upon Pascal, the earlier appreciative response broadened and the *Pensées* came to be admired for their elucidation of several themes then being exercised in discussion. Many an English reader must have found his mind prepared for parts of the *Pensées* by his growing agreement with the spirit of empiricism, and by the favourable reception he had previously given to the scepticism of Montaigne; but a fundamental motive for his ready acceptance of the newly available *Pensées* was the high estimation in which he was likely to hold French language and literature. As the fame of contemporary French literature spread to England, not least through the mediation of that exiled man of letters, Saint-Evremond, writers such as Boileau, Voiture, Rapin, and Molière, to mention only a few, were translated or copied, and English writers set their standards to a considerable degree in accordance with the tenets of French literary criticism. The years surrounding the turn of the century saw a great many translations from the French being made, and it may be recalled both Walker and Kennett translated other French authors besides Pascal. The interest of Kennett in the *Pensées* should, in fact, be partly seen as connected with his own literary pursuits and his translation of Rapin.

It is thus chiefly among literary men of the late Restoration period that the most conspicuous instances of English appreciation of the *Pensées* occur. Eager to follow where France had led, or at least affected by her example, English writers were drawn in part towards Pascal as an authority on style. Certain of his opinions and enough of his individualistic expression had survived the Port Royal edition to confer this reputation upon him—a reputation that had been assisted in France by his authorship of the *Lettres provinciales*; moreover, as those standards of clarity and simplicity in language favoured by the Royal Society increasingly gained acceptance, Pascal's combination of scientific and literary pursuits made him doubly impressive. Such initial approval promptly paved the way for the *Pensées* being esteemed for the number of fine sayings and perceptive comments they contained, which, usually for having summarized in a concise and eloquent manner some paradox in human life or nature, were borrowed for all purposes. Writers of various tastes demonstrate the current sympathy with Pascal in English literary circles either by quoting him directly, or by presenting as their own some of his most effective observations; and this form of popularity reached its peak in Pope's adaptation of several themes from the *Pensées* in *An Essay on Man*.

With the most outstanding immediate response to the *Pensées* in England largely arising out of this vogue for French literature, we shall review the nature of this new appreciation and generally attempt to assess Pascal's influence with that exerted by other French authors at the time. The traditional opinion has been that the *Pensées* considerably affected English thought in the early eighteenth century, intriguing and, on occasion, inspiring several English writers.[16] On closer examination, however, it rapidly becomes plain that most examples usually cited of Pascal's influence certainly utilized his images and expressions but placed them within a different context than either Pascal or his editors had intended. In English circles, the balance Pascal had struck between the claims of reason and faith remained attractive for a time, but, as deistic philosophies came to stress the pre-eminence of rational beliefs, the essentially Christian solutions he had offered to man's predicament were gradually rejected. Much to admire might still be found in Pascal's powers of description and figures of speech, but the total argument of the *Pensées* began to seem indefensible and its author's analysis of man to have been misapplied.

The theme that man is primarily motivated by self-love and the desire for pleasure enjoyed some fashionableness among English writers and thinkers of the late seventeenth century, through their acquaintance with the works of Malebranche and La Rochefoucauld as well as Pascal. The *Pensées* would not have reached John Dryden in time to have affected him significantly,[17] but, when his *Pastorals*, a translation of Virgil's *Eclogues*, appeared in 1697, they were accompanied by a preface by William Walsh, who referred to Pascal in this connection in his defence of the Roman poet against the criticisms of Fontenelle. Walsh, the later friend and confidant of Pope, found reason to accuse Fontenelle and his fellow-writers of 'immoderate self-love' in the practice of their craft, and provided illustrations for his charge:

There is generally more of the passion of Narcissus, than concern for Chloris and Corinna, in this whole affair. Be pleased to look into almost any of those writers, and you shall meet everywhere that eternal Moi, *which the admirable Pascal so judiciously condemns. Homer can never be enough admired for this one so particular quality, that he never speaks of himself, either in the* Iliad *or the* Odysseys: *and, if Horace had never told us his genealogy, but left it to the writer of his life, perhaps he had not been a loser by it.*[18]

Another example of Pascal's appraisal of this aspect of human nature particularly struck the playwright and critic, John Dennis. In 1698, by way of a reply to an attack by Jeremy Collier upon the morals of the English theatre, Dennis wrote *The Usefulness of the Stage, to the Happiness of Mankind, to Government, and to Religion*; and, setting out to prove that 'the Stage is instrumental to the Happiness of Mankind in general,' he proceeded to note it was universally acknowledged that 'Happiness consists in Pleasure.' Whatever man might do, 'whether in Spiritual or Temporal Affairs, whether in Matters of Profit or Diversion, Pleasure is, at least, the chief and the final Motive to it, if it is not the immediate one'; and, by way of clinching his argument upon 'our Spring and Fountain of Action,' Dennis referred to an extreme specimen: 'Now as 'tis Pleasure that obliges Man to preserve himself, it is the very same that has sometimes the Force to prevail upon him to his own Destruction. For, as Monsieur Pascal observes, The very Men who Hang, and who Drown themselves, are instigated by the secret Pleasure which they have, from the Thought that they shall be freed from Pain.'[19]

That Walsh's familiarity with the *Pensées* arose from the context of French literature is again shown when he invoked Pascal later in his preface while defending the desirability of a clear and natural style. The 'over-scrupulous care' of Fontenelle and others to make smooth connections in their writings had made modern compositions 'often-times tedious and flat'; instead, Walsh suggested, 'by the omission of them it comes to pass that the *Pensées* of the incomparable M. Pascal, and perhaps of M. Bruyère, are two of the most entertaining books which the modern French can boast of.'[20] Dennis, in contrast, may well have studied the *Pensées* in greater detail. In *The Grounds of Criticism in Poetry* (1704), he mentioned Milton's difficulty in *Paradise Lost* in making God speak convincingly of his attributes and power. Milton, he wrote, 'expresses himself with those Passions which in-deed are proper enough in the Poet, but never can be so in the Deity,' and he commended Cowley's note upon the *Davideis*, 'that God is to be introduced speaking simply.' It seemed to Dennis the case for this approach had been stated most persuasively by Pascal, and he proceeded to expand the original words into a small story:

And this puts me in mind of an extraordinary Argument of Monsieur Paschal, proving the Divinity of our Saviour by the Simplicity of his Stile; for, says he, our Saviour speaks of the sublimest Subjects, even the Glories of the Kingdom of Heaven, without being moved at all, which shews that he was really God: for suppose a Peasant, says he, or an ordinary Man should be carry'd to the Court of some Prince, as for example the Great Mogul, and there be shewn all his Riches, his Pomp, and his Power; this Peasant at his return would certainly speak of these things in extravagant terms, in terms that would sufficiently declare his Transport. But if the Mogul himself was to speak of them, he who had been always used to them, would speak without any Emotion. So, says Monsieur Paschal, if any one else had deliver'd any thing concerning the Glories of the Kingdom of Heaven, he would certainly have done it with Transport, nay tho he had been a Fanatick or an Impostor: for let those Divine Ideas come how they will, 'tis impossible for Man to think of them without being ravish'd by them. But our Saviour, who was God, and who consequently had been used to them from all Eternity, spoke of them unconcern'd.[21]

In 1697, shortly before making his attack upon the stage and publishing his edition of Moréri's dictionary, Jeremy Collier brought together under the title of *Essays upon several Moral Subjects* a number of pieces he had written during the previous few years. One of these, 'Of the Weakness of Human Reason,' comes near to being outright plagiarism of the twenty-fifth chapter of the *Pensées*, Collier at least having the grace to offer some passing acknowledgement to Pascal. The author's familiarity with French literature and philosophy had doubtless introduced him to a French edition of the *Pensées*, but the manner in which he paraphrased the text may be illustrated by a not untypical comparison. In Port Royal's version, the following passage was brief and its meaning clear:

Le plus grand Philosophe du monde, sur une planche plus large qu'il ne faut pour marcher à son ordinaire, s'il y a au dessous un précipice, quoy que sa raison le convainque de sa seureté, son imagination prévaudra. Plusieurs n'en sçauroient soûtenir la pensée sans paslir et suer. Je ne veux pas en rapporter tous les effets. Qui ne sçait qu'il y en a à qui la veüe des chats, des rats, l'écrasement d'un charbon, emportent la raison hors des gonds?

Under Collier's hand, however, these observations retained their broad intent, but underwent the same kind of superficial change and embellishment that would later be associated with the work of Kennett:

Another Instance of the Impotency of Reason may be taken from the Prevalence of Fancy. For Example, Let a Bridge somewhat broader then the space a Man usually takes up in Walking; be laid over a precipice, or deep River: Desire some eminent Philosopher to take a Turn or Two upon it for Meditation sake. I warrant you for all the Strength of his Notions he begs your Pardon. For tho' he can demonstrate, himself as safe as if he were upon a Bowling Green; yet he is so ridden by his Imagination that he dares not venture. And some are so struck, that the very Thought of such an Undertaking, will make them turn pale and fall a sweating. I need not run through all the particulars of this kind. 'Tis well known that the sight of a Cat, or the scratching of a Plate, will discompose some People almost into an Agony, and throw their Reason quite off the Hinges.[22]

Agreeing with this section in the Port Royal edition, Collier considered reason to be the most important human faculty, at the same time depicting its impairment by illness, old age, and local custom, and its manipulation by public opinion, education, and visual impressions; for, as he said, 'There are few Things Reason can discover with so much certainty and Ease, as its own Insufficiency.'[23] Elsewhere, he showed himself ready to hold faith in God a surer path to happiness, and, as a member and ultimately bishop of the Nonjurors, he provides a leading instance of the respect in which that group held Pascal's writings from a religious point of view. Attracted also to other Jansenist figures, Collier had knowledge of Pascal's life, and, in a later essay, recommended deists 'to look over Monsieur Paschal's Thoughts against Atheistical Indifference,' as well as works by Grotius and La Bruyère.[24] His own particular religious inclinations led him to believe, however, that the *Lettres provinciales* had portrayed Catholicism too adversely. In his dialogue, 'Of Lying,' first published in 1705, he incorporated an extract he had translated from the *Provinciales* illustrating the doctrines of equivocation and mental reservation, and then came forward with the following remark:

> Philotimus. *This is horrible Stuff! But you know this loose Casuistry is not allow'd by other Roman Catholics: The Divines of Paris, and the Clergy of the Diocese of Roan, remonstrate loudly against the Liberties in the Provincial Letters. The Faculty of Lovain, and the Archbishop of Malines, censure this Fencing against Lying. And it has likewise been since condemn'd by the Pope.*
>
> Philalethes. *You say right: and therefore I have no Design to charge it upon that Communion.*[25]

Jonathan Swift had some knowledge of Pascal, his library including a large number of French books; among them at different times were copies of the *Lettres provinciales* (Cologne, 1662, and 1669), the *Pensées* (Amsterdam, 1699), and La Bruyère's *Caractères . . . et ouvrage dans le gout de Theophraste et de Pascal* (Amsterdam, 1697), the last of which bore comments in Swift's hand.[26] Evidence of Pascalian influence in Swift's writings is disappointingly slight, and obscured by the fact that both men developed thoughts which had a common source for each of them in Montaigne; but Pascal the moralist observing man's wretched plight would no doubt have been remembered by Swift, though his pessimism was greater than Pascal's. Voltaire observed of *A Tale of a Tub* that 'Pascal n'amuse qu'aux dépens des jesuites; Swift divertit et instruit aux dépens du genre humain';[27] but a modern suggestion that Swift in that work might have been impressed by one of Pascal's reflections upon the distortion of human reason by appearances proved impossible to sustain, since the relevant passage in the *Pensées* would not have been available accurately or in full to the eighteenth-century reader.[28]

In the same year that Kennett's translation of the *Pensées* first appeared, the Jesuit William Darrell wrote with dismay that 'Pascal is to be met withal gay and brisk in the Ale and Coffee-Houses'; and, in view of such popular interest, it is not surprising to find during the succeeding years allusions to Pascal in the *Spectator* and similar writings by those who contributed to it, which were aimed towards a wide section of the reading public. Budgell's citation of Pascal's premature demise as a lesson in the consequences of physical neglect has already been mentioned; and the individual literary productions of Addison and Steele, whose partnership launched the *Spectator*, provide several further instances of familiarity with the celebrated Frenchman. Perhaps the anti-Catholic Steele was following the example of the *Lettres provinciales* when he wrote a satirical essay upon the state of affairs produced by unorthodox Jesuit missionaries in China;[29] and in the *Ladies Library*, which he published in 1714, he stressed the great importance of a good taste in books, and commended as a valuable and enjoyable accomplishment for a lady 'to be able to read Voiture, Racine and Boileau, or rather Paschal, among the French.'[30] The *Spectator* was partly directed towards a female audience, and, when presenting his translation of the *Lettres provinciales* in 1744, William Andrews recalled that both it and the *Ladies Library* had recommended 'Mr. Paschal to the perusal of our English Ladies.' It gave Andrews pleasure to believe in a resulting influence 'among the fair sex, in families where piety, ingenuity, or good sense remain.'[31] In 1704, Darrell had also testified with alarm and regret to the eager welcome given by 'the Shee-wits' to the *Lettres provinciales*; but his strictures can have made little headway, for the early eighteenth century marks the beginning of the lasting attraction shown by Englishwomen towards Pascal.

Since Addison frequently used Bayle's *Dictionnaire* as a source of materials for the *Spectator* and he was often to be found with it lying open upon his table, it is certain that he was familiar with the details of Pascal's life; and, in view of his friendship with the translator, we should be prepared for his having possessed a copy of Kennett's version of the *Pensées*.[32] In an essay he contributed to the *Guardian* (No.136, August 17, 1713), Addison drew upon Pascal to support his opinions regarding the ever-present uncertainties of life:

Some of our quaint moralists have pleased themselves with an observation, that there is but one way of coming into the world, but a thousand to go out of it. . . . I remember Monsieur Paschal, in his reflections on Providence, has this observation upon Cromwell's death. 'That usurper,' says he, 'who had destroyed the royal family in his own nation, who had made all the princes of Europe tremble, and struck a terror into Rome itself, was at last taken out of the world by a fit of the gravel. An atom, a grain of sand,' says he, 'that would have been of no significancy in any other part of the universe, being lodged in such a particular place, was an instrument of Providence to bring about the most happy revolution, and to remove from the face of the earth this troubler of mankind.' In short, swarms of distempers are everywhere hovering over us; casualties, whether at home or abroad, whether we wake or sleep, sit or walk, are planted about us in ambuscade; every element, every climate, every season, all nature is full of death.[33]

A frequently recurring topic in the periodical literature of this time concerned the dignity of human nature, a belief to which both Addison and Steele paid tribute. Writing in the *Tatler*, Addison confessed 'there is nothing that more pleases me, in all that I read in books, or see among mankind, than such passages as represent human nature in its proper dignity,' and he opposed those 'modish

French authors' and their English imitators who 'endeavour to make no distinction between man and man, or between the species of men and that of brutes.'[34] It was John Hughes in the *Spectator*, however, who chose explicitly to quote Pascal in vindication of the 'controverted Doctrine' against 'the Falsity of all Human Virtues':

'It is very disingenuous to level the best of Mankind with the worst, and for the Faults of Particulars to degrade the whole Species. Such Methods tend not only to remove a Man's good Opinion of others, but to destroy that Reverence for himself, which is a great Guard of Innocence, and a Spring of Virtue.

'It is true indeed that there are surprizing Mixtures of Beauty and Deformity, of Wisdom and Folly, Virtue and Vice, in the Human Make . . . . But as I began with considering this Point as it relates to Action, I shall here borrow an admirable Reflection from Monsieur Pascal, which I think sets it in its proper Light.

'It is of dangerous Consequence, *says he,* to represent to Man how near he is to the Level of Beasts, without shewing him at the same time his Greatness. It is likewise dangerous to let him see his Greatness, without his Meanness. It is more dangerous yet to leave him ignorant of either; but very beneficial that he shou'd be made sensible of both.'[35]

In the *Pensées*, Pascal had used his reflections to lead his readers to resolve imperfect human nature through the salvation offered by the Christian religion. To Hughes, on the other hand, he was merely one of several examples of men, among them Cato and Cicero, who had all treated this particular issue similarly. Though 'it is the Business of Religion and Virtue' to rectify our faults 'as far as is consistent with our present State,' Hughes did not really urge his readers forward; rather he suggested it was 'no small Encouragement to generous Minds to consider that we shall put them all off with our Mortality.' In comparable fashion, Budgell had made his reference to Pascal's views on hunting a polished digression from the story he was telling, and not to initiate the consideration of the world's futility; and elsewhere he set down such a Pascalian thought as 'we meet with as different Passions in one and the same Soul as can be supposed in two,' as an aside lightly rounding off an anecdote.[36]

Thomas Gordon (d. 1750), an essayist who edited the *Humourist* in the early seventeen-twenties, likewise referred to Pascal's views on human nature, but in a very derivative and confused manner. In a piece entitled 'Of Method in Writing,' he partly echoed the opinions of Walsh regarding Pascal's exemplary literary style, and afterwards abruptly broke into a summary of several of Pascal's best-known reflections set amid Stoic surroundings:

Tis most certain that they have very Good Grounds who make the Observation, That the too strict and over-scrupulous Care of Connexions renders the modern Compositions oftentimes tedious and flat. And by the Omission of them, it seems to me, that those noble Remains of the Emperor Marcus Aurelius, and the Reflections of the excellent Monsieur Paschal, are two of the most useful and entertaining Books which Antiquity, or the later Ages has produced . . . . *[Marcus Aurelius] says in another Place with that* (Brevitas Imperialis) *Imperial Brevity, which Pliny the younger so justly admires in Trajan, That the Extent of human Life is but a Point; that the Faculties of Sense and Perception are weak and unpenetrating; the Body slenderly put together, and but a Remove from Putrefaction, the Soul a rambling sort of Thing. Man is indeed compounded of Appetites inconsistent with each other, and of jarring Inclinations: It seems not improbable that we are the lowest Degree of rational Creatures, of a Nature between Angels and Beasts, lying open to Depredations of various Kinds, and harrass'd by the Excitements of Sense, and the Suggestions of Reason; for Human Nature, like a Frontier Country, is almost always the Seat of War.*[37]

All the evidence suggests that the general theme in the *Pensées* to which men with literary interests most responded was the analysis by the 'excellent,' 'admirable,' and 'incomparable' Pascal of man's paradoxical nature. Kennett had described the 'Reflexions upon Mankind' as 'so sprightly and vigorous, so penetrating, and sensible,' and, whichever particular facet appealed to English writers and thinkers individually, the opinion was one with which they seem to have concurred. Locke on man's insignificance, Petty and Southwell on the methods of human reasoning, Walsh on 'immoderate self-love,' Collier on the weakness of reason, Budgell on man's need of diversions, and Hughes on the dignity of man together represent an attraction towards Pascal as a moralist whose observations proceeded from valuable insights into man's true nature. In an age becoming confident of greater human capabilities, yet aware that man's actions frequently proceed from irrational motives, Pascal's discrimination between reason and the passions and his portrait of man as half angel, half brute, endowed with reasoning faculties yet swayed by impressions and circumstances largely beyond his control, summarized precisely that mixture of components other men were seeking to express themselves. Nor were the ultimate conclusions of the *Pensées* necessarily any less acceptable at first. It was Addison's intention in the *Spectator* not only to offer the public 'Papers of Humour and Learning,' but also 'several Essays Moral and Divine';[38] and, when religious topics were deliberately selected, they were approached with that combination of common sense and a regard for the mysteries of faith which mirrored the outlook of Addison himself. He applauded the manner in which 'the Gentlemen of Port-Royal . . . more eminent for their Learning and Humility than any other in France' had practised self-effacement in their writings; and his belief in the workings of the Holy Spirit and his conviction that a wise man would accept religion for his present and future happiness, rather than atheism, have some kinship with the position of Pascal.[39] His essays on the subject of Infinitude often echo sentiments from the *Pensées*, and, indeed, a comparison was subsequently drawn between Pascal's work and Addison's own unfinished *Evidences of the Christian Religion*.[40]

More often, however, the thoughts of Pascal at this time were treated with a polite gentility uncharacteristic of their implications; and, as deism with its largely rationalist solutions to the human predicament shaped that frame of mind increasingly typical of the eighteenth century, the early signs of departure from Pascal's total scheme of argument became more pronounced. A more intense preoccupation with the problems of human nature led to alternative answers to those offered in the *Pensées* being regarded as more legitimate. It is distinctive of this stream of opinion towards Pascal in England that, while his analysis of man continued to be admired for a time, still partly on account of the place occupied by the *Pensées* in French literature, the forms of his thought were the more ruthlessly extracted from their context and set within other designs of philosophy whose conclusions differed fundamentally from those of the original author. This development may be particularly observed in the writings of Prior, Arbuthnot, and Pope; and ironically, though Pope's *Essay on Man* has been hailed as the most outstanding example of Pascal's influence in a major work of the age, the distance of the *Essay*'s conclusions from those of Pascal is on a scale commensurate with its indebtedness in phrase and expression.

[III] The attitude of Matthew Prior towards those problems of human nature stated by Pascal illustrate some of the confusion into which an individual might be thrown by the conflict of opinions in transition. When a man was as personally acquainted with French society and literature as Prior, a knowledge of Pascal's writings might be predicted with some assurance. As well as two copies of the *Lettres provinciales* (Cologne, 1657, and 1685), he owned a copy of the *Pensées* (Paris, 1702),[41] and some of Pascal's observations left their mark upon his most ambitious poems. In *Solomon on the Vanity of the World* (1708), he impressively treated the subject of man's constant search for happiness, and very likely had Pascal's remarks in mind when he himself wrote of man's ambivalent position:

Amid Two Seas on One small Point of Land
Weary'd, uncertain, and amaz'd We stand:
On either Side our Thoughts incessant turn:
Forward We Dread; and looking back We mourn.
Losing the Present in this dubious Hast;
And lost Our selves betwixt the Future, and the Past. . . .
What shall amend, or what absolve our Fate?
Anxious We hover in a mediate State,
Betwixt Infinity and Nothing; Bounds,
Or boundless Terms, whose doubtful Sense confounds
Unequal Thought; whilst All We apprehend,
Is, that our Hopes must rise, our Sorrows end;
As our Creator deigns to be our Friend.[42] [III, 613-18, 644-50]

Prior's talents, however, were better suited for defining man's condition than for offering total remedies. The poet would be praised for his description of the sorrows of the human state, of how man's reason only tormented him with fruitless questions and revealed him at the mercy of his passions; but, beyond ending *Solomon* on a stoical note, Prior could only suggest that the most practicable way of assuaging human misery lay in 'some Interval from active Woe.' Hoping against hope his predicament might improve, man could find a measure of happiness in temporary pleasures. In *Alma: or, The Progress of the Mind* (1718), the poet developed some aspects of this theme with his more characteristic lightness of touch. Taking issue with the Aristotelian view, reinterpreted by Descartes, that the body follows the dictates of the mind, Prior sought to show instead that the mind is constantly affected by physical demands and sensations, and, in consequence, reason can never act alone; and, when discussing reason's limitations, he, like Pope after him, recollected Pascal's comments upon the effect of local custom and chose to dilate fancifully upon the phrase, 'Vérité au deçà des Pyrénées, erreur au delà.' As he wrote in 1721, again referring to the *Pensées*, 'Opinion is said to be the Queen of the World':

> *To close this Point, We need not roam*
> *For Instances so far from Home.*
> *What parts gay* FRANCE *from sober* SPAIN*?*
> *A little rising Rocky Chain.*
> *Of Men born South or North o' th' Hill,*
> *Those seldom move; These ne'er stand still.*
> DICK, *You love Maps, and may perceive*
> ROME *not far distant from* GENEVE.
> *If the good* POPE *remains at Home,*
> *He's the First Prince in* CHRISTENDOME.

Choose then, good POPE, *at Home to stay;*
Nor Westward curious take Thy Way.
Thy Way unhappy should'st Thou take
From TIBER'S *Bank to* LEMAN-*Lake;*
Thou art an Aged Priest no more,
But a Young flaring Painted Whore:
Thy Sex is lost: Thy Town is gone,
No longer ROME, *but* BABYLON.
That some few Leagues should make this Change,
To Men unlearn'd seems mighty strange.

But need We, Friend, insist on This?
Since in the very CANTONS SWISS,
All your Philosophers agree,
And prove it plain, that One may be
A Heretic, or True Believer,
On this, or t'other Side a River.[43]   [II, 503–28]

Nevertheless, in spite of his wishes to attain wisdom of uncontested clarity and govern his life accordingly, man in reality would do anything 'to ease the Pain of Coward-Thought'; and, in this Pascalian vein, Prior noted that not only do music, flowers, butterflies, anything pretty readily beguile his mind, but that chess and playing-cards have been purposely devised to enable man to forget himself.[44] Unable to believe the passions have their place in a beneficial design, as Pope later did, Prior again concluded that the only feasible, though inadequate, means of achieving some contentment was through the enjoyment of diversions. Rather than allow philosophical speculation to heighten our discomforts, we should delight in friendship, merriment, and wine.[45]

For Prior, fleeting moments of distraction could not wholly relieve every human misery, but they might console and were at least better than restlessly analysing the range of problems. In his life as in his verse, he was unable to provide a better alternative. Very much influenced by the scepticism of Montaigne, he was hostile to the claims of the rising sciences and considered the workings of pure reason a fantasy. Man's condition was not to be remedied through the assertions of materialistic and deterministic systems of philosophy; and, although some of Pascal's definitions might seem valid to him, Prior could not bring himself to accept the solutions offered through faith instead to his complete satisfaction. In default of proposing a genuinely comprehensive answer, Prior's doubts eventually led him to support a position Pascal had categorically rejected.

The principal literary works of John Arbuthnot, the Scottish mathematician and physician, were satirical, but it is his one excursion into serious verse entitled *GNOTHI SE' AUTON. Know Yourself* that demands attention here. Though written some years previously, this short meditation was not published until 1734 and then anonymously, the advertisement explaining that 'it may do good to some, and cannot hurt the reputation of the author.' Moreover, 'it contains some thoughts of Monsieur Pascal, which cannot make it less acceptable to the Public.'[46] This constituted an understatement, since from start to finish the poem largely followed the themes of Pascal's argument that man is 'by double nature, double instinct swayed,' and can only reach the greatest heights open to him when he becomes reconciled to his contradictions, rejects the explanations given by rival philosophies, and humbly accepts the answers offered him through faith.

The writing by Pascal which most influenced Arbuthnot in the composition of his poem appears, in fact, to have been the *Entretien de Pascal avec Saci*, first published in 1728, which dealt more directly with certain issues discussed in the *Pensées*. After an earlier acquaintance with Pascal's mathematical and physical discoveries, and also no doubt the *Pensées*, Arbuthnot must have seen in the *Entretien*'s contents a subject well-suited for imitation. A modern study has claimed the *Entretien* was 'unquestionably used,' and that in the later stages of the poem 'the indebtedness of Arbuthnot . . . is all but complete.'[47] It was then that the Scottish author was describing the failings of the philosophies of the Stoics and Epicureans, or, as Pascal would have it, of Epictetus and Montaigne:

> *Around me, lo, the thinking thoughtless crew,*
> *(Bewildered each) their different paths pursue;*
> *Of them I ask the way; the first replies,*
> *Thou art a god; and sends me to the skies.*
> *Down on this turf (the next) thou two-legged beast,*
> *There fix thy lot, thy bliss, and endless rest;*
> *Between those wide extremes the length is such,*
> *I find I know too little or too much.*

In such a predicament, all thanks should be given to the 'almighty power' for revealing the truth to man through scripture, 'the balm, the light, the guide of souls perplexed':

> *'O truth divine! enlightened by thy ray,*
> *I grope and guess no more, but see my way;*
> *Thou clear'dst the secret of my high descent,*
> *And told me what those mystic tokens meant;*

Marks of my birth, which I had worn in vain,
Too hard for worldly sages to explain;
Zeno's were vain, vain Epicurus' schemes,
Their systems false, delusive were their dreams,
Unskilled my twofold nature to divide,
One nursed by pleasure, and one nursed by pride:
Those jarring truths which human art beguile,
Thy sacred page thus bid me reconcile.[48]

Its closeness to Pascal's thought notwithstanding, Arbuthnot's approach credited mankind with remnants of former grandeur Pascal had been less inclined to allow. Seeing man more as a corrupted than a corrupt being, his deistic sentiments dominated Pascal's mysticism, resulting in, as one critic has said, 'a workmanlike statement of the sceptical approach to faith.'[49] Pascal had emphasized salvation as ultimately a process beyond human understanding, conferring upon man powers outside his reach; Arbuthnot in contrast conceived man here as sensibly though still paradoxically accepting divine help in order to develop those powers already latent in him:

Though by foul guilt thy heavenly form defaced,
In nature changed, from happy mansions chased,
Thou still retain'st some sparks of heav'nly fire,
Too faint to mount, yet restless to aspire;
Angel enough to seek thy bliss again,
And brute enough to make thy search in vain.
The creatures now withdraw their kindly use,
Some fly thee, some torment, and some seduce;
Repast ill suited to such different guests,
For what thy sense desires, thy soul distastes;
Thy lust, thy curiosity, thy pride,
Curbed, or deferred, or balked, or gratified,
Rage on, and make thee equally unblessed,
In what thou want'st, and what thou hast possessed;
In vain thou hop'st for bliss on this poor clod,
Return, and seek thy father, and thy God:
Yet think not to regain thy native sky,
Born on the wings of vain philosophy;
Mysterious passage! hid from human eyes;
Soaring you'll sink, and sinking you will rise:
Let humble thoughts thy wary footsteps guide,
Regain by meekness what you lost by pride.[50]

Both Prior and Arbuthnot show a readiness to use Pascal's thoughts irrespective of complete sympathy with their context, but the attraction of the *Pensées* for English moralists of the early eighteenth century is exhibited most strikingly and discordantly in Alexander Pope. Pope's interest in Pascal and his works began when he was young and lasted throughout his life. In 1711, at the age of twenty-three, he added a postscript to a letter to John Caryll, begging his pardon for the letter's length and offering the 'impertinent' excuse that 'I had not time enough (as Mons. Pascal said of one of his) to make it shorter.' Caryll, also a Catholic, was to be a longtime correspondent, and, in 1720, Pope expressed to him his admiration of Nicole's *Essais de morale*.[51] Several of Pope's other friendships were with men affected like himself by French writers and literary standards, and, when he produced the *Memoirs . . . of Martinus Scriblerus* in conjunction with fellow-members of the Scriblerus Club, among his contributions was a parody of Pascal's childhood genius in mathematics.[52] The importance of Pascal in Pope's thought is fully revealed, however, in his celebrated poem, *An Essay on Man*, published in 1733 and 1734. Borrowing freely from numerous sources, he brought together themes and sayings from Montaigne, Charron, and La Rochefoucauld, as well as Pascal, besides English authors and philosophers such as Locke, Shaftesbury, and Wollaston.[53] Although Pope left his distinctive mark on all he touched, it was soon recognized that the *Essay* was especially indebted to the *Pensées*; and, by turning certain of Pascal's leading observations into clever, finely-phrased verse, Pope in fact gave many English readers some of their most typical notions of Pascal's thoughts in what became one of the best-known works in eighteenth-century English literature.

The relationship between the *Pensées* and the *Essay on Man* was practically disavowed by Pope during the poem's composition, but confirmed emphatically afterwards. In December 1730, he wrote to Caryll, informing him of his hope 'to contribute to some honest and moral purposes in writing of human life and manners, not exclusive of religious regards,' and received the suggestion that he might appropriately read the *Pensées* in preparation. Pope wished as much secrecy as possible for the specific character of his project, and this could be reflected in his reply of February 6, 1731: 'Your recommendation of Pascal's *Pensées* is a good one (tho' I've been beforehand with you in it) but he will be of little use to my design, which is rather to ridicule ill men than preach to 'em. I fear our age is past all other correction.'[54]

Whatever the motives of this disclaimer, it was soon apparent that the thought of Pascal had guided several passages in the *Essay*, and not long after its publication Pope was even seeking to identify his work with the *Pensées*. Although the *Essay* met with great approbation in England and was initially welcomed in France, the French translations were critically examined by Jean Pierre de Crousaz, Professor of Mathematics and Philosophy at Lausanne, and then denounced by him in two attacks published in 1737 and 1738. Crousaz's chief purpose had been to detect signs of impiety and theological error amid the tendencies of Pope's philosophy, and, though many of his accusations were founded on the mistakes of the *Essay*'s translators, he particularly charged the author himself with a rationalistic optimism suspiciously close to the censured views of Leibniz and a materialism reminiscent of Spinoza. These damaging charges were roundly defeated in England by the future Bishop Warburton in *A Vindication of Mr. Pope's Essay on Man*, published first in letter form and finally appearing as a complete work in 1742. Pope was, however, led to inform Etienne de Silhouette, his principal French translator, that he had imitated Pascal at several points in the *Essay*, especially at the beginning of the second epistle; and, when Silhouette produced a new edition of his translation in 1742, he came to Pope's aid by drawing attention to no fewer than twenty-five instances in the poem where he considered a close resemblance existed to thoughts and phrases in the *Pensées*.[55]

In spite of these efforts, the *Essay* came under renewed attack in the same year when Louis Racine, the dramatist's nephew, on the basis once more of a misleading translation, challenged Pope's thought with being heretical, though adding he believed some of the *Essay*'s ideas had been developed by readers further than Pope had intended. A not unfriendly correspondence resulted in which Pope made perhaps the clearest statement of his own religious views, associating his thought explicitly with that of Pascal, whom Racine sanctioned, and thereby dismaying Voltaire and other sceptics who had sought to claim him as one of their own: 'Upon the whole, I have the pleasure to answer you in the manner you most desire, a Sincere Avowal that my Opinions are intirely different from those of Spinoza; or even of Leibnitz; but on the contrary conformable to those of Mons: Pascal & Mons. Fenelon: the latter of whom I would most readily imitate, in submitting all my opinions to the Decision of the Church.'[56]

Compared with Prior and Arbuthnot, the links between Pope and the thought of Pascal thus seem especially complex and full of inconsistencies. In spite of his early denial to Caryll, there is no doubt Pope made extensive use of the *Pensées* when writing the *Essay*, turning to both English and French versions; but what is more difficult to ascertain is the degree to which he personally was ready to associate himself with the conclusions his poem reached. The *Essay on Man*, by borrowing among other sources the images of Pascal but ignoring the pattern of his thought, was hailed by men of moderation and reason as a noble statement of elementary truths; but, when charged with having overlooked the part of revelation in religion, Pope defended himself by demonstrating how much his poem owed to the *Pensées*, and was ultimately prepared to confess that his own religious position was identifiable with that of Pascal. Faced with this difference between the philosophy of the poem and Pope's private views, yet with Pascal central to each, we need to investigate the intricacies of relationship between the place of Pascal's thought in the essentially reasonable *Essay* and the less conspicuous attitudes that prompted Pope's own 'Sincere Avowal.'

Reserving comment upon the discrepancies, we shall proceed first to examine the resemblances between the *Essay* and the *Pensées*; and, since some of the passages listed by Silhouette are too lengthy or indistinct to justify repetition here, this survey will be restricted to leading examples noted either by him or Pope's modern editors. Given Pope's desire to produce 'a general Map of Man,' the current literary preoccupation with the paradoxes of human nature, and his eclectic approach to the subject, Caryll's intuitions were correct that the *Pensées* might suitably add form and expression to his thinking; and the *Essay* reveals both the extent to which Pope had assimilated many of Pascal's reflections and the closeness of his borrowings to those made by his contemporaries. In the opening paragraph, writing of man's difficulty in obtaining a composite view of the universe and thus a true perspective on his nature, he epitomized observations that had already been developed by Locke:

> *He, who thro' vast immensity can pierce,*
> *See worlds on worlds compose one universe,*
> *Observe how system into system runs,*
> *What other planets circle other suns,*
> *What vary'd being peoples ev'ry star,*
> *May tell why Heav'n has made us as we are.*
> *But of this frame the bearings, and the ties,*
> *The strong connections, nice dependencies,*
> *Gradations just, has thy pervading soul*
> *Look'd thro'? or can a part contain the whole?* [I, 23−32]

The last phrase offers interesting proof of Pope's familiarity with the *Pensées* in Kennett's translation, which had recently appeared in its second and third editions. As Audra has pointed out, Pascal originally wrote, 'Comment se pourrait-il qu'une partie connût le tout?'; but for 'connût,' Kennett read 'contînt,' and proceeded to translate, 'For what possibility is there, that the Part should contain the whole?' The mistake was evidently not noticed by Pope and received a wider usage through his poem.[57] A little later, the couplet, 'Hope springs eternal in the human breast: / Man never Is, but always To be blest,' [I, 95-96], recalls Pascal's 'Ainsi nous ne vivons jamais, mais nous espérons de vivre; et nous disposant toujours à être heureux . . . .'[58] Other lines recall Pascal's arguments for acknowledging the limitations of human reason:

> *From pride, from pride, our very reas'ning springs;*
> *Account for moral as for nat'ral things:*
> *Why charge we Heav'n in those, in these acquit?*
> *In both, to reason right is to submit.*[59]   [I, 161-64]

The evidence accumulates from further passages that the *Pensées* provided a leading source for Pope's analysis of man. In Kennett's translation, man finds himself 'hanging, as it were, in his material Scale, between the two vast Abysses of Infinite and Nothing; from which he is equally removed'; and, apart from providing a new context, Pope merely expanded the details of Pascal's imagery:

> *Vast chain of being, which from God began,*
> *Natures aethereal, human, angel, man,*
> *Beast, bird, fish, insect! what no eye can see,*
> *No glass can reach! from Infinite to thee,*
> *From thee to Nothing!* . . . [60]   [I, 237-41]

It is above all in the second epistle, as Pope himself observed, that the impact of Pascal upon his thought was most pronounced, and nowhere more than in its famous opening:

> *Know then thyself, presume not God to scan;*
> *The proper study of Mankind is Man.*
> *Plac'd on this isthmus of a middle state,*
> *A being darkly wise, and rudely great:*
> *With too much knowledge for the Sceptic side,*
> *With too much weakness for the Stoic's pride,*
> *He hangs between; in doubt to act, or rest,*
> *In doubt to deem himself a God, or Beast;*
> *In doubt his Mind or Body to prefer,*
> *Born but to die, and reas'ning but to err;*
> *Alike in ignorance, his reason such,*
> *Whether he thinks too little, or too much:*
> *Chaos of Thought and Passion, all confus'd;*

> *Still by himself abus'd, or disabus'd;*
> *Created half to rise, and half to fall;*
> *Great lord of all things, yet a prey to all;*
> *Sole judge of Truth, in endless Error hurl'd:*
> *The glory, jest, and riddle of the world!*[61]   [II, 1-18]

The resemblance of these lines to the *Pensées* was plain to Pope's English expositors. Writing twenty years later in the *Adventurer* on writers whom Pope had imitated and improved, John Hawkesworth saw the final six lines here as clear proof that Pope had taken 'not only sentiments but even expressions' from Pascal; and, in 1756, Joseph Warton considered Pope's reflections as having been 'minutely copied.'[62] Although other influences may be discerned, the similarities of phrase conspire to make the overall indebtedness to the Pascal of Port Royal obvious. In fact, major portions of the passage may be largely reproduced in the very language of Kennett's translation:

(a)... to study Man ... [is] the proper Employment and Exercise of Mankind.
(b)We are placed here in a vast and uncertain Medium, ever floating between Ignorance and Knowledge.
(c)We have an Idea of Truth, not to be effaced by all the Wiles of the Sceptic: we have an incapacity of Argument, not to be rectified by all the power of the Dogmatist.
(d)What then is to be the Fate of Man! shall he be equal to God? or shall he not be superiour to the Beasts?
(e)If we think too little of a thing, or too much, our Head turns giddy, and we are at a loss to find out our way to Truth.
(f)What a Chimaera then is Man! what a surprising Novelty! what a confused Chaos! what a subject of Contradiction! A profess'd Judge of All things; and yet a feeble Worm of the Earth: the Great Depositary and Guardian of Truth; and yet a meer huddle of Uncertainty: the Glory and the Scandal of the Universe.[63]

Pope had entertained such views for many years,[64] but, as well as being familiar with Kennett's translation, the poet on this occasion consulted the *Pensées* in the French text of Port Royal. Since Pope chose to add 'riddle' to the 'Glory and the Scandal of the Universe' provided by Kennett, Audra has concluded that he mistook the word 'rebut' (outcast) in a French edition for 'rébus' (riddle), his error thus helping produce a famous phrase.[65] Other lines in the second epistle concerning the effect of the passions and egotism upon human reason [II, 39-42, 67-80] echo the *Pensées*, and Pope also gave new expression to Pascal's remarks upon the differences created by climate and latitude, appropriated earlier by Prior in *Alma*:

> *But where th'Extreme of Vice, was ne'er agreed:*
> *Ask where's the North? at York, 'tis on the Tweed;*
> *In Scotland, at the Orcades; and there,*
> *At Greenland, Zembla, or the Lord knows where:*
> *No creature owns it in the first degree,*
> *But thinks his neighbour farther gone than he.*
> *Ev'n those who dwell beneath its very zone,*
> *Or never feel the rage, or never own;*
> *What happier natures shrink at with affright,*
> *The hard inhabitant contends is right.*[66]   [II, 221-30]

In accordance with Pascal, Pope believed human pride to be 'a common friend' to all men amid the misfortunes of their predicament, while distractions might give temporary pleasures from infancy to old age [II, 271-82].[67] In the remainder of the poem, allusions to the *Pensées* are less frequent and specific. Pope drew more often from Montaigne in the third epistle, although, in his description of man as a 'thinking thing,' he possibly had in mind Pascal's comment that 'Man is a Reed; and the weakest Reed in Nature: but then he is a thinking Reed.'[68] In the fourth epistle, the debt to Pascal is a little more conspicuous. Certain lines on present and future happiness [IV, 67–72] broadly resemble similar reflections of Pascal;[69] and, when in the last stages the guiding truth for life was enunciated in the maxim 'Virtue alone is Happiness below,' Pope followed with a version of Pascal's argument of the wager:

> *The joy unequal'd, if its end it gain,*
> *And if it lose, attended with no pain. . . .* [70]   [IV, 315-16]

It is obvious from the *Essay* that Pope was greatly influenced by the *Pensées*, and several general similarities between the lives and characters of Pascal and himself have also been recognized. Both were invalids, both moralists and epigrammatic writers, both keen observers of man, and both Catholics. But, in spite of these associations, there are disagreements between the *Pensées* and the *Essay* which make the latter, although the most important example of the absorption of Pascal's thought by an English writer at this time, also a decisive sign of the gathering reappraisal of Pascal which would lead to the rapid decline of his reputation in English intellectual circles.

In his letter to Caryll, Pope had said that Pascal would 'be of little use to my design'; and, though perhaps he wished to keep the character of his projected work hidden from even his closest friends, he clearly had realised that the *Pensées*, though admirable in their way and useful, were too far removed in their solution of man's predicament to assist him much for what he had in mind. For all his dependence upon Pascal's portrayal of man, Pope was often fundamentally at variance in the *Essay* with his predecessor, and borrowed from Pascal only what was compatible with the philosophy he had already adopted for his new work. The latent poetry in the *Pensées* appealed to him, but not the theology, and, whereas Pascal had stressed man's wretchedness without God, Pope omitted doctrinal questions which formed so large a part of the Port Royal edition and optimistically assumed that man's position was as it should be. Seeing man first in relation to the universe rather than to God, Pope's all-embracing plan involved a chain of being, which Pascal had denied, and a settled scheme in which partial evil contributed to a greater good. In contrast to Pascal's depiction of man as an insoluble mystery, full of contradictory impulses, whom only faith can save, Pope attempted to expose man's pride and self-esteem, the causes of his unrest and dissatisfaction within the scheme of nature, and suggest that through love of his fellow-men his position might become tolerable and happy.[71]

To Pascal, no such certainty regarding any humanly formulated scheme was possible. In one of the passages in Kennett's *Pensées* from which Pope evidently borrowed, he had written, 'We are inflamed with a desire of piercing thro' All Things, and of building a Tower the top of which shall reach even to Infinity. But our feeble Edifice cracks and falls; the Earth opens, without bottom, under us, and buries our Devices in its Gulph.'[72] The final answers to man's condition were to be discovered solely through revelation and reconciliation with God. The motivations of the two authors, moreover, were quite opposite, and a modern critic has pointed out their difference, recalling Pope's statement to Caryll that his intention was not to preach:

> *Beyond mere problems of conduct Pascal's thought carried him to a solution of life which was essentially mystical. Pope, on the other hand, was glad to be a practical moralist. While Pascal was motivated by feeling and by experience which grew from personal conversion and shed light on all his writing, Pope based his thinking on books. Where the Frenchman was subjective and, with the zeal of a scientist, fervent, Pope tried at least to be impersonal. Here essential purposes differ: the aim of the one is to convert; the aim of the other is to instruct.*[73]

The *Essay on Man* is a monument to the esteem in which Pascal was held in England in the seventeen-thirties, but it is also the outstanding illustration of that transition in English opinion which, while admiring Pascal's handling of certain general topics in the *Pensées*, was nonetheless beginning to question radically the assumptions which his thought developed. In some respects, Pascal's reputation as a moralist and philosopher was then at its height. The *Pensées* had been influencing numerous English writers, and the *Essay* appeared soon after two new editions of Kennett's translation had made that version available again to the audience that had come into being since the early years of the century. For all Pascal's popularity, however, the *Essay* may also be regarded as symbolizing the start of a new, far more critical evaluation of the *Pensées* within English intellectual life, in which Pope was participating. It should not be forgotten that the poem was dedicated to his intimate friend, the freethinking Bolingbroke, who, in some fragments of essays he sent to Pope, charged Pascal with having falsely and impiously asserted that 'if there were no other life, the directions of reason for our conduct in this world would not be such as they are.' The religion of nature taught instead that morality was man's greatest interest and duty.[74] Such rationalist opinions were increasingly shared by many of Pope's more knowledgeable readers, and, although disseminating aspects of Pascal's thinking in poetic form to a large public, the *Essay* by its continuous popularity inexorably advanced the claims of reason rather than maintained Pascal's balance between reason and the Christian faith. In France, Voltaire, who as a young man made Pope's acquaintance in England, applauded the *Essay*, though not unreservedly, and in fact considered its arguments closely resembled those in the twenty-fifth chapter of his own *Lettres philosophiques*. In 1756, he was again delighted to note that Pope and he agreed upon the good fortune inherent in man's condition in opposition to Pascal's pessimism: 'Quand un Français et un Anglais pensent de même, il faut bien qu'ils aient raison.'[75]

Pope's affiliations with rationalist philosophy are clear enough, and the consequences of the Essay's publication must have been partly foreseeable to him; but he was also a Catholic, and therein lies the principal explanation for his concern to identify his poem with the thought of Pascal. Pope was conscious that in the *Essay* he had steered a narrow course between Christianity and deism, which was likely to win acceptance from English latitudinarians; but, when French translations were criticized for unorthodoxy, how better to defend his work and himself than to ally what he had written to the *Pensées*, which had previously received the Church's approval? The *Pensées* were widely admired explicitly for their religious character, and no other moralist from whom Pope had borrowed to such a large extent was so favoured by the ecclesiastical authorities. For the Catholic poet, caught in a comparable difficulty to Erasmus whom he had also once admired, this procedure must have seemed the best open to him.

But although Pope's identification of the *Essay* with Pascal may have been largely governed by the circumstances of Crousaz's attack, there were times when his personal attachment to the religion as well as to the reflections of Pascal broke through, making his letter to Louis Racine an honest expression of otherwise incongruent feelings. In some of his friendships and emotions, and in the manner in which he received the sacrament on his death-bed, we may observe a faith not too distant from that which Pascal and the Archbishop of Cambrai had come to typify. Pope might promote the sceptical and humanistic thought of his age in the *Essay* and continued no doubt to enjoy the *Provinciales*, but he sought to define his own religious position ultimately with reference to the intelligence and piety joined in those two figures. Such a disposition perhaps assisted him to link the *Essay* and the *Pensées* together in good conscience during the Crousaz controversy. For many men, however, Catholic and Protestant, such a unity of outlook would become increasingly difficult to maintain; and, indeed, where Pascal is concerned, Pope represents one of the last major successful attempts to achieve this during this period. In the future, much of English thought and writing would be still further marked by a preference for rationalistic beliefs, and a depreciation of the synthesis between faith and reason which had seemed appealing to an earlier generation. In his *Essay*, Pope had placed man upon an isthmus between opposing forces; but, during the years beforehand, Pascal in reality had been occupying a like position, mediating between the rival claims of faith and reason, and showing the pathway by which a man might pass to reconciliation with God. Already threatened, his place as a thinker was no longer as secure as it once had been; and, as rationalist opinions became more prevalent, the isthmus on which Pascal had set himself seemed to many Englishmen wholly untenable.

[IV] There can be little question that Pascal's influence upon early eighteenth-century Englishmen in matters of literature and philosophy was more pervasive than has been indicated here. Many of his most characteristic themes – his portrait of man's contrarieties, his analysis of 'l'esprit de géométrie,' his observations upon imagination, irregularity, and analogy in beauty and design, and his arguments upholding yet disqualifying the powers of human reason – whether agreed upon or not were provocative to contemporary intellectual enquiries. Other major works of the time, such as Mandeville's *Fable of the Bees* and Thomson's *Seasons*, may bear the impression of aspects of his thought;[76] but, as Pascal's reflections must often have mingled with similar views proceeding from other French and English thinkers, in the absence of unmistakable proof we can hardly label every allusion to some general topic discussed in the *Pensées* as revealing some specific knowledge of that work and its author. It has seemed better to provide a basis of fact for the assessment of Pascal's reputation, and, though this survey would be incomplete if no allowance were made for a more widespread effect upon the English mind, the addition of more indistinct examples here might prejudice the attempt to reach conclusions.

By the end of the third decade of the eighteenth century the initial popularity of Pascal among all sections of the reading public was at its peak. English familiarity with the *Pensées* was receiving a new impetus with the appearance of the second and third editions of Kennett's translation, and partial translations or quotations were common enough in books or periodicals to create suspicion that occasionally writers were borrowing from each other rather than from Pascal directly. His achievements in science, mathematics, and religious polemics had not yet appreciably lessened in the public eye, and his life was by and large still seen in the respectful terms of Kennett's preface. All in all, there is plenty of evidence to indicate that Pascal exerted a fair measure of influence in England during these years, and that the majority of opinions regarding this have to some extent been justified.

The evidence also overwhelmingly suggests, however, that many Englishmen tended to be selective in their appreciation. If we review those passages in the Port Royal edition of the *Pensées* to which English authors most frequently turned, it is immediately apparent that they drew heavily from the twenty-first through the twenty-sixth chapters and relatively seldom from the remainder. These chapters portraying man's contradictory nature, his powers and limitations as a rational being, his place in the universe, and his search for happiness were appropriated repeatedly, but, apart from the argument of the wager or an occasional isolated quotation, most other chapters were largely ignored; and this was especially true of those sections in which Pascal was exclusively concerned with defending Christian truths from the Bible. In view of the rise of scientific knowledge and the objective outlook which it fostered, what naturally appealed to English authors most in the *Pensées* at this time, apart from purely literary qualities, was Pascal's analysis of man, and man's understanding of himself and his world. Their interest falls recognizably within the line of approach inaugurated by Southwell and Petty out of the context of the Royal Society, being ably assisted by Pascal's 'very Mathematical Turn of Thought' with its emphasis upon clarity in expression.[77] Moreover, Englishmen are known for their love of paradox, and all these modes of appreciation surely reached their zenith in the second epistle of Pope's *Essay on Man*.

In consequence, we may conclude that the influence of the *Pensées* in England at this time was important, but it was also quite partial; and, on the whole, it is not among the better-known English writers that we should look for a comprehensive appreciation of Pascal's religion and philosophy as set forth in the Port Royal edition. As an intellectual force or a literary model in early eighteenth-century England Pascal is probably not of the same stature as Montaigne, Molière, or Boileau, and most English authors tended to respond only to those aspects of his thought which were illuminating to their own rationalist speculation. Their attraction to Pascal largely differentiated between the later group of chapters and the rest of the work, despite the attempted bias of the Port Royal edition, and was sufficiently strong to cause them for a while to utilize his characterizations of man while directing their own thoughts towards quite un-Pascalian conclusions.

Against this background, Pascal's reputation in England, centred upon his life and his authorship of the *Pensées*, next began to develop in two major directions. Several of his leading reflections were to become in some manner a permanent part of English thought in the eighteenth century, but the generation following that of Pope drew the boundary still more firmly between reason and the Christian faith. The deistic challenge, which had already impaired Pascal's conclusions, increasingly led many Englishmen to regard the whole of his thought with suspicion, especially when placed in relation to his life. A generation inspired by Newton's discoveries was less impressed by arguments of the reason's limitations, and Pascal and the *Pensées* inevitably came to be viewed more critically. As his reputation as a thinker had risen partly under the influence of French writing, so it would decline; and it is the story of the steady erosion of this reputation in English intellectual circles during the latter part of the century that we shall next investigate.

If, however, deistic beliefs were beginning to alter the prevailing view of Pascal by the seventeen-thirties, there had also come into existence by this time a body of opinion which, though touched in varying degrees by the rationalist thinking of the age, nevertheless valued Pascal with an attitude that was more exclusively religious.

Partly the result of a time-lag before the ideas and beliefs of the educated *élite* came to be more commonly accepted by other sections of society, and partly the choice of certain authors to emphasize the spiritual qualities of the *Pensées*, not necessarily at the expense of their worth as philosophy, this second major direction in which the appreciation of Pascal was developing gradually came to be widespread and popular; and, in several forms, it survived the breakdown of the association of reason and religion that would occur at some levels of thought in mid-eighteenth-century England.[78]

Examples of such an approach are to be found at an early stage in John Byrom, William Law, and the Wesley family; but there are other indications of its prevalence. One index for the general extent and nature of Pascal's reputation in England between 1730 and 1750 is the number of editions published of Pope's *Essay on Man*, but the devotional writings of Mrs. Elizabeth Rowe, which drew often and more directly from Pascal, appeared almost as frequently and seem to have been as widely read. The study of Pascal's reputation in England at this time would be too heavily concentrated upon intellectual circles if it did not pay attention to his appeal to an extensive audience which saw him with the eyes of popular piety. The growth and persistence of this trend with its rival interpretation of the human condition will demand our attention at a later point. In the meantime it should be borne in mind as a parallel and complementary development to the otherwise conspicuous decline in Pascal's reputation during the period now commencing.

CHAPTER FIVE

What a Hideous Monster is Fanaticism!

[I] Pope's *Essay on Man* extended familiarity with certain of Pascal's leading reflections and was received with widespread applause, but a state of tension had clearly arisen between the manner in which these reflections were being used and the ends towards which their author had originally directed them. Pope himself was attracted to the faith of Pascal yet was willing to forego its implications, and his ambivalence symbolizes a decisive moment in English attitudes towards the French moralist and his writing; for deistic and rationalist opinions increasingly assumed a more sceptical view of the essentials and conclusions of many of Pascal's arguments, and found his life much less edifying than had been the case before. Pope's friend, Bolingbroke, has already provided an illustration of the more totally critical approach to Pascal that was beginning to develop. In 1704, Kennett had presented the *Pensées* as the admirable culmination of a life of genius, but, by the mid-century, many leaders of English opinion had come to regard Pascal with hardly less hostility and suspicion than that which characterized the remarks of the *philosophes* in France. To men whose confidence in human abilities was steadily advancing, it was unacceptable and offensive to be reminded of human limitations by a figure whose life and thought, by their standards, had ended in a conspicuous denial of the virtues of reason.

Partly the result of a direct rationalist attack from abroad, the shift in Pascal's reputation among many intelligent Englishmen from a deceptively firm popularity to outright rejection at its most extreme was caused as much by their general acquiescence in deism, the eighteenth-century's distinctive form of religious belief. Addison and his friends might find Pascal's compromise between faith and reason agreeable and be sympathetic towards Kennett's recommendations, but such an harmonious frame of mind tended to yield before the growing preference to accept what could be precisely

131

known at the expense of the incertitudes of mystery and revelation. In this respect, some important forces producing the radical re-evaluation of Pascal proceeded from the writings of several men who, from one viewpoint or another, concerned themselves with religious controversy. Broadly questioning certain assumptions of traditional religion and treating many of Pascal's leading arguments as ill-founded or erroneous, they succeeded in undermining the appeal and credibility of the *Pensées*, limited the interest being shown by literary and other circles, and helped initiate a series of further adverse consequences.

The influence of deism with its emphasis upon man's new assurance of his place in the universe and the consistency of his happiness has already been noticed in the writings of Prior, Pope, and others, but its origins and the character of its controversial ideas should now be more specifically mentioned. Drawing upon the earlier teachings of Lord Herbert of Cherbury, the varieties of deist thinkers looked, in the main, unfavourably upon institutionalized churches and acts they regarded as superstitious, seeking instead to reduce religion's demands to belief in a natural order discernible by reason and in a supreme being best worshipped by the pursuit of an upright life. The widely shared reaction against the damaging effects of religious fervour, coupled with a confidence in the methods of thought that had resulted in notable scientific discoveries, gave an impetus to deistic thinking, sometimes in the direction of atheism, and intensified the conflict already in existence between freethinkers and the supporters of traditional Christianity.

During the opening stages of the deist controversy, the name of Pascal seems chiefly to have been invoked in Christianity's defence. Jeremy Collier recommended deists to read the *Pensées*, and further light is thrown on both the accuracy of the Jesuit Darrell's observation and the range of current debate when, in Charles Gildon's *The Deist's Manual*, Pascal was named in a conversation originating in a coffee-house. Gildon was a miscellaneous writer recently converted from deism, but who remained rationalist enough to defend the very Pascalian contention that reason, if properly used and willing to submit where its capacity ended, forms the natural path to the understanding and acceptance of revelation. Reason is the 'only Guide to God and Religion,' its enemies being 'Broachers of Heresies, and Superstition'; and, in the exchange between an atheist and a Christian, Pascal contributed an authoritative opinion to the latter's position:

Reason certainly (interrupted Philalethes) never deceives, nor is deceiv'd.
If justly follow'd (said Christophil) and unbiass'd by any Prejudice, or Passion; for then it will know when to decide, and when to submit; for, as St.

Austin says, Reason wou'd never submit, did it not find, that there was some Just Cause for its Submission; and it is but Just, that it submit, when it Judges it self, that it ought to do so. For if Reason never submitted, says Mr. Pascal, there would be nothing Supernatural, or Mysterious in Religion, and if it never was to be Judge, Religion would be Absurd, and Ridiculous.[1]

Seeing such importance being placed on human reason in support of traditional Christian belief, we might expect the argument of the wager to be considered a useful ally in checking the spread of deistic teachings. Though not wholly original, it had been among the first features of the *Pensées* to arouse English interest, Locke incorporating it into his widely-read *Essay* and Kennett drawing attention to Pascal's 'Essay against this Spirit of Indifference,' though regarding it as 'a way of arguing' rather than a fully conclusive proof. Earlier, in 1664, Archbishop Tillotson had recognized the applicability of its basic reasoning process when, in his famous sermon, 'The Wisdom of being Religious,' he contrasted the religious man and the atheist. Having in the first instance proposed that 'if the Arguments for and against a God were equal, and it were an even question whether there were one or not,' he concluded that 'the hazard and danger is so infinitely unequal, that in point of prudence and interest every man were obliged to incline to the affirmative'; and he subsequently repeated his belief that it was 'a monstrous folly to deride these things.'[2] Archbishop Dawes of York made use of the wager in a poem against the atheists, and the future Bishop Berkeley's knowledge of the *Pensées* enabled him to follow closely the argument as developed by Pascal, when he spoke on the theme of immortality at Trinity College, Dublin, in January 1708:

Whatever effect brutal passion may have on some or thoughtlessness & stupidity on others yet I believe there are none amongst us that do not at least think it as probable the Gospel may be true as false. Sure I am no man can say he has two to one odds on the contrary side. But wn life & immortality are at stake we should play our part with fear & trembling tho 'twere an hundred to one but we are cheated in the end. Nay if there be any the least prospect of our winning so noble a prize. & that there is some: none, the beastliest libertine or most besotted Atheist, can deny.[3]

To one leading though erratic deist, however, such caution seemed unwarranted and liable to render a most serious matter of decreased value; and, accordingly, a strong challenge to the validity of Pascal's argument was made by the third Earl of Shaftesbury, a man educated partly under Locke's supervision and much indebted to French thinkers. Though describing in his *Letter Concerning Enthusiasm* (1708) how life's pursuits are habitually chosen to obtain one's best advantage, Shaftesbury eventually rejected the reasoning of Pascal, which his mentor had followed, as unconvincing and inadequate:

And thus it is in religion. We are highly concerned how to beg right; and think all depends upon hitting the title, and making a good guess. 'Tis the most beggarly refuge imaginable, which is so mightily cried up, and stands as a great maxim with many able men, 'that they should strive to have faith, and believe to the utmost; because if, after all, there be nothing in the matter, there will be no harm in being thus deceived; but if there be anything, it will be fatal for them not to have believed to the full.' But they are so far mistaken that, whilst they have this thought, 'tis certain they can never believe either to their satisfaction and happiness in this world, or with any advantage of recommendation to another. For besides that our reason, which knows the cheat, will never rest thoroughly satisfied on such a bottom, but turn us often adrift and toss us in a sea of doubt and perplexity, we cannot but actually grow worse in our religion, and entertain a worse opinion still of a Supreme Deity, whilst our belief is founded on so injurious a thought of him.[4]

But a more serious blow to the trustworthiness of the *Pensées* had begun to develop from another quarter. The growing value attached to rational proofs led several proponents of a natural religion to concentrate their attacks upon the supernatural features of Christian belief; and, if the argument of the wager were a form of self-deception, how much more might the accounts of special instances of divine revelation and interruptions of the natural order, as related in the Old and New Testaments, affront the powers of human reason? In 1696, John Toland had published his *Christianity not Mysterious*, seeking to diminish the importance of such elements in the Christian faith, and his successors found prophecies and miracles a rich field for the exposure of human credulity. Anthony Collins, Thomas Woolston, and Matthew Tindal were among those who, in their various works, similarly placed the biblical record under close scrutiny, using textual discrepancies to support their deductions; and their general conclusion was that such extraordinary occurrences, hitherto considered incontrovertible proofs of the truth of the Christian religion, could never again be regarded as valid supports for its claims. Henceforth Christianity should be judged by the degree of its accordance with the natural scheme.

The *Pensées* in the Port Royal edition were particularly vulnerable to attacks of this kind. The tendency today is to regard as less important that section of the work which, on the grounds that unaided reason can go no further, advances the claims of Christianity through the biblical record and its teaching. This second and final part of Pascal's total argument, however, formed in the Port

Royal edition a large and central portion of the volume. There Pascal upheld the fulfilment of prophecies and God's special dispensation towards the Jews as marks of the authenticity of the Christian heritage, and the editing committee had also compiled a whole chapter of his thoughts on miracles. To Basil Kennett, indeed, Pascal had unusual skill in determining and communicating the truths to be found in Scripture, possessing 'accurate Knowledge,' 'peculiar discernment,' and a 'singular Art of illustrating and comparing different Texts,' all enhanced by his sincere intentions and 'his truly Christian Heart.'[5]

There can be little question that the *Pensées* were known to most leading deist writers, as the formulation of their arguments usually displays impressive familiarity with works of religion and philosophy. The clearest evidence is found in the case of Anthony Collins, perhaps the most appealing of the radical English deists. In 1724, Collins published *A Discourse of the Grounds and Reasons of the Christian Religion*, questioning the authority of the prophecies, but this aroused so many rebuttals that he felt obliged three years later to make a reply entitled *The Scheme of Literal Prophecy Considered*. His aim as before was first to show how many defenders of Christianity had rested its final claims upon the record of prophecies fulfilled, and then to demonstrate how weak and absurd these widely acknowledged proofs in fact were. In Collins' extensive library were copies of the *Lettres provinciales* and certain rejoinders as well as the *Pensées*, and the testimony of Pascal he quoted from the last might have been expressly designed for him to cast doubt upon its author's plausibility:

The celebrated Pascal says, La plus grande des preuves de Jesus Christ, ce sont les propheties. C'est aussi à quoi Dieu a le plus pourvû; car l'evenement qui les a remplies est un miracle subsistant depùis la naissance de l'Englise jusqu'à la fin. And again he says, Quand un seul homme auroit fait un livrel des predictions de Jesus Christ pour le tems & pour la maniere, & que Jesus Christ seroit venu conformément à ces propheties, ce seroit d'une force infinie.[6]

Whether seeking to reform or demolish the Church, the effect of these assaults was ultimately to discredit the importance of prophecies and miracles, and, with respect to the *Pensées* of Pascal, to disqualify a major part of that work for serious consideration by many men who prided themselves on their reasoning abilities. During the course of the eighteenth century, men of intelligence came in large numbers to view miracles as being one of the chief barriers to a realistic faith instead of a fundamental support, and to regard believers as regrettably still dependent upon superstition; or, following the revered Locke, they regarded such belief as temporarily justified if it induced persons less endowed with reason than themselves to adopt a life of uprightness and sobriety. The freethinking spirit the deists engendered likewise found Pascal's opposition to classical pagan philosophies and the scepticism of Montaigne questionable, and was inclined to regard Mohammed as a fellow-seeker after truth rather than as the false prophet Pascal had cast him. As for the Jews, the new tendency was to reduce their traditional importance and redefine their place in universal history; and in 1746, Edmund Law, a follower of Locke and later Bishop of Carlisle, so redirected one of Pascal's reflections on the chosen people towards his general contention that, under divine guidance, man was progressing in religion at the same rate as in other branches of knowledge.[7] The growth of these attitudes must have helped persuade many a reader to confine his interest to those chapters where Pascal's analysis of the nature of man still had some pertinence to discussion; and the *Pensées* as a whole increasingly took on an old-fashioned appearance, being valued now mostly by the less educated or by those whose concept of religion in some way found necessary the interventions of an all-powerful Deity.

In spite of the force of the deist challenge, the hope once expressed by Boyle that the new learning might create a fuller understanding of the Christian faith nonetheless held firm among many leaders of religious opinion. They remained opposed to several of the deists' extreme conclusions, but were prepared to adjust their own defences and find a measure of agreement with their adversaries. The established church had often in the past adopted a tolerant attitude towards the place of reason in religious enquiry; and, though rational proofs for faith were increasingly held to be important in most denominations, the impact of deism is perhaps most noticeable in the Church of England. The inroads caused by deistic beliefs and the resulting effect upon Pascal's reputation at certain levels of organized Christianity is graphically set forth in the journal of the Nonjuror John Byrom, who recorded a discussion he and others had with Joseph Butler, Bishop of Bristol, at the home of the philosopher, David Hartley, in March 1737. Illustrating the differences that could exist among men of strong religious convictions, the conversation is especially revealing of the position of Bishop Butler, a man so indicative of the rising state of mind in intellectual circles:

They talked of Sir Is. Newton having writ his books with a view to religion, and Dr. Butler said that Sir Isaac always thought that prophecy was the great proof of the Christian religion; and Monsieur Pascal was mentioned and some part of his life, which not being represented right, I remembered how it was, and told them, and saying that he was such a genius for mathematical knowledge, and that at last he showed the truly great man and left it for knowledge of a superior kind. We entered into a kind of dispute about prophecy, and I said I thought the Old Testament for prophecy and the New for miracles, and that miracles were the readiest proof; upon which arose an argument and talk about reason and authority, they being for reason and I for authority.[8]

The distance between Butler's and Pascal's thought is less immediately but just as significantly apparent in the character of Butler's best-known work, *The Analogy of Religion, Natural and Revealed, to the Constitution and Course of Nature*, published in 1736 after twenty years in writing. His chief purpose in the *Analogy* was to challenge and disprove those deistic speculations which sought to base religion wholly upon reason. In brief, he tried to show that the various objections raised against Christianity could be satisfactorily answered by analogies drawn from nature; but that ultimately, though reason and conscience may be our guides, it is only through the light of revelation that a full understanding of religion may be obtained. The underlying argument throughout, as he moved from one proposition to another, was in support of probability—that, to a prudent man, the teachings of Christianity, including those resting upon revelation, are more likely to be true than not. This approach was summarized in one of the *Analogy*'s introductory passages:

Probable evidence, in its very nature, affords but an imperfect kind of information; and is to be considered as relative only to beings of limited capacities. For nothing which is the possible object of knowledge, whether past, present, or future, can be probable to an infinite Intelligence; since it cannot but be discerned absolutely as it is in itself, certainly true, or certainly false. But to us, probability is the very guide of life.[9]

Such a view is reminiscent of Pascal's wager, and, though the argument had gained common usage among philosophers and continued to be of more specialized interest to mathematicians, Butler's familiarity with Pascal makes it likely he was conversant with Pascal's reasoning in a more than general way. Comparisons have often been drawn between the two men, and some resemblances exist in their patterns of thought and the presentation of their arguments – though not in their literary styles – in their austere lives, and in their sensibility of the misery and confusion of the world.[10] There may also be echoes of the *Pensées* in Butler's sermons upon human nature. But beyond these broad impressions, a profound dissimilarity separates the *Pensées* from the *Analogy*, making the *Analogy*, for all its aims, point more in the direction of mid-eighteenth-century rationalism than to the balance between faith and reason represented by Pascal. In this respect, Butler's approach to Pascal, insofar as it can be ascertained, resembled that of Pope, being influenced by the *Pensées* yet deviating from the conclusions of Pascal's thought. When the conversation at Hartley's home had ended and Butler had left, some comments were made by the other participants which emphasized the differences already implicit between Byrom and the bishop. Byrom expressed a desire to have Butler's temper and calmness, 'yet not quite, because I thought he was a little too little vigorous,' and his friends seemed to agree, one saying he wished Butler had spoken more earnestly.[11]

The seeming detachment and lack of fire Byrom and his friend noticed in Butler indicated the bishop's apparent unwillingness to appreciate that kind of faith which ultimately characterized the position of Pascal. As Mossner has pointed out in his study of Butler, a broad gulf in fact separated the two men:

Pascal had at once greater doubts and greater faith than Butler, but his faith was not derived from reason. In Butler there is no subtle underlying conception that 'the heart has its reasons which the reason does not know,' no intuition of the ultimate reality of things. The Analogy *states clearly that "religion is not intuitively true, but a matter of deduction and inference." Butler is too much a rationalist to admit of even a tinge of enthusiasm; his religion is always prudential rather than spiritual. It is akin to the time-spirit much more closely than that, for instance, of William Law, who may be allowed to bear a distant affinity to Pascal. Nor, again, is there more than a superficial resemblance between Pascal's celebrated wager and Butler's doctrine of probability. The latter is derived from Locke's theory of knowledge and claims merely to put religious belief on the same plane as belief in scientific hypotheses. The former stakes the will to believe against future torment. In Butler, the greater the probability, the greater is the faith; in Pascal, the lower the possibility, the greater the faith. Pascal is drawn to the faith of the inveterate gambler by the heaviness of the odds against him. Butler, representative of the middle-class, appeals to the middle-class temperament of carefulness and canniness. He plants his feet firmly on the ground.*[12]

Pascal gladly admitted his scepticism that reason could produce faith; Butler still preferred to grope his way with the help of reason, conscience, and experience, but seems to end, in Stephen's words, 'as far from joyful confidence as from blank despair.'[13] The *Analogy*, for all the thoroughness of its arguments, has not surprisingly been credited with advancing scepticism as much as serving as a discouragement, and its relationship with the thought of Pascal is eventually a tenuous one. The trend of their arguments and their reasoned approach to the topics discussed associate the two men as writers of a certain type of Christian apology; but, though Butler was ultimately upon religion's side, his caution and his absence of spiritual fervour divide him from Pascal and make his work representative of the willing compromise with rationalist philosophy that was becoming a characteristic feature of many churchmen and laymen alike. The *Analogy* to a large degree distilled the controversial themes of Butler's generation, and the decline of Pascal's effectiveness as a thinker in England may be partly measured by the decision to depart from the accentuations of the argument of the wager by one who would have surely merited inclusion among Shaftesbury's 'able men.' Indeed, to some Catholics it could seem there was a strange justice at work; for, if Pascal had achieved early fame in England by excoriating the Jesuits' teachings on probability, he was now fast becoming the victim of a not unrelated argumentative process.

Full of inconsistencies and paradoxes though they are, the writings of another bishop portray some further trends in attitudes towards Pascal. William Warburton, Bishop of Gloucester, came to the defence of Pope's *Essay on Man*, and at about the same time was also ready to uphold at least one of Pascal's views more directly. In the second part of his lengthy work, *The Divine Legation of Moses Demonstrated*, upholding the special authority of the Jewish revelation, he made use of Pascal's remarks on the perils of being an innovator in an attack upon his longtime antagonist, Henry Stebbing:

Therefore when my learned Adversary, in order, I will believe, to advance the Christian Faith, would discourage Christian Industry, by calumniating, and rendering suspected what he is pleased to call Experiments in Religion, it is, I am afraid, at best but a Zeal without knowledge. Indeed, M. Pascal ascribes this contempt of experiments to a different cause — 'Ceux qui sont capables de inventer sont rares,' says he. 'Ceux qui n'inventent point sont en plus grand nombre, & par consequent, les plus fortes; et voila pourquoi, lors que les Inventeurs cherchent la gloire qu'ils meritent, tout ce qu'ils y gagnent, c'est qu'on les traite de Visionnaires.' It is true, if men will come to the study of Scripture with unwashen hands, that is, without a due reverence for the dignity of those sacred Volumes, or, which is as ill, with unpurged heads, that is, heads stuffed with bigot systems, or made giddy with cabalistic flights, they will deserve that title which Pascal observes is so unjustly given to those who deserve best of the Public. [14]

About ten years later, however, Warburton was apparently inclining towards discrimination between Pascal as a brilliant and quotable thinker and those aspects of his religious beliefs he considered to have departed from sensible practice. In a letter to his younger friend, Bishop Hurd of Worcester, in 1752, he referred to a grammar of Port Royal as written while its authors were 'Divines, and Philosophers, and Critics, and long before they became Schismatics and Fanatics'; and on another occasion, in a sermon entitled 'The Influence of Learning on Revelation,' he paid tribute to Pascal, with Boyle, Newton, Locke and others, as men of science 'no less respectable for their sincere belief of Christianity.'[15] But it was Hurd who perhaps best caught the nature of Warburton's later views on Pascal when he chose to compare *The Doctrine of Grace*, written against John Wesley in 1762, with the *Lettres provinciales*. In Hurd's opinion, their singular merit in composition would cause each work to be read 'when the sect, that gave occasion to it, is forgotten; or rather the sect will find a sort of immortality in this discourse.'[16]

It is symptomatic of the sceptical tendency prevalent among the leaders of the Church of England to find Warburton largely abandoning an appreciation of Pascal as a spiritual figure, and only recognizing him for his contributions to science and rational philosophy. Bishop Hurd was in some ways similarly persuaded. As an orthodox theologian, he was prepared to make polemical use of those defences of prophecy by 'the profound and reflecting M. Pascal,'[17] but he questioned other aspects of Pascal's religion and had no illusions how his final years compared with those of Addison. In this respect, he showed himself in full accord with what had developed into a substantial body of opinion:

Thus our Addison, like the admirable Pascal, closed his valuable life in meditating a defence of the Christian Religion. One is not surprised to find this agreement in the views of two such men; the one the sublimest genius, and the other the most cultivated, of modern times. But there was this lamented difference in their story. The spirit of Jansenism, falling on a temper naturally scrupulous, and a constitution always infirm, threw a sombrous fanatic air on Pascal's religious speculations, as it did on his life: while our happier countryman, by the benefit of better health and juster principles, maintained a constant sobriety in the conduct of each.[18]

The extent to which reason triumphed over faith among many leading Anglicans is underscored by the fact that, had these men perhaps retained a closer understanding of the religious faith of Pascal, they might have been more favourably inclined towards Wesley instead of attacking him; for, as we shall see, the identification of Wesley and his movement with the Pascal of the *Pensées* is one of the most arresting features of Pascal's reputation in England in the later part of the eighteenth century. Hurd's polished allusion to the *Provinciales*, however, recalls that in another area the spirit which had once animated Henry Hammond to see in Pascal a potential ally against the sinister forces of Rome still prevailed among later divines. What warmth of feeling Pascal might be shown by prelates and the English church as a whole was now more likely to derive from similar motives to those which had caused the original translation of the *Provinciales* than upon any appreciation of the *Pensées*.

Although relations with the Gallican Church were often cordial and its leaders frequently the object of considerable respect, English opinion in general was hardly less hostile towards Catholicism than in the previous century. In spite of this, 'no Protestant, however uncompromising, could altogether withhold his admiration from a Fénelon, a Pascal, or a Bossuet,' and the liking for these three French men of religion rested on the manner in which each of them in his own way had stood distinct from the body of the Roman Catholic Church. Besides his authorship of *Télémaque*, Fénelon's piety and simplicity of life led many besides Pope to hold him in high regard, and, during the War of the Spanish Succession, Marlborough had seen that his estates were protected and had supplied him with wagons of grain. Bossuet's defence of Gallican liberties recalled for many Englishmen the struggle of their own national church to assert its independence. As for Pascal, the particular attraction he exerted proceeded from a selection of his qualities. He fascinated cultivated readers by his literary style and appealed to many because of his upright character, although he might seem mediaeval and, sometimes, too much of a loyal Papist. At bottom, however, he delighted Englishmen generally by the vigour with which he had led the Jansenist assault on the Jesuits.[19] In the face of numerous attacks upon large segments of his personality and thought, Pascal was thus able to maintain among Englishmen something of the image of a noble enemy, and his reputation in that regard, though modified by the changing temper of the times, remained relatively unaltered.

[II] Pascal's deteriorating reputation as author of the *Pensées* owed much to the contrary tendencies of eighteenth-century English thought, but the decline was hastened by criticism originating from his fellow-countrymen. The movement in French intellectual life towards a strong belief in human reason, progress, and enlightenment caused those aspects of Pascal bearing the odious marks of an age of faith to be seen as detracting from his feats of mind still deserving admiration. Of all the foreign sources influencing Englishmen on this issue, there can be no question that the damaging attacks of Voltaire predominated. Acquaintance with his writings cannot totally explain why much of English opinion came to estimate Pascal less favourably than before, but Voltaire's leadership of eighteenth-century European rationalism was bound to bring his views to the notice of a wide audience. His antagonisms towards Pascal began to form the basic assumptions of many educated men, and were echoed by several of Pascal's English critics; and even those like John Wesley who came to Pascal's defence often felt obliged to define their appreciation with some reference to Voltaire's opposing attitudes.

Part of his relentless offensive against traditional religious beliefs and institutions, the refutation of Pascal was one of Voltaire's lifelong preoccupations, beginning with the attachment of fifty-seven *Remarques sur les Pensées de Pascal* as a final chapter to his *Lettres philosophiques* in 1734. This was followed by additional *remarques* in 1742, and by attacks scattered throughout his prose and poetry, his works of philosophy and history, his novels and his correspondence. The onslaught did not end until his death in 1778; indeed, it seems the last writings he sent to the printer were ninety-four new *remarques* to accompany his re-edition of Condorcet's version of the *Pensées*.[20] This prolonged attack was sustained by his conviction that Pascal was Christianity's most formidable representative; and, pleased that reason and common sense were making such advances, Voltaire launched his last discharge by claiming victory was in sight since his opponent's spirit now stood alone against the forces of the age: 'De tant de disputeurs éternels, Pascal est seul resté, parce que seul il était un homme de génie. Il est encore debout sur les ruines de son siècle.'[21]

It is important to recall that the first group of *remarques* was published during an acute struggle between the Jansenist and Jesuit parties in France affecting political life as well as purely religious matters; and, though no lover of the Jesuits, Voltaire was inclined to think worse of the Jansenists for the severity of their doctrines and their current activities. He therefore chose to challenge the *Pensées* in part as the most influential work the Jansenist movement had produced. His hostility towards their author, however, was already proceeding from more deeply-rooted objections, for he believed Pascal's brilliant reaffirmation of traditional Christian doctrine presented perhaps the supreme obstacle to the furtherance of enlightened opinions and practices. Prepared to recognize Pascal's stature in certain fields, Voltaire nevertheless came to identify him as an enemy of the human race—and increasingly as a personal enemy too–whose influence it was necessary to destroy. Waterman has epitomized the crucial reasons for this implacable animosity:

As long as Jesuits fought Jansenists, as long as any political or religious group persecuted dissenters, as long as any kind of injustice was perpetrated in the name of God or Mammon, Voltaire could never lay down his pen, and he could not cease worrying about the influence of the great Pascal. Nor did he often fail himself to give justice where justice was due. He defended both Jesuits and Jansenists whenever they were persecuted and down-trodden. He staunchly upheld the right of both sides to free expression of opinion and equal justice under law, and specifically he reproached the enemies of Arnauld and Pascal for failing to recognize their genius. But the die was cast: the magnificent and dangerous Pensées *had to be refuted in order to further the progress of mankind.* [22]

Voltaire concentrated his attack upon Pascal's belief in the duality of human nature, which the author of the *Pensées* had claimed Christianity alone could satisfactorily explain. From the outset, he took violent exception to the view that man's misfortunes are the most obvious signs of his fall. Pascal had seen man as a complete enigma to himself, understandable only through the doctrine of original sin, but Voltaire was convinced that man is fundamentally a natural being, the happiest of animals, and his state one on which we should congratulate ourselves. Far from being a collection of people vainly seeking distractions, society realizes the needs of its members and is cemented by their respect for one another. Pascal's pessimism was further questionable since experiences such as his, and ideas of the duality of man's nature, are quite unknown to most of the human race. Illness, abnormal strain, and self-preoccupation had affected his mind, causing him to lose that hope which should carry a normal person through depressions and temporary setbacks. Rather than muse on his situation in a metaphysical or religious fashion, man should patiently take steps to improve it, applying his rational faculties to affairs at hand and to the promotion of justice and happiness throughout the world. There was much to encourage belief in human progress, and, though Pascal might assert all reason must give way to feeling, no conclusive proof for this existed; 'notre raisonnement se réduit à céder au sentiment en fait de goût, non en fait de science.' [23] Other targets for Voltaire's scorn were Pascal's defence of the Jews' place in history, his belief in the worth of biblical prophecies and miracles, and any instance of Jansenist teachings clearly visible in Pascal's thought.

In all his attempts to dismiss the *Pensées*, and with them the reputation of Pascal as an apologist, Voltaire's approach essentially remained one of ridicule. As Cassirer has noted, he carefully avoided pursuing Pascal to the real centre of his religious thinking and the ultimate depths of his problem, seeking rather to combat him on a more superficial, self-explanatory level.[24] The two men were markedly different, and Pascal's defenders were not successful in altering the tone of debate in consequence. Voltaire hoped to render Pascal's arguments either absurd, refusing to grapple with their fundamental theses, or deluded, representing Pascal towards the end of his life as pitifully rejecting belief in the obvious potentialities of man. Concluding it to be more 'reasonable' to accept the human condition with all its faults as natural and even perfectible rather than bad, he thought it useless to try to prove any theory of human depravity valid or necessary. Only through faith might these sorry views of humanity be held at all, and faith was a discredited mode of apprehension.

Other *philosophes*, notably Diderot and Condorcet, supported Voltaire, and the conflict aroused wide interest. Largely owing to the degree of toleration existing and the absence of dramatically opposing forces entangling politics with religion or philosophy, the confrontation between religion and rationalism in England was less pronounced than that occurring in France; but under Voltaire's influence men of reason there also came to see Pascal and his *Pensées* as a standing rebuke to the propositions they shared with the *philosophes*. Hopes for the perfectibility of man appeared to rest on hypothesis, and achievements of reason and science seemed guilty of that intellectual pride Pascal had condemned; for, by founding his Christian apology on what might be observed in man himself, Pascal had met objective analysis on its own ground. Believing in the inerrancy of the scientific method, the *philosophes* and their sympathizers were confronted by an admitted genius who inexorably argued that reason alone could never ennoble mankind. Other victories might be won, but, until Pascal's compelling defence of Christian doctrine was demolished, eighteenth-century optimism lay fundamentally open to denial. The *Pensées* revealed the Enlightenment's Achilles' heel, and Condorcet's edition of 1776 represented a heroic effort to reclaim all he could for his party's cause, and thereafter hang Pascal with his own rope after years of scorn and dispute had failed to finish him.

The opinion has frequently been expressed that Voltaire's first *remarques* are peculiarly associated with England. There is much agreement that his thought underwent a notable development during temporary exile there between 1726 and 1729, and it has even been argued that he began to write his first major attack upon Pascal while the guest at Wandsworth of Everard Falkener, a merchant whom he admiringly saw rise to be an ambassador and Postmaster-General. Voltaire's connections and acknowledged talents introduced him to social and literary circles, and his keen observation of English life—usually to French disadvantage—was shown when the *Lettres philosophiques* appeared.[25] The twenty-fifth chapter consisting of the *Remarques* stands in some contrast to the rest of the work, which mostly describes and evaluates religion and government in England, as well as leading figures in science and literature; and the evidence suggests Voltaire added this last chapter at a late stage after consultation with his French publisher, to render more likely his work's acceptance by the Jesuits. In certain respects, however, it does not seem to be wholly misplaced. A major theme of the other sections is the author's advocacy of a reasoning outlook, and to oppose Pascal was but extending and making use of arguments mentioned when reviewing Locke and other English proponents of the new learning. Moreover, it seems fair to suppose that current English interest in Pascal as scientist, writer, and thinker had not remained unnoticed by Voltaire; for the second edition of Kennett's *Pensées* was published during his stay, shortly followed by another, and Pascal's depiction of man was then intriguing several English authors. The extent to which Voltaire assimilated English deistic thought is a matter for debate, but he surely cannot have been forgetful while composing his *remarques* of any views on Pascal he may have read or heard expressed; whether contrived or not, he scattered several references to English life among his outspoken comments.[26]

Owing to anticipated difficulties with French censors, the *Lettres philosophiques* appeared first in English a year beforehand, in 1733, translated by a minor literary figure, John Lockman; but, although well-received, it was not until the second English edition eight years later that the *Remarques* were placed with the rest of the translation, being the separate work of 'R.E.M.'[27] Other editions followed, mostly containing the *Remarques*, and a study of English libraries later in the century reveals that the *Lettres* were widely read, along with Voltaire's works as an historian, an epic poet, and a writer of tales. In the seventeen-sixties, the first collection of his writings in English was published under the direction of Thomas Francklin and the novelist, Tobias Smollett.[28] Seemingly the first opportunity for the English reader to sample Voltaire's opinions on Pascal had been offered in 1739, when the appropriate volume of a new translation of Bayle's *Dictionnaire* had appeared. The ten-volume *General Dictionary, Historical and Critical* was not only 'interspersed with several thousand Lives never before published,' but also carried further comments inserted by the translators; and, though the entry on Pascal was in most respects unchanged, the additional comments assume considerable importance when attached to the new concluding words of the article itself: 'Mr. Voltaire has made animadversions on several of his *Thoughts concerning Religion.* I shall give a specimen in one or two of them.' Voltaire's criticisms of Pascal's wager had already been quoted in the notes, but, in extracts from the *Remarques* in the *Lettres philosophiques* that followed here, attention was turned to Pascal's understanding of the nature of man, and, more briefly, his ideas upon beauty.[29]

With a tribute to Pascal's genius and eloquence introducing the selection, Voltaire announced that 'the more I respect them, the more I am persuaded, that he himself would have corrected many of those thoughts which he had thrown at random on paper.' The *Pensées*, as they stood, were open to most serious objections:

It is my opinion that Mr. Pascal's design, in general, was to exhibit mankind in an odious light. He strenuously endeavours to represent us all as wicked and unhappy. He writes against human nature in pretty near the same manner as he wrote against the Jesuits. He ascribes to the essence of our nature, such things as are peculiar to some men only; and speaks injuriously, but at the same time eloquently, of Mankind. I shall be so free as to take up the pen, in defence of the human species, against this sublime misanthropist. I dare affirm that we are neither so unhappy, nor so wicked as he declares us to be.

One of Pascal's most typical observations upon man's wretchedness in this world was placed next, linked, as in the *Lettres*, with Voltaire's ringing condemnation of its pessimism and unreality. Tradition holds that a letter from Falkener prompted Voltaire in this defence of mankind:

'*When I consider man's blindness and misery, and the astonishing contrarieties which are seen in his nature; and when I behold the whole universe dumb, and man unenlightned, left to himself, and wandering, as it were in this nook of the universe, without knowing who placed him there; what he is come to do; and what will become of him after death; I return back terrified, as a man who having been carried, when asleep, into a frightful desart island, should awake without knowing where he is, or knowing how to get out of this island: hence I wonder that mankind are not seized with despair, when they consider the wretchedness of their condition.*'

As I was perusing this reflection, I received a letter from a friend who lives in a far-distant country. His words are as follow.

'*I am at this time just as you left me; neither gayer nor more sad, neither richer nor poorer. I enjoy perfect health, and am blest with all things that make life agreeable; undisturbed with love, avarice, ambition, or envy; and will venture, so long as these things last, to call myself a very happy man.*'

Many men are as happy as my correspondent. It is with men as with animals. Here a dog shall eat and lie with his mistress: there another turns the spit, and is equally happy; a third shall run mad, and is knocked on the head. As to myself, when I cast my eyes on London and Paris, I do not see any cause to throw me into the despair mentioned by Mr. Pascal. I see a city, that does not resemble in any manner a desert island, but, on the contrary, populous, rich, well governed; and where men are as happy as far as is consistent with their natures to be: what wise man would attempt to hang himself, because he does not know in what manner God is seen face to face, and because he cannot unravel the mystery of the Trinity? He might as well plunge into despair, because he has not four feet and a pair of wings.

Why should any one endeavour to make us consider our Being with horror? Our existence is not so wretched as some people would make us believe it to be. To consider the universe as a dungeon, and all mankind as so many criminals who are carrying to execution, is the idea of an Enthusiast: to suppose that the world is a seat of delights, where we ought to meet with nothing but pleasures, is the dream of a Sibarite: but to conclude that the earth, mankind, and animals are what they ought to be, in the disposition of Providence, is, in my opinion, thinking like a wise man.[30]

The publication of the *General Dictionary* bearing Voltaire's attacks meant that the English public not only had renewed access to details of the life and writings of Pascal as Bayle had presented them, but could also read on the same pages denunciations of Pascal's understanding of man by his most effective and persistent antagonist. These attacks were damaging in themselves, but, by implicating the person of Pascal with the defects of his thought, they threw into stronger relief many features of his character, giving a new turn to Bayle's remark that Pascal had been 'a Paradoxical Individuum of Human kind.' Several editors were responsible for this production, chief among whom was the Rev. Thomas Birch, an historian and biographer who later served as Secretary of the Royal Society; and, since another was John Lockman, we may presume the inclusion of some of Voltaire's most eloquent and destructive criticisms is particularly attributable to him, as well as their translation.[31]

The impact of this amalgamation of Bayle's portrait of Pascal with refinements by Voltaire was not eventually restricted to the *General Dictionary's* readers. English dictionaries of a similar nature had already begun to use and incorporate Bayle's work, many of his startling ideas being so successfully absorbed that eventually the original is hardly traceable in its new form.[32] It is therefore no surprise to find the entries on Pascal in encyclopaedias and dictionaries published in England later in the century bearing a recognizable affinity to the facts and opinions expressed in Birch's standard English version of the *Dictionnaire*; and, in this respect as much as any other, Bayle truly became 'an adopted son.'

The first edition of the *Encyclopaedia Britannica* (1768-71) did not contain an article on Pascal, but the second included a short account of his life emphasizing his youthful precocity and the degrees to which he carried self-mortification—renouncing all pleasures and wearing a belt with sharp points—in language reminiscent of Mme. Perier as presented by Bayle. Far more attention was devoted to the *Lettres provinciales* and Voltaire's praise for them than to the *Pensées*, the latter being very briefly described as 'a work against atheists and infidels . . . [which] has been much admired.'[33] Likewise reflecting opinion as much as informing it, a very similar article appeared in 1784 in the *New and General Biographical Dictionary*, the author giving as his sources Mme. Perier's life of her brother, Bayle's *Dictionnaire*, and the seventeenth-century Adrien Baillet's *Jugemens des sçavans*. This entry concluded by remarking on Pascal's celibacy in a strongly questioning manner, touched with despair:

Here then was a genius of the first order, led by a false religion, in whose chains he was so fast bound, as never to entertain even a thought of getting loose; led, I say, to think ill of, and to discard, a sure and most unerring dictate of the natural law, as in some degree opposite to the revealed, and so make God to contradict himself. But he was not the first great genius, that had been so led; nor will he be the last.[34]

In 1723, William Bond had purloined certain of Bayle's words on Pascal without reservation, apparently considering they enhanced what had been an unusual life but also an uplifting and instructive one. Some other writers remained similarly untroubled, but the circulation of Voltaire's challenges increasingly conspired to set the details of Pascal's well-known life in an unpromising light, while feeding the growing dissatisfaction with aspects of his thought. As Voltaire had realized, it was an easy task to attack the *Pensées* through the figure behind them, thereby showing them as the random jottings of a visionary invalid, whose maladies and hallucinations had overcome his superb mental gifts; and, by 1750, a number of English rationalists were taking up the chorus of the French *philosophes*. One may picture many an Englishman then chancing upon the *Spectator*'s description of Pascal as a noble but sickly individual, who wrote on

MⁱBLAISE PASCHAL.

G. Vertue Sculp.
1744

PLATE 5 Frontispiece from vol. 1 of *The Life of Mr. Paschal, with his Letters Relating to the Jesuits,* trans. William Andrews (London, 1744)

the misery of man, and, comparing him with the robust and level-headed Sir Roger, withdrawing any sympathy in his repugnance. The sense of distance widened when, in 1749, a reprint of Kennett's translation bore the customary passage from Budgell's essay on its title-page, but reduced it to a few lines relating only Pascal's sufferings. Such a personality had become abhorrent to the rationalist and sceptic, and he accordingly tended to reject the *Pensées* too; but, in those areas of English religious life where an experiential faith survived or was reawakened, Pascal continued to be revered, and his pessimistic view of human nature was often held more to his credit than to his lasting dishonour.

[III] However much the *Pensées* might languish from opposition or neglect, eighteenth-century England's interest in the *Lettres provinciales* and some aspects of their author's life still remained unshaken. Pascal's exposure of Jesuitism had won the lasting approval of all staunch Protestants, and, as we have noticed, Anglicans in particular were inclined to count him almost as their own. The new trend in appreciation, which viewed the *Provinciales* as pleasurable as well as provocative reading, is embodied in a new translation published in 1744. Times had changed since the days of the Popish Plot, and the work was given rather the semblance of a classic rediscovered than a sensational revelation. The hostility towards Catholicism was indisputable but less crudely conveyed; instead of 'Sicut Serpentes,' the title-page now carried a quotation from Juvenal:

> . . . *Felicia tempora quae te*
> *Moribus opponunt: habeat jam Roma pudorem.*[35]

Elegantly produced in two volumes and offering handsome engraved portraits of Pascal and Arnauld by George Vertue,[36] this new edition also reflected current biographical interest by including Mme. Perier's life of her brother with the letters, and listing it as a comparable attraction.

The translator was a Nonjuror, William Andrews, a native of Croscombe, Somerset, who, as a deacon, had declined to proceed to the priesthood since he could not in good conscience take the necessary oath of abjuration. Living for many years at Wedmore, he devoted himself to literature, and fitted up a study over the church porch there, in which surroundings we may imagine his leisurely version of the *Provinciales* was made. Andrews died at Bath in 1759 and was buried in that city's abbey. Reputedly a modest man who denied any intention of promoting· controversy, he sent forth his translation inscribed only with his initials.[37]

Andrews partly justified his efforts on the grounds that the old translation, last printed nearly seventy years before, was unavailable, 'in very few hands, and in a dress not so modern,' as well as having been defective. He shared some of his forerunner's sympathies, however, for he also expressed the hope he might be striking a small but useful blow against the ever-menacing power of Rome: 'So much has been apprehended lately, both by Church and State from Jesuitical maxims, that the best pens and the greatest authority have been employed to suppress them. If I can but contribute my mite to so salutary an end, I pretend to no better apology for troubling the public.' Like Hammond, Walker, and Kennett before, Andrews necessarily sought excuses for Pascal's Catholicism; for, 'though Mr. Paschal is no Jesuit, yet it is plain enough from his letters that he is a strenuous Papist.' Accepting that several of Pascal's views differed from those of the Church of England, he had nonetheless been pleased to find that, on the important issues of the Pope's supremacy and transubstantiation, Pascal in some respects upheld Anglican teaching. Steele's suggestion of Pascal for the edification of ladies was witness to the suitability of his works, and, in general, Andrews had no doubt of their merits. 'My author, in the original, wants no advocate,' he wrote, Pascal's reputation being 'so well known to the learned world, that nothing I can say can add any thing to his fame.' Interestingly he continued, 'his works are his best vouchers, and amongst those, the following Letters relating to the Jesuits have always had the precedence.'[38]

In tones less urgent than the seventeenth century's, Andrews reflected a moderated antagonism towards Rome, and, though he still made his purpose unmistakable, his version's straightforward text and cultivated manner also helped advance Pascal as a figure of importance in literature. English fears of foreign, Catholic domination remained latent and a renewed presentation of the *Provinciales* must have been widely welcomed, but educated men were by now more ready to enjoy the *Provinciales* for their satirical qualities than as material for controversy. Issues once so crucial had become less stirring and relevant; but Pascal's eloquence and humour remained the same, and Voltaire's admiration also publicized the *Provinciales* at the expense of the *Pensées*. An analysis of loan records from eight English cathedral libraries extending over this period implies that, though neither work was borrowed very frequently, the *Provinciales* were definitely in greater demand than the *Pensées*; and they were quite often requested at the Bristol Library.[39]

Elsewhere the overall impression of English tastes is much the same. For the Rev. William Cole, antiquary, visiting the church of St.

Etienne du Mont, it was sufficient to note in his diary that 'Pascal the Jansenist & cutting Writer of the *Lettres provinciales*' was buried there.[40] As a modern classic, the *Provinciales* also exerted stylistic influence within a literary *genre*. The *Letters of Junius* were probably formed upon the model of Pascal's, their author more successfully preserving his anonymity; and, though the contents of Charles Jenner's *Letters from Altamont* show no obvious relation to the work which they recall, the choice of form and a quotation from Pascal on the title-page are indicative enough.[41]

The *Provinciales* thus maintained for Pascal some distinction as a master of expression and wit, but they achieved this to an unusual degree in the eyes of Edward Gibbon, who selected the work as one of three which had particularly contributed to the formation of his outlook as an historian. Remarking upon his private reading as a youth at Lausanne, he recalled he had learned from the *Provincial Letters* of Pascal 'to manage the weapon of grave and temperate irony, even on subjects of ecclesiastical solemnity.' Almost every year, he noted, he had perused them with new pleasure.[42] Gibbon's library at his death included three copies of the *Provinciales* (Cologne, 1698, Paris, 1754, and Leyden, 1761) and one of the *Pensées* (Paris, 1761), all in French as befitted his almost native familiarity with the language and his frequent residence abroad.[43] Owing much also to Bolingbroke and Voltaire for his manner of writing, there can be little doubt that Gibbon spoke with honesty of the influence of the *Provinciales* upon the *Decline and Fall*. Hunting for traces of that 'grave and·temperate irony' in Gibbon's history can assume the proportions of a minor pastime, and Young has drawn attention to what he considered some prime specimens:

> . . . *his mingling of truth and malice in an innocent antithesis is often of the purest Pascalian quality, as for example when he writes of the Popes' attitude to the Filioque clause: 'They condemned the innovation but they acquiesced in the sentiment.' Or more broadly (and there is plenty of fun in Pascal):*
>
> *In the last and fatal siege of Syracuse, her citizens displayed some remnant of the spirit which had formerly resisted the powers of Athens and Carthage. They stood about twenty days against the battering-rams and catapultae, the mines and tortoises of the beseigers, —really it seems as if Gibbon, who thought Lord Heathfield of Gibraltar 'a glorious old fellow,' had for once taken fire —'and the place might have been relieved if the mariners of the Imperial fleet had not been detained at Constantinople in building a church to the Virgin Mary.' Pascal would have condemned the irreverence, but no one would have enjoyed the expression of it more keenly.*[44]

Certain other aspects of Pascal's reputation similarly flourished, his fame as a scientist remaining largely intact. In 1752, the Rev.

John Brown did not find Pascal's religious interests disqualifying him from inclusion among numerous distinguished persons of ancient and recent times who symbolized the desirable union of rational powers with strong imagination; and, in 1765, Goldsmith linked Pascal with Huygens, Boyle, and others as having 'improved philosophy by producing new objects of speculation.'[45] A steady interest in the well-known stories of Pascal's early years is also apparent, partly out of the increased attention then being paid to childhood as an indicator of future promise. Pascal was a natural choice to demonstrate the belif that genius was announced by the display of precocious talents, and his youthful mathematical and physical discoveries were inevitably seen as heralding his future achievements. In a vein reminiscent of the *Memoirs . . . of Martinus Scriblerus*, Laurence Sterne named Pascal in a conversation between Yorick, his father, and Uncle Toby upon certain prodigies of childhood, 'some of which left off their substantial forms at nine years old, or sooner, and went on reasoning without them.'[46] More seriously, the Rev. John Mainwaring described the young Handel secretly playing the clavichord by night to escape his father's disapproval, and continued:

And here it may not be unpleasing to the reader, just to remind him of the minute and surprising resemblance between these passages in the early periods of Handel's life, and some which are recorded in that of the celebrated monsieur Pascal, written by his sister. Nothing could equal the bias of the one to Mathematics, but the bias of the other to Music: both in their very childhood outdid the efforts of maturer age: they pursued their respective studies not only without any assistance, but against the consent of their parents, and in spite of all the opposition they contrived to give them.[47]

In 1764, the compiler of *Anecdotes of Polite Literature*, discussing early evidence of mathematical genius, rightly quoted from the Abbé Dubos that 'the adventure which happened to Monsieur Paschal, has been published by so many different hands, that it is known all over Europe';[48] and occasionally the more remarkable tales from Pascal's life would reappear in biographical miscellanies in later English journals and magazines.

Although the *Pensées* were now largely overlooked by literary men, the success of the *Spectator* still prompted many subsequent writers to copy its style and content, and an essay appearing in the *World* (No. 92, October 3, 1754) was clearly inspired by Budgell's story commenting upon Pascal. This periodical numbered several leading men of fashion among its contributors, and, after describing a company of drinking men in whose revels he had reluctantly joined, the author in thir instance proceeded to reflect:

When I considered that, perhaps, two millions of my fellow-subjects passed two parts in three of their lives in the very same manner in which the worthy members of my friend's club passed theirs, I was at a loss to discover that attractive, irresistible and invisible charm (for I confess I saw none) to which they so deliberately and assiduously sacrificed their time, their health, and their reason; till dipping accidentally into monsieur Paschal, I read upon the subject of hunting the following passage. 'What, unless to drown thought' (says that excellent writer) 'can make men throw away so much time upon a silly animal, which they might buy much cheaper in the market? It hinders us from looking into ourselves, which is a view we cannot bear.' That this is often one motive, and sometimes the only one of hunting, I can easily believe. But then it must be allowed too, that if the jolly sportsman, who thus vigorously runs away from himself, does not break his neck in the flight, he improves his health, at least, by his exercise. But what other motive can possibly be assigned for the Soaker's daily and seriously swallowing his own destruction, except that of 'drowning thought, and hindering him from looking into himself, which is a view he cannot bear?'

The writer in the *World* did not refer directly to Pascal's life, but his conclusions were similar to those of his predecessor. Whereas Budgell had written he would hunt like Sir Roger de Coverley 'as the best Kind of Physick for mending a bad Constitution, and preserving a good one,' his adapter recommended the example of 'Cantabrigius,' who, he said,

... drinks nothing, and rides more miles in a year than the keenest sportsman, and with almost equal velocity. The former keeps his head clear, the latter his body. It is not from himself that he runs, but to his acquaintance. Internally safe, he seeks no sanctuary from himself, no intoxication for his mind. His penetration makes him discover and divert himself with the follies of mankind, which his wit enables him to expose with the truest ridicule, though always without personal offence. Chearful abroad, because happy at home, and thus happy, because virtuous.[49]

Such peripheral interest in the *Pensées* heightens the contrast between that work being largely ignored by cultivated men or considered uncongenial, while the *Lettres provinciales* received their applause. Although Port Royal was still highly regarded even by such a figure as Lord Chesterfield—'Inform yourself what the Port Royal is,' he wrote to his son[50]—the number of publications in English of works relating to the community declined as the eighteenth century progressed, paralleling the disappearance of the *Pensées* themselves. The relative neglect of Pascal and his thought after their previous high standing is nonetheless occasionally surprising; for example, Horace Walpole, whose correspondence invariably contains opinions on anything and anybody, nowhere mentioned Pascal. A man as informed as he upon subjects of conversation in England and France cannot have been unfamiliar with current views on Pascal, and his library at Strawberry Hill contained a four-volume edition of the *Provinciales* (Amsterdam, 1734-39), as well as Jesup's *Lives of Picus and Pascal.*[51] Walpole's apparent disinterest may perhaps be best explained by a strong antipathy towards Pascal's character and the *Pensées*, and also by an understandable tendency to associate his works with the reading tastes of religious groups and social classes other than his own. In 1744, Berkeley was calling the contradictions of human nature, torn between flesh and spirit, beast and angel, earth and heaven, 'a vulgar theme';[52] and the evidence accumulates to suggest that men of Walpole's intelligence were inclined to judge Pascal as a spent force, the *Provinciales* alone having stood the test of time, and as a man who in most respects fully deserved Voltaire's description of 'this sublime misanthropist.'

[IV] A foretaste of the final stages of the eighteenth-century process whereby English ambivalence towards Pascal's understanding of man and religion turned into vehement disapproval may be obtained from some correspondence between two intellectually-minded ladies, the famous blue-stocking Elizabeth Carter and her younger friend, Catherine Talbot, the exchange taking place in 1748. Mrs. Carter was presumably no stranger to Pascal, having in 1739 translated Crousaz's attack on Pope's *Essay on Man*; and Miss Talbot, as a member of the household of the future Archbishop Secker of Canterbury, was also able to write knowledgeably about him. Having already promised twice that she would give her views, Miss Talbot eventually did so with zeal, though confessing her misgivings for Pascal's personality and his Catholicism:

My book has been Pascal; and I fancy, if you had walked with me, we should have agreed very tolerably in our thoughts of him. The thing that left a disagreeable impression on your mind, must have been his life, which presents one with so gloomy a scheme of goodness, as would make any body very unhappy that should think to imitate him. But in his book itself wherever I have dipped accidentally, it has given me the highest pleasure.

Miss Talbot was especially attracted to the reflections in the *Pensées* on man's greatness and misfortunes; taken together, these seemed to her to give the justest notions of life, 'nor is it at all painful to consider the dark side of this prospect, when one knows that unless things are by wilful folly put out of their due course, the sunshine is to be continually gaining ground.' His thoughts, she found, uplifted human emotions beyond our fellow-creatures in this world to objects on a higher plane, and she proceeded to copy out some remarks of Pascal's on life's transitoriness, which had particularly impressed her:

'Il est injuste qu'on s'attache, quoi qu'on le fasse avec plaisir, et volontairement: je tromperais ceux en qui je ferai naître ce desir, car je ne suis la fin de personne, et n'ai de quoi le satisfaire. Ne suis je pas prête à mourir? et ainsi l'objet de leur attachement mourra donc?'

I give you only part, the whole is good; but yet this excellent man, and most superior genius, drew very wrong consequences from these right principles, and for fear of being too much beloved, seems to me to have grown into a harshness, and austerity of behaviour to his friends, that must in a very blameable degree have given them uneasiness. Let but human creatures be beloved like human creatures, and there is no danger of going too far: and surely it is one of the highest duties for people to render themselves as amiable as they can. . . .

I cannot have done yet with my friend Pascal, for I do highly admire him as a genius, love him as a saint, and pity him as a papist. 'Tis quite terrible and amazing to see how he renounced his understanding, his ease, and his life, from such wrong principles, as but in any thing but matter of duty, he could not have seen the absurdity of. That ever it should come into any one's imagination, that to renounce all the comforts and accommodations of life, and to shut one's eyes on all the fair beauties of this world, was the way to raise our love, and gratitude to the beneficent author! Yet this is the comfortless horrid doctrine of strict popery, and those good hearts that have been awed by it into error and wretchedness deserve equal compassion and esteem.[53]

Miss Talbot's hopes for agreement with Pascal's observations on the bounds of friendship received scant sympathy, however, for Mrs. Carter's views led her instead to see the extract in the context of her estimate of its author's character:

I am much obliged to you, dear Miss Talbot, for your excellent comment on Pascal. If unfortunately for him you had not quoted his own text, from a belief that you had only honestly represented his meaning, I should have been tempted to have gone through the whole book; but there are some painters, whatever the originals, who make all their pictures angels: and you seem to make every author you quote, speak good sense. I much question whether I should not write a book myself, if you would promise to write a comment on it. En attendant, I am going in the spirit of controversy to oppose this favorite author of yours, who seems to have founded his notions of duty rather on the basis of a severe and gloomy temper, than on the cheerful, social, goodnatured spirit of the Gospel. He is however most highly to be esteemed and compassion-

ated, for having turned the edge of that severity chiefly on his own ease; and his character in many respects deserved the greatest esteem.

To illustrate her belief that the passage in question contained 'a great deal of false reasoning,' the older lady then broke into French, thinking it 'but pure complaisance to quarrel with Mr. Pascal in his own language.' Challenging him with many inconsistencies of thought and mistaken conclusions upon human life and nature, she admitted 'you will certainly think I am going to write a book in good earnest.' Miss Talbot seems thereafter to have felt unequal to much further argument, and hastened towards the optimistic religious position of her *confidante*:

All that in Pascal is unsociable, harsh, and gloomy, I utterly disclaim.... These things are done with a very good meaning, but surely a mistaken one, and while we are continued in this world, we ought thankfully to make, and think, and speak the best of every thing in it, that is innocent; common good breeding and goodnature teach us this kind of behaviour at the most ordinary entertainment that is made for us. And shall this fair world have been formed with such exquisite art, and inexhaustible bounty purely for us, and this life so carefully preserved by an ever watchful Providence, only to be disliked and railed at, and so far as we can and dare, scorned, and refused? Well, are we agreed now? Or will you take the other side of the question? Poor wretched creatures that we are, the best of us are forced to run a little wrong on the right side, lest we should err too far on the other, and more dangerous. Yet indeed we have much in us too that is noble and amiable, and the thought that these excellencies shall in due time be perfected by the giver of them, and made for ever to approach nearer their divine original, may make us amidst all our infirmities look round upon one another with joy, fondness, and admiration.[54]

This well-behaved clash between the two ladies clearly ended in a victory for the benevolence of the Creator and the 'cheerful, social, goodnatured spirit' whereby he would have his children live. Significantly, agreement between them was most forthcoming upon the manner of Pascal's life, for, as the insinuations of Bayle aided by the open attacks of Voltaire took firmer hold, the increasing practice was wholeheartedly to condemn the man himself as pathetic and inexplicable. Notable among these radical opponents of Pascal, to whom we shall now turn, was David Hume, the Scottish philosopher and historian, whose strong sceptical opinions inevitably caused him to form an unfavourable estimate. Already familiar with Bayle's *Dictionnaire*, Hume made the first of his visits to France between 1734 and 1737 and there began his acquaintance with the works of

Voltaire, who, with other *philosophes*, had a profound and lasting effect upon his intellectual development.[55] The influence of French hostility towards Pascal is plain in Hume's short piece, *A Dialogue*, published in the seventeen-fifties. Treating the basis of morals, one participant in this discussion held them to be founded upon 'the maxims of common life and ordinary conduct'; but the question was then raised how men whose habits and outlook have differed markedly from the more normal lives of their contemporaries have still been regarded as worthy of imitation. To show that both good and bad possibilities exist in 'artificial' lives and manners, Hume drew an illustration from Diogenes, 'the most celebrated model of extravagant philosophy,' and chose as a modern parallel Pascal, 'a man of parts and genius . . . and perhaps too, a man of virtue, had he allowed his virtuous inclinations to have exerted and displayed themselves.' The resulting contrast clearly stated some preference on the speaker's part:

The foundation of Diogenes's conduct was an endeavour to render himself an independent being as much as possible, and to confine all his wants and desires and pleasures within himself and his own mind: The aim of Pascal was to keep a perpetual sense of his dependence before his eyes, and never to forget his numberless wants and infirmities. The ancient supported himself by magnanimity, ostentation, pride, and the idea of his own superiority above his fellow-creatures. The modern made constant profession of humility and abasement, of the contempt and hatred of himself; and endeavoured to attain these supposed virtues, as far as they are attainable. The austerities of the Greek were in order to inure himself to hardships, and prevent his ever suffering: Those of the Frenchman were embraced merely for their own sake, and in order to suffer as much as possible. The philosopher indulged himself in the most beastly pleasures, even in public: The saint refused himself the most innocent, even in private. The former thought it his duty to love his friends, and to rail at them, and reprove them, and scold them: The latter endeavoured to be absolutely indifferent towards his nearest relations, and to love and speak well of his enemies. The great object of Diogenes's wit was every kind of superstition, that is, every kind of religion known in his time. The mortality of the soul was his standard principle; and even his sentiments of a divine providence seem to have been licentious. The most ridiculous superstitions directed Pascal's faith and practice; and an extreme contempt of this life, in comparison of the future, was the chief foundation of his conduct.

In spite of unusual beliefs and behaviour, both men had met with widespread admiration, placing in doubt the possibility of any universal standard of morals. The evident risks of eccentricity, however, caused the other party in the conversation to reaffirm his faith in those morals derived from rational habits and common usage. In his view, an experiment 'which succeeds in the air, will not always succeed in a vacuum'; and, if men forsake the maxims of common reason and set their own, 'no one can answer for what will please or displease them.' The natural principles of their mind would not function with the same regularity as they would, if such men were 'free from the illusions of religious superstition or philosophical enthusiasm.'[56]

Hume's opposition to Pascal was particularly devastating in another area where the influence of the French thinker had already been severely weakened; for, of all the eighteenth century's attacks upon such proofs for Christianity, his essay, 'Of Miracles,' is usually accounted the most decisive in destroying the effectiveness of this traditional defence. The idea of such an essay first occurred to him when he heard at the Jesuit college of La Flèche of some supernatural happenings alleged to have recently taken place there. He finally concluded 'that no testimony is sufficient to establish a miracle, unless the testimony be of such a kind, that its falsehood would be more miraculous, than the fact, which it endeavours to establish'; and, applying this maxim to both miracles and prophecies, he developed his argument with reference to well-known instances from religion and history. Like other works of their kind, the *Pensées* would have come under scrutiny and by implication have been dismissed, but Hume also directed his attention separately to the miracle of the holy thorn. Describing the acceptance of its authenticity both in and out of the community of Port Royal, he voiced his suspicions but granted the unusual learning and probity of witnesses to the healing wrought on the niece of 'the famous Pascal, whose sanctity of life, as well as extraordinary capacity, is well known.' Hume early clarified these remarks, adding that Pascal had also been 'a Believer in that and in many other Miracles, which he had less opportunity of being inform'd of'; and, when he revised the essay in 1768, he further contrasted 'the great names of Pascal, Racine, Arnaud, Nicole' with 'such despicable materials,' and poured scorn upon a cure having been 'really performed by the touch of an authentic holy prickle of the holy thorn, which composed the holy crown, which, etc.'[57]

The new confidence of the age in drawing the boundary between reason and madness inescapably caused the former to be prized more highly than before and made the latter more liable to be regarded with horror; and, in this connection, Pascal's peculiarities received further critical appraisal as the object of pathological study. In his 'Miscellaneous Observations on the Influence of Habit and

Association.' Thomas Percival, a Lancashire doctor and author and one of the noted medical men of his day, described the case of Simon Browne, a dissenting minister 'seized with melancholy.' Here, he held, was an example of partial insanity co-existing with general intelligence in an individual, and, to support his conclusions, he drew attention to the life of Pascal:

I am inclined to believe, that the celebrated M. Paschal laboured under a species of insanity, towards the conclusion of his life, similar to that of Mr. Simon Browne. And, having hazarded such a surmise, it is incumbent on me to shew, on what it is founded. This very extraordinary man discovered the most astonishing marks of genius in his childhood; and his progress in science was so rapid, that at the age of sixteen, he wrote an excellent treatise of Conic Sections. He possessed such a capacious and retentive memory, that he is said 'never to have forgotten any thing which he had learned.' And it was his practice, to digest and arrange in his mind, a whole series of reflections, before he committed them to writing. This power was at once so accurate and extensive, that he has been heard to deliver the entire plan of a work, of which he had taken no notes, in a continued narration, that occupied several hours. But it is related, by the editor of his Thoughts on Religion and other Subjects, *'that it pleased God so to touch his heart, as to let him perfectly understand, that the Christian religion obligeth us to live for God only, and to propose to ourselves no other object.' In consequence of this persuasion, he renounced all the pursuits of knowledge, and practiced the most severe and rigorous mortifications; living in the greatest penury, and refusing every indulgence, which was not absolutely necessary for the support of life. It appears from some of his pious meditations, that this resolution of mind proceeded from the visitation of sickness. And the following solemn addresses to the Deity clearly indicate an imagination perverted by the most erroneous associations.*

The prayers of Pascal quoted by Percival gave thanks for sickness and 'divorce from the pleasures of the world,' requesting that 'I may look on myself as dead already, separated from the world, stripped of all the objects of my passion, and placed alone in thy presence.' The resulting diagnosis ignored the suggestion that Pascal's religion had its admirable features; it was merely the product of a diseased state of mind:

Was it consonant with soundness of understanding, for a man to take a sudden disgust at all the liberal studies, and innocent enjoyments, which had before engaged and gratified his mind? And was it not as much the fiction of a distempered fancy, that God enjoined poverty, abstinence, and ignorance, to one possessing rank, fortune, and the noblest endowments of the mind, as the belief of Simon Browne, that he was divested of that rationality, which at the same time he so eminently displayed? Whenever false ideas, of a practical kind, are so firmly united, as to be constantly and invariably mistaken for truths, we very justly denominate this unnatural alliance Insanity. And, if it give rise to a train of subordinate wrong associations, producing incongruity of behaviour, incapacity for the common duties of life, or unconscious deviations from morality and religion, Madness has then its commencement. [58]

Like his contemporary, Joseph Priestley, Percival was a convinced Unitarian, and, in their writings published in the seventeen-eighties, the rationalist offensive demonstrably nears its peak. Ably attempting to redefine Christianity upon a wholly rational basis, Priestley was inevitably antagonistic towards the type of religion Pascal had come to represent, and inserted the following brief portrait into his *Lectures on History and General Policy*:

Hardly any thing gives us a more affecting view of the weakness and inconsistency to which the mind of man is liable, than to see men of sound and clear understandings, in most respects, and of upright honest hearts, fall into sentiments that lead to gross and painful superstitions. A most remarkable instance of this was Pascal, one of the greatest geniuses, and best men, that ever lived. He entertained a notion that God made men miserable here in order to their being happy hereafter; and in consequence of this he imposed upon himself the most disagreeable mortifications. He even ordered a wall to be built before a window of his study, from which he thought he had too agreeable a prospect. He also wore a girdle full of sharp points next to his skin, and while he was eating or drinking any thing that was grateful to his appetite, he was constantly pricking himself, that he might not be sensible of any pleasure. His sister too, who was a woman of fine sense and great piety, actually died of thirst, as she thought, to the glory of God. [59]

The climax was reached in 1789 when two articles appeared in the *Gentleman's Magazine*, both in the form of letters written from Edinburgh and signed 'Eusebius.' Their author told that he was 'born and bred a Presbyterian,' though having 'little of the sour leaven of fanaticism' in his composition, and he offered his remarks after having recently read some reflections on Sunday observance in the same periodical. The first letter, which bears repeating in some detail, described a Sunday he had just spent in a village in Westmorland. Riding near Windermere, he had heard a church bell and 'felt a strong desire to join in the exercise of public worship.' Shown into the parson's pew, he found the parson's family decent and attractive, and the clergyman, when he appeared, 'a portly middle-aged man, in whose countenance sat peace, plenty, and good-will to all mankind.' The service was conducted with every indication of reverence, and the parson delivered his sermon upon the Psalmist's words, 'The earth is full of the goodness of the Lord.' This plain discourse contained 'a great deal of that pleasing, rational, and elevating system of religion' which the traveller wished could be heard more often. The Almighty was represented as a being of boundless beneficence, who had made every living creature for the perception of happiness, but none more than man, 'by multiplying to him the sources of enjoyment, and endowing him with the capacity of deriving either use or pleasure from all the objects of creation.' The parson then pursued his joyful theme by comparing it with more pessimistic views:

Shame to those teachers of a severe and gloomy creed, who paint the Supreme Being in the horrid colours of their own distempered minds or vitiated hearts! . . . how shocking the thought, that the Divinity should resemble what is monstrous in humanity!—'The Christian,' says the gloomy fanatic, 'is born to affliction—few and evil are his days—sorrows encompass him from his cradle—dangers surround him on every side—hell gapes under his feet—the paths of life, indeed, are strewed with pleasures; but these are the snares of the tempter, which God permits to be thrown in the way of his creatures, to try their resolution, to exercise their Christian forbearance, and to purify them for himself.'—How false, my children, how distorted is this picture of religion!—Did God then create man to be miserable?—did he form him to be the victim of tyrannic caprice?—Shocking impiety!

The great end of existence was rather 'to be happy yourselves, and contribute to the happiness of your fellow-creatures,' and the sermon concluded on that benevolent note.

The author afterwards informed the parson he had been 'truly edified,' and consequently received an invitation to dinner. Family life at the parsonage next aroused his admiration, and he found pleasing the sight of the village youth merrily playing country sports on the green, looking on the Sabbath as an occasion, too, for relaxation and amusement. He then resumed his journey, deeply impressed by all he had seen and heard, treasuring his memory of the chance meeting as one of the most fortunate days of his life.[60] In parting, however, he told his readers they should soon expect a second letter offering a picture of a different kind; and when, a month later, the promised letter appeared, the contrast was most extreme, illustrating from actual example all the sermon had portrayed with disdain. In the principles and life of the Westmorland parson the author had seen religion 'in its most amiable garb,' but now he proceeded to give 'genuine anecdotes of one whom the

French at this day boast of as an honour to their nation'—Blaise Pascal.

We need hardly say that, though due tribute was paid to Pascal's 'premature and most acute genius,' the stories given were almost without exception those relating to his ascetic habits and the more repellent features of his piety—how he persuaded his younger sister to enter a convent, his refusal to be waited on, his iron girdle, and his physical debilitation and early death. The picture was admittedly most unpleasant, unrelieved by any of the winning virtues present in the Westmorland parson, and portraying a man absurdly driven by the belief that happiness could only be obtained through self-denial and mortification. The author finished by dramatically pointing to the great and obvious divergences between the two figures he had described:

Two very opposite characters are delineated in these letters; yet both acting upon the same principle, a desire of regulating their life according to what they believe to be the will of their Creator. See the country-clergyman, a man of plain common-sense, without pretension to talents, or to superiority of intellect, instilling into his flock the love of the Supreme Being, as the Father of mercies, delighted with the happiness of his creatures. Behold him, with heart-felt delight, discharging the duties which he owes to society as a husband, a father, and a friend. The innocent enjoyment of life he represents as a duty of religion. Happy in himself, he diffuses happiness on all around him. —View next the celebrated Pascal. —Endowed by nature with a genius to enlighten and improve mankind, to advance the glory of God, by contributing to the good of society —he conceives that mortification is necessary for his soul's welfare. He believes it an act of piety to extinguish in the breast of a sister the voice of nature urging to the blissful duties of a wife and of a mother, and exults in the thought, that the austerities which shortened her life were the price of her eternal salvation. —Pursuing for himself the same course, he solicits pain and affliction, becomes the voluntary victim of incurable disease, and dies, for the glory of God, a premature death.

Who can hesitate a moment to determine which of these men entertains the most worthy ideas of the Divine Being? —Who will hesitate to exclaim, 'If Religion is amiable, what a hideous monster is Fanaticism!'[61]

It is intriguing that these two essays may well have been written by James Boswell, who elsewhere recorded his sincere pleasure on receiving a gift of the *Pensées* from Dr. Johnson.[62] In the strong likelihood of their coming from Boswell's pen, it would appear they were either intended as rhetorical—in which case, Boswell may have hastily drawn together some provoking facts and opinions, probably from an encyclopaedia, and presented them with an eye for sensa-

tion; or that they did, to some extent, reflect some genuine misgivings about the life of Pascal which lay behind an appreciation of his
religious writings. With his legal training, Boswell would have possessed the skill to grasp the two sides of a case; and, like certain other
figures of the period of whom we have knowledge, he might not
have found it necessarily incongruous to hold in his mind conflicting
points of view on a subject such as this without achieving reconciliation. As it stands, however, the essay on Pascal marks the high point
of late eighteenth-century English suspicion, contempt, and
ridicule.

As we contemplate the rise of English opposition to Pascal which
culminated in these outbursts, it is conspicuous how much English
rationalist opinion as well as French saw him as embodying essential
contradictions to several of its most cherished and essential beliefs.
In spite of some feeling for his stature in the past, Pascal in so many
ways typified the unnatural to an age which equated nature with its
ideas of order, happiness, and God. His advocacy on behalf of
prophecies and miracles had been a primary flaw; but when, to this,
was added the record of his strange, superstitious conduct, much of
his life and character seemed also to deny everything that might be
worthy in the practice of religion. As Hume implied, if 'artifical' lives
had to exert any influence upon morals, the example of Diogenes
was preferable. To an age in sympathy too with Pope's proclamation
of the desirable union of self-love with social, Pascal's isolation made
him appear a pathetic, utterly misguided figure, who had erred
against that common sense which should attend the daily worship of
a Supreme Being. Compared with the Westmorland parson, he
seemed an enthusiast of the most irrational and despicable sort. It
was not that there was no place for him in the eighteenth century's
understanding of melancholy; Lady Mary Wortley Montagu wrote
despondently that she was 'as full of moral Refflections as either
Cambray or Pascal,' and Edward Young's *Night Thoughts* were from
an early date claimed to bear associations.[63] But, on the whole, men
and women conversant with the sceptical trends of the period grew
disinclined to appreciate the *Pensées* and the author who produced
them, considering the *Lettres provinciales*, which they enjoyed, almost
as a happy accident. It was left to a later generation to discover that
Pascal's mediaeval gloom could take on an interestingly Gothic
palor.

The transformation of what might have been decent obscurity
into open enmity in England would probably have been unlikely
without the agency of Voltaire. Many Englishmen might sense some
discomfort from Pascal's enfeebling views, but the issues at stake

were made far clearer for them through the circulation of the direct attacks of the century's most brilliant antagonist. Voltaire's charges of misanthropy carried several stages further the dissatisfactions with Pascal's analysis of man to be deduced from Pope and other English writers; and, by being linked with Bayle's portrayal, they also caused English readers to see in the genius they had once admired a vivid symbol of the weaknesses holding man back from enjoying a greater earthly happiness. Rationalist opposition never reached the intensity shown by the *philosophes* in France, but Pascal in England likewise had his outspoken adversaries, and several examples of their hostility bear the signs of French precedents.

Although English attacks upon Pascal were thus in part an offshoot from the French, there are nevertheless certain features which make this a distinct episode from the larger, simultaneous controversy. The place of the *Pensées* in the development of English deism has been noticed, and the argument of the wager was challenged or adapted in the minds of English thinkers; but, instead of any systematic rebuttal of Pascal's thought or any onslaught as wide-ranging as that by Voltaire, English denunciations came rather to centre far more upon Pascal personally. This no doubt displays the influence of Bayle at first- or second-hand, but it surely proceeded too from the English interest at that time in biography. The zest with which some rationalists took up the cudgels of assault handed them by Voltaire and applied them to Pascal's life is occasionally surprising, and leaves the impression that, through familiarity, they had come to regard his career as providing the best target for their offensive. By way of Mme. Perier, Bayle, Jesup, and the *Spectator*, Pascal had long been established as a figure of historical significance, and criticism might not have been so articulate if some need had not been felt to rid English opinion of his standing as a stranger admitted to its midst. In England, however, he not only suffered through concentration upon his shortcomings as an individual, but drew upon himself further distrust on account of his Catholicism. His translators had all attempted to reconcile his thought with English Protestantism; but, as English hostility increasingly took shape, Pascal was evidently at the mercy of anti-Catholic emotions as well as of rationalist fervour. Though, to Voltaire, *l'infâme* might be largely synonymous with the Roman Catholic Church, national prejudices helped give the English verdict of Pascal's fanaticism a flavour of its own.

A variety of attitudes central to eighteenth-century rationalism therefore contributed to the English depreciation of Pascal; and their success against this declared enemy is reflected in the fact that, after the middle of the century, no English version of the *Pensées* was made available for over fifty years. But, however much belief in reason came to assume the characteristics of a faith in the minds of some, its authority was never fully recognized as quite supreme; and, accordingly, it is to the area of religion that we should look for the most definitively English features of this controversy.

CHAPTER SIX

The Absolute Need
of Continual Light

[I] The state of religion in eighteenth-century England was generally marked in both the established church and the various denominations by a spirit of moderation and reasonableness that frequently seems to have amounted to indifference. Although the Church of England contained men at all levels who sought to discharge their duties conscientiously, many clergy were often more concerned with their own advancement through political and other connections; and in the sects, now fewer than before, sobriety and conservatism were often the most noticeable features. In part a reaction against the emotional factiousness of the preceding age, these prevailing sentiments were also induced by the new rationalist climate of opinion; and, as the more dangerous challenges of deism were repelled or accommodated, many areas of English religious life came to exhibit a decline in original thought and sometimes an equanimity concerning the future of the Christian faith. As the examples of Bishops Butler and Warburton have shown, the resulting attitudes towards Pascal in such company—to some extent respectful but more conspicuously marked by alienation and a fashionable distrust—did not greatly differ from those shared by most educated people of their social standing.

A form of religious belief which stressed the mind's satisfaction while neglecting or explaining away the needs of the heart was bound ultimately, in the nature of things, to bring forth some response from those considering themselves spiritually deprived. Some features of the previous century's religion continued in strength, often because they were more understandable and reassuring than many contemporary arguments. That *The Pilgrim's Progress* went through more than fifty editions in its first hundred years is remarkable proof of the steady appeal of a work created in an atmosphere of earnestness and old controversies. But the reaction to the eighteenth-century church's lack of essential vitality is seen most clearly, however, in the searchings of particular individuals and in the new religious movements of the time. The era is commonly described as the Age of Reason, but in England, as elsewhere, it was also characterized by an unresolved tension between the forces of reason and the Christian faith, which gave rise to expressions of belief conceived in the face of rationalist advances, or out of discontent with existing religious organizations. Though in many cases distinctly influenced by contemporary currents of thought and not inevitably separated from some appreciation of rationalist philosophy, these new forms of belief nevertheless looked to religion for a satisfaction often experiential in quality, rather than for its worth as an inherited collection of teachings conveniently reconcilable with scientific evidence or ethical pronouncements from other sources. They also emphasized afresh that the nature of man might be redeemed solely through God's saving grace.

The leading English contributions to the dispute upon the legacy of Pascal proceeded from these circumstances. The mounting disapproval among English rationalists was expressed by many voices, who, having in some measure their chosen lines of attack, usually struck at similar aspects of Pascal's thought and personality, and often echoed current French hostility. Pascal's English defenders, however, are more unique, and they tended to speak more as individuals. Sometimes seen in the company of other Port Royal writers, but also as a figure on his own, Pascal occupied a secure place in the affections and esteem of men and women wishing to maintain or rediscover a more spiritual understanding of religion; and, despite the breaking of rationalism's association with his representation of the Christian faith, the appreciation of Pascal by such groups of opinion lasted throughout the century. Forsaken by many for the more cultivated attractions of the *Lettres provinciales,* the *Pensées* as Port Royal had presented them retained elsewhere their reputation as a devotional classic, and occasionally were regarded as a work that might act as a signpost on the path towards mysticism.

In the early years of English familiarity with the *Pensées,* Pascal had been widely esteemed for his 'truly Christian heart'; but, as the eighteenth century progressed, sympathy with his thought came to be largely restricted to circles commonly held less typical of the general movement of religion. The Nonjurors favoured Pascal, the Wesley brothers and their associates in the beginnings of Methodism read and commended him, there are other examples of various kinds of admiration for his piety, and, in Scotland, he attracted the interest of a group of contemplative men and mystics, chief among whom was Lord Forbes of Pitsligo. The last of these may most suitably be described first; for, as well as providing a distinct incident in this narrative, features of Scottish regard for Pascal the devotional writer are not without a bearing upon developments in England.

[II] Until now our attention has been fastened upon the growth of Pascal's reputation in England, but signs of an early acquaintance with his career and writings lie open to discovery in Scotland too. In 1670, James Gregory, recently appointed professor of mathematics at St. Andrew's after study abroad, mentioned his familiarity with the *Lettres de A. Dettonville* in correspondence with John Collins;[1] and Pascal's work was also known to John Craig and John Keill. The *Pensées* were soon noticed by Sir George Mackenzie, king's advocate during the persecution of the Covenanters and a man devoted to the advancement of learning. Appearing in 1690, his 'Essay on Reason' treated the questions 'How weakly Men reason in matters of greatest Importance,' and 'Whence proceeds it that Man is so unreasonable, and how to improve our Reason,' Mackenzie towards the end being led to observe:

Men may think me insolent when I tell them that they understand not themselves; but they should bear this from me, who would willingly wish that they could justly tax me of a Lye in it. But for my Security I must put them in mind, that Monsieur Paschal told them before me, that he had laid aside the Study of the Mathematicks, because few understood to converse with him in it, and betook himself to consider Man; as thinking that a Subject so near, and of such Concern to every one, that all could not but understand it; and yet he found this less understood than the other.[2]

Pascal's chief influence, however, was exerted in the area of Scottish religious thought, this being facilitated by traditional links with France. Associations with Port Royal established during the Commonwealth years later contributed to doubts of orthodoxy at the Collège des Ecossais, and to the frequent admonition of Catholics in Scotland.[3] The Scottish national church throughout the seventeenth century was divided upon the question of episcopacy, and, though Presbyterians were receptive to developments affecting their fellow-Calvinists in France and Holland, the impact of French religious movements is most visible among those men who agreed with the superintendence of bishops, and placed special importance on the concept of the Church as a spiritual society. If Anglican acceptance of Pascal's religious writings was primarily in response to their polemical or intellectual qualities, Scottish appreciation most plainly grew from the search of individuals wishing to achieve a more inward and personal faith. In that quest, the *Pensées* seem naturally to have been preferred to the *Provinciales,* and assisted towards the expression of a certain type of mysticism.

Robert Leighton, Archbishop of Glasgow, may be regarded as the forerunner of this school, which was linked together by personal ties. Appointed Principal of Edinburgh University in 1653, he was afterwards persuaded to become Bishop of Dunblane before proceeding to Glasgow in 1670. Humbly interpreting a modified form of his office in the hope that he might thus help in healing the divisions of Presbyterianism, he regretfully acknowledged the powerful forces against him and finally resigned his position, spending his last years in acts of charity and private devotions. As a young man he had been impressed by Jansenists he had encountered in France and Flanders, these, his friend Bishop Burnet tells us, having struck him as 'men of extraordinary tempers . . . who studied to bring things, if possible, to the purity and simplicity of the primitive ages; on which all his thoughts were much set.'4 Such contacts were periodically renewed and encouraged Leighton in his own pursuit of a life of quiet contemplation. He also attempted to instil qualities of holiness in those whom he might persuade in the Scottish church, though not without a due regard for learning; and, at his death in 1684, his library contained several works associated with Port Royal, including books by Saint-Cyran and Arnauld as well as Pascal's *Pensées.*5

One follower of Leighton's example was Henry Scougall (1650–78), son of the Bishop of Aberdeen, who travelled several times to the Continent in pursuit of spiritual improvement. Returning from one of these journeys, he was persuaded by Bishop Burnet to publish *The Life of God in the Soul of Man,* which appeared shortly before his death. Immediately hailed by all ranks of religious opinion in Scotland, this devotional work gave its author, like Pascal, a saintly reputation, and its qualities were acknowledged in England by Whitefield and the Wesleys. The sermon at Scougall's funeral was preached by his close friend, George Garden (1649-1733), who also held an academic appointment at Aberdeen. Garden's mystical tendencies, however, grew more pronounced with the years, and, in 1701, he was suspended from the ministry for approving the teachings of Antoinette Bourignon, a Flemish enthusiast, who had attacked organized religion in all forms. Garden's wide reading and his search for the essentials of Christianity brought him eventually to the *Pensées,* for, in 1710, he wrote of an 'excellent thought of Mr. Paschal' to be found in Kennett's translation: 'The prophets have interwoven particular prophecies with those concerning the Messiah, that neither the prophesies concerning the Messiah should be without their proof, nor the particular prophecies without their fruit.'6 Continuing to care for those members of his former congregation adhering to episcopacy after the withdrawal of state support in 1690, Garden was reconciled to Anne's supremacy in the Church, but declared himself a Jacobite in 1715. Subsequently imprisoned, he escaped to France, and after his return by 1720 devoted his remaining years to promoting a High Church theology.

Garden's attraction to the strange writings of Mme. Bourignon had developed from dismay at the current state of much religious exposition. In 1699, he complained openly of 'a certain driness and deadness in most of writings and sermons nowadays about divine things, that they do not at all touch the heart: . . . There was never more preaching than in this age, yet never a greater spiritual famine.'[7] Others in Scotland found themselves in agreement, and, like Garden, tried to learn both from Mme. Bourignon and from Mme. Guyon, a famous French Quietist who had provoked a notable controversy between Fénelon—who defended her—and Bossuet. After an unhappy marriage, Mme. Guyon had entered upon a life of religious devotion under a spiritual director, seeking in the Quietist manner to attain a state of pure faith, devoid of any act of will and oblivious to all distinct ideas. If such perfect unity with God were reached, outward acts of piety became unnecessary, sin impossible, and even hopes of eternal salvation were set aside.

Through correspondence and personal meetings, Mme. Guyon became known to Garden, and, in 1717, he was at her bedside when she died. The religious tendencies of another Scot, Andrew Ramsay, led, however, to his conversion to Catholicism and prolonged residence in France. Ramsay's origins are obscure, but, in the course of his wanderings. he visited Fénelon, becoming first his secretary and eventually his literary executor. Gaining fame as an interpreter of the Archbishop's character and writings, he published a popular biography in 1723, thereby attracting the notice of the Old Pretender, who appointed him tutor to his sons as Fénelon had instructed the young Duc de Bourgogne some thirty years before.[8] After receiving a doctorate from Oxford in 1730, Ramsay maintained connections with English intellectual life, and it was through him that Pope learned of Louis Racine's criticisms of *An Essay on Man*.[9] His interests were very tied to the memory of his former master, and, when he referred to Pascal, it was usually by way of comparison. Although an anti-Jansenist, he recalled similarities between Fénelon's 'Doctrine of Pure Love' and that expressed by Port Royal authors and Pascal, and esteemed the literary style of Pascal, Bossuet, and Fénelon, though believing he could 'shew faults and negligences.'[10]

By far the most striking example of Scottish appreciation of Pascal, which combined distrust of dogmatic theology, loyalty to the Stuarts in exile, and the search for greater spiritual contentment, is provided by Alexander Forbes, Lord Forbes of Pitsligo (1678-1762). A supporter of the Jacobite cause in both rebellions, which led to great personal hardships and disgrace, Forbes visited France as a young man, this permanently shaping his approach to religion. He remained an Episcopalian, but the effect of Fénelon and Mme. Guyon upon him resulted in his remaining in correspondence with Quietists afterwards, and he continued to study mystical writers and practice their manner of devotions. Forbes was well-read, as shown by his numerous quotations from recent French and English, as well as classical, authors which featured in his *Essays, Moral and Philosophical*, published in 1734. He particularly favoured Pascal, and the degree of his concurrence with the themes and spirit of the *Pensées* is outstanding.

Forbes' indebtedness to Pascal is nowhere more striking than in his 'Essay on Self-Love,' the principal part of this volume. The second section, 'The Change made on Self-Love, by the Fall,' is wholly a commentary upon some reflections Pascal had once written:

*As the Fall of Adam is concluded by all Christians, (from the Authority of sacred Writ) to have made a strange Alteration upon all the Powers and Faculties of human Nature; so Mr. Pascal gives different Accounts of Self-Love before the Fall, and after it. He says, "Man was at first created with two kinds of Love: the one for God, the other for himself: but with this Condition, that the Love for God should be infinite; that is, without any other End but God alone; and that the Love for himself should be finite, and leading to God as the End. (*rapportant à Dieu.) *Man in that State not only loved himself without Sin, but he could not lawfully have ceased to love himself. When Sin enter'd into Man, he lost the first of those Loves; and the Love of himself, having remain'd alone in that great Soul of his, which was capable of infinite Love, this Self-Love spread itself, and overflow'd the vast Space which the Love of God had forsaken: and thus he loved himself alone, and all things for himself; or, in other Words, he loved himself infinitely."*

To Forbes, the arguments supplied by Pascal constituted proof against some of the more extreme beliefs in man's greatness then gaining currency. To see the Fall as the French apologist had done 'makes the Injustice of Self-Love certainly no less than it was before, and the Folly of it infinitely greater.' If man, uncorrupted, loved himself 'only with such an inferiour and subordinate kind of Love as Mr. Pascal represents,' how could he now in corruption and misery love himself with a supreme and ultimate love 'as if he were the Deity itself?' Even some of the deists found that kind of claim wildly extravagant, and it was shocking to common sense, 'tho' Christianity were out of the question.' He then gave his own summary of man's predicament, recalling with approval that 'Mr. Pascal does not pretend to account for the Fall of Man, but only tells by way of History.' After man has accepted the fact of his apostasy and realised the level to which his self-esteem has brought him, he may seek the charity of his 'great Author,' which enables him to be undeceived 'both from within himself, and from the Defects of the inferiour Creation' – an interpretation generally reminiscent of the reasoning employed in the *Pensées*.[11]

Later in his essay, Forbes' interest in Pascal's analysis of human nature is further shown by his remarks upon the corrupting effects of self-love:

> *But we see in fact, that a Man led by his own Interest will ruin every thing committed to his Trust, when he can do it with impunity, and will even venture on the highest Punishment and Infamy when the Temptation is great. This made Mr. Pascal say,* Le moi est haïssable: "*Self is a hateful thing, both because it is unjust in making it self the Center of all things, and oppressive to others, in designing to subject them to it self: for every selfish Man is a common Enemy, and would be the Tyrant of all others if he could." Again, "Our Inclinations ought to stand towards the Publick: and this Byas towards ourselves, is the first Spring of all Disorder, in War, in Politicks, in Oeconomicks."*
>
> *'Tis this Byas towards ourselves, which spoils all. In War it makes Disputes about Command, and just so in Politicks; and even in Church-matters, the desire of Pre-eminence is a great Spring of Division. The same selfish Byas is the Ruin of Domestick Affairs, not only as it occasions what is call'd bad Oeconomy; but, which is of more importance, as it destroys the tenderest and closest Unions.*[12]

As he proceeded, the trend of Forbes' thought continued to remain close to the themes of the *Pensées*, drawing other illustrations from them. Pascal was commended for exposing how little philosophers had understood the true causes of man's nature, which might only be obtained through the message of revelation. 'No body,' he wrote, 'shews better than Mr. Pascal the opposite and imperfect Schemes of the Philosophers, for want of that Discovery of the Fall.'[13] But it was when finally treating the love of God, that the harmony of Forbes' own religious inclinations with the thoughts of Pascal received their fullest expression. Maintaining that only in the pure love of God can 'the whole of Man's Duty and Happiness' be found, he strengthened his argument by drawing upon the best testimony he knew:

> *St. Augustine gives a Reason for that great Duty, besides the point of Justice, from the Design of our Existence and the Nature of our Soul. He says, "God*

hath made us for himself, and our Heart must be unquiet till it rests in him."
Mr. Pascal likewise (after taking a View of all the Hurry and Amusement we
are engaged in, and the different Springs that move us) concludes, "That
Man can find no Rest, neither in himself nor in the Creatures, but in God
alone."

The reader was then referred to an 'Addition,' designed, like
other brief appendices, as 'an Explanation of some Terms, and a
Collection of some Citations to support the Essay.' This consisted of
two passages from the twenty-sixth chapter of Kennett's *Pensées*,
describing man's restlessness of soul and constant search for distraction before finding happiness in God. Forbes himself wished to
clarify Pascal's phrase that man seems to prize recreation as his
sovereign good: 'By Recreation Mr. Pascal means not only Men's
Diversions (and some harmless ones cannot be condemn'd) but the
serious Business of their Lives, as will appear by the Strain of the
whole Section. And that serious Business St. Augustin puts upon a
level with the Plays of Children.'[14]

Further quotations from the *Pensées* were liberally scattered
throughout the dialogues comprising the rest of the volume. Discussing the nature of the soul, Forbes turned to the author he admired
for a remark on human mortality; 'a little earth is cast upon the Head
(says Mr. Pascal) & *en voila pour jamais*.'[15] In the second dialogue, 'A
Short Account of the World,' a conversation on Augustine's theme
of 'the World divided into two cities' produced the following exchange between Aemilius and Lucinus upon a recurrent theme:

AE. *Is not Pride the third branch or stream of Self-Love, the most raging
and impetuous of all?*

L. *No doubt: it makes Cities and Kingdoms desolate, and the Earth a Field
of Blood.*

AE. *This Spirit also discovers it self most universally. Mr. Pascal says,
"Vanity has taken so firm a hold on the Heart of Man, that a Porter or a
Turnspit can talk big of himself, and is for having his Admirers: Philosophers
do but refine upon the same Ambition."*[16]

Pascal's assessment of the rival philosophies of the Stoics and
Epicureans was noted,[17] and, when later discussing the equality of
men by nature, Aemilius was led to observe:

*Every Man has something in him of the Mathematician, the Mechanick,
the Lawyer, the Statesman, the Mountebank; and so of all other Trades or
Professions. A Man, no doubt, may mistake his Genius, and enter upon a
wrong Trade; but still he may know some little thing of his Business, tho' as*

little as you please. Mr. Pascal observes, "There is a wide difference between a Genius for the Mathematicks, and a Genius for Business or Policy." The French word is Finesse, *which is not always taken in a bad sense. He shews at some length the different Principles on which those Professions are founded; and drawing to a conclusion, he says, "But then 'tis certain, between both, that a false Genius will neither make a Geometry Professor, nor a Privy Counsellor."*[18]

The conversation reviewed the accidental manner in which offices and positions seem frequently to be assigned; but, in Lucinus' opinion, the abuse of authority was a lesser evil than the probable situation if everyone's wish for power were satisfied. He went on to say, 'Mr. Pascal has a pretty Illustration of this Subject, which Mr. Kennet translates with some Humour,' and Forbes helpfully directed the reader's attention to a footnote:

How wisely has it been ordain'd, to distinguish Men rather by the exterior shew, than by the interior Endowments! Here's another Person and I disputing the way. Who shall have the preference in this case? Why, the better Man of the two. But I am as good a Man as he: so that if no Expedient be found, he must beat me, or I must beat him. Well; but all this while, he has four Footmen at his back, and I have but one. This is a visible advantage: We need only tell Noses to discover it. 'Tis my part therefore to yield; and I am a Blockhead if I contest the point. See here an easy Method of Peace, the great Safeguard and supreme Happiness of this World.

As Aemilius observed, however, less overt demonstrations could sometimes be just as effective:

But the odds of four Footmen to one, is a real Distinction of Power as well as of Figure; 'tis a sort of Life guard to a great Man. 'Tis even remarkable how far a bare Name will go, without much attendance, or much Money, to secure a Man from Insults, and to keep those who have a dependence upon him in some order among themselves. So that Name and Rank have a magical kind of Power in the World, which, as things now stand, is of no small benefit.[19]

Forbes' writings show that, through acquaintance with French Quietism and his knowledge of the intellectual life of his day, he was greatly drawn towards Pascal as a moralist and religious writer, and, most centrally, to Pascal's conviction that man can find wholeness only by accepting revelation and seeking union with God. Bearing a philosophical outlook, he was not so impartial in his beliefs as to wish to present them to unfair advantage; as he wrote of the 'Essay on Self-Love,' 'I took all the care I could, that it might have no Air of a Religious Dissertation.'[20] His manner of reaching conclusions ac-

cordingly bears some resemblance to Pascal's, and of his admiration
for the type of Christian faith Pascal represented there can be no
doubt. Forbes' letters mention Pascal, and his *Thoughts concerning
Man's Condition*, written in 1732, not unexpectedly bear many overtones. This appreciation is the more noteworthy since Forbes was
capable of critical distinctions between the *Pensées* in French and in
Kennett's translation, and his familiarity suggests a detailed study of
the work. A high point in Pascal's reputation among British authors
of the eighteenth century surely occurs in a conversation on the
remains of human virtue in 'A Short Account of the World':

> L. *'Tis agreeable to leave the gloom, and to consider what remains after
> such a melancholy Shipwreck. We did not indeed speak much of the Fall, nor
> can it be represented by Mortals. If such an Event had been capable of
> description, Milton's Imagination had bidden fair for it. Pascal's reasoning
> to evince the fact, from the Contrarieties of human Nature, is very fine.*
> AE. *All he writes is so.*[21]

Doubtless the *Pensées* were known to others in the north-east of
Scotland also inclined towards mysticism, such as Lord Deskford,
Pitsligo's kinsmen the fourteenth and sixteenth Lords Forbes, and
the physician James Keith. The Franco-Scottish world in which all
these men moved was not uncommon to Scots of the early eighteenth century, who sought to fashion a life which political and
ecclesiastical changes had made impossible for them in their own
country alone. Their Jacobite sympathies directed their hopes towards Versailles and Saint-Germain, and, as Catholic exiles often
came to favour Jansenist teachings, the High Church proclivities of
Scottish Episcopalians made them also susceptible to religious
trends encountered in France. Especially desirous that piety should
complement and irradiate learned argument and church discipline,
they found their needs considerably satisfied by the discovery of
mystical movements of their own and other times. The *Pensées*, as
reverently presented by Port Royal, instinctively appealed to them as
they attempted under difficult conditions to develop a more fully
devotional and spiritual life.

Although their Jacobitism proved disastrous for Episcopalians,
the known regard for the *Pensées* perhaps entered into the decision
to publish Kennett's translation in Edinburgh in 1751.[22] Except in
the obvious case of Forbes, however, Pascal appears to have been
appreciated by Scotsmen more in the company of other devotional
writers than for what he contributed alone. While Hume and Boswell were reacting against the narrow rigidities of Presbyterianism
each in his own way, Pascal largely remained for a certain type of

Scottish reader a valued member of a company which included Augustine, à Kempis, Fénelon, and Scougall.

[III] Since their interests were often mutual, Scottish Episcopalians tended to regard the Nonjurors in England as their natural friends and allies, and the history of both movements is characterized by adherence to increasingly lost causes, compensated by the distinction of spiritual revival. From time to time during this study, reference has been made to individual Nonjurors, men who, in various ways, were drawn to the *Lettres provinciales* or the *Pensées,* and also to the examples of Fénelon and Bossuet. The party had its origins when, in 1689, clergymen of the Church of England were required to swear allegiance to William and Mary or forfeit their benefices and other offices. Nine bishops and about four hundred other clergy considered such action inconsistent with their integrity, regarding themselves as still bound by previous oaths to James II, and withdrew or were removed from their positions. Their numbers were augmented when, on the exiled king's death in 1701, the clergy were further required to recognize William III and his successors according to the Act of Settlement as kings both by right and law, and to abjure the Pretender; and, in 1714, a similar declaration of loyalty was demanded with respect to George I, which also stated that the Pretender had no claim whatsoever.

The defiant clergy whose consciences thus led them into the wilderness included many of the most learned and upright men in the Church of England; and, indeed, the decline of the Anglican Church's vitality during the eighteenth century was to some extent caused by the withholding of their talents. Strictly interpreting the oaths they had taken earlier, many of the original group—men such as the saintly Thomas Ken, Bishop of Bath and Wells—lived in hope of a compromise, perhaps by the Pretender's conversion to Protestantism, which would make the accession of William and Mary in retrospect a temporary emergency. Hostile to Catholicism, as Andrews' translation of the *Lettres provinciales* shows, and not necessarily active Jacobites, they regarded themselves as the true remnant of the Church of England which would one day resume its rightful place of leadership; but, as prominent members died or made their peace with the government of Anne, and as difficulties grew in continuing an apostolic line, the party diminished and came to be mostly represented by a generation of men distinguished chiefly for their piety, their learning, and the strength of their convictions. Although Jacobite sympathies were latent in many Anglican clergy especially in the years following the Hanoverian succession, the

Nonjurors withdrew increasingly from active political affairs, as well as from regular church life, and occupied themselves in quieter, more private pursuits. In this regard, William Andrews seems not to have been untypical.[23]

The example of Scottish Episcopalians strengthening their High Church theology and their own sense of holiness in the face of alienating circumstances is paralleled by the practices of certain Nonjurors; and, of those whose religious outlook mirrored some appreciation of the *Pensées,* the most noteworthy are John Byrom and William Law. A graduate of Cambridge who declined a fellowship because he would not take the oaths required of a clergyman, Byrom mixed in the intellectual and literary life of his day, writing poetry himself though his principal means of support lay in teaching a system of shorthand he had invented. Since a copy of the third edition of Kennett's translation of the *Pensées* was in his library, there can be little question that an entry in his journal for January 19, 1731, records in an engagingly casual manner its acquisition with two shirts and cravats, and some gingerbreads. Byrom's library also included other books by Pascal—two editions in French of the *Pensées,* and three copies of the Provinciales;[24] and his journal later shows that he considered some passages from their author as suitable for shorthand practice as extracts taken from the *Spectator:* 'Monday, 7th [April, 1735]: Mr. Nelson and Duann in the coffee room; went to Melmoth's about nine, drank chocolate there, stayed till twelve talking about Mr. Law again; he had writ a good deal from a foolish Spectator of Steele's and some other author; appointed Friday to meet again and for him to write out Pascal's prayers.'

This particular exercise was apparently not a complete success, since the pupil later complained of the prayer he had transcribed that 'he could not relish, that he should not be able to read, that it was so very exact, and seemed to think it difficult.'[25] Byrom's admiration for Pascal once led him, as we have seen, to defend his testimony upon prophecies and miracles in discussion with the formidable Bishop Butler; but another attraction of the *Pensées,* however, was undoubtedly their meditative qualities, which prompted him to paraphrase into the form of popular hymnology Pascal's short profession of faith, contained in his life by Mme. Perier. The simple and open-hearted manner in which these sentiments were expressed suggests that Byrom had not merely undertaken a literary experiment, but was endeavouring simultaneously to render a statement of his personal religious feelings. The result is the clearest example of identification with Pascal which has come down from the Nonjuror tradition:

I love and honour a poor humble State,
Because my Saviour Jesus Christ was poor,
And Riches, too, that help us to abate
The Miseries which other Men endure.

I render back no Injuries again,
Because I wish the Doer's Case like mine,
In which nor Good nor Evil, as from Men,
Is minded much, but from an Hand Divine.

I aim sincerely to be just and true,
For my Good-will to all Mankind extends;
A Tenderness of Heart, I think, is due
Where stricter Ties unite me to my Friends.

Whether in Conversation or alone,
Still to my Mind God's Presence I recall;
My Actions wait the Judgment of His Throne,
And 'tis to Him I consecrate them all.

These are my Thoughts, and briefly thus display'd;
I thank my Saviour for them ev'ry Day,
Who of a poor, weak, sinful Man has made,
A Man exempt from Vice's evil Sway.

Such is the Force of His Inspiring Grace,
For all my Good to That alone I owe;
Since, if my own corrupted Self I trace,
I'm Nothing else but Misery and Woe.[26]

A reader also of Mme. Guyon and the German and Dutch mystics of the later Middle Ages, Byrom was too sociable and practical a man to pursue them far in the arrangement of his life; and Pascal's uncomplicated expression of piety, with its references to everyday life, was of the kind finally most acceptable to him. Like many of his contemporaries, he was also influenced by William Law, the High Churchman and Nonjuror, who, of all the party, achieved the widest reputation as a religious writer and developed farthest a mystical understanding of Christianity. Law's library contained a number of books by Port Royal authors, among them a copy of the first edition of Kennett's translation of the *Pensées;*[27] and, in 1740, he and two followers, one of them the aunt of the historian Gibbon, retired to lead a devotional form of life together in the Northamptonshire

village of Kings Cliffe. Perhaps Law knew of Pascal as a polemicist
too, one critic considering that his *Three Letters to the Bishop of Bangor*
(1717) 'may fairly be put on a level with the *Lettres provinciales*
... both displaying equal power, wit, and learning.'[28] In Leger's
opinion, Law drew upon the *Pensées* in two instances in his *Practical
Treatise upon Christian Perfection* (1726), when describing the nature
and design of the Christian faith.[29] The sole end of Christianity, he
believed, was 'to deliver us from the misery and disorder of this
present state, and raise us to a blissful enjoyment of the divine
Nature,' and he related the effect produced on man by knowledge
acquired through revelation:

*As happiness is the sole end of all our labours, so this divine revelation aims at
nothing else.*

*It gives us right and satisfactory notions of ourselves, of our true good and
real evil; it shews us the true state of our condition, both our vanity and
excellence, our greatness and meanness, our felicity and misery.*

*Before this, man was a mere riddle to himself, and his condition full of
darkness and perplexity. A restless inhabitant of a miserable disordered world,
walking in a vain shadow, and disquieting himself in vain.*

But this light has dispersed all the anxiety of his vain conjectures.

Shortly afterwards Law commented on man's ambivalent nature,
concluding with a reflection also borrowed in general terms from
the *Pensées:*

*... would we think, and act, and live, like Christians, we must act suitably to
these terms of our condition, fearing and avoiding all the motions of our
corrupted nature, cherishing the secret inspirations of the Holy Spirit, opening our minds for the reception of the divine light, and pressing after all the
graces and perfections of our new birth.*

*We must behave ourselves conformably to this double capacity, we must
fear, and watch, and pray, like men that are always in danger of eternal
death, and we must believe and hope, labour and aspire, like Christians that
are called to fight the good fight of faith, and lay hold on eternal life.*

*This knowledge of ourselves makes human life a state of infinite impor-
tance, placed upon so dreadful a point betwixt two such eternities.*[30]

The works of Pascal do not appear to have been a major source of
Law's theology, which, with its emphasis upon the indwelling of
Christ in the soul, became increasingly akin to that of the German
mystic, Jakob Boehme.[31] In Law's case in particular, it seems that the
Pensées, though suggestive, were not considered a record of experi-
ence in the same category as, for example, the writings of Tauler, à
Kempis, Ruysbroeck, or St. John of the Cross. Pascal's thoughts and

the example of his life would be valued in the initial stages of a quest for greater holiness, but, beyond that, especially in Port Royal's version, the *Pensées* were too reasoned and insufficiently abstracted from the world to guide or sustain the central impetus. Although the extent of Law's indebtedness to Pascal is therefore questionable, his own devotional writings were nevertheless often associated with the *Pensées* wherever such instruction was appreciated during the eighteenth century.

Perhaps the most abiding feature of Nonjuror interest in Pascal consisted, however, in the manner in which some sympathy for his writings was kept alive at the universities. During the early years of the century, both English universities, which alone trained clergy, contained numerous supporters of the Nonjurors' doctrinal views who were amenable to the prospect of a Stuart restoration. Both Byrom and Law achieved distinction at Cambridge; but, during the years after the death of Anne, Oxford became recognized for its particular attachment to High Church theology, often accompanied by sentiments of Jacobitism, figures such as William King, Principal of St. Mary Hall, helping to provide this reputation. In light of earlier interest in Pascal at that university, it is not altogether surprising to see his writings renewing their appeal in familiar surroundings among devout men, who sought also to maintain their religion's independence from the depredations of Catholicism.

This was the Oxford, affected by the rationalist thought of the age but conservative in its religious instincts, which the Wesley brothers knew and where they first attempted to practice a more exacting form of Christianity. It should not be forgotten that both the Rev. Samuel Wesley and his wife were strong adherents of the High Church party, and that Mrs. Wesley was once a firm supporter of the Stuart cause. After learning of Pascal at home, a measure of continuity was therefore preserved when John and Charles Wesley entered the university where, in 1728, the Nonjuror antiquary, Thomas Hearne, was writing 'Paschal's Thoughts is a practical book much admired by some.'[32] Wesley's existing knowledge of the *Pensées* and their author was thus enabled to reach a fuller understanding within the academic community, touched by the Nonjuror outlook, in which he and his brother found themselves.

[IV] The attempts to revive Christian fervour and belief among the unregenerate and apathetic are the most strikingly positive feature of English religious life in the eighteenth century; and, of these, the founding of Methodism was the most permanently successful, largely through its comprehensive approach to the Christian faith and its highly efficient organization. The part played by Pascal in the origins of Methodism is not as great as that of Law or the Moravian, Peter Böhler, but the influence was an important one, especially during the more formative years of John and Charles Wesley; and, though Pascal attracted them primarily as a writer of spiritual conviction, John Wesley also came to value his reasoned defence of Christianity as an aid to the desirable growth of a strong intellectual belief among his followers.[33]

The acquaintance of the Wesleys with Pascal began in their childhood. It has long been recognized that the remarkable character of their mother so affected their lives that John, in particular, can in no way be fully understood without reference to her religious instruction. To a constant concern for her children's spiritual condition, she brought a wide background of reading from works of theology and devotion, among which the *Pensées* of Pascal figured prominently. Some evidence of her liking for Pascal's reflections, as must have been transmitted to her sons, may be found in a dialogue she wrote of a supposed conversation between herself and her eldest daughter. Entitled *A Religious Conference between M[other] and E[milia] . . . Written for the Use of my Children.* 1711/12, this interesting document shows plainly that Mrs. Susannah Wesley, like others at that time, esteemed Pascal for his definition of the relationship between faith and reason:

E. *Ought we, then, to discard our reason from having anything to do in matters of religion?*

M. *By no means. For though it is of itself too weak and insufficient to direct us the way that leads to eternal life, yet when enlightened and directed by God's Holy Spirit, it is of admirable use to strengthen our faith: and those are alike to blame that either indulge or despise it. A little learning and study will serve to convince us that there are innumerable things which surpass the force of human understanding. Nor is it hard for an honest mind that is willing to know the truth, to discern when reason ought to submit, and where it is able to comprehend; where it should doubt, and when it should rest assured. And if we would act reasonably, we shall neither stifle the principles of reason, nor build too much upon them: for by doing the first, we make our religion childish and ridiculous, and by the other we exclude all supernatural assistance and mysterious truths from it, and thereby cut off all hopes of salvation by Jesus Christ, as M. Pascal has well observed.*[34]

Elsewhere in the dialogue, Mrs. Wesley drew from the *Pensées* to support her argument that, though man's mind might be superior to his body, 'yet the whole system of intellectual powers is not fit to be opposed in value to the lowest degree of moral goodness or virtue';[35]

and, in 1722, writing to her brother, Mr. Annesley, upon her happiness in spite of her infirmities, she once again found occasion to take a quotation from Pascal:

This world, this present state of things, is but for a time. What is now future, will be present, as what is already past once was; and then, as Mr. Pascal observes, a little earth thrown on our cold head will for ever determine our hopes and our condition; nor will it signify much who personated the prince or the beggar, since, with respect to the exterior, all must stand on the same level after death.[36]

Leger has described Mrs. Wesley as 'une lectrice assidue des *Pensées*,'[37] but it cannot have been solely from her that John and Charles Wesley first learned of Pascal; their father, the Rev. Samuel Wesley, Rector of Epworth and a poet of some distinction in his lifetime, also thought highly of Pascal's writings. In an essay generally known as *Advice to a Curate*, published soon after his death in 1735, he suggested a number of comparatively recent religious books for study, remarking that the works of Messieurs de Port Royal and of Pascal were 'worthy their character,' and of the latter that 'he has, indeed, most surprising thoughts, and it is enough to melt a mountain of ice to read him.'[38] Probably some recollections of their upbringing lay behind the sentiments of the eldest son in the family, Samuel the younger, when, in 1739, he showed concern for the possible effects of John Wesley's exertions upon his health. 'I should be very angry with you, if you cared for it,' he wrote, 'should you have broken your iron constitution already; as I was with the glorious Pascal for losing his health, and living almost twenty years in pain.'[39]

With such a background, we not unexpectedly find both John and Charles Wesley turning to Pascal in their early efforts to pursue what they conceived to be their calling. To other evidence of the popularity of the *Pensées* at Oxford at that time may be added John Wesley's note in February 1726 that he had heard a sermon at St. Aldate's by a member of Lincoln College on the mind's dependence on its relationship to the will, which may well have been indebted to Pascal's reflections;[40] and to Wesley, his brother Charles, and the other members of the 'Holy Club,' the ascetic practices of Pascal must have seemed as praiseworthy as his intellectual and spiritual qualities. Other French religious figures, such as Fénelon and Quesnel, would attract him during the course of his life. Wesley, however, did not exclude himself from all social relationships, and, in 1730, began to correspond with a young widow, Mary Pendarves, signing himself in literary fashion by the name of 'Cyrus.' His continuing familiarity with Pascal is evident from a letter he wrote to her in 1731:

Who can be a fitter person than one that knows it by experience to tell me the full force of that glorious rule, 'Set your affections on things above, and not on things of the earth'? Is it equivalent to 'Thou shalt love the Lord thy God with all thy heart, soul, and strength'? But what is it to love God? Is not to love anything the same as habitually to delight in it? Is not, then, the purport of both these injunctions this, —that we delight in the Creator more than His creatures; that we take more pleasure in Him than in anything He has made, and rejoice in nothing so much as in serving Him; that, to take Mr. Pascal's expression, while the generality of men use God and enjoy the world, we, on the contrary, only use the world while we enjoy God?

How pleasingly could I spend many hours in talking with you on this important subject![41]

The complexities of Wesley's later years at Oxford and in his relations at that time with his family make it hard to analyse satisfactorily the forces under which he was acting. Soon after he had obtained his degree, however, when he was beginning to think more seriously about taking Holy Orders, he read à Kempis, Scougall, and Jeremy Taylor's *Rules and Exercises of Holy Living* and *Holy Dying,* all of which left a great and lasting impression upon him. After discovering Law's *Practical Treatise* and *Serious Call to a Devout and Holy Life,* his interest led to a meeting with their author in 1732 which resulted in a close association. As a theologian and spiritual guide, Law's effect upon the Wesleys during a critical period of their development was considerable. At the time of his early acquaintance with Law's works, John Wesley was, moreover, especially attracted towards Arminianism, a doctrine to which the Nonjurors strongly adhered; and, without being one of the major forces upon which their relationship was built, the sympathy of both the Wesleys and Law with Pascal within an Anglican tradition they largely shared no doubt helped provide a basis for mutual understanding. Soon after his friendship with Law began, Wesley published his first book, *A Collection of Forms of Prayer, for Every Day in the Week,* for the use of his pupils at Oxford, in which traces of several authors have been discerned, among them Fénelon and Pascal;[42] and it is striking that, not long afterwards, Charles Wesley twice commended the reading of both Law and Pascal to others for their spiritual improvement.

During the next few years, the record of Pascal's influence in the origins of the Methodist movement is largely supplied through Charles Wesley's journal. In 1735, he accompanied his brother on their mission to Georgia, and, like John, was much impressed by the courage and simple faith of some Moravians travelling with them. Neither of the Wesleys, however, found their stay in Georgia satisfactory, and Charles left Savannah the following year for England. Obliged to break his journey at Boston, he was taken ill with 'the flux,' but managed to set down some reflections on his general state: 'Sat., October 16th. [1736]. My illness increasing, notwithstanding all the Doctors could do for me, I began seriously to consider my condition; and at my evening hour of retirement found benefit from Pascal's prayer in sickness.'[43]

Charles nevertheless still hoped to return to Georgia, and he spent the next year waiting in England, visiting members of his family, and reading his favourite authors – among them Pascal[44] – while he attempted unsuccessfully to persuade the Anglican authorities to allow Moravian cooperation in the colony. Convinced of the necessity of the conversion experience, he proceeded to conduct all his relationships with that end in view; and, calling on his sister, Kezia, and finding her in tears longing to obtain the love of God, he prayed over her, blessed God from his heart, and used Pascal's prayer for conversion. By this 'she was much affected,' begging him to write it out for her; and that evening she was similarly moved when he read Law's account of redemption.[45]

During 1738, both brothers now having returned from Georgia and resigned their positions, they made the acquaintance of Peter Böhler, a Moravian bishop and a man of deep piety, who greatly assisted in leading John and Charles Wesley towards their separate but practically co-instantaneous conversions. Charles Wesley afterwards began to preach in what was regarded as an irregular fashion, and, in August 1739, he started his itinerant ministry. Shortly before, he chose to return briefly to Oxford, and, on July 1, preached before the university. His sermon was apparently well received, but his visit provoked some questioning about the early Methodists by the Dean of Christ Church, Dr. Conybeare, himself an able controversialist who supported a rational approach to religion. The Dean spoke to him 'with unusual severity' against field-preaching and the example of Whitefield, explaining away all inward religion and union with God; and, to Charles, this was unmistakable proof of the abhorrence with which the conventional world would regard his mission. A few days later, he had a second conference with Dr. Conybeare, who again 'used his utmost address to bring me off from preaching abroad, from expounding in houses, from singing psalms.' The Dean further denied justification by faith alone 'and all vital religion'; but Charles Wesley recorded that, for whatever reason, he 'promised me, however, to read Law and Pascal.'[46]

George Whitefield, another member of the Oxford 'Holy Club,' was closely associated with the Wesleys at first, though soon developing an independent career as a travelling evangelist. Between 1739 and 1741, he made the second of his many journeys to America; and, when travelling between Delaware and Savannah, he disembarked at Lewis Town. The comments in his journal on his reception there show that he too had some familiarity with Pascal, and found one aspect of his life an affecting example:

Sunday, May 25 [1740]. Preached twice from a balcony, to about two thousand, the church not being capable of holding them. In the evening, discoursing on Abraham's faith, a great many, and some even of the most polite, wept much; but, alas! when I came to turn from the creature to the Creator, and to talk of God's love, in sacrificing His only begotten Son, Jesus Christ, their tears, I observed, dried up. I told them of it. We can weep at the sufferings of a martyr, a man like ourselves; but when are we affected at the relation of the sufferings of the Son of God? Pascal, I have been informed, always wept when he read of our dear Lord's passion. Though weeping be not always a sign of grace, yet, I think it is an evidence of the hardness of our hearts, and a want of a due sense of sin, when we can remain unmoved at the account of the sufferings of a dying Saviour.[47]

If indeed any element of Law's mysticism had entered into John Wesley's appreciation of Pascal, this was decisively rejected after his experiences in Georgia and with his growing recognition of what his true ministry should be. In a letter to his brother, Samuel, in 1736, he had described the writings of the mystics as 'the rock on which I had the nearest made shipwreck of the faith';[48] and, shortly after returning to England, he broke with Law, whom he found unable to realize the nature of his spiritual crisis. Wesley's condemnation of mysticism was rooted in his growing suspicion of the more speculative kinds of thought and of solitary religion, being convinced that, since mysticism often broke away from historical Christianity, its intricacies and contradictions might lead many people into delusions. His devotion to the means of grace, and particularly to the authority of Scripture, caused him, from thenceforward, to speak out unceasingly against what he considered to be mysticism's dangers.

But, as Green has commented, 'Wesley's strong repudiation of the Mysticism of his own age . . . did not wholly close his mind against the worthier elements of mystical religion or the exemplary piety of individual mystics';[49] and there is abundant evidence that, although Pascal might display undesirable symptoms in his expression of Christianity, Wesley continued to value him for his distinctive qualities, and recognized that his arguments for religious faith could inspire the Christian life and strengthen it against other creeds and philosophies. In 1745, he again acknowledged Pascal's appeal to himself by arranging for the *Pensées* to be placed among 'the books we should keep for our own use at London, Bristol, and Newcastle.'[50] The most impressive proof of his newly defined appreciation, however, is found in his decision to include the *Pensées* in one of his more ambitious undertakings, the *Christian Library*.

Designed 'for the use of those that fear God,'[51] this extensive collection appeared between 1749 and 1755, being 'Extracts from and Abridgments of the choicest pieces of Practical Divinity which have been publish'd in the English Tongue.' The works represented had been chosen in accordance with Wesley's plans for the instruction of his followers, and he attempted, by excising their contents of error and controversy, to supply his readers with the best of the Christian heritage for their ready use. The branch of the Church to which an author had belonged was no disqualification if his works were profound and intelligible, but mystics were avoided. Like many other men of the century, Wesley in his own way stood firmly against a total reliance upon the emotions, and instead upheld a more balanced and well-informed understanding of the Christian faith in which the emotions played a necessary, but not a dominant, rôle. To educate his followers in Christian doctrine was consistent with those forces that had shaped him at home and university, and, through the *Library* and other means, he sought passionately to replace ignorance by knowledge among the members of his societies.[52]

A considerable portion of the *Christian Library* consisted of sermons and other works by noted divines from the sixteenth to the eighteenth centuries, among them Barrow, Cudworth, Burnet, South, Tillotson, Cotton Mather, Jonathan Edwards, and Wesley himself. A biographical interest was obvious, which extended from Clarke's *Lives of Eminent Men* to accounts of the martyrdoms of Ignatius and Polycarp. Bunyan's *Holy War* was represented, also five essays by Abraham Cowley and devotional works by Jeremy Taylor, Fénelon, and Scougall. The *Pensées*, as Wesley offered them, would appear to have been drawn from the Edinburgh edition (1751) of Kennett's translation, the title-page bearing the abbreviated quotation from the *Spectator*. By far the larger part of Kennett's work was reproduced, a few passages relating to sceptical philosophy being deleted, chapter x on the Jews shortened, and chapter xii, 'Against Mahomet,' omitted entirely. No really significant changes and no remarks by Wesley himself are detectable, and we may assume that, as in the case of so many volumes in the *Library*, Wesley

THOUGHTS

O N

RELIGION,

And other

SUBJECTS.

B Y

Monfieur *PASCAL.*

Had that incomparable Perfon Monfieur *Pafcal* been a little more indulgent to himfelf, the World might probably have enjoyed him much longer : Whereas, through too great an Application to his Studies in his Youth, he contracted that ill Habit of Body, which, after a tedious Sicknefs, carried him off in the Fortieth Year of his Age: And the whole Hiftory we have of his Life till that Time, is but one continued Account of the Behaviour of a noble Soul ftruggling under innumerable Pains and Di-ftempers.　　　　　　　*Vide Spectator*, Vol. II. N° 116.

PLATE 6 Title-page of John Wesley's edition of the *Pensées* in his *Christian Library* (Bristol, 1749–55), vol. XXIII.

did not take time to edit the *Pensées* meticulously. Once the decision to incorporate a work in the *Library* had been taken, this was proof enough to him that its contents were suitable for his readers; and Kennett, of course, had already excluded some passages particularly favouring the Catholic Church.

The *Christian Library* thus helped render the *Pensées* familiar and acceptable to early Methodists, and also displays to clear view an important part of the estimation Wesley had developed of Pascal. Admiring him as a prophet of personal grace, Wesley valued him, too, as a thinker who had not dissociated spiritual certainty from intellectual belief, but had rather tried to relate the two; and, aware that Pascal's religion consequently stood opposed to current confidence solely in man's abilities, he especially appreciated him for typifying what he considered to be the surest Christian defence against the misguided use of reason. He evidently knew of the opinions of Voltaire, for, while on a return voyage from Ireland in October 1752, during the years when the *Library* was being issued, he entered in his journal: 'I read over Pascal's *Thoughts*. What could possibly induce such a creature as Voltaire to give such an author as this a good word, unless it was that he once wrote a satire? And so his being a satirist might atone even for his being a Christian.'[53]

Generally hostile to contemporary French authors, Wesley wrote in 1781 that Montesquieu was unworthy of the praise bestowed upon him, having imagination, but not judgment or solid learning; 'I think, in a word, that he was a child to Monsieur Pascal, Father Malebranche, or Mr. Locke.'[54] Five years earlier he had also depreciated the abilities of unassisted reason in a letter he wrote to Miss Mary Bishop, a well-educated lady who kept a school at Bath:

Although I am thoroughly persuaded that those reasonings are in great measure from a preternatural cause, and therefore chiefly to be resisted by continuing instant in prayer, yet I think Christian prudence not only permits but requires you to add other means to this. That which I would especially recommend is reading, particularly Pascal's Thoughts *(in the* Christian Library) *and the first two tracts in the* Preservative against Unsettled Notions in Religion. *These temptations are permitted to give you a deep and lasting conviction of the littleness and weakness of your own understanding, and to show you the absolute need wherein you stand of continual light as well as power from on high.*[55]

With a similar purpose in view, Wesley gave his followers further opportunities for instruction in the religion and witness of Pascal. During four months of 1787, the *Arminian Magazine*, which he had founded in 1778 to promote acceptance of his belief in universal redemption, presented an entire chapter from his version of the *Pensées*, entitled 'Thoughts on the Misery of Man,' extracted from 'a late writer.'[56] Among those who had assisted him in the selection of books for the *Christian Library* was the Rev. Philip Doddridge, head of a large dissenting academy, and it is not surprising that, when planning the curriculum of Kingswood School, Wesley specified that the *Pensées* should be read in the second year of the pupils' final training for the ministry.[57] One of his best-known sermons, 'The Important Question,' also shows him seeking to communicate Pascal to his audience. Preaching upon the text, 'What is a Man profited, if he shall gain the whole world, and lose his own soul?' he opened his address by saying:

There is a celebrated remark to this effect, (I think in the Works of Mr. Pascal,) that if a man of low estate would speak of high things, as of what relates to kings or kingdoms, it is not easy for him to find suitable expressions, as he is so little acquainted with things of this nature; but if one of royal parentage speaks of royal things, of what concerns his own or his father's kingdom, his language will be free and easy, as these things are familiar to his thoughts. In like manner, if a mere inhabitant of this lower world speaks concerning the great things of the kingdom of God, hardly is he able to find expressions suitable to the greatness of the subject. But when the Son of God speaks of the highest things which concern his heavenly kingdom, all his language is easy and unlaboured, his words natural and unaffected; inasmuch as, known unto him are all these things from all eternity.[58]

Wesley's admiration of Pascal nevertheless had its limits. In *Thoughts on a Single Life,* he advocated the avoidance of all needless self-indulgence, but stated, 'I dare not add Monsieur Pascal's rule,–Avoid all pleasure.' This was impossible without destroying the body, and neither did God require it from us, since our enjoyment of life should add to his glory; and Wesley alternatively suggested, 'avoid all that pleasure which anyway hinders you from enjoying him; yea, all such pleasure as does not prepare you for taking pleasure in God.'[59] Our final glimpse of Wesley's appreciation, however, perhaps because of his age or the particular circumstances, summarizes the lifelong effect the *Pensées* exercised upon him and reveals the depth of his feeling for Pascal's essential faith. In April 1790, less than a year before his death, he wrote to his nephew, who had become a Roman Catholic a few years before but had since shown signs of indifference to all forms of religion; and, by his choice of Christian examples, he affirmed once again his commitment to a piety which transcends denominations, and, maybe inad-

vertently, linked Scougall's devotional writings with these predecessors in discipleship:

*Dear Sammy, —For some days you have been much upon my mind. I have been
pained concerning you, and have been afraid lest I should feel, when it was
too late, that I had been wanting in affection to you. For ought I to see you in
want of anything and not strive to supply your want? What do you want? not
clothes or books or money. If you did, I should soon supply you. But I fear you
want (what you least of all suspect), the greatest thing of all—religion. I do not
mean external religion, but the religion of the heart; the religion which
Kempis, Pascal, Fénelon enjoyed: that life of God in the soul of man, the
walking with God and having fellowship with the Father and the Son.*[60]

Other men who, in some way, enter into the story of early
Methodism shared the interest of the Wesleys in Pascal, one of these
being the Rev. John Newton, who, though standing apart from the
movement, was a warm admirer of its leaders. Also known for his
friendship, while Vicar of Olney, with the poet, William Cowper,
Newton was previously engaged in the slave trade, and, between
1755 and 1760, held the position of tide surveyor at Liverpool.
Whenever contrary winds prevented ships from entering harbour,
his occupation allowed him leisure to pursue his self-education and
religious interests, and one entry in his diary records, 'much of ye
day (when not in business) reading Hervey, Parschal, Cowper and ye
Scriptures.'[61] After his ordination in 1764, Newton remained at
Olney for sixteen years, when he moved to a parish in London. At
some time in his life he acquired a copy of the second English edition
of the *Lettres provinciales,* which may once have belonged to Milton,
and possibly that work helped arouse his strong opposition to
further toleration of Roman Catholics. Pascal's influence is not
clearly present in Newton's works, however, neither has a search
through the writings and correspondence of Cowper revealed any
obvious signs of indebtedness. Although the lives of Cowper and
Pascal suggest occasional parallels, and Cowper translated the
poems of Mme. Guyon, any close relationship between the *Pensées*
and his own religious thought is probably conjectural.[62]

John William Fletcher (1729-85), born de la Fléchère, was a native
of Switzerland who, after studying at the University of Geneva,
embarked upon a military career. His hopes of a commission being
frustrated, he was engaged as a private tutor in England, and, much
impressed by the Methodists, was eventually ordained in the Church
of England. A close friendship developed with the Wesley brothers,
but, on declining an itinerant ministry, he chose to become Vicar of

Madeley in Shropshire, where he remained for the rest of his life. Fletcher's greatest service to Methodism was in writing *Checks to Antinomianism*, called forth by the threatened schism in the movement between the Calvinist and Arminian parties. In the heated controversy over the doctrines of election and predestination, Fletcher defended the less confining Arminian position with a keenness of logic reminiscent, perhaps, of the *Lettres provinciales*.[63] Elsewhere in his writings, Fletcher valued Pascal for much the same qualities which characterized John Wesley's appreciation, seeing the faith of Pascal as an excellent defence against the purely rationalist approach to religion. He was fully aware of the charges brought against Pascal by Voltaire, and, in his *Eulogy on the Christian Philosophers,* he vigorously upheld Pascal against his detractors:

Pascal was one of the best writers, the finest geniuses, and the greatest mathematicians that France has produced. In his conduct and writings he has fully demonstrated, that philosophy perfectly accords with Christianity. Superficial philosophers are frequently among the incredulous, but the truly learned consider it an honour to be believers. The system of Descartes tends to demonstrate the existence of a God: and though Voltaire has frequently ridiculed the devotion of Pascal, he has done justice to that of the great English philosopher, in his Elements of Newton's Philosophy.[64]

In a letter written in July 1761, Fletcher defended 'experimental religion' against what he believed to be the dangerous tendency to insist upon 'rational goodness, benevolence, &c., exclusive of feelings in the heart.' To know the peace and love of God was impossible under this 'easy scheme,' according to the testimony of 'some of the best and wisest of men,' and he proceeded to cite Pascal as a case in point, regretfully alluding to the partial decline of his fame:

Pascal, the strength of whose reason was so much celebrated in the last age, thought that peace and love, unfelt, and consequently unenjoyed, were of as little service to him as a painted sun to a plant under snow, or the description of some beautiful fruits to a man starved with hunger. Take one of his thoughts:—

"To know God speculatively is not to know him at all. Heathens knew him to be the infallible author of geometrical truths, and supreme disposer of nature. The Jews knew him by his providential care of his worshippers, and temporal blessings, but Christians know God as a God of consolation and love, a God who possesses the hearts and souls of his servants, gives them an inward feeling of their own misery, and his infinite mercy, and unites himself to their spirits, replenishing them with humility and joy, with affiance and love.'[65]

Like John and Charles Wesley, however, Fletcher appreciated Pascal fundamentally for his piety, as a letter offering consolation that he wrote in 1777 indicates:

My dear companion in tribulation, and in the patience of Jesus. Peace be multiplied unto you, and resignation by the cross of Jesus. I bear your foot on my heart, and cast my heart on Him, to whom all burdens are lighter than a feather. Paschal said, when the rod of tribulation was upon him, "Now I begin to be a Christian," meaning a follower of the Man of sorrows. By his pierced feet may yours be eased.[66]

Both Wesley and Fletcher upheld Pascal against the attacks of Voltaire, but the strongest direct support was offered by Robert Sandeman (1718-71), a leading member of a small sect known as the Glasites, which, wishing to return to a more primitive Christianity, had broken away from Presbyterianism. The sect was not noted for its educated ministry, but Sandeman achieved prominence in 1757 when he published his *Letters on Theron and Aspasio,* a critical reply to James Hervey, who had recently upheld the Calvinist party's arguments in the theological controversy then dividing the Methodist movement. Hervey's work had occasioned a reply from Wesley himself, and Sandeman, though not directly involved, supported Wesley in opposing the determinism which characterized Calvinist doctrine. When discussing the relation of reason to religion, Sandeman deliberately chose to challenge his opponent by comparing the opinions of Pascal and Voltaire:

Paschal, whom I mention as a person respected by philosophers for his uncommon abilities, could observe the original dignity of human nature, like that of a decayed palace, from the greatness of its ruins. But our author is charmed with the beauty and order of the ruins themselves. By reading Voltaire's remarks on Paschal's thoughts, one may see how differently men think, or affect to think on this subject; and may likewise have a good opportunity of trying by his own thoughts, in the contrast of sentiments, which side bears the greatest weight or appearance of truth.

Pascal's reflections on man's blindness and misery, and his consequent despair, were then placed next to Voltaire's rejoinder upon the pleasant, orderly life of London or Paris, cities 'where mankind are as happy as it is consistent with their nature to be.' The remarks of Voltaire, which some of Hervey's propositions were made to resemble, were considered by Sandeman, however, to be shallow, and vulnerable to a more searching examination:

With the same charming prospect is the mind of our author relieved from all difficulties arising from the dark side of things. He forms to himself a high notion of the difference betwixt the appearance of human nature in its savage, which he then calls its original state, and its appearance when refined by education in civilized nations. From the excellency of the latter the dignity and glory of human nature arises to his view. . . . And where can we have a more full view of all this beautiful scene than in London and Paris, the capitals of the two most civilized nations? And in these where to better advantage than among people of refined taste and manners, or those who compose the politest assemblies?

In contradiction, the world's greatest cities at their peak, 'from Nineveh down to those of our own times,' had always been noted for the extent of their wickedness, 'and that even under the wing of decorum.' It was deplorable that, 'as our taste refines, we learn to distinguish nicely, and to sin grossly'; for current conventions of society in both England and France openly tolerated the practice of vice and strove to conceal the extent of human degradation.[67] In short, Pascal's perceptions were more truthful.

The evidence supplied by the Wesley family and others connected with the origins of Methodism is unusual in recording an unbroken appreciation of the writings of Pascal extending throughout the entire century. From his first acquaintance with the *Pensées* as a child until the end of his life, Pascal exerted a constant influence upon John Wesley, which survived the decline of his fortunes in other circles; and, by a process which drew from the opinions of the High Church party at Oxford and the religious needs of the wider public amongst whom Wesley and his associates moved, but turned from the mystical leanings of Law towards a concern for the practical Christian life, Pascal's former reputation in England as a genius who had combined impressive powers of reason with deep spiritual understanding achieved a renewal—though placing him in a more exclusively religious setting than before. Moreover, as Pascal's life was becoming uncongenial to the rationalist, his witness amid his afflictions seemed to Methodists worthy of emulation, not broadly differing from many another saintly biography presented as a lesson in the *Arminian Magazine*.

The primary appeal of Pascal to the Wesleys and their movement thus derived from his personal testimony to the essentials of the Christian faith, which, by its realistic note and its ultimate dependence upon Scripture, avoided that mysticism Wesley abhorred; but it also arose from a high regard for the clarity and logical thoroughness of his thought. Men of reason as well as men of faith, the

Wesleys were ready to value both aspects of Pascal, irrespective of denominational boundaries; and, especially by including the *Pensées* in his *Christian Library*, John Wesley endorsed their author with unmistakable approval to his numerous followers and sympathizers. His support of Pascal against the claims of unrestricted reason therefore did not proceed from the emotional outlook, which tended to dominate in Whitefield, but from an educated assessment of the benefits made available for a proper understanding of the Christian faith by the quality of Pascal's arguments and insights.

The recurring controversy between the Calvinist and Arminian parties provided, among other things, an opportunity for the public airing of opinions upon the association or separation of reason and the means of redemption. Wesley's Arminian views caused him to believe that man has an element of choice in accepting or refusing God's offer of salvation, and that reason might play an important part in bringing him to the decisive stage. In this respect, he considered the religion of Pascal one of the best examples of a balanced intellectual and spiritual belief, free from the excesses of either, as his mother had once taught her children. A combination of these in the Christian might withstand the assaults of rationalists and sceptics and the seductions of pure emotionalism, and would illuminate an alternative, more authentic way to the achievement of perfection. Wesley's evaluation of Pascal, and his efforts to persuade others to think likewise, thus form eighteenth-century England's most ambitious endeavour to preserve and re-emphasize his importance as an intellectual and religious figure, in contradiction to the strictures being more typically expressed by the age.

[V] Concentration upon leading figures in English religious life of the eighteenth century has already provided us with several instances of the manner in which Pascal's *Pensées* continued to inspire and instruct numerous men and women. Since its arrival in England, the Port Royal edition had been valued as an aid to the development of Christian piety and understanding,[68] elements of such an interest entering into the presentation of Jesup's *Lives of Picus and Pascal,* and causing the later editions of Kennett's translation to be directed to an increasingly exclusive religious audience. Such appreciation persisted, though often unobtrusively, and forms an underlying theme whose further exploration draws a diverse collection of men and women into our picture.

The works of Mrs. Elizabeth Rowe are little known today, but, in her lifetime and afterwards, they were extravagantly praised by such literary authorities as Prior, Pope, and Johnson. The daughter of a nonconformist minister, she first became known for her poems, but later achieved still wider popularity with the publication in 1728 of *Friendship in Death; in Twenty Letters from the Dead to the Living.* These writings and their supplement, *Letters Moral and Entertaining,* expressed her faith in immortality and her desire to rekindle religious feeling in those who had turned aside; and their appeal was such that *Friendship in Death* and the later *Devout Exercises of the Heart* were frequently reprinted during the remainder of the century.

Mrs. Rowe borrowed freely from elsewhere, quotations from the Bible, other religious books, and a number of English and French authors abounding in her pages; and the assistance she gained from the *Pensées* and works proceeding from the Port Royal community is very apparent. She had been taught French by Henry Thynne, son of her patron, Lord Weymouth, and her 'Thoughts on Death,' translated from Nicole's *Essais de morale*, appeared as part of *Friendship in Death*.[69] Her marked tendency to renounce worldly things once led Catherine Talbot to comment to Mrs. Carter on an unfavourable resemblance to Pascal;[70] but, though Pascal's chief attraction for her was as an uplifting devotional writer, she also found him excellent for giving focus and an improved literary form to her rather pedestrian sentiments. Some of her shorter pieces, in fact, consisted of little more than lengthy quotations from the *Pensées*.

A typical sample of her use of Pascal in this manner is found in the fifth of the *Letters Moral and Entertaining,* concerned with the pleasant prospects of immortality. Mrs. Rowe began by expressing satisfaction with her supposed correspondent's curiosity in this most important subject:

If immortality is the pride and happiness of human nature, why should it not be mentioned with the same gaiety with which we talk of other agreeable things? The other world is at least a greater novelty than this; nor is it such a glorious round of action, to eat, to drink, and sleep, that people should have an aversion to think, if not to try, what a variety of enjoyment a future life will give them. But to forget this is the design of all the thoughtless amusements the wit of man can invent. What Monsieur Paschal says is perfectly just.

A well-known passage from the *Pensées* followed, commenting upon man's inability to live happily with himself, and his unceasing search for diversions. The rest of the letter was brief, Mrs. Rowe bringing the long quotation to a close for fear 'you will certainly think I am going to transcribe the whole book'; and the overall impression is of a short composition built around one of Pascal's reflections rather than of an incidental quotation in the context of her own remarks.[71]

Mrs. Rowe's high regard for Pascal caused her to find an apt quotation to accompany her views on several of her preferred subjects—religious indifference, man's search for happiness, and the goals of human wisdom.[72] A reference in a letter to the Countess of Hertford contains her fullest praise; and, though lavishly worded, it suggests the genuine feelings which the *Pensées* were capable of arousing in her, and why she had once before described Pascal as 'one of the greatest men in the world':

I should have begun my Japan table as soon as I came home, if Les Pensees de Pascal *had not accidentally come in my way, and given my thoughts a situation superior to all earthly things. In reading that book I lose every care, and grow independent on all below the skies; the trifling hopes and fears of human life vanish before a more important interest, while I yield to the evidence of these just reflections.*[73]

Like Isaac Watts, Mrs. Rowe enjoyed a reading public spread through most religious groups; and, since death and a future life were naturally subjects of intense and universal concern, her appreciation of Pascal in the context she chose would have been similar to that of many in her audience. Already a figure of some fame, Pascal's essentially religious qualities now gave him an affectionate reputation amid what might be described as the world of popular piety. In these surroundings, the *Pensées* were valued for their place on a bookshelf of devotional literature, and a letter of 1749 from a country vicar on a neighbour's death reveals precisely the company in which they found themselves:

The last time I saw him I dined and spent the afternoon with him, and never saw him look better or more cheerful; so that I had little thought of never seeing him more. What was his employ when disengaged from the necessary business of his situation may be easily guessed, by the books then lying on his table: 'The whole Duty of Man,' 'Reading's Life of Christ,' and a 'Discourse on Death,' with 'Mons. Paschal's Thoughts.' In short, I always considered him as a great and bright example; and apprehend every day's future experience will tend to fix that notion in me.[74]

The *Pensées* were not only regarded by such readers as a spiritual guide, but, as in the case too of Mrs. Rowe, as a source for authors composing works of that general kind, often with the improvement of morals in view. *The Rule of Life*, another classic which went through numerous editions, consisted of selected quotations from notable authors, and included such hortatory lines as 'The ingenious M. Pascal kept always in Mind this Maxim, Avoid Pleasure and Superfluity.'[75] *The Power of Religion on the Mind*, a book by an American Quaker which gained an English following, praised the humility and simplicity of Pascal's heart.[76] In *Sermons to Young Men*, William Dodd, a society preacher eventually hanged for forgery, used Pascal, rather insincerely it would seem, to support his denunciation of gaming and his advocacy of the industrious employment of time;[77] and, in 1760, the *Christian's Magazine*, of which Dodd was editor, carried a biography of Pascal for the enlightenment of its readers. Drawing its material but not its opinions mostly from the *General Dictionary*, this study cordially commended Pascal's father for the religious exemplar he set his son, upheld Pascal's enquiries into 'those great and capital articles, which concern Christianity in general,' and concluded by quoting Sewell's poem on his epitaph. The author was also inclined to see Pascal's reluctance to engage in only the most innocent conversation as a virtue to be desired, in a society where the reformation of manners had become a matter for religious action:

And indeed it would be well, if this caution of M. Pascal's was observed a little more exactly at the tables of Christians, of the more polite especially; where too frequently discourses are heard, which cannot fail to spread dissoluteness, and in many cases, it is to be feared, prophaneness, amongst servants, and the lower order of mankind. What an account must those have to make hereafter, who have been so far from using their riches and eminence to the service of God and religion, that they have made them the only splendid means of disseminating more universally vice and infidelity![78]

The grounds for Dr. Johnson's esteem for the *Pensées* have their connections with this devotional theme, which, at bottom, unites English religious sympathies towards Pascal during the eighteenth century. Like Wesley, Johnson was influenced as a young man by the writings of Law, and during his lifetime also came to admire à Kempis and Jeremy Taylor as well as Pascal. Although, as his prayers demonstrate, he was a deeply spiritual man, he constantly sought to expand and strengthen his religious faith with the aid of proofs from reason. The bounds within which he conducted his religious enquiries avoided mysticism, and he welcomed anything that would help make Christianity seem rational. Profoundly aware of the importance of religious emotions, he was, like Wesley, opposed to too great a dependence upon them, though on differing grounds; and each of them strongly censured over-confidence in reason's powers.

Johnson, however, not only appreciated Pascal for the quality of his faith, but also saw him from the viewpoint of a literary critic, regarding at least one of his definitions with interest. In an essay in the *Rambler* (No. 92, February 2, 1751), he wrote:

It has been long observed, that the idea of beauty is vague and undefined, different in different minds, and diversified by time or place. It has been a term hitherto used to signify that which pleases us we know not why, and in our approbation of which we can justify ourselves only by the concurrence of numbers, without much power of enforcing our opinion upon others by any argument, but example or authority. It is, indeed, so little subject to the examinations of reason, that Paschal supposes it to end where demonstration begins, and maintains, that without incongruity and absurdity we cannot speak of geometrical beauty. [79]

Johnson also held Pascal's style in high regard, for, in a letter to Miss Frances Reynolds, written in 1781, he began his advice on the possible publication of her 'Essay on Taste' by commenting that it contained 'such depth of penetration, such nicety of observation, as Locke or Pascal might be proud of.'[80]

Other aspects of Pascal's achievements also no doubt appealed to him. Although he had a liking for general truths and for ethical philosophy, he was not greatly attracted to more abstract kinds of speculation; but he possessed the habit of engaging in mathematical calculations to alleviate the depressions from which he frequently suffered, and possibly he was drawn to Pascal for his mathematical proficiency. Several stories of Johnson's preoccupation with mental arithmetic have been transmitted, and Mrs. Thrale recorded a conversation involving Pascal upon the concept of infinity, which occurred, she tells us, 'in the Coach as we were airing one Day between Brighthelmston and Rottenden, I think in the Year 1769':

I mentioned to him one day Soame Jennings's Refutation of Paschal, as thus: —

Infinity —says the French Geometrician —tho' on all sides astonishing, is most so when connected with numbers; for the Idea of infinite Number —& infinite number we know there is —can hardly find room in the human Mind, but stretches it still more than the Idea of infinite Space. Our English Philosopher on the other hand exclaims; —I mean Soame Jennings —let no man give his tongue leave to talk of infinite Number, for infinite Number is a Contradiction in Terms; if [it] is Numbered, it is not infinite I'll warrant it. What do you say to these contenders Mr Johnson? —why I say replied he, that Numeration is infinite, for Eternity might be employed in adding Figure to Figure, or if you will better comprehend me —Unit to Unit; but each Number is finite, which the possibility of doubling it easily proves; besides, stop where you will; you will find yourself as far from Infinitude as ever. —So much for his Arithmetick. [81]

The clearest expression of Johnson's attitudes towards Pascal, however, is found not in his opinions as man of letters nor in his somewhat neurotic addiction to mental calculations, but in the record he has left of his spiritual life. Like Pascal, he firmly believed in the limitations of the human mind and in arguments for Christianity from prophecies and miracles; and, if the emphasis in his Anglicanism was upon life in this world rather than in the next, this did not prevent him from being sensitive to the dimensions against which Pascal's life had been lived and his thoughts conceived. When Johnson's library was sold after his death, it did not contain any books by Pascal; but during his lifetime he possessed a copy of the *Pensées*, prefaced, apparently, by Mme. Perier's life of her brother, to which he turned in moments of despondency. While travelling in Kent in 1768 for the benefit of his health, he wrote in his diary one night that, at the start of his sixtieth year, he had spent the day 'in great perturbation,' unwilling to terrify himself by accounting for time that had passed. At church he had been unusually distracted, and, in an attempt to relieve his nearly constant distress, he had read 'a great part of Pascal's Life.' The same day, 'it came into my mind to write the history of my melancholy,' but on this he intended to deliberate; for, 'I know not whether it may not too much disturb me.'[82]

On Good Friday, April 2, 1779, he noted in a similar vein that, after attending church with Boswell, he had returned home to read the Scriptures and given Boswell a copy of the *Pensées* 'that he might not interrupt me.'[83] The same incident was recorded by Boswell, who also mentioned that he preserved the book with reverence; 'His presenting it to me is marked upon it with his own hand, and I have found in it a truly divine unction.'[84] Boswell's feelings for Pascal, though, seem to have been somewhat variable, and the evidence suggests that, while valuing the gift of the *Pensées*, he could on occasion hold strong alternative opinions regarding the life of their author.

Further testimony of Johnson's high regard for Pascal is provided by Hannah More, whose literary abilities had introduced her to social and intellectual circles in London. An enthusiastic admirer of Port Royal and its writers throughout her life, she met Johnson at the home of Mrs. Garrick in 1781, the great Doctor first lightly, then seriously talking about her favourite authors:

He reproved me with pretended sharpness for reading 'Les Pensees de Pascal,' or any of the Port Royal authors, alleging that as a good Protestant, I ought to abstain from books written by Catholics. I was beginning to stand upon my defence, when he took me with both hands, and with a tear running down his cheeks, 'Child,' said he, with the most affecting earnestness, 'I am heartily glad that you read pious books, by whomsoever they may be written.'

On another occasion, however, Hannah More indicates that, although he deeply admired Pascal, Johnson's opinions did not necessarily extend to include all aspects of Port Royal and Jansenism:

Our conversation ran very much upon religious opinions, chiefly those of the Roman Catholics. He took the part of the Jesuits, and I declared myself a Jansenist. He was very angry because I had quoted Boileau's bon mot upon the Jesuits, that they had lengthened the creed and shortened the decalogue; but I continued sturdily to vindicate my old friends of the Port Royal.[85]

The attraction of the *Pensées* for Johnson, as for many another reader desirous of Christian fortitude, was thus essentially that of a tested companion to whom he might turn to compose and redirect his despondent thoughts. In such circumstances, Pascal's analysis of man seemed valid, and his life worthy of careful consideration. From his exchange with Hannah More, and his earlier interest in Pascal upon beauty and infinity, we may assume that Johnson also admired the *Pensées* for combining perceptive enquiry with spiritual depth; for the Jesuits had traditionally placed importance upon informed religious understanding, and Port Royal itself had gained a reputation for lamentable traces of enthusiasm. The possibility of Boswell having held varying estimations of Pascal in his mind further recalls that, while it was widely held, as the *Christian's Magazine* commented, that 'M. Voltaire and M. Pascal have very different ideas of the Christian Religion,'[86] these opposite attitudes were not in reality wholly exclusive. For an eminently rational man such as Johnson to value Pascal's spirituality, and for an apostle such as Wesley to approve of Pascal's rational abilities and deprecate his excesses of devotion, confounds some neater classifications of this period, and suggests that, in spite of recognized rifts in opinion, room existed for the contrary tendencies to meet together. It illustrates in some measure the ambiguities present in eighteenth-century English thought that, on a topic so full of implications as the life and religion of Pascal, this could be so; and it also testifies that some appeal remained in his original balance between reason and faith for a society whose impressions of him were often sharply divergent, but which were less likely still to exhibit such extremes as those occurring in France.

The appearance of Hannah More, after glimpses of the religion of John Newton, Cowper, and the *Christian's Magazine*, acts as a reminder that, if the richness of English religious sensibility was proceeding in any common direction, it was towards that outlook described as Evangelical. The need of an inner faith, of the inspirational light of which Wesley wrote to Mary Bishop, came to be accepted by men and women of other classes than those generally found in the Methodist societies, who likewise grew prepared to look with some favour upon Pascal, and rediscovered the attractions of the Port Royal *Pensées*. By the end of the century, new factors were entering in, notably the re-examination of rationalist philosophy under the impact in England of the French Revolution. The consequent reaction, and Pascal's new-found appeal for Romantic writers, contributed to a more concerted fusion of opposing views than that which had characterized occasional individuals during the years beforehand.

CHAPTER SEVEN

This Strange Combination

[I] Though moderating tendencies existed, the division of opinion upon the merits of Pascal's personality and the value of his thought constitutes the most palpable feature of his reputation in eighteenth-century England. With the century's progression, those of his readers who followed the rationalist trends of the age became inclined to think little of the *Pensées* and their author; for others, his earlier reputation as an intelligent writer on matters of religion still seemed warranted, particular qualities being sometimes realized anew. As we examine the fortunes of Pascal in the seventeen-nineties and in the opening decades of the nineteenth century, some examples of these rival attitudes will be found persisting; but, under the influence of fresh developments in the political and intellectual spheres, the currents of hostility increasingly moderated their attacks, and, without abandoning certain strictures, began to concede to him a qualified admiration.

The causes of the decline of Pascal's standing in English intellectual circles were several, but there is no doubt that considerable force was exerted by the highly critical opinions of Voltaire. Supplying many of the chief arguments against Pascal, Voltaire's known antagonism to accepted religious beliefs appealed both to advanced sceptics, familiar with French thought, and to other persons of lesser abilities who were attracted by the prospect of setting such beliefs in question. Much as Voltaire was admired by many for his literary and historical achievements, and for symbolizing the movement towards a more rational society, the evidence nonetheless points to a diminishing favour in England by the end of his life and to an almost universal unpopularity during the time of the French Revolution. The conservative instincts of eighteenth-century Englishmen, proud of their political and religious settlement and doubtful that any more successful system was possible, led them to be suspicious of the direction French intellectual life had taken. It appeared that, led by Voltaire, the *philosophes* were bent upon the destruction of traditional religion; and, since, according to English political belief, the principal purpose of organized religion was to uphold the civil government, this was regarded with utmost alarm. His opinions, once so fascinating, were increasingly seen as a constant incitement to dangerous free-thinking, and, in spite of his distrust of popular movements, to political and social change; and men such as Priestley, whose views were held to resemble those of Voltaire, were severely castigated.[1]

With the advent of the French Revolution, and the spectacle of the more extreme exhortations of the *philosophes* being determinedly put into practice, thereby threatening the security of England itself, it naturally followed that Voltaire became 'the inevitable target for the missiles thrown by disturbed complacency, pessimistic piety, realistic caution and panic fear.'[2] Englishmen readily saw the events in Paris as the fearful outcome of a conspiracy of minds which they had watched distrustfully during previous years; and their assumption that Voltaire had been the mastermind was apparently confirmed by the revolutionaries' admission of his influence and the extravagant honours he posthumously received. *Emigré* priests did much to persuade the general public that there was no sin of which he had not been capable, and the Abbé Barruel's *Memoirs Illustrating the History of Jacobinism* (1797) informed readers by exaggerated stories and with emotional arguments that his hand lay behind all crimes committed during the Revolution, also spreading tales of the horrors he had suffered on his deathbed.[3] The reputation of Voltaire in England, once largely characterized by generous appreciation, now underwent such a change that, until well into the nineteenth century, he was widely condemned and vilified.

A predictable consequence of this intense hostility was a re-evaluation of the former objects of Voltaire's antagonism; and, while his criticisms and the insinuations of Bayle did not entirely cease to shape English attitudes, the reputation of Pascal clearly rose at this moment as Voltaire's was plunging sharply down. Even before the Revolution, there are indications that Voltaire's offensive had run its course. In 1779, an English reviewer of Bossut's edition of Pascal's works commented that it had become difficult to judge their author fairly. Infidels regarded him as 'an austere enthusiast,' believers as 'an unparalleled genius,' and, since there was no party of which he was not either the defender or the adversary, 'his merit has been seldom estimated with impartiality.'[4] In the spring of 1789, a correspondent in the *Gentleman's Magazine* reacted against the religion of Priestley by comparing it with what he had found in the *Pensées*:

Though I do not hold it necessary to abide by every thing that is said by Mons. Pascal, yet more just and noble sentiments of God and his only son Jesus Christ, more edifying instructions concerning man and the means of his salvation, meet my mind in these imperfect fragments, than in all the rapid and copious effusions of Dr. Priestley.

There are [those] who think, that the enterprising and restless genius of the said Doctor has bewildered his understanding in divine truths; and that, through his great charity, he is anxious that this blessed state should become general to all the good people of these realms, Jews as well as Christians.[5]

Following the outbreak of the Revolution, the opinions of William Seward, an anecdotal writer well-known to Johnson and his circle, provide some of the first instances of new evaluations of Pascal under the pressure of events. For several years Seward contributed a column entitled 'Drossiana' to the *European Magazine;* and a brief but rather disjointed note of his, published while the Terror was raising English fears to a new intensity, dramatically portrayed Pascal as a pillar of law and order whose wisdom had been disastrously forgotten. His neglected virtues of this kind now conferred a new respectability upon his life and character:

The modern French seem to have imagined themselves much wiser than this learned and acute countryman of their's. He says, "La puissance des Rois est fondée sur la raison, & sur la foiblesse du peuple." According to him, his present countrymen in their adoration of reason,
                    Insaniri docent ratione.
They tell the world to worship reason,
That is, rank sacrilege and treason.
    In his "Thoughts written about the Year 1650*," he says, "Qui auroit eu l'amitie du Roi d'Angleterre (Charles Premier), du Roi de Pologne (Casimir Cinq), & de la Reine de Suede (Christina), auroit il cru pouvoir manquer de retraite & d'azyle au monde?" How applicable is this to some late Revolutions in Europe, and what a lesson for men to see----quam fraglili loco Starent superbi. ---Senec.*
"Jamais on ne sait le mal si pleinement & si gaiement," says this acute writer, "que quant on le sait par un faux principe de conscience." How well this observation applies to all religious and political persecutions! The leaders in general know but too well what they are doing, the rest follow them tete baissé, *as sheep do the head of the flock.*

Mention was made of Pascal's prayers, which 'are extremely pious and eloquent, and remind us very much of those of the late Dr. Johnson," also of his precocity as a geometrician.[6] Similar approval was extended by the *Universal Magazine* in December 1797, which quoted Pascal on man's true dignity deriving from his powers of thought, and associated him with some observations by Johnson on the consequent need to strive for a greater perfection.[7] The same periodical shortly before, also in its series 'Opinions and Reflections of celebrated Men,' had quoted Bayle's comments upon Pascal's devotions in a manner leaving a generally favourable impression;[8] and, in 1798, Seward in the *European Magazine* likewise drew from Bayle, his remarks further reflecting the new acceptance Pascal was beginning to receive:

It was said of this sublime genius, that his conduct, his humility, his mortification, and his piety, would mortify infidels much more than if twenty missionaries were set upon them.

He used to say, that a Divine was much better employed in making mankind perceive the beauty and the majesty of the Christian religion, than in dryly proving the truth of it.

A very excellent little devotional book might be made from a judicious selection from "Les Pensées de Pascal."[9]

Seward presented his views upon Pascal most thoroughly, however, in his popular *Anecdotes of some Distinguished Persons*, appearing at this time. Admitting that 'Pascal had, in common with many other learned men, some weaknesses, upon which humanity will ever drop a tear,' he nonetheless regarded him as 'acute and amiable,' and 'perhaps one of the best men that ever lived.' Having commended the honesty of the *Pensées* as well as the craftsmanship of the *Lettres provinciales*, he again vested his remarks with an urgent note of topicality. In her biography, Mme. Perier had told of Pascal's loyalty during the Fronde and his stated opposition to rebellion; and, in the present situation, such an example deserved to be recalled:

Pascal, like many excellent and studious men, seems to have had a horror of politics. "In a Republican Government, as that of Venice, it would be a great crime," says he, "to attempt to introduce a King, or to oppress the liberty of any people to whom God has given it. In a Monarchical Government, it is not possible to violate the respect that is owing to the Sovereign, without a species of sacrilege. Besides," adds this great man, "a civil war, which is the general consequence of the alteration of a form of government, being one of the greatest crimes that can be committed against the happiness of mankind, it is impossible to speak against it with too much indignation." Pascal subjoins in a note with great simplicity, "I have as great a dread of this crime as of murder and of robbing on the highway. There is nothing, I am sure, that is more contrary to my nature than this crime, and to commit which I should be less tempted."[10]

This change in attitude apparently did not affect the editors of the *Encyclopaedia Britannica*, for, though their new article upon Pascal concluded with a tribute to his genius by Bossut, it generally repeated most of the stories of his discoveries and peculiarities that had been circulating for the past half-century and more. Greatly expanded from the entry in the second edition, it described in detail his asceticism and illnesses, and attributed his supposed mental derangement to the effects of a carriage accident, an explanation supported by Voltaire. More attention was paid to the *Lettres provinciales* than to the *Pensées*, and the writer was obviously much indebted to Bayle, Voltaire, and other French sceptics for the tone and content of his presentation. This account of Pascal's life and achievements must have remained for several years one of the most influential of its kind, being reprinted without alteration in the fourth and fifth editions of the *Britannica*.[11]

The *New and General Biographical Dictionary*, on the other hand, displayed more awareness of trends in opinion. In 1784, it had considered Pascal's celibacy as scorning 'a sure and most unerring dictate of the natural law'; but, fourteen years later, although its short life of Pascal was much the same, the *Dictionary's* final opinion was more charitable:

> *To err on the side of rigour, is not the usual fault of genius: but Pascal was in all respects singular, and differed, not only from ordinary men, but from other men of genius. With every deduction that can be made for a few errors arising out of his education, Pascal was undoubtedly one of the ornaments of human nature; and if a few have rivalled him in talents, no man of equal eminence perhaps can be found, who lived so innocently as Pascal.*[12]

Certain other writers who, in some way, also sought to portray the range of human achievements were willing to share in the current reappraisal. In *Sketches of a History of Literature*, Robert Alves found a new appeal in Pascal's wager, and believed it to be a strong argument in favour of Christianity that Pascal, like Newton 'a genius, so profound, inquisitive, and mathematical,' should have accepted its claims as true; and, in a course of Oxford lectures, Henry Kett, an observer of the Revolution's first stages, again upheld Pascal's faith with that of Newton and numerous other famous men, while patriotically asserting his own conviction in 'the truth and the importance of the Christian Revelation, the value of ancient learning, the dignity of science, and the excellence of the British Constitution.'[13]

In the *European Magazine*, Seward had expressed some hope that the *Pensées* might again be made available to the public; and Pascal's new-found appeal is best demonstrated by the appearance, in 1803, not of a 'judicious selection' but of a wholly new translation of the Port Royal *Pensées,* the first edition in English since that in Wesley's *Christian Library.* The decision to undertake such a project had been made by Thomas Chevalier (1767-1824), descendant of Huguenot refugees and an active member of the Baptist denomination, who had a notable career as a surgeon and anatomist. Entitling his volume *Thoughts on Religion, and Other Important Subjects,* he also added a memoir by way of introduction, commenting on particular elements of Pascal's life and writings in ways that reveal the influence of contemporary events upon him. The significance of Chevalier's observations lies chiefly in the evidence they present of a new understanding of Pascal being defined in contradiction to the opinions of Voltaire; but his remarks upon Pascal's character and achievements are also of interest as the estimations of a man who combined religious certitude with considerable intellectual abilities. Moreover, Chevalier brought a professional eye to accounts of the deterioration of Pascal's health and well-being.

Finding the life of Pascal most instructive, especially in view of so many accomplishments within so brief a span, Chevalier, like most biographers, first described Pascal's childhood and his early discoveries in geometry. Others had found these stories incredible, but he did not question their authenticity and came strongly to the young mathematician's defence. 'Why,' he asked, 'should a man be presumed incapable of such discoveries because he wrote in defence of Christianity, and because his name was Pascal, any more than if it were Euclid, Archimedes, or Newton?' Pascal's subsequent progress 'perfectly accorded with this extraordinary elicitation of his talents.' Chevalier further chose to differ from some other commentators by seeing Pascal's education by his father as having produced more unfortunate effects than special benefits, which lasted during the remainder of Pascal's life:

Private education has undoubtedly in some instances great advantages. But it is too apt to be rendered abortive by excessive indulgence where application is disliked; and to leave a mind which is too intent upon study, without that wholesome variety of intercourse, which at once enlivens the fancy, counteracts the bad influence of intense application on the health, and often opens the way to those connections in after life, by which its cares are sweetened and its sorrows lessened, and the sum of usefulness and happiness is increased. The good or bad effect, however, of either one system of education or the other, does not depend so much on itself, as on the disposition of the student. In point of health, at least, it appears probable that Pascal sustained some disadvantage, by not enjoying a more free and lively intercourse with young men of his own standing; and that, though naturally endowed with wit and animation, he contracted a degree of narrowness and austerity in his notions and habits, which he never afterward shook off. He who associates only with the young will never be wise, but the rigidity of age should not continually cramp the sinews of youth.[14]

In spite of his illnesses which caused him perpetual discomfort, 'Pascal, though unhealthy, was still Pascal ever active, ever enquiring,' and the memoir continued with an account of his experiments and discoveries in the realm of physics. His growing concern with religion was described, but, though such an example was generally commendable, 'it must not, however, be forgotten, that Pascal was a Catholic; and the reader will perceive by some passages in this volume, that he was not quite free from the superstitious credulity of the Romish Church.' Pascal's way of life should not be foolishly copied, but it nonetheless exhibited aspirations fundamentally deserving of approval:

By living for God alone, Pascal undoubtedly meant to live entirely employed in the study of religion, and in the practices of devotion, self-denial, and charity: Duties common to every Christian, in proportion to his opportunities and ability. It is not, however, in the power of every one to pursue these duties, like Pascal, in a state of sequestration from the lawful and ordinary engagements of civil society. To live to God, is to live in obedience to the will of God. Our relative duties to society, are a part of his will concerning us: and the blind devotee, who thinks himself at liberty to neglect his business, his family, his neighbour, his king, or his country, under the pretence of living to God, is egregiously mistaken. Yet let us not too hastily compare even him to the sordid fool, who suffers earthly considerations and projects to engross the whole of his care, and under the pretext of duty to mortals like himself, disregards the calls of the Gospel of Salvation, and turns his back on the only source of true wisdom, happiness, and blessing.[15]

Later remarking that Pascal's asceticism had attained a degree of strictness 'that has seldom, if ever, been exceeded, even in Catholic Countries,' Chevalier still considered hasty judgments inappropriate. Even his iron belt, set with sharp points, did not necessarily make Pascal an object of ridicule: 'A contrite papist, whom superstitious prejudice has wounded with an aculeated girdle, or encumbered with a ponderous fetter, though laughed at or derided by the world, may be more acceptable in the sight of the discerner of hearts, than the wild reformer who treats him with disdain, and makes his own liberty the cloak for his folly.'[16]

Sentiments deploring the excesses of rationalism soon grew to become one of Chevalier's principal themes. Discussing the *Lettres provinciales,* he saw Pascal's views of religious dissension as equally applicable to scenes of political strife: 'When men thirst for dominion, and above all, when they thirst for revenge, every opposition fires and enrages them, and any thing will serve for a pretext to depreciate, or even to destroy their opponents.' The manner in which the Jesuits had handled 'problems not solvable by human penetration' provided but one example of recurring human efforts 'more intent on prying into that which is secret, than on regarding that which is revealed,' which had resulted in 'inextricable difficulty and error.' Turning directly to the *philosophes* and those influenced by their thought, he considered Voltaire's praise for the *Provinciales* to have been insincere in light of his hostility towards the Jansenists. Voltaire, however, had cared nothing for religious opinions of any kind, seeing them all as unimportant and subjects only for mirth; 'Jesuitism and Jansenism, Popery and Protestantism, things sacred and things profane, were all taxed to make sport for this prince of buffoons.'[17]

The Jesuits had been expelled from France and the Society dissolved, 'an event in which all other parties, both infidel and Christian, found occasion to rejoice,' but its cursed leaven had never ceased to be active; and, 'under the more specious and plausible names of Illuminism and Philosophy,' had now returned in an even more insidious and terrifying form, 'producing vices more gigantic, and barbarities more atrocious, than its fiercest opponents ever ascribed to it before.'[18] The recent occurrences in France had thereupon caused Chevalier, like Seward and others, to respond to Pascal's political conservatism, which he found especially praiseworthy:

Another discriminating feature in his character must not be forgotten; namely his loyalty to the King. Pascal was no anarchist. He had too much sense to pluck the jewels out of a monarch's crown, and scatter them among a mob; nor would he ever have helped to dethrone his lawful Sovereign, in order to set up a traitor. During some insurrections which occurred while he resided in Paris, he took a distinguished part in opposition to the faction with which they originated; and said, that sooner than join with persons who promoted rebellion, he would go out as a common assassin, or a robber on the highway. He saw through the cobweb pretexts under which the disaffected and disappointed cloak their endeavours to overturn an established order of things, and thoroughly understood all the pick-lock machinery with which they go to work.[19]

The edifying manner of Pascal's death was described, and his epitaph set down. Turning to the *Pensées*, Chevalier voiced his regret that their author had not survived to finish his design; nevertheless, 'the cause he meant to defend, remains on a firm and immovable rock, against which the gates of hell shall never prevail.' Discussing the problems experienced by the original editors, he saw their published work as having 'general excellence, beauty, and originality . . . [which] will always make them interesting to a sober and judicious reader.' Mention of textual difficulties, however, gave Chevalier the opportunity to launch his bitterest attacks against Voltaire, seeing him as wholly responsible for the text as well as the notes of his edition of the revised version by Condorcet:

It was for this very reason that Voltaire thought he should hardly do enough to undermine the influence of Christianity in the world, if he suffered so popular a book as The Thoughts of Pascal *to be circulated only in their original state. He therefore undertook to corrupt them in a way, which exhibits one of the most singular specimens of literary artifice that has ever been imposed upon the world.*

The artifice alluded to was that of publishing an edition of the Thoughts of Pascal, with Notes *by Voltaire himself. In this edition he differently arranged, or rather disarranged the Thoughts themselves, so as to destroy much of their beauty and force. Some new passages were inserted, taken from manuscripts of Pascal to which he had access; and in the introduction of which he has taken care to blend some abominable things of his own invention, for the purpose of making Pascal appear as great an hypocrite as himself. Added to this, he has also introduced into the body of the work, and under the running title of 'Pascal's Thoughts,' a discourse, intended to bring the immortality of the soul into question. The Phraseology of many of Pascal's Thoughts is also changed; and the notes are added here and there, in order to make some passages appear laughable, others weak, and others absurd. Nothing can be more clear than that Voltaire's design in this publication was of the most abandoned kind; and that it was sent abroad on purpose to disseminate his own pernicious and abominable sentiments with the greater success among the readers of Pascal, who would not have been so likely to see them in any other way; and in order at the same time to weaken the energy of Pascal's observations, by exhibiting them in an unconnected and mutilated form.*[20]

Drawing attention to examples of Voltaire's hostility, Chevalier singled out his attacks upon Pascal's analysis of human nature and his comment that all recent apologists of Christianity were like reeds surrounding an oak in order to support it; 'we may root up these reeds without prejudicing the oak.' Such a remark plainly exposed the nefarious intent of Voltaire's opposition:

This passage discovers the cloven foot of its author, whose only object in rooting up the reeds was to prejudice the oak. A work in defence of Christianity, consisting of sententious observations, at once forcible in argument, and popular in style, like the Thoughts of Pascal, was perhaps more directly calculated to serve as an antidote to the writings of Voltaire, than any that could have been published expressly against them. For Voltaire's perpetual endeavour was to assail Christianity, not with any regular system of argument, for of that he was incapable, but by short jokes and low ridicule, which might make it an object first of sport, and afterward of contempt. The step therefore which he took to discredit the Thoughts of Pascal, is equally a mark of his own malice against the truth, and of the merit of a work, the good effect of which he thought it necessary to counteract by such insidious means.[21]

But, as Chevalier admitted, to repeat Voltaire's criticisms further might only extend their circulation, and he drew his memoir to a close by justifying the need of his translation on account of the poor quality and unavailability of those by Walker and Kennett. His primary object had been 'to communicate the sentiments of Pascal in his own stile,' and he welcomed any other attempt to do better; but his quite commendable efforts clearly met with some success, for a second edition was brought out three years later.[22]

Chevalier's belief in the ability of Pascal's religion to deflect the assaults of militant rationalism stands out as the dominant reason why he embarked upon his task. The skill with which the *Pensées* exposed human errors and proved the necessity of submission to the truths of revelation evidently struck this nonconformist as offering timely lessons to a distraught age. His approach to Pascal was reverent, and his account of the progress of his subject's afflictions more understanding and charitable than the medical opinions of Percival not many years before. If, at times, Chevalier's hostility towards Voltaire tended to prejudice his judgment, this was, perhaps, excusable in the circumstances; for, as English opinion recoiled at the apparent results of the teachings of Pascal's adversaries, his religious qualities and his support of established governments suddenly seemed as desirable and relevant as the activities of his opponents seemed disastrous.

From here we shall proceed to examine how a new understanding of Pascal's life and writings gradually arose in two major directions. The Evangelical party, which sought to combat religious indifference with a more vital faith, gave a more definite form to the existing appreciation of Pascal as a devotional writer and a Christian example; and, with renewed fears of Roman Catholicism, English opinion also found the *Lettres provinciales* again a useful weapon on behalf of the Protestant cause. Equally important is the emergence during this period in other quarters of a broader estimation of Pascal, which partly agreed with the sceptics' condemnations but was prepared to find in him several splendid qualities. His individuality and unquestioned genius won the admiration of the Romantic writers, and their sympathy with his harmonization of religion and philosophy steadily gained a wider acceptance. Both these trends, not unrelated within the context of the times, contributed to laying the foundations which would establish his appeal as a thinker of note among the Victorians.

[II] In light of her religious sympathies, it is not surprising to find Hannah More also reacting strongly against the effects of the Revolution in France. As she increasingly turned from writing plays to the publication of religious books and tracts, her views became closely identified with those of the Evangelical party, which sought to practise a Christian humanitarianism in contrast to the disinterested benevolence upheld by the rationalists. Her fellow-Evangelicals encouraged her to write against the Jacobin threat, and when, in 1815, she chose to survey the events of the period, she charged Voltaire for having been one of 'the avowed adversaries of Christ,' who became 'strenuous subverters of order, law, and government.' Describing the growth of his evil influence, she recalled the effectiveness of his ridicule had once seemed irresistible, and that his epigrams had received fashionable approval. At length, 'the parasite of princes, and the despot of literature, sounded the trumpet of Jacobinism,' and 'the political and moral world shook to their foundation.' Britain first awoke, 'roused by the warning voice of Burke,' and 'enthusiasm was converted into detestation.' The seditious and infidel impulses Voltaire had cultivated for so long were finally checked by public indignation at their outcome, peace was restored, kings reinstated in their rightful thrones, 'and many of the subjects of the King of kings, it is hoped, are returned to their former allegiance.'[23]

The blend in Hannah More of a high moral tone, a concern to apply the essentials of Christianity to a troubled world, dismay at the failure of existing churches to do so, and a firm confidence in the Protestant virtues of the Church of England, were characteristics shared among Evangelicals, especially the 'consistent Christians' of the Clapham Sect, who placed great emphasis upon the possession and exercise of vital religion. In such a setting, Miss More's appreciation of the Port Royal authors, which had caused Johnson to call her 'the Jansenist,'[24] flourished and grew, and throughout her life she continued to display an uncommon zeal for the spirituality of Pascal in the company of his associates. For all her adulation and the personal help she acknowledged from reading their works, her interest was essentially directed towards practical ends. Visiting Oxford in 1781, she was dismayed that no copy of a favourite book on the history of Port Royal could be found in the libraries; but, though warmly recommending it, she confessed to a friend it contained 'some Popish trumpery, and not a little mystical rubbish.'[25] Like Johnson and Wesley, she admired Pascal for his powers of intellect; and, in one of her earlier serious works, *An Estimate of the Religion of the Fashionable World* (1790), she praised his rational approach to the mysteries of the Christian faith:

> *The example of Pascal has proved that as much rhetoric, and logic too, may be shown in defending Revelation as in attacking it. His geometrical spirit was not likely to take up with any proofs but such as came as near to demonstration as the nature of the subject would admit. Erasmus, in his writings on the ignorance of the monks, and the Provincial Letters on the fallacies of the Jesuits, while they exhibit as entire a freedom from bigotry, exhibit also as much pointed wit, and as much sound reasoning, as can be found in the whole mass of modern philosophy.*

But, as she also wrote, true belief could not be achieved without a quickening of the spirit, and it was in verifying this that Pascal's appeal for her ultimately lay:

> *It is doing but little, in the infusion of first principles, to obtain the bare assent of the understanding to the existence of one Supreme Power, unless the heart and the affections go along with the conviction, by our conceiving of that power as intimately connected with ourselves. A feeling temper will be but little affected with the cold idea of a geometrical God, as the excellent Pascal expresses it, who merely adjusts all the parts of matter, and keeps the elements in order. Such a mind will be but little moved, unless he be taught to consider his Maker under the interesting and endearing representation which revealed religion gives of him.*[26]

On numerous occasions throughout her life, Hannah More reaffirmed her sympathy with the type of Christian faith which Pascal and Port Royal represented. In 1805, she wrote to William Wilberforce of being 'so fascinated with these writers, that I scarcely ever look into another book,'[27] and a few years before she had commented on Law's *Serious Call to a Devout and Holy Life* that 'few writers except Pascal, have directed so much acuteness of reasoning and so much pointed wit to this object.' Elsewhere she cited Pascal with Selden and Grotius as examples of learned men who had yet dedicated themselves to the advancement of religion, and quoted him with approval on the integrity of the author of the Pentateuch.[28]

In a letter of 1811, she mildly criticized Addison for having failed to resemble Pascal more closely. His spirit had been very devout, and his *Evidences of the Christian Religion* were admirable; still, he seemed not to have 'entered into those deep views of evangelical truth' which abounded in Pascal and Fénelon, among others.[29]

Miss More's talents as an author achieved their greatest success in her religious novel, *Coelebs in Search of a Wife* (1808), in course of which she eloquently upheld Pascal on man's predicament. The narrator at one point reflected upon the London scene, which 'presents every variety of circumstance in every conceivable shape, of which human life is susceptible.' The charitable societies organized to alleviate ignorance and misery brought to mind Hamlet's exclamation, 'What a piece of work is man! How noble in reason! How infinite in faculties! In action how like an angel! In compassion how like a God!' The city, however, also revealed another side to human nature. The contrast between splendid virtue and disorderly vice, 'the extremes of all that is dignified, with the excesses of all that is abject,' inevitably provoked also the cry 'in the very spirit of Pascal, O! the grandeur and the littleness, the excellence and the corruption, the majesty and the meanness, of man!' The sight of members of parliament indulging in personal recriminations, 'the interests of an empire standing still, the business of the civilised globe suspended,' made one lament human nature's infirmities; and, 'soaring a flight far above Hamlet or Pascal,' recalled the words of the Psalmist, 'Lord, what is man that thou art mindful of him, or the son of man that thou regardest him.'[30]

When the Pope's vicar-general in England, the Rev. Joseph Berington, felt obliged to object to signs of anti-Catholicism displayed in *Coelebs,* he not unnaturally remarked upon the contradictions in Miss More's attitude to Pascal. In an exchange of correspondence in 1809, he accused her of falsification and peremptory judgment of certain Catholic doctrines and practices, and of having failed to understand fully the religious position of those Catholic authors she admired. 'Can you persuade yourself,' he asked, 'that your favourites, Fenelon and Pascal, held those detestable principles, which you unblushingly impute to their religious belief?' In her reply, which met with the vicar-general's satisfaction, Hannah More politely suggested he had misconstrued what she had written, and offered to explain her appreciation of Pascal and other spiritual writers:

I honour good men whatever be their religious persuasion, but I honour their virtues without adopting what appears to me to be their errors. I am too zealous in my own faith not to admire zeal in the opposite party. . . .

It is true, Sir, I am not unacquainted with your best divines. After near twenty years' search, I have put myself in possession of almost all those excellent authors Messieurs de Port Royal. *In no writers have I found a more exalted devotion. Pascal, Nicole, Saint François de Sales make also a part of my little library. On the other hand, I have perused with profit and pleasure, Bossuet, Bourdaloue, Massillon, &c. You yourself, Sir, have taught me to admire St. Bernard. My strong objection to some of your doctrines by no means interferes with my cordial respect for those good men who hold them.*[31]

Hannah More's love for Pascal and his 'evangelical truth' was shared by others among the more devout and progressive Anglicans of the day. Wilberforce described the *Pensées* as 'a work highly valuable, though not in every part to be approved; abounding in particular with those deep views of religion, which the name of its author prepares us to expect.'[32] Such cordiality was not, however, unanimous within the Church of England. The course of the French Revolution seems to have strengthened rather than changed the bias of certain individuals who had grouped the faith of Pascal with that of Wesley as undesirable forms of religion; and, in 1806, Miss More described a representative of this tradition, whose outlook had grown more rigid in face of events:

We have had here for four or five days on a visit, a clergyman of superior learning; a very respectable, correct man, but one of the most strenuous disciples of the Daubinian school—of that school he is an exact, though, perhaps, rather favourable specimen, on account of his natural mildness of character; which happy temperament, however, does not in the least remove his prejudices, or diminish his unrelenting hatred of those writers, whom it is the fashion to call evangelical; but which you and I had rather distinguish by the name of spiritual. . . . When I spoke of spiritual religion, and the sort of writers whom I thought likely to promote it, he declared he had never read one devotional book. I ventured to recommend Pascal, upheld as his reputation is by mathematics on one side and brilliant wit on the other, and Nicole, whose strength of argument I hoped might gain some quarter for his serious piety; but he will soon find out that their talents will not cover that multitude of sins which their spirituality involves, and that Jansenism is only methodism in French. The misery is, that these fiery polemics read only one side of the question; and if, through natural mildness, they should ever be disposed to relax, the monthly appearance of the Antijacobin Review new braces their slackening bigotry, and rekindles the smouldering embers of immortal hate.[33]

In view of the Evangelical party's satisfaction with Pascal, it is a foregone conclusion to find him receiving frequent attention in the pages of the *Christian Observer,* 'conducted by Members of the Established Church,' which was founded in 1802 to make known the Evangelicals' position. The very first issue acquainted readers with the *Discours sur la condition des grands*, and the *Pensées* were repeatedly cited for their excellence during the ensuing years.[34] Hannah More must have been humbly gratified when the *Observer's* review of *Hints towards Forming the Character of a Young Princess* (1805) found her work occasionally recalling 'the venerated memory' of 'those invaluable authors,' Pascal and Fénelon.[35] Another reviewer, examining *Letters to a Friend, on the Evidences, Doctrines, and Duties of the Christian Religion* (1812) by the mathematician, Olinthus Gregory, held Pascal in particularly high esteem. He had been, perhaps, the first to realize the 'peculiar suitableness' of the Gospels to man's condition; and, had his work been completed, he doubtless 'would have left little to do in this province of theology.' The subsequent recommendations of this contributor were almost limitless:

His work, indeed, as it is, is a mine of profound thought and evangelical divinity. No library is complete which does not contain it, and no tutor discharges his duty to his pupil who does not initiate him in it; who does not warn him of the mischievous arts by which Voltaire in his edition labours to impair it; who does not stimulate him to think out the train which the great author has suggested, and fill up the chasms which he has left.[36]

The extent of Evangelical interest in Pascal was most fully displayed in 1814 and 1815, when the *Observer* carried an extensive review of a new French edition of the *Pensées*, followed by a prolonged serial biography. Much of the review was devoted to a refutation of the disparaging notes of Voltaire and Condorcet, which the edition in question still included; but, though he defended Pascal against the 'Holy Philosophical Church,' the writer was inclined to regard some of Pascal's views on the vanity of human happiness—'the *sunk foundation* of his remarks'— as too strict and possibly harmful. The gloomy portraiture of man's lost and depraved condition omitted the 'bright spots' deriving from the arts and domestic affections, which were the innocent blessings of merciful Providence; and he considered that the presentation of so many 'signs of wrath and penal misery' would cause some enquirers after truth to shrink back in fear, doubting any attractions in the religion Pascal sought to advocate. There was much in the *Pensées*, however, that gained his warm approval. The arguments for the acceptance of Christianity had 'all the merit of novelty'; and Pascal's voice, 'now raised with authority, as if from Mar's [*sic*] Hill, to proclaim the unknown God, and now, in measures awful and piercing as the lamentations of a prophet, mourning over the misery of man,' identified him as one with à Kempis, Fénelon, and Nicole. These were Catholics who, 'whatever they might be in their creed, were in the temper of their hearts essentially Protestant.'[37]

The *Observer's* biography revealed still more precisely certain trends in appreciation which English opinion would increasingly follow, and was in itself undoubtedly influential in shaping emerging attitudes. Narrating Pascal's life in an elevating style, it saw a valuable lesson at practically every turning. The early discoveries should stimulate youthful imagination, and Pascal's devotion to the Bible as a practical book conveying the spirit and genius of Christianity was an uplifting example of submission to the revealed will of God. His patience in his illnesses eminently illustrated the beautiful sentiment that 'religion is like precious odours, most fragrant when it is burnt or crushed,' and his renunciation of superfluities only emphasized his spiritual commitment. His judgment of the medically explainable miracle of the holy thorn was regrettably obscured by his Catholic allegiance and the perilous circumstances of Port Royal. The *Pensées,* however, contained 'various and almost inimitable excellencies,' and made 'forcible and pathetic appeals to the hearts and consciences of his readers'; they worthily represented Christianity as 'the only balm and cordial' able to soothe the multiplied miseries of human existence, and brighten the gloomy avenues of death.

Pascal's life, in short, resembled that of Enoch—a man who 'walked with God.' His unselfishness, his love of poverty, and his kindly acts merely underlined the totality of his surrender, and even his extreme peculiarities were entitled to respect. In a passage surely adapted from Chevalier's memoir, the author argued that 'a poor mistaken Papist, wounded by a girdle, or bleeding under a scourge, with a broken and contrite heart,' was yet nearer God's kingdom than 'a proud, insolent, intolerant professor of religion, who, with a less exceptionable creed, is lamentably deficient in the graces of humility, self-denial, and charity.' The love of God could produce strange effects upon human nature; but, quoting from Bacon, who retained his fame as a Christian philosopher in spite of the tide against rationalism, the result in Pascal to this biographer was understandable and to be admired:

A servant of God must often be contented to appear, before the superficial observation of a mere worldly man, as a paradoxical character, exhibiting inconsistencies, which he is unable to reconcile. The contrasts which meet and coalesce in the mind of a sincere Christian, have been thus beautifully displayed by the illustrious Verulam. "*He bears a lofty spirit in a mean condition; he is rich in the midst of poverty, and poor in the midst of great riches; though tossed and shaken, he is as mount Zion, that cannot be moved: he is a lion, and a lamb; a serpent, and a dove; a reed, and a cedar; as sorrowful, yet always rejoicing; as having nothing, yet possessing all things.*"[38]

The acceptance of Pascal by the Evangelical party, exemplified most clearly in Hannah More and the *Christian Observer*, brings to a climax the approval given him by English Protestantism during the period under consideration. The original English sympathy for the Jansenists and Port Royal in the seventeenth century had survived to reappear more intensely than ever before, greeting Pascal as one of a small number of Catholics, who, for all their errors, belonged to the company of true believers. Certain bounds, it is true, existed to the willingness of the Evangelicals to identify completely with him, apart from some elements of his Catholicism. They were inescapably heirs to the Age of Reason, and, although they valued Pascal's intellectual powers, some of his arguments now seemed dated or unacceptable. In 1814, the *Observer* was led to remark that 'on the topic of miracles, Pascal is unsatisfactory, and will be peculiarly so to an English reader who has traversed the same ground under such masters as Locke, Butler, and Paley'; and, as we have seen, his denial of the possibilities of purely human happiness seemed on occasion too bleak. Writing to his friend, John Thornton, in 1807, the future Bishop Heber rejected any likelihood of 'that cold-blooded indifference which Pascal cants about' resulting towards one's fellow-creatures from a greater devotion to God.[39] But the essentials necessary for their approval were strikingly present.

The Evangelicals' stress upon the necessity of conversion, justification by faith, and the authority of Scripture as the rule of faith were all to be encountered in the *Pensées;* and their conclusions regarding man's need for salvation in an age of political and industrial revolution did not differ fundamentally from those Pascal had stated earlier. His acts of charity suited their ideas of Christian philanthropy, and his rejection of needless luxuries, far from arousing suspicion, largely appealed to a group ready to denounce worldly pleasures. His character throughout his illnesses was a lesson in suffering bravely borne, and his death a perfect ending to a life of estimable discipleship. The French Revolution had made religion fashionable again, and conduct which had been branded fanatical now seemed to betray desirable qualities. In seeking to guide earlier indifference or hostility to Christianity towards higher goals, the Evangelicals found much in Pascal and the *Pensées* which they gladly embraced in their task.

The delight Hannah More showed in Pascal and Port Royal was rivalled, if not exceeded, by her friend, Mary Anne Schimmelpenninck (1778-1856). Born into the Society of Friends and later a Moravian, this lady first became acquainted with the Port Royal authors through books lent her by Miss More, and was immediately drawn to their type of religious faith. Her zeal was such that, in 1814, she and her husband travelled to France and visited, among other places, the farmyard scene where stood the ruins of Port Royal. In her account, she described the several 'stations,' including the church where Pascal had been buried, at which pilgrims to Port Royal twice yearly made their devotions. Every association with Pascal was greeted with rapture – a dessert of peaches from a tree he was said to have planted, the sight of a well for which he had once contrived some ingenious machinery, also 'a sort of dismantled hovel, or seed-house, the remains of a cell which Pascal used as a study.' In contrast to the desolate palace of Versailles, once the seat of Port Royal's enemies, the former monastery was still regarded by many as hallowed ground, suggesting to Mrs. Schimmelpenninck's mind an 'awful lesson' of the fate of absolute power when unsanctified by religion.[40]

Surely at this point some attempt to analyse the appeal of Pascal to Englishwomen would not be inappropriate, Mrs. Schimmelpenninck being merely the latest in a long line of such devotees. The Jesuit Darrell first commented on the predilection of English ladies for Pascal's works, and the examples of Elizabeth Rowe, the mother of the Wesleys, Catherine Talbot, and Hannah More – to mention only the most conspicuous – have shown its permanence and given some indications of its nature. In all likelihood, the attraction lay in the spectacle of a great mind discoursing from a sickbed upon fundamental truths, in language that was nobly but simply expressed. Pascal's skill in reaching the crux of the themes he discussed in a manner sincere yet elusive, thereupon offering to transport his readers to spiritual certainties, intrigued and drew loyal followers from his female audience, and his sufferings would have elicited instincts of protection and care. Perhaps the essence of his magnetism (for such it seems to have been) was captured best by George Eliot, who, at the age of fourteen, had herself received the *Pensées* as a school prize. In an early nineteenth-century setting, she described Dorothea Brooke as knowing many passages of the *Pensées* by heart, and thinking that to marry the Reverend Edward Casaubon, a pale church historian, 'would be like marrying Pascal. I should learn to see the truth by the same light as great men have seen it by.'[41]

The staunch Protestantism of the Evangelicals, and the sentiments of Chevalier who had seen in the Jesuits and the *philosophes* merely variations on the theme of human arrogance, demonstrate the durability also of Pascal's reputation as the brilliant exposer of reprehensible Catholic practices. Often considered a Protestant in all but name, he remained liable to be summoned to English Protestantism's aid whenever new threats seemed to arise; and such an occasion once more occurred in 1814 when the Jesuits, suppressed in 1773 owing to widespread dissatisfaction, were restored as an order. The resulting fears prompted a new translation of the *Lettres provinciales*, which in character recalled the editions of the seventeenth century rather than the relative detachment of Andrews' work, its predecessor. The translator, whose identity is unknown, had some interest in the *Provinciales* as literature, but a strongly-worded short history of the Jesuits was inserted by way of introduction, this being followed by the papal bull for the Society's revival, which 'those who feel as men and think as Christians, will read . . . with no ordinary sensations.' Probably by another hand, the history charged 'this, *nominally*, religious order,' which had 'wormed itself into almost absolute power,' with every type of unscrupulous wickedness, and recalled its many actual and attempted crimes against rulers and governments, including the Jesuits' support of the Jacobite cause. The Society had been very rightly abolished, and its restoration should give rise to the gravest alarm.[42]

Ardent anti-Catholic feeling, to which the issue of Catholic emancipation no doubt contributed, was very evident in a fresh translation of the *Pensées*, published in Edinburgh in 1825, and drawn from a new edition of Pascal's works by Berthou. This was the labour of the Rev. Edward Craig of St. James' Episcopal Church in that city, whose hope was that Pascal might now be known 'according to his real merits'; and, in a manner reminiscent of Basil Kennett over one hundred years before, he claimed that the time and thought he had spent had given him 'among the happiest and most gratifying portions' of his life. It would be ample reward if his version afforded readers 'even a moderate share' of this pleasure. Again like Kennett, however, he considered by no means all the work suitable to be published:

The first three chapters of the original work have been left out, as not being connected immediately with its general object. And the translator does not hesitate to avow, that he has withheld a few passages, which occur occasionally, on the subjects of the peculiar tenets of the Romish Church; because he did not feel warranted, by the mere wish to record faithfully in a translation, all the sentiments of an Author, to circulate what he believes to be dangerous error, and which, from the strength and accuracy of other statements among which it was found, might lead some weak minds astray. Had the task of original publication devolved on him, he would have felt differently: for it is right that every man should have a fair opportunity of giving his opinions to the world. But in making a translation for the benefit of a subsequent age, it is perfectly equitable to select that which common consent has stamped with its approbation, and to leave out the few remains of prejudice and unscriptural opinion, which might borrow, from the sanction of such a name, an influence that they ought not to have.

In an accompanying memoir of Pascal's life, which bore some resemblance to the biography in the *Christian Observer*, Craig repeatedly censured the iniquities and despotism of Rome, and likened the Jansenists to the present minority seeking to bring the 'English and Scottish Establishments' to precise and literal accord with their articles and confessions. Pascal's decision to devote himself to religion rather than science was applauded as the act of an elevated mind, and Craig discussed the *Pensées* with much admiration. One feature in particular aroused his enthusiasm:

It is this extensive knowledge of human nature which constitutes the peculiar charm of the Pensées. *They who read it, feel that the writer gets within their guard; that he has, from experience, the power of entering into the secret chamber of their conscience, and of exhibiting to them the many evils which would otherwise lie there unmolested, but which, seen in the light in which he placed them, must be recognized as their own. The arguments of such a writer must have weight; and it is almost natural to feel, that he who has so thorough a knowledge of the disease, may be followed also in his recommendation of a remedy.*

Charges of misanthropy were rebutted by examples of Pascal's charity, which resembled that of the Scottish preacher and philanthropist, Thomas Chalmers, and the circumstances of his death were described in great detail. As he concluded, Craig praised Pascal for battling against the evils of Rome, and voiced regret that he had not been allowed to exercise his talents in the reformation of the Church of France. Darkly he recalled that 'Louis de Montalte could never be forgiven, by that deep designing body of men, whom he had exposed'; and, pausing on this note, he went so far as to suggest Pascal might, in fact, have been murdered by the Jesuits. The nature of his fatal illness could not be satisfactorily determined by his physicians, and there were many well-authenticated instances of the Jesuits having poisoned their enemies:

It would be cruel indeed to charge the Jesuits, as a body, with more than the enormous load of guilt which lies upon their heads; but knowing as we do historically, their dark machinations, their bitter and unmitigable hate, and their bold admission of the principle, that the end sanctifies the means — knowing also that no individual ever did more than Pascal did to sting them to the quick, and to bring all their rancour and malice in its deadliest form upon his head, it is impossible to look at the suspicious circumstances of his death-bed, without fear and indignation.

Wholly lacking the mystical inclinations of his Scottish Episcopalian predecessors, Craig's intense Protestant sympathies finally led him to regard Pascal's decease as calamitous, and the dissolution of Port Royal a tragedy, from which all of France's more recent troubles might be traced:

With the death of Pascal, and the banishment of his friends, all rational hope of the reformation of the French church ceased. "Darkness covered the people — gross darkness that might be felt." And from that day to this, successive woes have fallen, in almost unmingled bitterness, on that irreligious and careless people. What further evils may yet assail them, time will unfold; but even now, increasing darkness gathers round. The sad lessons of experienced suffering, are already thrown aside; and darker superstition frowns, while she forges for them new and heavier chains. In the prospect of the gloom that lowers upon that melancholy country, and in the belief that the torch of truth in the hand of the Jansenists, and of their great champion, might have dispelled it, the friends of true religion may well take up the friendly lamentation which mourned over the tomb of Pascal, the loss sustained by his country in his untimely fall, and say, Heu! Heu! Cecidit Pascalis.[43]

Commending the translation of 'this very valuable work,' a Methodist reviewer explained, 'Mr. Craig is a sterling Protestant; so that he is not rendered either blind or indifferent to the monstrous errors of the Church of Rome, by the genius and piety of Pascal.'[44] In the nineteenth century, as always, it seems Pascal could be retrieved from his Catholic surroundings by his English friends and be claimed largely as their own. The world of popular piety still regarded him as a helpful writer and a Christian example; and, at the same time as Craig's *Pensées* were published, a shortened version of Kennett's translation appeared,[45] while, a few years before, Wesley's *Christian Library* with its treatment of the *Pensées* had been reprinted. If Craig's sentiments at Pascal's illnesses and early death, and his condemnation of Catholicism, triumphed over a more reasoned approach, this apparently was to the taste of many readers; and, reflecting these interests, which the Evangelical party represented at a more refined level, the *Pensées* over the following decades appeared in numerous editions, demonstrating in itself how considerably Pascal spoke to the Victorians' religious needs.

[III]   While the rationalism of the *philosophes* was being denounced by the Evangelical party and other ranks of Christian opinion in a rebirth of religious confidence, its claims as an all-sufficient system of thought were also arousing doubts in another quarter. Without rejecting the rôle of reason, changing interests in the closing years of the eighteenth century began to attach importance to the ability of the mind and emotions to transcend information acquired wholly through objective analysis. In part the outcome of that strain in the Enlightenment represented by Rousseau, the Romantic movement was accordingly more ready to appreciate the intangible nature of religious faith than were its sceptical predecessors. The Age of Reason had idealized the detached, level-headed man, but greater attention was now paid to the exceptional character or genius, whose perceptions and achievements set him high above his fellows; and depression or love of solitude came to arouse interest rather than dismay. In the writings of leading English Romantics, particularly Coleridge, we find expressed a new intellectual admiration for Pascal, mixed with a reaction against French rationalism, once an earlier enthusiasm for the Revolution had waned.

The first signs in Coleridge of this new understanding of Pascal occur in a letter he wrote to Thomas Poole of Nether Stowey from Germany, in 1799, after hearing of the death of his infant son. Sceptics had weighted Pascal's balance of faith and reason heavily on the side of the latter, but Coleridge was impressed by his arguments for faith, and willing to recognize that knowledge might be usefully gained from non-rational belief. Pascal's arguments were all the more acceptable to him for having been quoted in a work by Friedrich Heinrich Jacobi, a philosopher in whom he was then absorbed:

I read your letter in calmness, and walked out into the open fields, oppressed, not by my feelings, but by the riddles, which the Thought so easily proposes, and solves—never! A Parent—in the strict and exclusive sense a Parent—! *to me it is a* fable *wholly without meaning except in the* moral *which it suggests—a fable, of which the Moral is God. Be it so—my dear dear Friend! O let it be so! La nature (says Pascal) 'La nature confond les Pyrrhoniens, et la raison confond les Dogmatistes. Nous avons une impuissance à prouver, invincible à tout le Dogmatisme: nous avons une idée de la vérité, invincible à tout le Pyrrhonisme.' I find it wise and human to believe, even on slight evidence, opinions, the contrary of which cannot be*

proved, & which promote our happiness without hampering our Intellect.
—My Baby has not lived in vain—this life has been to him what it is to all of
us, education and developement.[46]

An entry in his notebook four years later shows the continuing effect
of Pascal upon him as a genius, the quality of whose insights often
overruled the laboriously reached assumptions of more ordinary
men: 'It has been long my sincere wish, & (for that all our Habits
partake of human Frailty) my *pride*, to try to understand, in myself,
& to make intelligible to others, how great men may err *wildly*, yet not
be mad—that all opinions that can be understood & are not contrad.
in terms have more to be said for them than Bigots and Pedants &
Sciolists suppose. —Paschal!!—'[47]

The similarities between Pascal's thought and Coleridge's outlook
was remarked upon by Henry Crabb Robinson, an intimate of
Coleridge's circle and also devoted to German thought. Their conversation had once concerned miracles and the historical evidence
for belief in Christianity; and, again in contrast to the rationalists'
position, Coleridge confessed he found miracles no obstacle to
Christianity's acceptance, if comprehended within the greater
scheme of faith:

He went so far as to affirm that religious belief is an act, not of the
understanding, but of the will. To become a believer, one must love the
doctrine, and feel in harmony with it, and not sit down coolly to enquire
whether he should believe it or not.

Notwithstanding the sceptical tendency of such opinions, Coleridge added,
that, accepting Christianity as he did in its spirit in conformity with his own
philosophy, he was content for the sake of its divine truths to receive as articles
of faith, or perhaps I ought to say, leave undisputed the miracles of the New
Testament, taken in their literal sense.

In writing this I am reminded of one of the famous sayings of Pascal, which
Jacobi quotes repeatedly: 'The things that belong to men must be understood in
order that they may be loved; the things that belong to God must be loved in
order to be understood.'[48]

The Romantic outlook also more readily emphasized man's capacity for misery and wickedness as well as for good, and, in an essay in
his journal, the *Friend* (No. 1, June 1, 1809), Coleridge clearly
showed his assessment of Pascal took into account the pessimistic
views of human nature for which the French thinker had been so
much condemned. According to his creed, universal testimony
showed that 'whatever humbles the heart and forces the mind inward' acquaints us with new self-realization. 'From Pascal in his

closet, resting the arm, which supports his thoughtful brow, on a pile of demonstrations,' to the poor, pensive Indian who seeks the missionary in the American wilderness, 'the humiliated self-examinant feels that there is Evil in our nature as well as Good, an Evil and Good for a just analogy to which he questions all other natures in vain.' The great definition of our humanity is our conscience, which no scientific or wholly rational explanation can solve.[49] The changing mood of the times is further indicated by the fact that, whereas two or three decades before this aspect of Pascal's thought would have aroused indignation from most men of Coleridge's intellectual stature, it was now given the appearance of an obvious truth.

Once fervent in support of the Revolution, Coleridge eventually became disenchanted, and considered the *philosophes* and their followers to have deviated from the spirit of France he admired. Pascal, Mme. Guyon, and Fénelon represented more the France that he loved; otherwise, 'France is my Babylon, the Mother of Whoredoms in Morality, Philosophy, Taste.' 'How indeed,' he asked, 'it is possible at once to *love* Paschal, and Voltaire?' His reflections upon who might truly represent the national spirit led him later to jot down the idea that Descartes, Malebranche, Pascal, and Molière were the last generation in whom Gothic blood had predominated over Celtic.[50]

Attracted to Pascal's brilliance and his mingling of religious faith with philosophical reason, Coleridge was also captivated in a different manner by the *Lettres provinciales*. A letter he wrote from Keswick to his patrons, Sir George and Lady Beaumont, in 1803, reveals his delight on discovering that work, illustrating once again its unusual ability to intrigue men of broad interests:

My dear & honored Friends! my spirit has been with you day after day. Yesterday Afternoon I found among Southey's Books a Tetraglott Edition of Paschal's Provincial Letters / I seized it, O how eagerly! It seemed to me as if I saw Lady Beaumont with my very eyes; and heard over again the sounds of those words, in which she had expressed her enthusiastic Admiration of him. Tho' but a wretched French Scholar, I did not go to bed before I had read the Preface & the two first Letters. They are not only excellent; but the excellence is altogether of a new kind to me. Wit, Irony, Humour, Sarcasm, Scholastic Subtilty, and profound Metaphysics all combined — & this strange combination still more strangely co-existing with child-like Simplicity, Innocence, unaffected Charity, & the very soul of Christian Humility. — And the Style is a robe of pure light.[51]

Coleridge apparently borrowed this copy of the *Provinciales* from Southey for the purpose of learning Italian, and took it with him when he left for Malta and Italy in 1804; he also took a Port Royal

Italian grammar. In July of that year, his notebook records several examples of Italian idioms and grammatical usage taken from the early letters. Certain comments he wrote in the margin of the *Provinciales* reveal his continuing pleasure. The first letter was 'admirable,' and the second 'at least equal to the first.' 'What life,' he added, 'is given even to a Theological Controversy by the Introduction of Character and Drama!'[52] Witnessing Roman Catholicism at close hand also led him to a greater awareness of Pascal's more serious purpose, for at the end of the book he remarked:

> There can be no doubt, that the Jesuits only accommodated their doctrines to the manners and opinions of the Catholics—this indeed Paschal confesses—these horrid opinions therefore and this utter subversion of moral feelings and notions must have been the fruit of the essentials of the Catholic Church—yes! and truly is so at this very day. Other orders may not have written as openly as the Jesuits; but they really act on the same principles. —This I know.[53]

Besides possessing the *Provinciales*, Southey also knew the *Pensées*, though evidently only in the edition prepared by Condorcet with notes by Voltaire. In his commonplace book, he noted four quotations from Condorcet's preface and his eulogy of Pascal, and then proceeded to write down five short extracts from the *Pensées*, all in French. The reflections particularly attracting Southey's attention are too few and varied to indicate very much why Pascal appealed to him; but, in view of his introduction by way of Voltaire and Condorcet, it is intriguing that the thoughts of Pascal he chose were essentially related to such problems as the limitations of rationalist philosophy, and the difficulty of persuading the rest of the world to adopt new schemes and ways of thinking.[54] Very likely, Southey's interest was in part derived from his recognition of Pascal's ability to describe his own state of mind as his belief in the aims of the French Revolution turned to disillusionment.

Clear proof of Wordsworth's familiarity with Pascal's writings is lacking,[55] though his literary associates talked of them and the *Pensées* became known to some members of his family circle. In 1824, Sara Hutchinson wrote that she and John Monkhouse were reading the *Pensées* 'with more delight than with any Book we ever before rec^d,' and two years later, when family fortunes experienced a sharp loss, she reminded her cousin of some thoughts in times of calamity from 'our Friend Pascal.'[56] Dorothy Wordsworth, however, recorded her distinctive critical opinion, when she wrote to Lady Beaumont in 1806 to thank her for transcribing a passage from Pascal:

It is a beautiful passage indeed — very beautiful; but there is always a some-thing wanting to the fulness of my satisfaction in the expression of all elevated sentiments in the French language; and I cannot but think, simple as the conception is, and suitable as is the expression, that if Pascal had been an Englishman having the same exalted spirit of piety and the same genius, and had written in English, there would have been more of dignity in the language of the sentences you have quoted, and they would have been more impressive.[57]

A forceful voice of respect for Pascal from among this Lakeland group of writers came from Hazlitt, whose stormy career and radical opinions tended to break his once close relationships. Hazlitt knew the *Provinciales,* and, in 1807, apologized for the length of his own reply to Malthus' *Essay on the Principle of Population* with the still graceful excuse Pascal had delivered.[58] His appreciation, how-ever, was evidently of a more fundamental kind, for, when, in 1819, he publicly accused William Gifford, one of his leading critics, of misrepresentation, he chose to end with some personal reflections on the sort of reputation by which he would like to be remembered:

I have some love of fame, of the fame of a Pascal, a Leibnitz, or a Berkeley (none at all of popularity) and would rather that a single enquirer after truth should pronounce my name, after I am dead, with the same feelings that I have thought of theirs, than be puffed in all the newspapers, and praised in all the reviews, while I am living. I myself have been a thinker; and I cannot but believe that there are and will be others, like me. If the few and scattered sparks of truth, which I have been at so much pains to collect, should still be kept alive in the minds of such persons, and not entirely die with me, I shall be satisfied.[59]

Not surprisingly the *Quarterly Review,* to which Gifford was a contributor, seized upon this confession to provide amusement for its readers, describing the letter as 'more than commonly ridiculous'; but it is worth noting that, in its comments, the *Review* did not question the stature of Pascal himself, only Hazlitt's identification:

. . . we are favoured with the writer's own opinion of himself, and he therein gravely informs the world that the object of his literary labours is the fame 'of a Pascal, a Leibnitz, or a Berkeley!' and plainly intimates that he expects to be classed with them after his death. There is something beyond all farce or caricature in this angry buffoon's self-satisfied assumption of a seat amongst these three great men, whom Religion, Genius, Philosophy and Science raised almost above the nature of mortals — and this too, immediately after a more striking display than we remember to have seen elsewhere of Mr. Hazlitt's peculiarities. We doubt whether a Dutch sign-painter would make his own

apotheosis equally ludicrous: even if he were to depict himself recumbent at the
table of the Gods, with trunk hose, grasping a tobacco-pipe with one hand,
and striving to purple his lips in nectar with the other.[60]

'Hazlitt is scurvily treated,' observed Robinson after reading this
issue of the *Review*, 'but it is mere retaliation and what he merits.'[61]
Hazlitt's opinion of Pascal would have been informed, and his mis-
fortune surely lay in having openly mentioned feelings more suited
to a private occasion. His wish for 'the fame of a Pascal, a Leibnitz, or
a Berkeley,' however, stands in great contrast to the confession of
faith Pope had made nearly eighty years before, and illuminates an
important aspect of Pascal's new intellectual popularity. The Augustan poet had finally admitted distinctions existed between exem-
plars of faith and human reason, but Hazlitt, like other Romantics
desirous of a spiritual as well as a rationally-grounded religion, was
led to see in Pascal, Leibniz, and Berkeley equal benefactors of
mankind. In revolt against the more extreme forms of rationalism,
and searching for more than the Unitarianism of their youth might
offer, Coleridge and Hazlitt each discovered Pascal's attractions as a
religious philosopher and proceeded to direct their understanding
of him to a more imprecisely defined goal than he had attained.

As Pascal's religious thought was thus acquiring new popularity
among the Romantic writers, a steady interest was maintained elsewhere in other aspects of his career. In a history of the Royal Society,
the chemist Thomas Thomson paid tribute to Pascal as mathematician and man of science; and the *Edinburgh Review* in 1812 praised
his discoveries on atmospheric pressure, describing him as 'a genius
which burst forth like a meteor, and after a few bright corruscations,
was lost in darkness.'[62] The widest agreement upon the merits of any
one achievement of Pascal could doubtless still be brought together
around the *Lettres provinciales*. In addition to perennial anti-
Catholic interest, their appeal was constant to that multitude of
readers seeking diversion in the realms of literature and satire. The
Monthly Magazine believed their author had 'perhaps excelled every
writer in the refined delicacy of his ridicule,' and Hannah More
expressed her hope that the attractions of Pascal's work might be 'an
honest bait' to lead readers to his more spiritual writings. Many, she
believed, had 'been induced to read Cowper's 'Task' by 'John Gil-
pin,' 'Pascal's Thoughts' by his 'Provincial Letters,' and Doddridge's
Works by his Letters.'[63] When the *Encyclopaedia Londinensis* published its article on Pascal in 1821, an accompanying engraving, which
incorporated a single book in its design, portrayed the *Provinciales*;[64] and, seeing the popularity of these letters against the

PASCAL.

PLATE 7 Plate from the *Encyclopaedia Londinensis*
(London, 1810–29), vol. XVIII.

Jesuits from Coleridge to the most casual reader, it perhaps becomes understandable how, in 1812, the *Monthly Magazine* could introduce a short selection from the *Pensées* with the observation that they 'were once overvalued, and are now forgotten.'[65]

The Evangelical party and the Romantic writers had recently found much to admire in the *Pensées* and the character of their author; but the crucial stage in the rehabilitation of Pascal after the previous century's antagonism involved the acceptance of some validity in his views on human nature by the inheritors of the rationalist school, and the communication of their altered views to a broad segment of English opinion. His analysis of man had earlier provoked the severest differences, and, though a considerable reappraisal had already taken place, those universal sources of reference, the encyclopaedias and dictionaries, still tended to reiterate the judgments upon him handed down by the previous generation.[66] The time was ripe for a comprehensive reassessment of Pascal's life and achievements, stamped with an air of authority; and, in the views of Dugald Stewart, the Scottish philosopher, we find presented a sober, judicious analysis, prepared to appreciate where appreciation might be due rather than praising or condemning Pascal outright, which would considerably guide the future shape of Pascal's nineteenth-century reputation.

Stewart's comments were lucid and magisterial, but their importance was increased by the extent to which they received circulation. His interpretation of Pascal was contained in his *Dissertation: Exhibiting the Progress of Metaphysical, Ethical, and Political Philosophy, since the Revival of Letters in Europe,* which began to appear in 1815 as a supplement to the *Encyclopaedia Britannica;* but rival encyclopaedias soon introduced their readers to his views, and his evaluation was freely quoted by several other writers.[67] He began by questioning the accuracy of Pascal's existing general reputation. Although his name was 'more familiar to modern ears, than that of any of the other learned and polished anchorites, who have rendered the sanctuary of *Port-Royal* so illustrious,' his fame in England seemed to proceed more from superficial acquaintance or questionable taste than from a first-hand knowledge of his works. A great mathematician and physicist, Pascal was now chiefly celebrated for the *Lettres provinciales;* but, in Stewart's belief, the well-known enthusiasm of Gibbon for that work was enough to 'account for the rapture with which it never fails to be spoken of by *the erudite vulgar* in this country.' He could not help suspecting that 'it is now more praised than read,' and even Gibbon would probably have laid it aside had it not been for his fascination with ecclesiastical controversies and

Roman Catholicism. Apart from its literary interest, however, the *Provinciales* had nonetheless set a good example by demolishing an edifice of casuistry through common sense and satire:

In one respect, the Provincial Letters *are well entitled to the attention of philosophers; inasmuch as they present so faithful and lively a picture of the influence of false religious views in perverting the moral sentiments of mankind. The overwhelming ridicule lavished by Pascal on the whole system of jesuitical casuistry, and the happy effects of his pleasantry in preparing, from a distance, the fall of that formidable order, might be quoted as proofs, that there are at least some truths, in whose defence this weapon may be safely employed;—perhaps with more advantage than the commanding voice of Reason herself. The mischievous absurdities which it was his aim to correct, scarcely admitted of the gravity of logical discussion; requiring only the extirpation or the prevention of those early prejudices which choke the growth of common sense and of conscience: And for this purpose, what so likely to succeed with the open and generous minds of youth, as Ridicule, managed with decency and taste; more especially when seconded, as in the* Provincial Letters, *by acuteness of argument, and by the powerful eloquence of the heart? In this point of view, few practical moralists can boast of having rendered a more important service than Pascal to the general interests of humanity. Were it not, indeed, for his exquisite satire, we should already be tempted to doubt, if, at so recent a date, it were possible for such extravagancies to have maintained a dangerous ascendant over the human understanding.*

Thus firmly placing Pascal on humanity's side, Stewart went on to remark upon the *Pensées* in language often not far removed from that of former critics. Finding various reflections 'equally just and ingenious,' and others 'truly sublime,' he considered not a few 'false and puerile' and the whole unconnected fragment 'deeply tinctured with that ascetic and morbid melancholy, which seems to have at last produced a partial eclipse of his faculties.' At the same time, however, when referring to Voltaire's consequent attacks, 'several of which it is impossible to dispute the justness,' he also commented upon that author's 'levity and petulance' and his 'many very exceptionable strictures.' The overall impression received was that, while Stewart was ready to sympathize to some extent with Voltaire's assaults, he was not willing to engage in any rationalist crusade, and regarded the *philosophe* with mixed feelings. He later spoke concerning Pascal of 'the sad history of this great and excellent person,' but it is plain from his assessment that, ultimately, the less attractive features of Pascal's life and writings were superseded by a more just appreciation of his genius. Moreover, although Stewart still saw the

Provinciales as the more important work, he considered the reflections in the *Pensées* clearly worth attention and, occasionally, quite remarkable. His estimation of Pascal, *'that prodigy of parts,* as Locke calls him,' may not have been over-favourable, but its attempt at detachment and its mellowing mood represent a significant shift from the hostility of comparable sources in the previous century, and assisted in cementing a new phase in appreciation by Pascal's British audience.[68]

Strong rationalist opinions did not entirely cease, but when, in 1826, an abridgement of Bayle's *Dictionnaire* in English was published, the entry on Pascal was totally restricted to anecdotes of his childhood genius, with no mention of his thought or later career.[69] The old descriptions must not have been held as important as they once had seemed. Another perspective, which enabled Pascal's audience to look beyond traditional charges or loyalties, and relate him to the context of his times, was suggested by Macaulay. Taking the position that 'it is the age that forms the man, not the man that forms the age,' he believed the careers of Voltaire and Pascal might have been interchangeable if each had lived in the period of the other:

Voltaire, in the days of Lewis the Fourteenth, would probably have been, like most of the literary men of that time, a zealous Jansenist, eminent among the defenders of efficacious grace, a bitter assailant of the lax morality of the Jesuits, and the unreasonable decisions of the Sorbonne. If Pascal had entered on his literary career, when intelligence was more general, when the church was polluted by the Iscariot Dubois, the court disgraced by the orgies of Canillac, and the nation sacrificed to the juggles of Law; if he had lived to see a dynasty of harlots, an empty treasury and a crowded harem, an army formidable only to those whom it should have protected, a priesthood just religious enough to be intolerant, he might possibly, like every man of genius in France, have imbibed extravagant prejudices against monarchy and Christianity. The wit which blasted the sophisms of Escobar—the impassioned eloquence which defended the sisters of Port Royal—the intellectual hardihood which was not beaten down even by Papal authority, might have raised him to the Patriarchate of the Philosophical Church.[70]

The signs multiply on further examination that a new trend in English understanding of Pascal was now under way, in which Romantic sentiment and a chastised rationalism would frequently join. The emergence of these new intellectual forces and the increasing number of editions of Pascal's works, soon drawing upon an improved text in the case of the *Pensées*, in fact make the year 1830 a natural ending for this pursuit after his adventures. Among men in positions of intellectual leadership, the truths in many of his insights had come to be relished, in spite of some misgivings over his apparent pessimism and ascetic way of life; but, on the whole, these eccentricities were now considered the price of brilliance, rather than the expression of fanaticism, and did not deny Pascal his place as a thinker of importance. His embodiment of excellence in many fields fascinated the new age, and the implications of his thought for so many issues intrigued a wide audience and aroused its imagination. It is indicative enough that, when the next new translation of the *Pensées* was published, it had been retitled *Thoughts on Religion and Philosophy*.[71] We take leave of Pascal at this moment, as a new generation of admirers was gathering strength; and, to illustrate vividly the direction in which their appreciation would proceed, we may turn to one of the definitive statements of mid-nineteenth-century opinion which appeared in the *Edinburgh Review* in 1847. Commenting upon the revised edition of the *Pensées* by Faugère, this appraisal spoke of the 'Rembrandt-like depth of colouring' in Pascal's representation of man's nature — sombre, but with bursts of light shining through—and severely reproached Voltaire for his verdict of misanthropy; and its picturesque summary of Pascal's talents and qualities dramatically portrayed the mingled feelings of pleasure and awe with which many a Victorian reader would respond:

On the whole, in contemplating the richly diversified characteristics of this exalted genius in its different moods and phases—the combination of sublimity and depth with lightness and grace—of the noblest aptitudes for abstract speculation with the most exquisite delicacy of taste and the utmost sensibility of feeling—of profound melancholy with the happiest and the most refined humour and raillery—the grandeur of many aspects of his character, and the loveliness of others, we seem to be reminded of the contradictory features of Alpine scenery, where all forms of sublimity and beauty, of loveliness and terror, are found in singular proximity; where upland valleys of exquisite verdure and softness lie at the foot of the eternal glaciers; where spots of purest pastoral repose and beauty, smile under the very shadow of huge snowy peaks, and form the entrance of those savage gorges, in which reign perpetual sterility and desolation; in which the very silence is appalling—broken only by the roar of the distant cataract, and the lonely thunder of the avalanche.[72]

Pascal in America

The fortunes of Pascal in England have been described, abundantly demonstrating that his characteristic thoughts affected a great many educated persons—churchmen, poets, essayists, men of science, and philosophers. At first sight, it is by no means obvious that Pascal should also have been familiar to a number of Americans during the colonial period and the early years of the Republic. He made no outstanding contribution to any aspect of American thought, and what effect he had has not, it seems, warranted any study in contrast to the influence of Voltaire, Montesquieu, and Rousseau. The scattered evidence available does suggest, however, that he was regarded with some interest wherever his writings and achievements were known, adding slightly to our understanding of intellectual currents in America and of certain individuals there during the Age of Reason. A major fascination naturally lies in who read or referred to him; but, on a small scale, the reactions to his work and thought also illuminate the American episode in the eighteenth-century conflict between faith and reason, and may help define the extent of American involvement in it. With English evaluations as background, it may also be possible to discern a distinctive American vision of Pascal, and to compare it with contemporary English views.

Throughout the period in question, knowledge of Pascal in America derived primarily from either French or English sources, since no American edition of any of his works was published until the eighteen-twenties; and, in light of the many corresponding intellectual interests and the constant flow of books across the Atlantic, it is not surprising English influence was at first practically exclusive. Pascal's fame in England chiefly began with the translation of the *Lettres provinciales* in 1657. Retitled 'The Mysterie of Jesvitisme,' its sensational exposure of the Jesuits strongly appealed to English Protestant opinion; and, as a ready market existed for books of a religious kind in New England, copies of the *Provinciales* were before long making their way there. The splendid library belonging to John Winthrop, Jr., Governor of Connecticut, and added to by his son and grandson, included the first English edition; and, among the clergy, Ebenezer Pemberton, pastor of Boston's Old South Church and a fellow of Harvard College, owned 'the Mystery Jesuitism' as well as two English versions of another Jansenist work, Nicole's *Essais de morale*. An inventory of books mostly the property of the Rev. George Curwin of Salem listed 'Mons. Paschal's Mystery of Jesuitism. With Cuts.'[1] Books on New England shelves often resembled those read by Virginia planters, and we find Col. Ralph Wormely of Middlesex County possessing 'the mistery of the Jesuitts' at his death in 1701.[2]

Simultaneously, Pascal's skill at mathematics and his notable experiments on atmospheric pressure also received some attention. Men like Cotton Mather who followed the activities of the Royal Society would have had some familiarity with Pascal's scientific work, since the Frenchman's discoveries prompted several of Boyle's investigations and were not infrequently referred to in early issues of the *Philosophical Transactions*. More particularly, it may be worth mentioning that *Compendium Physicae,* a textbook which drew attention to Pascal's barometric experiment on the Puy de Dôme, was adopted by Harvard Collège in time to have visible effects upon Commencement theses in 1687, and remained in use until 1728.[3]

Cotton Mather, in fact, presents us with the first of several tantalizing problems concerning the degree of acquaintance with Pascal's writings in the case of representative American figures. Keenly interested in religion and all its ramifications, among them the contributions reason and science might bring to a fuller understanding of Christianity, he must have heard at some time of Pascal, and quite probably saw the *Provinciales* and the *Pensées;* but, in the absence of concrete evidence, we can only suppose this occurred. Grounds of a sort exist, however, for claiming that Mather was at any rate versed in the details of Pascal's life. This was not impossible, for Pascal had been celebrated as a brilliant thinker during his lifetime, and biographical sketches praising his combination of genius and sanctity soon began to appear in dictionaries and elsewhere. Such knowledge must have spread to America, with a curious result, for, when Governor William Stoughton of Massachusetts died in 1701, the epitaph inscribed on his tomb in Dorchester bore a very close resemblance to the wording written for Pascal by his friend Aimonius Proust de Chambourg, and afterwards publicized.

Tradition, it seems, has attributed Stoughton's epitaph to Mather, but Mather's range of learning and interests would certainly have

PLATE 8 Tomb of Governor William Stoughton of Massachusetts (d. 1701), in the Burial-ground, Dorchester, Mass. See further, page 285, n5.

equipped him for such a conception. The most elaborate of early stones in the Dorchester graveyard, perhaps the work of a foreign artist, its words are chiefly altered from the original's where the achievements, not the characters, of the two men differed. They created an immediate impression on Judge Samuel Sewall, who, in 1704, recorded that he 'rid into the Burying place, and read Mr. Stoughton's Epitaph, which is very great';[4] but opinion on the whole has felt uncomfortable with the glowing tribute set forth at second hand in memory of the austere presiding judge at the trials of the Salem witches. Still, Mather's involvement in the affair led to a close association with Stoughton; and, though he may, if he were the author, have chosen Pascal's epitaph primarily for its stylistic qualities, he may also have conceived it as the most fitting eulogy available he could adapt and offer respectfully to a man who, to his mind, embodied the finest Puritan virtues.[5]

In 1688, the *Pensées* first appeared in English, being followed in 1704 by Kennett's better translation, which was republished several times. In the shortened version released by Pascal's friends at Port Royal, unexceptionably describing the divisions within human nature and indicating their remedy through salvation, the work spoke to Englishmen and Americans of various religious persuasions; and it had an extra appeal in its clearly phrased aphorisms and expressions. In England, it soon became fashionable for authors to draw quotations from the *Pensées* to add force to their own arguments, and their writings would have added to American impressions of the famous Frenchman. In a religious context, we find, in 1710, Ebenezer Pemberton similarly citing Pascal and commending him in an election sermon preached before the Governor and other dignitaries of Massachusetts:

*It is a divine as well as wise and just Remark, made by * One of the greatest Masters of Thought in the Last Age, that Persons of Quality and Character ought to have two Sets of thoughts, by which to regulate their Conduct: by the One they are to view themselves in their State of distinguishing Elevation, which is not from Nature, but Arbitrary Establishment; by the Other they are to take a prospect of themselves in their Natural Condition of Infirmity, and Equality with the rest of Mankind. The bright Idea of their Dignity and Power must be temper'd with the more cloudy Idea of their Frailty: A Seperation of these will lead into gross Illusions, and betray into Errors fatal to themselves, and their Dependents: But an happy Union of these will afford light to direct them in the bright tracts of Substantial Glory; and forcible arguments to engage them to such a management, as shall be glorious to themselves, and happy to the World.*[6]
*Monsieur Paschal.

The *Pensées* evidently became as generally known among the limited American public as the *Provinciales* had been. Although the library of Robert Carter in Virginia was undistinguished in books of philosophy, it contained a copy of 'Paschal's Thoughts.' In England we have noticed how the Port Royal version, the only version the eighteenth century knew, was valued also as a work for devotions; and, in New England, according to one critic, the *Pensées* became as widely read as any work by the later European Calvinists. This may have been the cause of its recurring appeal to Samuel Johnson, first president of King's College (Columbia), New York. In a list Johnson kept of books he read between 1719 and 1756, he first recorded reading 'Mr. Paschal's Thoughts on Religion' in the year following his leaving Yale in 1719. He read it again in 1730-31 while rector of the Episcopal Church at Stratford, Connecticut, and for a third time in 1746-47 still holding the same position. In 1745, the Rev. Ebenezer Parkman of Westborough, Mass., noted 'Read Thoughts on Religion.'[7] The *Pensées* likewise had a following among Quakers. A wealthy merchant, John Smith, son-in-law of James Logan, jotted down that he had read the work, and an English copy (1751) belonged to Anthony Benezet.[8]

If the nature and extent of Cotton Mather's awareness of Pascal present a puzzle, in the case of Jonathan Edwards' they are even more intriguing. Similarities have often been drawn between the two pioneers, by authors as opposite as Oliver Wendell Holmes and Perry Miller, the latter observing that, in the *Freedom of the Will,* 'there are arresting parallels between the minds of Edwards and Pascal.'[9] The only clear reference to Pascal Edwards left occurs in the notebook in which he listed the titles of books he wished to remember, and information about where they could be secured. There the following entry appears: 'The Life of Monsieur Paschal Collected from the Writings of Madam Perier his Sister Greatly Commended in an Advertisement at the end. of Mons Paschals thoughts with such Expressions as these that this Single Life is more than an 100 Sermons & would do more towards the Reforming the Libertines of the (Present) Age than if you should Let Loose twenty missionaries upon them.'[10]

From this we may deduce that Edwards at some stage saw a copy of the *Pensées* in English, and, at any rate, read among the advertisements an insertion regarding Jesup's *Lives of Picus and Pascal.* Such an advertisement, containing the same quotation from Bayle, in fact appeared at the back of the second edition of Kennett's translation (1727). Living as Edwards did in rural Massachusetts, he was acutely aware of being isolated from the intellectual centres of the time, and tried strenuously to counteract this. To what extent he drew upon

Pascal, if he actually read the *Pensées,* is hard to determine. Holmes suggested the title of Edwards' regrettably best-known sermon, 'Sinners in the Hands of an Angry God,' might be reminiscent of Pascal's phrase 'dans les mains d'un Dieu irrité,' and other slight coincidences in expressions both of them used may exist as well. There are also, of course, obvious differences between the two men; as Holmes wrote, 'if they had met in this world, Pascal would have looked sadly on Edwards as a heretic, and Edwards would have looked sternly on Pascal as a papist.'[11]

But some resemblances are indeed striking – the saintliness of both men, their tendencies towards asceticism, their skill as controversialists, and the overwhelming sense each of them had of the littleness of man and the greatness of God. If Pascal was a mathematical prodigy, Edwards rivalled him in the field of natural history, as his short treatise 'Of Insects' demonstrates; and, although, as Miller has pointed out, the mystical tendencies in Edwards never lost sight of the psychology learned from Locke, Edwards recorded spiritual experiences in his life which bear comparison with Pascal's 'night of fire.' Both were men of great intellectual stature and deep piety, though separated in several ways; and it may suffice to say that, if Edwards read the *Pensées* at all deeply, he must have found in them much that was appealing and congenial. Like Mather and Pemberton in their time, he recognized that, as the experimental philosophy opened up new vistas for thought, systematic reason consequently ruled out the possible intervention of divine grace. In the best of the Puritan tradition, he therefore attempted to make a restatement of the Christian faith with the aid of the new philosophy, and would doubtless have been in a position to appreciate the efforts of Pascal's perceptive mind working with a similar spirit and purpose.

By the middle years of the century Pascal's American reputation had broadly developed along established English lines, though slightly later and less comprehensively in the minds of Americans to whom his writings were less available. The shreds of evidence suggest, however, that what interest existed was more exclusively religious than in England, where a literary and philosophical evaluation became a vital part of fashionable attitudes. By the seventeen-forties, arbiters of English opinion began to prize man's rational faculties as supremely important, and challenged or neglected to involve themselves in the contrary conclusions of Pascal. Voltaire's charges of misanthropy spread their influence too; and, though in some circles – among the early Methodists, for example – Pascal's manner of life and his sceptical view of human capabilities were considered to provide valuable lessons for serious Christians, informed men on the whole were liable to look on him with varying shades of disapproval.

In contrast, American intellectual development created a situation in which disputes of reason and science with religion did not dominate the eighteenth century to nearly the extent that happened in eighteenth-century Europe. Among the first settlers the scientific outlook had been considered desirable and valid, and the transition was rather from Puritanism to an enlightened Puritanism than dramatically from one system to another. Most prominent individuals were actually a highly interesting combination of traits deriving from both intellectual worlds. Nevertheless, while many Americans continued to have some appreciation of Pascal as a religious figure, some shift in taste resembling that in England is discernible. The advent of deism in colonial America caused a reappraisal of his works, and, as in England, men were drawn now to the *Provinciales* for the author's cleverness and wit. Here Benjamin Franklin offers a nice case in illustration. Soon after beginning his apprenticeship to a Boston printer, he discovered a translation of the *Provinciales;* but, in that Puritan setting, he obtained such pleasure from reading it that, rather like Gibbon, he later returned to it on repeated occasions.[12] Perhaps it was due to Franklin's efforts that, when the Library Company of Philadelphia was founded in 1741, it announced its possession of the *Provinciales* in French, apparently ordered, as well as an English translation given by one David Bush.[13] Philadelphia, as one might expect from its size and character, was a city in which Pascal was not unknown. Although a search has not revealed any French copies of Pascal's works being imported there by booksellers during the century's second half, English and French copies were sometimes otherwise offered for sale; and the Library Company gradually increased its holdings of books by Pascal, among them an English translation of the *Pensées* given by the Rev. Samuel Preston.[14] Pascal's likeness would no doubt have been known there too from several possible sources, but an incident recorded in 1778 by Pierre du Simitière, an immigrant artist and designer of medals, may be mentioned. In June of that year, du Simitière noted in his diary that Capt. John Montresor, Engineer-in-chief of the British Armies in America, had presented him with a collection of bronze medals of famous Frenchmen, among them one commemorating Blaise Pascal.[15]

After the mid-century Americans, too, became increasingly conscious of their membership in a culture spanning the Atlantic, and extending beyond the community of English-speaking peoples; and, out of the close relationship with France during the War of

Independence, we find French copies of Pascal's works joining English versions as sources of personal acquaintance. When John Adams, a novice at diplomacy in Paris in 1778, asked for advice in learning the best French, he was recommended among other books 'Pascalls provincial Letters,' which he purchased and later took back with him to Massachusetts.[16] In 1785, James Madison wrote to Thomas Jefferson, asking him to procure a number of books in Paris on his behalf, including the *Provinciales,* and both he and Adams subsequently referred to Pascal in their separate correspondence.[17] Jefferson, himself, seems to have known Pascal mostly through English versions, for, when his library was sold to Congress in 1815, it contained a copy of Kennett's translation of the *Pensées* (1749) and of Andrews' translation of the *Provinciales;* but there is evidence that, at an earlier date, he had also owned a two-volume French edition of the *Pensées.* A prominent Virginian of the previous generation, William Byrd II, possessed the *Provinciales* in French, and the second volume of Jefferson's *Provinciales* is inscribed 'Peyton Randolph,' presumably the name of its former owner. Jefferson set his initials in both volumes of this set, and we have record they were bound for him in calf with gilt in 1807; but no quotations or extracts from Pascal were set down by Jefferson in his commonplace book.[18]

Other records indicate that, around 1800, Pascal's works were singly or severally available in most American centres of population. The Boston library possessed the *Provinciales* and the *Pensées,* and, in South Carolina, Charleston readers could find the *Provinciales* translated by Andrews. Among colleges, Harvard in 1790 owned three copies of the *Pensées* and one of the *Provinciales,* Yale in 1823 possessed the *Pensées*, and Brown in 1793 a copy of each.[19] The impression on the whole persists that the *Pensées* retained a greater following in America than in England; but this is not to say that Pascal was at all well-known in America compared to some other writers, and his absence has been noted from eighteenth-century American periodicals. The assaults of Voltaire moreover cannot have spread as they did in England, for nowhere, it seems, did an American leave record of associating his name and Pascal's together.[20] The only conspicuous example of a rationalist attack, comparable to those made in Europe, is provided by David Rittenhouse, who, turning to the Pensées shortly before his death in 1796, acknowledged he read them with pleasure; but, according to his early biographer, 'that pleasure . . . was diminished, when he learned, what was often the state of Pascall's mind: – a state of melancholy and gloom: and sometimes even of mental derangement.'[21]

It can be no coincidence that Rittenhouse's opinion had developed in Philadelphia, the centre of the Enlightenment in

America, the city most open to European ideas, and to which the radical Priestley, who had violently attacked Pascal, came seeking refuge in 1794. But, as far as Pascal's reputation was concerned, it was an American phenomenon that, hardly had the ripples from the European storm arrived, than they were challenged by the new intellectual forces of the nineteenth century. In America, a strong rationalist offensive was, for several causes, denied a proper opportunity for growth, and the largely broad and generous approach to Pascal's various achievements moved forward to receive redefinition without any shock of interruption. The French Revolution's excesses provoked denunciations of Voltaire and the *philosophes* from pulpits as threats to law and order in the young republic; and the relative absence of emerging rationalist critiques of Pascal in America may signify their rapid yielding to a revived appreciation, in which reason, religion, and the new Romantic interest in what the Enlightenment had sought to obliterate all played a part.

The persistence of a strong religious acceptance of Pascal is clear from the attention paid him in evangelical magazines and by Protestants aroused by the restoration of the Jesuit order in 1814, the latter ultimately leading to the first American publication of the *Provinciales* in 1828.[22] As in England at that time, American Protestants were disposed to regard Pascal as one of their own in all but name, and such attitudes were conspicuous in a three-part article upon Pascal and the *Provinciales* which appeared in issues of the *Christian Disciple*. Although, like many a zealous Protestant, the author had some difficulty in reconciling his admiration for Pascal with his Catholicism, he enthusiastically approved his unmasking of the Jesuits and many of his personal qualities. The focus of the article, however, was upon the seventh letter of the *Provinciales,* which described an 'astonishing' conversation between Pascal and a Jesuit on the subject of duelling; and the author concluded with an impassioned plea to end the current practice of fighting duels, in which the defence offered by its advocates was likened to that elaborated by the Jesuits. Duelling was fortunately less of a social problem in New England than in the southern and western states, but its evil effects demanded its abolition everywhere. Pascal's motives were those of a true Christian, and arguments of 'Jesuitical refinement' should yield to the example of the apostle Paul, who 'displayed more true courage, in exposing his character and life in the cause of virtue and religion, than has appeared in all the duels that ever have been fought by gentlemen.'[23]

Contemporary with this harnessing of Pascal to the cause of social improvement and the reformed religion, we find elsewhere his spiritual qualities gaining a different acceptance in the eyes of Benjamin Rush. The knowledgeable Philadelphia physician found an interest in Pascal through his medical studies; and, whereas his fellow-citizen, Rittenhouse, had seen Pascal's religious thoughts lamentably as the product of a diseased state of mind, Rush was ready to believe they contained important elements of truth which accorded with the results of his own investigations. In his short paper, 'On the Different Species of Phobias,' he first listed eighteen types of phobia he had observed, and then commented:

For these maladies of the mind, there are two infallible remedies, viz. reason and religion. The former is the sure antidote of such of them as originate in folly, —while the latter is effectual in those species, which are derived from vice. "I fear God (said Pascal) and therefore I have no other fear."—A belief in God's providence, and a constant reliance upon his power and goodness, impart a composure and firmness to the mind which render it incapable of being moved by all the real, or imaginary evils of life.[24]

Rush, in 1812, again commended Pascal's good sense when discussing the fear of death and steps taken to remedy its obsession:

As much of the fear of death is produced by the dread of the pains which attend it, let us inform our patients that these pains are by no means universal, that they are less severe than the pains of many common diseases, from which there are daily recoveries, and that heaven has kindly furnished us with several remedies, which remove or mitigate them. "It is less distressing to die (says Mr. Pascall) than to think of death." This I believe is strictly true in most cases.[25]

Pascal no doubt remained a familiar author in Virginia also,[26] but it is rather in New England that we most readily find a continuing interest during the early nineteenth century. John Adams' reading of the *Provinciales* in Paris evidently stayed in his mind, for, in 1816, he was writing to Jefferson with renewed enthusiasm for that work and its author:

I do not like the late Resurrection of the Jesuits. They have a General, now in Russia, in correspondence with the Jesuits in the U.S. who are more numerous than every body knows. Shall We not have Swarms of them here? In as many shapes and disguises as ever a King of the Gypsies, Bamfie[l]d More Carew himself, assumed? In the shape of Printers, Editors, Writers School masters etc. I have lately read Pascalls Letters over again, and four Volumes of the History of the Jesuits. If ever any Congregation of Men could merit, eternal Perdition on Earth and in Hell, According to these Historians though like Pascal true Catholicks, it is this Company of Loiola. Our System however of Religious Liberty must afford them an Assylum. But if they do not put the Purity of our Elections to a severe Tryal, it will be a Wonder.[27]

From the records left by the Adams family, John Adams' discovery of Pascal plainly founded a family tradition, descending particularly to his son. In a eulogy on John Quincy Adams, delivered at his death by Edward Everett, Pascal was mentioned as one of the authors stamped on his memory, French having been to him as a second mother-tongue. The father's library had contained a single copy of the *Provinciales*, but that of the son included the first edition (Cologne, 1657), a later four-volume edition (Cologne, 1739), a two-volume set of the *Pensées* (Geneva, 1778), and a set of the works of Pascal published in Paris in 1819.[28] Among the books John Quincy Adams advised his son, Charles Francis, to read for self-improvement and preparation for a public career were the great letter-writers, Pliny, Voltaire, and Pascal; and, without drawing any comparison between the two French antagonists, Charles noted in his diary in 1827 that the *Provinciales*, 'though upon antiquated subjects,' had pleased him. The style was pure, 'and the controversial eloquence which it displays is the reason that it has been recommended by my Father.'[29]

The young Adams' introduction to Pascal was not only through his father but by way of the lectures on French literature by George Ticknor, which he had attended in 1824 as a Harvard undergraduate. Emphasizing Pascal's asceticism and the literary qualities of the *Provinciales*, Ticknor's evaluation reflected European rationalist views, but, like Dugald Stewart, he by no means presented his subject without attractions. Between 1815 and 1819 Ticknor had studied in Europe, and his resulting treatment of Pascal, as shown in the manuscripts of his lectures, reveals an awareness of emerging perspectives and a desire to communicate the conclusions he had reached. He acknowledged one of his sources was Bayle, and considered it a tragedy that, having written the *Provinciales*, Pascal had sunk back into penances and mortifications. In that state of mind he had written the *Pensées*, a little book, intensely devotional and containing sublime thoughts on God and his works, but often 'degraded by the peculiar views he had of religious and human nature.' In spite of these shortcomings, Pascal was to Ticknor a fundamentally impressive and fascinating figure. Some aspects of his life might seem remote and unpleasant, but censures could not wholly detract from the quality of the *Pensées* any more than the distance of the *Provinciales* could lessen their excellence:

But the seal of Genius is on everything he touched. His false conclusions are drawn with the most admirable and earnest eloquence; and the very misanthropy, which it gives us so much pain to witness in a heart intended to have

*known only the most gentle affection—has something almost sublime about it
from the self-sacrifice by which we are sure it was bought & which was more
cruel to him than all his mortifications.*

*Indeed, on whatever side we consider Pascal's character, there is something
remarkably striking and original that fastens our attention. We have nothing
in common with him in all our opinions & feelings—and yet we are drawn to
him by an irresistible attraction.*[30]

The evidence does not reveal that Pascal occupied a symbolic
position in America during the Age of Reason comparable to the
place he held in the intellectual life of France, and, to a lesser degree,
England. He was not as well-known, and the harmonies of enlightened Puritanism did not readily offer a battleground for antagonistic views about him. If, however, Pascal made any contribution at all
to developing American thought—if, for all the limited knowledge
of him and his works, an irresistible attraction constantly made itself
felt—in what manner was his influence exerted? It has been argued
that, while the optimism of Franklin and others fashioned one
aspect of the American character, an absorption remained in the
dark mysteries of human nature, and it is as a reinforcement to the
latter that Pascal's life and writings in America should surely be seen.
As in England, his analysis of man, based as far as possible on
rational premises, had an appeal from the beginning, and so had the
Provinciales; but perhaps his having placed supreme value on religious truth, his retreat from human company, and his discovery of
salvation eventually through revelation and the scriptures, also
made him seem to Americans a type whose interests and psychology
were particularly akin to their own. One might well imagine that
reading the *Pensées* with the Bible at hand, shut up in a snow-covered
farmhouse, could set many a New England farmer on the path to a
religious revival in the spring. It was perhaps fitting, then, that it was
in rural Amherst, Massachusetts, that the first American edition of
the *Pensées* was published, in 1829.[31]

This American attachment to Pascal's view of man's defects and
mortality is noticeable as we observe the formation of some
nineteenth-century literary figures. Emerson recalled admiring
Pascal in his youth, and keeping a copy of the *Pensées* in his pew at
church to read when the sermon was dull. 'Stern & great, old-
fashioned-theological but with sublime passages,' he described it,
and his early journals show he sometimes jotted down passages on
the contradictions in human nature.[32] A concern with those parts of
man which reason cannot entirely illuminate became the preoccupation of other writers. To disregard the horrors attendant upon

man's existence was the ultimate foolishness to Melville. Here is Ishmael meditating upon evil:

The truest of all men was the Man of Sorrows, and the truest of all books is Solomon's, and Ecclesiastes is the fine hammered steel of woe. "All is vanity." ALL. This wilful world hath not got hold of unchristian Solomon's wisdom yet. But he who dodges hospitals and jails, and walks fast crossing grave-yards, and would rather talk of operas than hell; calls Cowper, Young, Pascal, Rousseau, poor devils all of sick men; and throughout a care-free lifetime swears by Rabelais as passing wise, and therefore jolly; — not that man is fitted to sit down on tomb-stones, and break the green damp mould with unfathomably wondrous Solomon.[33]

A recent critic has observed that, if Pascal was reputedly troubled by the hallucination of a gulf which opened beside him, Hawthorne's obsession was his haunted chamber, and Poe's the grave. We know Hawthorne once read Pascal, and Poe apparently liked to quote from the *Pensées* that most of our ills spring from our inability to live at ease with ourselves.[34] Never rejected to the extent that he was in France or England, Pascal's introspective influence eventually dominated his other characteristics in a country which otherwise grew into holding so many fundamental Enlightenment beliefs; and perhaps it could not have been more appropriate that, among the very earliest examples of his presence in America, should have been the lines on Governor Stoughton's tomb.

CHAPTER ONE

1 T. B. Macaulay, *The History of England from the Accession of James II*, II, 51.

2 The principal evidence for the exact date of publication of the first English edition of the *Lettres provinciales* is found in the copy possessed by George Thomason (d. 1666), the noted London book-collector. Hand-written on the title-page is the date of August 31 [1657]. The Latin translation of Pierre Nicole appeared in 1658, followed before the end of the century by translations into Italian and Spanish. See discussion in Paule Jansen, *De Blaise Pascal à Henry Hammond: Les Provinciales en Angleterre*, pp. 25–27; also Ruth Clark, *Strangers and Sojourners at Port Royal*, pp. 102–103.

3 [Blaise Pascal], *Les Provinciales: or, The Mysterie of Jesuitisme* (London, 1657), [title-page]. For a definitive French text of the *Provinciales*, see Pascal, *Oeuvres*, ed. Léon Brunschvicg and others (Paris, 1908–21), vols. IV–VII, hereafter referred to as Pascal, *Oeuvres*.

4 Specific reasons for the Jesuits' unpopularity included their secret activities during the reign of Elizabeth I, their suspected organization of Catholic plots under both the Queen and her successors, anti-Spanish feeling, and, under Charles I, anti-French feeling also. For a brief analysis of this profound hostility under the Stuarts, see David Mathew, *Catholicism in England, 1535–1935*, pp. 69–70.

5 Jansen, *De Blaise Pascal à Henry Hammond*, p. 26. When the Cologne edition of 1657 appeared, there must have been time for its preface to be borrowed for the first English edition. The English edition of 1658, however, made use of the entire Cologne edition.

6 Anthony à Wood, *Athenae Oxonienses*, ed. Bliss, IV, 382–85.

7 [Antoine Arnauld (?)], *A Journall of all Proceedings between the Jansenists, and the Jesuits* ... (1659), [title-page].

8 Clark, *Strangers and Sojourners*, p. 105; Jansen, *De Blaise Pascal à Henry Hammond*, p. 88.

9 Ibid., pp. 61–64.

10 Ibid., pp. 64–84. It is often said John Evelyn was the translator of the *Lettres provinciales*, an error largely caused by an entry in his diary for January 2, 1665, mentioning the publication of a related work with a similar English title translated by him. Both French and English writers have shared in the confusion, and, though Evelyn's participation has been refuted (for instance in Jansen, *De Blaise Pascal à Henry Hammond*, pp. 86-88), this does not seem to have affected every writer on this subject. One recent study has seen Evelyn's hand clearly displayed in the style of the translation, both in the prose and in the short poem contained in the *Provinciales*; see Pierre Janelle, 'Pascal et l'Angleterre,' pp. 154–59.

11 [Arnauld (?)], *A Journall of all Proceedings*, To the Reader.

12 These first enquiries had been made by Dr. Richard Steward, Dean-designate of St. Paul's and Provost of Eton, and Sir George Radcliffe; Clark, *Strangers and Sojourners*, p. 54. For accounts of two important later attempts at union, see G. Lambin, *Les rapports de Bossuet avec l'Angleterre*, and Edmond Préclin, *L'union des églises gallicane et anglicane*.

13 *Provinciales* (London, 1657), Preface. It was not until 1659 that Pascal appears to have been named as the author of the *Provinciales* for the first time, in a Jesuit defence.

14 An extensive bibliography of books of this kind is given in Clark, *Strangers and Sojourners*, pp. 278–91.

15 G.E.B. Eyre and C.R. Rivington (eds.), *A Transcript of the Registers of the Worshipful Company of Stationers: from 1640–1708 A.D.*, II, 150.

16 [Blaise Pascal], *Les Provinciales* (London, 1658), Advertisement.

17 Ibid., Preface.

18 Ibid., Additionals to the Mystery of Jesuitisme, p. 115.

19 For these two writings, see Pascal, *Oeuvres*, VII, 278–99, 308–27.

20 Pierre Jarrige and others, *A further Discovery of the Mystery of Jesuitisme* (1658), Preadvertisement [p. 1].

21 Joseph Gillow, *A Literary and Biographical History of the English Catholics*, III, 50–52.

22 [Jacques Nouet and François Annat], *An Answer to the Provinciall Letters Published by the Jansenists* . . . (1659), Preface.

23 Ibid., pp. 481–82.

24 Ibid., pp. 487–89.

25 Ibid., pp. 505–13.

26 [Gabriel Daniel], *The Discourses of Cleander and Eudoxe upon the Provincial Letters* (1704), To the Reader [p. 8].

27 [Antoine Arnauld and others], *To Mystérion tés Anomias: Another Part of the Mystery of Jesuitism or The new Heresie of the Jesuites* . . . (1664), p. 48.

28 No doubt the phrase also commended itself by its general allusion to what had been obscure, and, perhaps, by being similar to the biblical words "mystery of iniquity."

29 Samuel Clarke, *Medulla Theologiae: or The Marrow of Divinity* ...(1659), To the Christian Reader [p.1].

30 Richard Baxter, *A Key for Catholicks, To open the Jugling of the Jesuits* ... (1659), Epistle Dedicatory [p. 14].

31 Ibid., pp. 20–21, 351.

32 Ibid., pp. 278–79.

33 Ibid., pp. 58–62. It should be noted that Baxter clearly recognized the author of the *Provinciales* as a Catholic, but did not reconcile this fully with his approval of him as Jansenist–thus demonstrating a recurring dilemma for English Protestants. He again cited the *Provinciales* when he made a brief reference later to material differences between Jesuits and Jansenists (pp. 127–28), and when he commented unfavourably upon the moral practices of the Jesuits (p. 229).

34 Ibid., p. 335.

35 John Wilson, *The Cheats*, ed. Nahm, p. 220 (Act v, sc. iv, ll. 11–37); for comment, see also pp. 91 – 92, 276 – 77.

36 For Scruple's arguments on gluttony, see ibid., pp. 152 – 53 (Act I, sc. v, ll. 92 – 108), also pp. 92 – 93, 251; on simony, p. 224 (Act V, sc. iv, ll. 130–37), also p. 278; on abortion, pp. 162–63 (Act II, sc. iii, ll. 75–104), also pp. 127, 254.

37 [Theophilus Gale], *The True Idea of Jansenisme, both Historick and Dogmatick* (1669), A Premonition.

38 Ibid., p. 73. Gale also referred (pp. 8–9) to the sixteenth letter in which the Jesuits had claimed that for many years Port Royal had been the centre of a Jansenist conspiracy.

39 Ibid., Preface [pp. 18–19].

40 *Bibliotheca Oweniana* (1684), pp. 23, 29.

41 See discussion in John Milton, *Works*, ed. Patterson and others, XVIII, 581; and in John Milton, *Life Records*, ed. French, IV, 199, and V, 129. This particular copy later passed into the possession of the Rev. John Newton, friend of the poet William Cowper.

42 Clark, *Strangers and Sojourners*, p. 112.

43 [Nicolas Perrault], *The Jesuits Morals* (1670), Advertisement [p. 9].

44 [Anon.], *Fair Warning To take heed of Popery* ... (1674), pp. 18, 36–50, 54, 62, 65.

45 David Clarkson, *The Practical Divinity of the Papists Discovered to be Destructive of Christianity and Men's Souls* (1676), Advertisement [pp. 1–2].

46 Jeremy Taylor, *The Whole Works*, ed. Heber and Eden, I, ccv–ccviii; VI, 249.

47 Compton was the author of *The Jesuites Intrigues* (London, 1669), while to Stillingfleet is attributed the preface to *The Jesuits Loyalty, Manifested in Three several Treatises* ... (London, 1677). Burnet translated *A Decree made at Rome ... Condemning some opinions of the Jesuits and other Casuists* (London, 1679), and also contributed a preface.

See discussion in Jansen, *De Blaise Pascal à Henry Hammond*, pp. 44–51.

Stillingfleet's copies of the *Provinciales* were in the following editions: Cologne, 1665 (Latin); Cologne, 1666 (French); Cologne, 1684 (the four-language edition in French, Latin, Spanish, and Italian). He also owned a reply by Gabriel Daniel entitled *Les entretiens de Cléandre et d'Eudoxe* (Amsterdam, 1696), which had first appeared in 1694; N.J.D. White, *A Catalogue of Books in the French Language, Printed in or before A.D. 1715, remaining in Archbishop Marsh's Library, Dublin* (1918), p. 142. Burnet owned a Latin edition of the *Provinciales* (Cologne, 1658) and an edition in French, as well as several replies; *Bibliotheca Burnetiana* [1716], pp. 9, 32, 34–40. While travelling in France as a young man, Burnet sought acquaintance with the Jansenists, and his library reveals an extensive interest in the movement's literature.

48 Perrinchief owned the *Provinciales* in the Cologne edition of 1657 (Bodleian Library, *MS Rawl.* D.878). Plume owned a copy of the first English edition, and of the Latin edition of Cologne, 1665; S.G. Deed, *Catalogue of the Plume Library at Maldon, Essex*, p. 131.

49 [Anthony à Wood], *The Life and Times of Anthony Wood . . .*, ed. Clark, III, 167.

50 E.H. Plumptre, *The Life of Thomas Ken, D.D., Bishop of Bath and Wells*, II, 298; *A Collection of Excellent English Books . . . Being the Library of the Most Reverend Father in God, Dr. Tillotson* [1695], p. 9.

51 This information has been kindly supplied to me by the Deputy Keeper of Archbishop Marsh's Library.

52 Supra, n. 10.

53 John Evelyn, *Diary*, ed. E.S. de Beer, III, 393.

54 Robert Boyle, *Works*, ed. Birch (1772), VI, 295.

55 Clark, *Strangers and Sojourners*, p. 112n.

56 Ibid., p. 108; Evelyn, *Diary*, III, 393n.

57 [Arnauld and others], *To Mystérion tés Anomias*, Epistle Dedicatory.

58 Clark, *Strangers and Sojourners*, pp. 108–109; John Evelyn, *Diary and Correspondence*, ed. Bray, III, 143.

59 Evelyn, *Diary*, III, 397.

60 Ibid., III, 431; [Pierre Nicole], *The Pernicious Consequences of the New Heresie of the Jesuites against the King and the State* (1666), Dedicatory Preface.

61 [Blaise Pascal], *The Mystery of Jesuitism, Discovered In certain Letters . . .* (London, 1679). It would appear the name at any rate of Escobar had become synonymous with perverted casuistry, as it had in France. In his *Satires upon the Jesuits* (1678–81), the poet John Oldham ridiculed both him and Suarez; E. F. Mengel, Jr. (ed.), *Poems on Affairs of State: Augustan Satirical Verse, 1660–1714*, II, 19–20.

62 [Anon] *The Missionarie's Arts Discovered . . .*, pp. 3, 41–44, 66, 73.

63 Evelyn, *Diary*, IV, 539.

64 Clark, *Strangers and Sojourners*, pp. 1–12. In her work, Miss Clark has given a comprehensive account of relationships between the Jansenists of France and Holland, and the British Isles. For Pascal's references to Conry and Sinnich, see *Oeuvres*, XI, 104–105.
65 Clark, *Strangers and Sojourners*, pp. 14–39. Pascal referred to the term "Calaganes" in the eleventh letter of the *Provinciales*; *Oeuvres*, V, 328.
66 Thomas Birch (ed.), *A Collection of the State Papers of John Thurloe, Esq.* (1742), I, 618–23.
67 Clark, *Strangers and Sojourners*, pp. 52–53.
68 Godefroi Hermant, *Mémoires*, VI, 575–78.
69 Pascal, *Oeuvres*, XIII, 92–93, sec. 176.
70 [Nouet and Annat], *Answer to the Provinciall Letters*, p. 484.
71 M.V. Hay, *The Jesuits and the Popish Plot*, p. 151.
72 Thomas White, *A Letter to a Person of Honour* (1659), To the Reader.
73 Ibid., pp. 13–14.
74 [Nouet and Annat], *Answer to the Provinciall Letters*, p. 485.
75 Clark, *Strangers and Sojourners*, pp. 226–27.
76 C.-A. Sainte-Beuve, *Port-Royal*, III, 223n.
77 [Daniel], *Discourses of Cleander and Eudoxe*, To the Reader.
78 Charles Dodd (pseud. for Hugh Tootell), *The Church History of England, From the Year 1500, to the Year 1688. Chiefly with regard to Catholicks . . .* (1737–42), III, 519.
79 Pasquier Quesnel, *Correspondance*, ed. Le Roy, II, 267–69, 272–74.
80 Hilaire Belloc, *Pascal's 'Provincial Letters,'* p. 13.
81 For example, a new translation of the *Provinciales* was published in 1816, in answer to the restoration of the Jesuits as an order; while several translations appeared in the mid-nineteenth century, when fears arising from the growing influence of the Oxford Movement and the re-establishment of a Catholic hierarchy were at their height. Among anti-Catholic literature appearing at that time was *Cases of Conscience: or, Lessons in Morals . . . Extracted from the Moral Theology of the Romish Clergy* (London, 1851), by 'Pascal the Younger.'

CHAPTER TWO

1 This letter, dated February 17, 1648, is printed in Pascal, *Oeuvres*, II, 212–14.
2 Ibid., VIII, 255.
3 The possibility of Pascal having been influenced by Hobbes has been discussed by Gilbert Chinard, *En lisant Pascal*, pp. 35–82.
4 Pascal, *Oeuvres*, VIII, 251–52.
5 Isaac Barrow, *Theological Works*, ed. Napier, IX, 111–19.
6 Henry Oldenburg, *Correspondence*, ed. Hall and Hall, I, 234–35. In another letter, ibid., 225, Oldenburg referred to the friendship he had made with Pascal.

7 For details of the competition, see Pascal, *Oeuvres*, VII, 337–47; VIII, 15–19.

8 A fragment of Pascal's reply is printed with comment, ibid., VIII, 133–42. Wren's son, Christopher, in his *Parentalia: or, Memoirs of the Family of the Wrens* (1750), pp. 242–43, listed among his father's papers letters to and from Pascal and a letter from Hobbes on Pascal's published solution, as well as that to Carcavy. If the description of the last was correct, it would seem the original problem was also sent to the churchman and mathematician, Seth Ward.

9 Pascal, *Oeuvres*, VIII, 204.

10 Ibid., 155–78.

11 Wallis' vigorous complaints of his treatment in the competition are mostly given in the preface to *Tractatus Duo. Prior. De Cycloide . . .*, and he repeated his charges in a treatise following addressed to the Dutch physicist, Huygens; John Wallis, *Opera Mathematicorum* (1693 – 99), I, 489 – 569. See also his correspondence with Huygens in Christiaan Huygens, *Oeuvres complètes*, III, 307–308, 519–20.

12 Huygens, *Oeuvres*, II, 364–65, 535; III, 56. The *Lettres de A. Dettonville* were published first separately and then in collected form during the winter of 1658–59: see Pascal, *Oeuvres*, VIII, 247–88, 325–84; IX, 1–149, 187–204.

13 Huygens, *Oeuvres*, III, 57, 85 – 87, 126 – 27. For a study of Pascal's rôle in the dispute, see Ernest Jovy, *Pascal inédit*, I, 462 – 561; and more briefly with respect to Wallis, J.F. Scott, *The Mathematical Work of John Wallis, D.D., F.R.S.*, pp. 151–55.
    Mention may here be made that, in the nineteenth century, French scholars were intrigued by the alleged discovery, amid numerous autograph letters of historical interest, of correspondence between Pascal and a wide range of his contemporaries, including practically every scientist of note. Among these letters were 27 to Barrow, 76 to Boyle, 33 to Hobbes, 6 to Hooke, 3 to and 14 from Milton, 176 to and 11 from Newton, 5 to Wallis, and 1 to Wren.
    One of the letters to Newton (who would at the most have been an undergraduate of nineteen) stated, 'Je vous envoye divers problesmes qui ont esté autrefois l'objet de mes préoccupations touchant les lois de l'abstraction [*sic*], afin d'exercer vostre génie,' and offered the advice, 'Travaillez, estudiez; mais que cela se fasse avec modération.' It is not surprising the whole collection was quickly revealed as a clumsy forgery. For an account of the episode, see H. L. Bordier and E. Mabille, *Une fabrique de faux autographes ou récit de l'affaire Vrain Lucas*.

14 Isaac Newton, *Correspondence*, II, 75n; H.W. Turnbull (ed.), *James Gregory Tercentenary Memorial Volume*, p. 91; S.P. Rigaud (ed.), *Correspondence of Scientific Men of the Seventeenth Century*, I, 119–20, 123.

15 Rigaud, *Correspondence of Scientific Men*, I, 139, 186; II, 459, 533. For the *Traité du triangle arithmétique*, see Pascal, *Oeuvres*, III, 433–598.

16 Oldenburg, *Correspondence*, III, 237.

17 Rigaud, *Correspondence of Scientific Men*, II, 5, 454−56; also I, 122, for a similar example.

18 Oldenburg, *Correspondence*, II, 480; IV, 390−91. A similar, but apparently quite original machine, made by Samuel Morland, was the subject of some exchange of information between Oldenburg and his chief French correspondent, Henri Justel, in 1668.

19 Oldenburg's interest in further works by Pascal, first expressed in 1668 (ibid., IV, 321−22), continued for several years; in 1675, Leibniz informed him that he had hopes of manuscripts being found (Wallis, *Opera Mathematicorum*, III, 620). In 1670, Collins wrote Gregory that he had heard of a fuller, second edition of the *Traité du triangle arithmétique* having been printed (Turnbull, *James Gregory Tercentenary Memorial Volume*, p. 138).

20 Rigaud, *Correspondence of Scientific Men*, I, 186−87.

21 Newton, *Correspondence*, I, 341n.

22 Rigaud, *Correspondence of Scientific Men*, II, 14−15.

23 Pascal had published his *Expériences nouvelles touchant le vuide* (*Oeuvres*, II, 53−76) in 1647, and his account of the famous experiment the following year at the Puy de Dôme shortly after it had taken place (ibid., 363−73). His contributions to science have been defined and reviewed by Isabel Leavenworth, *A Methodological Analysis of the Physics of Pascal*.

24 Boyle, *Works*, ed. Birch, I, 14. For an account of the relationship of Boyle's research into air pressure to that of Pascal and others, see J. B. Conant (ed.), *Robert Boyle's Experiments in Pneumatics*.

25 Boyle, *Works*, I, 151−56,

26 Hobbes had based the views in his *Dialogus Physicus* (1661) partly upon certain misunderstandings, and partly upon his belief that a subtle matter filled all of space. Boyle replied with *An Examen of Mr. T. Hobbes his Dialogus Physicus de Natura Aëris* in 1662 (*Works*, I, 186−242). Boyle gave a brief description of Pascal's experiment with the bladder in his defence against Line, ibid., 154.

27 Henry Power, *Experimental Philosophy, In Three Books: Containing New Experiments Microscopical, Mercurial, Magnetical* (1664), pp. 96 − 98, 104, 116, 131−32.

28 For the *Traitez*, see Pascal, *Oeuvres*, III, 143−292. This work has been translated by I. H. B. and A. G. H. Spiers and published as *The Physical Treatises of Pascal*.

29 Huygens, *Oeuvres*, V, 42, 70, 80.

30 Boyle, *Works*, II, 745−46. Pascal's experiment involving a man underwater is described in *Oeuvres*, III, 183−84.

31 See particularly Boyle, *Works*, II, 753, 758−59, 781, 783−84.

32 Ibid., 796−97. For an account of Pascal's original experiment, see *Oeuvres*, III, 189−90.

33 Boyle, *Works*, II, 759, 784.

34 Boyle, for example, writing in 1669 upon Pascal's 'noble attempt' to imitate the Torricellian experiment with water, commented that

subsequent knowledge of the atmosphere's variations had created additional factors for analysis; ibid., III, 209.

35 John Keill, *Introductio ad Veram Physicam*, Preface [p. 6].
36 Boyle, *Works*, v, 684–90. The experiment was carried out by Col. John Windham, assisted by Thomas Nash and John Warner. These papers were eventually published in 1692 as *The General History of the Air designed and begun*.
37 Oldenburg, *Correspondence*, II, 547.
38 John Lough, 'Locke's Reading during his Stay in France (1675–1679),' VIII, 229–58.
39 John Harrison and Peter Laslett, *The Library of John Locke*, pp. 100, 191, 204, 276, 278; J.L. Axtell, 'Locke, Newton and the Two Cultures,' p. 174.
40 Gabriel Bonno, 'Les relations intellectuelles de Locke avec la France (D'après des documents inédits),' XXXVIII, 132.
41 Henri Ollion and T.J. De Boer (eds.), *Lettres inédites de John Locke à ses amis Nicolas Thoynard, Philippe van Limborch et Edward Clarke*, p. 49.
42 John Lough (ed.), *Locke's Travels in France*, 1675–1679, p. 282.
43 See Wolfgang von Leyden, 'Locke and Nicole,' XVI, 41–55. Locke's translation of these three essays by Nicole was first published in 1828; the appearance of a rival translation during the time he was in France probably deterred him from seeking to have his own printed.
44 Bonno, 'Relations intellectuelles de Locke,' 59–62, 244–47.
45 R.I. Aaron and Jocelyn Gibb (eds.), *An Early Draft of Locke's Essay. Together with Excerpts from his Journals*, p. 81. The break in the opening sentence results from Locke having written at that point in shorthand.
46 Bonno, 'Relations intellectuelles de Locke,' 60–61: Pascal, *Oeuvres*, XIII, 155–56, sec. 234 (P.R., ch. xxxi, para. 15); ibid., 111–12, sec. 194 (P.R., ch. i, para. 1). Regarding the marginal note, see von Leyden, 'Locke and Nicole,' 43.
47 Aaron and Gibb, *Early Draft of Locke's Essay*, p. 82: Pascal, *Oeuvres*, XIII, 147, sec. 233 (P.R., ch. vii, para. 1, 2): Bonno, 'Relations intellectuelles de Locke,' 61–62.
48 John Locke, *An Essay Concerning Human Understanding*, ed. Fraser, I, 364–65 (Bk. II, ch. xxi, para. 72).
49 Aaron and Gibb, *Early Draft of Locke's Essay*, pp. 84, 86: Pascal, *Oeuvres*, XII, 73–74, sec. 72 (P.R., ch. xxii).
50 Bonno, 'Relations intellectuelles de Locke,' 59–60.
51 Locke, *Essay*, II, 215–16 (Bk. IV, ch. iii, para. 24).
52 Bonno, 'Relations intellectuelles de Locke,' 246.
53 See discussion, ibid., 246–47.
54 Locke, *Essay*, I, 7: Pascal, *Oeuvres*, XIII, 56–57, sec. 139 (P.R., ch. xxvi, para. 1).
55 Locke, *Essay*, I, 10. This phrase occurs near the end of the sixteenth letter; Pascal, *Oeuvres*, VI, 292. It was, however, not wholly original.
56 For a discussion of this and some other general similarities, see R.I.

Aaron, *John Locke*, p. 300; also D. G. James, *The Life of Reason: Hobbes, Locke, Bolingbroke*, pp. 111−14.

57 Locke, *Essay*, I, 199−200 (Bk. II, ch. x, para. 9). For Mme. Perier's reference to Pascal's memory, see Pascal, *Oeuvres*, I, 99; for Nicole's eulogy of Pascal, see ibid., x, 314−16.

58 Voltaire, *Oeuvres complètes*, ed. Moland, XXXI, 11−12.

59 Francis Atterbury, *Sermons and Discourses on several Subjects and Occasions* (1761), II, xxxix−xi : Locke, *Essay*, I, 351−52 (Bk. II, ch. xxi, para. 56): Pascal, *Oeuvres*, XIII, 132, sec. 219 (P.R., ch, xxix, para. 43): ibid., 103, sec. 194 (P.R., ch. i, para. 1). The translation from Pascal would appear to be Atterbury's own.

60 Quoted in Clark, *Strangers and Sojourners at Port Royal*, p. 127.

61 Robert Hooke, *Diary*, 1672−1680, ed. Robinson and Adams, pp. 146, 148; *Bibliotheca Hookiana*, p. 32.

62 Bodleian Library, *MS Rawl. D. 878*, fols. 39 − 59.

63 Dugald Butler, *The Life and Letters of Robert Leighton*, pp. 591−92: N. J. D. White, *A Catalogue of Books . . . in Archbishop Marsh's Library, Dublin*, p. 142: *Bibliotheca Burnetiana*, p. 39.

64 Olivier Leroy, *A French Bibliography of Sir Thomas Browne*, p. 88.

65 Among the numerous comparisons made between Browne and Pascal are those by Walter Pater, *Appreciations. With an Essay on Style*, pp. 136−38; Sir Edmund Gosse, *Sir Thomas Browne*, pp. 65−67; Olivier Leroy, *Le Chevalier Thomas Browne*, pp. 120−26, 153−55, 189−90; W.P. Dunn, *Sir Thomas Browne: A Study in Religious Philosophy*, pp. 53, 172.

66 R. W. Ladborough, 'Pepys and Pascal,' x, 133−39: Pascal, *Oeuvres*, XII, 9−16, sec. 1, 2 (P.R., ch. xxxi, para. 2).

67 *The Petty-Southwell Correspondence*, 1676−1687, ed. Lansdowne, pp. 148−49, 152, 155.

68 Sir William Petty, *The Petty Papers*, ed. Lansdowne, II, 198−99.

69 *Petty-Southwell Correspondence*, pp. 158−59. For a discussion of this and other references to Pascal in the correspondence, see Lord Edmond Fitzmaurice, *The Life of Sir William Petty*, 1623−1687, pp. 299−301.

70 *Petty-Southwell Correspondence*, pp. 165, 169.

71 Ibid., pp. 172−73.

72 Ibid., pp. 192, 208.

73 *Bibliotheca Rayana*, p. 29; *Bibliotheca Digbeiana*, p. 97. Ray owned a copy of the first English edition of the *Lettres provinciales*, and Digby the first of Evelyn's two translations of Jansenist works. In addition to the *Pensées* already mentioned, Hooke's library contained the *Lettres de A. Dettonville*, the *Traité du triangle arithmétique*, and two editions of the *Lettres provinciales* (London, 1658, and Cologne, 1669); *Bibliotheca Hookiana*, pp. 17, 19, 51, and appendix, p. 11. Hooke also recorded in 1678 purchasing the second edition of 'Paschalls Hydrostaticks' (*Diary*, pp. 355, 364).

74 Oldenburg, *Correspondence*, II, 311−12.

CHAPTER THREE

1 Blaise Pascal, *Monsieur Pascall's Thoughts, Meditations, and Prayers* . . . ,trans. Joseph Walker (London, 1688), [title-page]. The second of the supplements, originally written as were all of them under the pseudonym of Dubois de la Cour, had already been published in translation as *An Excellent Discourse Proving the Divine Original, and Authority of the Five Books of Moses* (1682). The translator, who knew of both the *Pensées* and the discourse upon them, was apparently William Lorimer.

2 [M. A. de la Bastide], *An Answer To the Bishop of Condom's Book; Entituled, An Exposition of the Doctrin of the Catholick Church, upon Matters of Controversie*, [trans. Joseph Walker] [1676]. This book also appeared in a London edition; see Edward Arber (ed.), *The Term Catalogues, 1668–1709 A.D.* . . ., I, 256.

3 *News for the Curious; A Treatise of Telescopes* . . . , trans. Joseph Walker (1684); Matthieu de Larroque, *The History of the Eucharist*, trans. Joseph Walker (1684). See also Arber, *Term Catalogues*, II, 73, 81. *News for the Curious* was also published in another edition that year in London as *Astronomy's Advancement;* ibid., II, 84.

4 [C. Vischard de Saint Réal], *Caesarion, or Historical, Political, and Moral Discourses*, trans. Joseph Walker (1685). See also Arber, *Term Catalogues*, II, 149.

5 *Monsieur Pascall's Thoughts* (1688), Epistle Dedicatory.

6 [De la Bastide] *An Answer to the Bishop of Condom's Book*, Epistle Dedicatory.

7 De Larroque, *History of the Eucharist*, Epistle Dedicatory.

8 *Monsieur Pascall's Thoughts* (1688), Epistles Dedicatory.

9 De Larroque, *History of the Eucharist*, Epistle Dedicatory.

10 [Saint Réal], *Caesarion*, Epistle Dedicatory.

11 *News for the Curious* . . . (1684), Epistle Dedicatory.

12 *Monsieur Pascall's Thoughts* (1688), Epistle Dedicatory to *A Discourse upon Monsieur Pascall's Thoughts,* etc. The quotation from Donne would appear to have been drawn from his poem *Metempsychosis,* especially stanzas VI and XXIII–XXXI; John Donne, *Complete Poetry,* ed. Shawcross, pp. 307–29. The reference has been briefly discussed by Pierre Janelle, 'Pascal et l'Angleterre,' p. 163.

13 *Monsieur Pascall's Thoughts* (1688), Epistle Dedicatory.

14 N. Hodgson and C. Blagden, 'The Notebook of Thomas Bennet and Henry Clements (1686–1719); With some Aspects of Book Trade Practice,' VI, 37, 39.

15 [William Newton], *The Life of the Right Reverend Dr. White Kennett, Late Lord Bishop of Peterborough* (1730), p. 61.

16 Quoted in G.V. Bennett, *White Kennett, 1660 – 1728, Bishop of Peterborough*, p. 255. That study and the article on Basil Kennett in the *Dictionary of National Biography* have provided much of the foregoing information. In Basil's case, the surname was usually spelt with one 't,' but, since his brother White and other members of the family

wrote 'Kennett,' that version has seemed preferable here.

17 Blaise Pascal, *Thoughts on Religion, and Other Subjects* [trans. Basil Kennett] (London, 1704), Preface of the Translator.

18 Basil Kennett, *Sermons Preached on Several Occasions, to a Society of British Merchants, in Foreign Parts* (1715), p. 65; Pascal, *Oeuvres*, XIII, 421, sec. 530 (P.R., ch. xxviii, para. 44; Kenn., pp. 279–80).

19 Kennett, *Sermons*, pp. 356–57; Pascal, *Oeuvres*, XIV, 129–31, sec. 692 (P R., ch. xiii, para. 17, 18; Kenn., pp. 114 – 15).

20 The edition of 1704 continued to be advertised for several years, and, in March 1715, Henry Clements, who had succeeded to Thomas Bennet's bookselling business, purchased ten copies through subscription (Hodgson and Blagden, 'Notebook,' 168). Such evidence must indicate a steady demand for Kennett's translation.

21 For the editing committee's preface, see Pascal, *Oeuvres*, XII, clxxx–cxcix; for Mme. Perier's biography of Pascal, see ibid., I, 35–121.

22 Louis Moréri, *The Great Historical, Geographical and Poetical Dictionary* (1694), II [article, 'Paschal (Blaise)'].

23 Louis Moréri, *The Great Historical, Geographical, Genealogical and Poetical Dictionary* (1701), II [article, 'Paschal (Blaise)'].

24 L. P. Courtines, *Bayle's Relations with England and the English*, pp. 154–55.

25 Pierre Bayle, *An Historical and Critical Dictionary* (1710), IV, 2464–71.

26 Jeremy Collier, *Essays upon several Moral Subjects: Part III* (1702), pp. 79–80.

27 *Spectator* [by Joseph Addison, Richard Steele, and others], ed. Bond, I, 478–79; Pascal, *Oeuvres*, XIII, 52–65, 69–70, sec. 139, 143 (P.R., ch. xxvi, para. 1, 2, 3; Kenn., pp. 217–18, 223–26).

28 [Alexander Pope and others], *Memoirs of the Extraordinary Life, Works, and Discoveries of Martinus Scriblerus*, ed. Kerby-Miller, pp. 107 – 108. The membership of the Scriblerus Club also included Congreve, Atterbury, Lord Oxford, and Gay.

29 George Berkeley, *Works*, ed. Luce and Jessop, VI, 28. See also Pascal, *Oeuvres*, I, 98.

30 Edward Jesup, *The Lives of Picus and Pascal, Faithfully Collected from the most Authentick Accounts of them*, [Title-page].

31 D. A. Stauffer, *The Art of Biography in Eighteenth Century England*, I, 467; II, 134. For all the apparent similarities between Pico and Pascal, it is odd in one respect that Jesup should have combined their biographies. Pascal described Pico's thesis, *De omni scibili*, as having a title 'qui crève les yeux,' and such inevitably inadequate attempts to embrace the whole of knowledge as 'fastueux' (Pascal, *Oeuvres*, XII, 81–82, sec. 72). These remarks were not likely to have been known to Jesup, however, as they are not in the Port Royal *Pensées*.

32 Jesup, *Lives of Picus and Pascal*, Dedication to *The Life of the Celebrated Monsieur Pascal* . . . .

33 Ibid., Preface to *The Life of the Celebrated Monsieur Pascal* . . . .

34   Ibid.; see also Pierre Bayle, *Oeuvres diverses* (1727–31), I, 194–95.
     For the advertisement referred to, see Blaise Pascal, *Thoughts on
     Religion, And other Curious Subjects*, trans. Basil Kennett (London,
     1727), publisher's notice following p. 315. The place of the *Nouvelles
     de la république des lettres* in English literature has been discussed by
     Courtines, *Bayle's Relations with England*, pp. 62–71.
35   Jesup, *Lives of Picus and Pascal*, Preface to *The Life of the Celebrated
     Monsieur Pascal* ....
36   Ibid. The original Latin epitaph, for convenience, is given in the
     Appendix, note 5; see also Pascal, *Oeuvres*, X, 312–13. It was written
     by Pascal's friend Aimonius Proust de Chambourg, Professor of Law
     at the University of Orléans.
37   Jesup, *Lives of Picus and Pascal. The Comparison between Picus and
     Monsieur Pascal*, pp. 87–92.

CHAPTER FOUR

1   Blaise Pascal, *Pensées de M. Pascal sur la religion et sur quelques autres
    sujets* (Paris, 1678); an authoritative account of the very complex
    story of the *Pensées* has been given by Louis Lafuma, *Histoire des
    Pensées de Pascal, 1656 – 1952*. For a list of the numerous editions,
    see also Albert Maire, *Bibliographie générale des oeuvres de Blaise Pascal*,
    vol. IV.
2   Condorcet's comments on the text of his edition together with his
    Eloge de Pascal appear in Marquis de Condorcet, *Oeuvres*, ed.
    O'Connor and Arago, III, 567–662. Of special interest is that edition
    of Condorcet's version of the *Pensées* published in 1778, with notes
    by Voltaire.
3   Blaise Pascal, *Oeuvres*, ed. Charles Bossut (1779), vol. II. Bossut
    divided the *Pensées* into two sections, the first dealing with
    philosophy, morals, and *belles-lettres*, and the second with matters of
    religion.
4   Victor Cousin, 'Rapport à l'Académie française sur la nécessité
    d'une nouvelle édition des Pensées de Pascal.'
5   Blaise Pascal, *Pensées, fragments et lettres*, ed. Prosper Faugère.
6   For Brunschvicg's version, see Pascal, *Oeuvres*, vols. XII–XIV. Other
    leading editions in accordance with similar principles have been by
    Havet (1852), Gazier (1907), and Strowski (1921). For a survey of the
    approaches taken by the various editors, see Sister Marie Louise
    Hubert, *Pascal's Unfinished Apology*, pp. 1–25.
7   Blaise Pascal, *Pensées sur la religion et sur quelques autres sujets*, ed.
    Louis Lafuma (1951). Chevalier (1925), Souriau (1933), and Stewart
    (1950) are recent editors who have referred to Pascal's outline.
8   These details are taken from the 1704 edition of Kennett's transla-
    tion.

9 The changes made in the text of the *Pensées* by the Port Royal committee have been carefully noted by Lafuma in his edition of the *Penseés*. A compelling call for a detailed analysis of the structure, contents, and style of the Port Royal *Pensées* and of the philosophy Port Royal's alterations created has been made by M.M. Vamos, 'Pascal's *pensées* and the Enlightenment: the Roots of a Misunderstanding,' xcvii, 7−145. The substantial comparison given there of the leading differences between the Port Royal edition and the *Pensées* of today develops certain material and views contained in Vamos, *Pascal's Pensées in England, 1670 − 1776*. The Port Royal edition eventually contained 443 fragments, Brunschvicg enumerating 924 and Lafuma 991 altogether.

10 Pascal, *Oeuvres*, xiii, 127, sec. 206.

11 An outstanding example of Walker's mistakes occurs on p. 81 of his translation, when he turned ' . . . qu'ils [les Juifs] sont forméz exprés pour estre les heraults de ce grand avenement' into 'they are made on purpose to be the Hero's of this great design' (P.R., ch. viii, para. 1). Elsewhere, regarding Pascal's wager, he chose to see 'un infini' as 'an Infinite Being' instead of infinity, and several times robbed arguments of their greatest emphases by reducing key phrases to platitudes or mistranslating fundamental grammatical constructions.

12 Lord Forbes of Pitsligo, *Essays, Moral and Philosophical, on Several Subjects* (1734), pp. 155n, 165.

13 Voltaire, *Letters concerning the English Nation* (1741), pp. 199n, 207n, 222n, 232n. It is ironic that 'R.E.M.' produced the best English version then available of those fragments Voltaire had selected, placing them side by side with examples of Voltaire's scorn for their author.

14 Blaise Pascal, *Thoughts on Religion, and Other Important Subjects*, [trans. Thomas Chevalier] (London, 1803), pp. 70−71; see also Kennett's translation of the *Pensées* (1704), p. 185.

15 See Pascal, *Oeuvres*, xiii, 52, n.3, with regard to the authorship of certain passages on diversions appearing in the Port Royal edition which were familiar to English readers of the eighteenth century.

16 For instance, Louis Charlanne in *L'influence française en Angleterre au* xviie *siècle*, pp. 340−41, commented upon the manner in which the *Pensées* as well as the *Lettres provinciales* aroused English interest and admiration; and, in *La vie posthume des Pensées*, Bernard Amoudru considered it an established fact that Pascal had numerous readers, imitators and critics in England (pp. 59−63.)

17 L.I. Bredvold, *The Intellectual Milieu of John Dryden*, p. 119. An adaptation of Pascal's argument of the wager possibly appears in Dryden's *Don Sebastian* (Act I, sc. i), acted and printed in 1690.

18 John Dryden, *Works*, ed. Scott and Saintsbury, xiii, 338: Pascal, *Oeuvres*, xiii, 367−68, sec. 455 (P.R., ch. xxix, para. 18). Fontenelle had criticized Virgil in his *Discours sur l'églogue*. This preface has

often been attributed to Dryden (see discussion in Bredvold, p. 119n), and also to Dr. Knightly Chetwood, Dean of Gloucester, but it seems clear Walsh should be regarded as its author.

19 John Dennis, *The Critical Works*, ed. Hooker, I, 148–49: Pascal, *Oeuvres*, XIII, 324–25, sec. 425 (P.R., ch. xxi, para. 1). Collier's notorious work was entitled *A Short View of the Immorality, and Profaneness of the English Stage* (1698). Interestingly, after allowing for the book's faults, Macaulay was of the opinion it was worthy of great merit: 'To compare Collier with Pascal would indeed be absurd. Yet we hardly know where, except in the *Provincial Letters*, we can find mirth so harmoniously and becomingly blended with solemnity as in the *Short View*. In truth, all the modes of ridicule, from broad fun to polished and antithetical sarcasm, were at Collier's command. On the other hand, he was complete master of the rhetoric of honest indignation'. *Edinburgh Review*, LXXII (1840–41), 521.
It may be noted that Dennis' reference to Pascal here was more incidental than a part of his main contention. Pascal did, in fact, express himself with some hostility towards the theatre, and was regarded at a later date as one of its principal censors. Conceivably, Dennis had some sympathy with Pascal's condemnation of the treatment of love on the stage, for, in *A Large Account of the Taste in Poetry* (1702), he remarked upon the dangerous passions that could be aroused in spectators; Dennis, *Critical Works*, I, 284.

20 Dryden, *Works*, XIII, 339–40.

21 Dennis, *Critical Works*, I, 353: Pascal, *Oeuvres*, XIV, 235, sec. 797 (P.R., ch. xiv, para. 4; Kenn., p. 122).

22 *Pensées* (1678), p. 189: Pascal, *Oeuvres*, XIII, 5–6, sec. 82 (P.R., ch. xxv, para. 7): Jeremy Collier, *Essays upon several Moral Subjects: In Two Parts* (1697), I, 218–19.

23 Collier, ibid., I, 215. For some comments upon the relations between the thought of Pascal and Collier, see Kathleen Ressler, 'Jeremy Collier's Essays,' pp. 226–27, 274–76.

24 Collier, *Essays upon several Moral Subjects: Part III* (1720), pp. 146–47.

25 Jeremy Collier, *Essays upon several Moral Subjects: Part IV* (1725), pp. 178–81. The passage translated by Collier appears in the ninth letter (Pascal, *Oeuvres*, V, 204–206).

26 T.P. Le Fanu, 'Catalogue of Dean Swift's Library in 1715, with an Inventory of his Personal Property in 1742,' vol. XXXVII, Section C, 272; H.H Williams, *Dean Swift's Library*, pp. 4 and 8 of library catalogue facsimile. Swift gave one copy of the *Provinciales* (Cologne, 1669) to his friend, the Rev. Daniel Jackson, the book eventually passing to the Irish statesman and orator, Henry Grattan: *The Rothschild Library*, II, 628.

27 Voltaire, *Oeuvres complètes*, XL, 193.

28 For an investigation of possible relationships between the thought of Pascal and Swift, see Emile Pons, 'Swift et Pascal,' XLV, pp. 135–52;

but in 'Swift et Pascal: note complémentaire,' v, 319–25, Pons admitted his conclusions were not really convincing. Swift's own *Thoughts on Various Subjects* bears little resemblance to Pascal's.

29 *Spectator*, IV, 448 – 53 (No. 545, November 25, 1712); see also Charlanne, *L'influence française en Angleterre au* XVIIe *siècle*, p. 341.

30 *The Ladies Library* (1714), I, 23.

31 Blaise Pascal, *The Life of Mr. Paschal, with his Letters Relating to the Jesuits*, trans. William Andrews (London, 1744), I, Preface to the Reader. The appeal of Pascal's writings to Englishwomen, such as Mrs. Elizabeth Rowe, the mother of the Wesleys, and, especially, Hannah More, will be examined later.

32 *A Catalogue of the Valuable Library of the late celebrated Joseph Addison, Secretary of State, &c* . . . (1799), p. 13.

33 Joseph Addison, *Works*, ed. Hurd and Bohn, IV, 257: Pascal, *Oeuvres*, XIII, 92–93, sec. 176 (P.R., ch. xxiv, para. 14; Kenn., pp. 203–204). A later critic considered the satire on the country gentry which the tales of Sir Roger de Coverley eventually became to have rivalled the standard of the *Lettres provinciales*: *Monthly Magazine*, IX, 3.

34 Addison, *Works*, II, 49–50.

35 *Spectator*, IV, 417–18 (No. 537, November 15, 1712): Pascal, *Oeuvres*, XIII, 316, sec. 418 (P.R., ch. xxiii, para. 7; Kenn., pp. 196–97). Hughes was known to Bishop White Kennett, collaborating with him on a work of English history.

36 *Spectator*, IV, 527 (No. 564, July 7, 1714): Pascal, *Oeuvres*, XIII, 315–16, sec. 417 (P.R., ch. iii, para. 13; Kenn., p. 43).

37 Thomas Gordon, *The Humourist* (1720–25), II, 130–31. The themes Gordon was recalling appear in chapters iii, xxi, and xxii of the Port Royal edition.

38 *Spectator*, IV, 547 (No. 571, July 23, 1714).

39 Ibid., 519 (No. 562, July 2, 1714); III, 431 (No. 381, May 17, 1712).

40 Ibid., Nos. 565, 571, 580, 590; see Bishop Hurd's remarks in Addison, *Works*, V, 103n.

41 H.B. Wright, *Matthew Prior: A Supplement to his Biography*, pp. 173, 261, 264.

42 Matthew Prior, *Literary Works*, ed. Wright and Spears, I, 377–78: Pascal, *Oeuvres*, XII, 70–92, and XIII, 88–90, sec. 72 and 172 (P.R. ch. xxii, and ch. xxiv, para. 12; Kenn., pp. 186–92, and 202–203). Shortly before in this poem [III, 223–24], Prior expressed similar thoughts to Pascal's on hope surmounting experience.

43 Prior, I, 498–99: Pascal, *Oeuvres*, XIII, 215–16, sec. 294 (P.R., ch. xxv, para. 5; Kenn., p. 208). For his essay, 'Opinion,' see Prior, *Literary Works*, I, 586–99: Pascal, *Oeuvres*, XIII, 10, sec. 82 (P.R., ch. xxv, para. 5; Kenn., pp. 207–208). In *Solomon*, Prior had also followed Pascal when he alluded to the tricks distance and perspective play upon the sight [I, 185–88], and man's difficulty in achieving a fixed viewpoint for observing the world:

In Vain We measure this amazing Sphere,
And find and fix it's Centre here or there;
Whilst it's Circumf'rence, scorning to be brought
Ev'n into fancy'd Space, illudes our vanquish'd Thought.   [I, 536–39]

44 Prior, *Literary Works*, I, 513 [III, 480–91]: Pascal, *Oeuvres*, XIII, 52–65, sec. 139 (P.R., ch. xxvi, para. 1, 2, 3; Kenn., pp. 215–35).

45 Prior, *Literary Works*, I, 515–16. Prior's attitudes and dilemmas have been examined by M. K. Spears in four articles: 'The Meaning of Mathew Prior's *Alma*,' XIII, 266–90; 'Matthew Prior's Attitude toward Natural Science,' LXIII, pt. 1, 485–507; 'Some Ethical Aspects of Matthew Prior's Poetry,' XLV, 606–29; 'Matthew Prior's Religion,' XXVII, 159–80.

46 G.A. Aitken, *The Life and Works of John Arbuthnot*, p. 436n. In this edition, both the poem as published and its earlier manuscript form are printed together. The final version has undergone much improvement, conceivably at the suggestions of Pope.

47 L. M. Beattie, *John Arbuthnot, Mathematician and Satirist*, pp. 377, 381. For the *Entretien de Pascal avec Saci*, see Pascal, *Oeuvres*, IV, 23–57.

48 Aitken, *Life and Works of John Arbuthnot*, pp. 438–39.

49 H. N. Fairchild, *Religious Trends in English Poetry*, I, 168; see also discussion in Beattie, p. 381.

50 Aitken, *Life and Works of John Arbuthnot*, p. 439. It is interesting to find Pascal soon appearing again in an essay also entitled 'Know Thyself' in the *Gentleman's Magazine*, reprinted from a recent issue of the *London Journal* and signed 'R. Freeman.' The writer sought to prove the wisdom of his maxim chiefly through illustrations drawn from universal experience, 'as Authority hath very little Weight in the present Age'; and he described the amusing results when a man trained for one position in life suddenly exchanges it for another, such as a magistrate becoming a coachman or a clergyman a bricklayer. Although Freeman treated the subject very differently from Arbuthnot and with no real philosophical scheme, his essay is reminiscent of several reflections in the *Pensées*, and he concluded with an allegorical story from 'the celebrated Mr. Paschal, whose Judgement was no less solid than his Wit was piercing,' upon 'the Condition of the Great, especially Princes, in this World'; *Gentleman's Magazine*, VIII (1738), 354–55. The story was taken from Pascal's first *Discours sur la condition des grands*, published in 1670 by Nicole as part of his *Essais de morale* from records of conversation: Pascal, *Oeuvres*, IX, 359–73. By 1724, five English editions of the *Essais* had appeared.

51 Alexander Pope, *Correspondence*, ed. Sherburn, I, 129; II, 43. When Joseph Spence wrote concerning Pope's *Odyssey* in 1726, he made use of the same quotation from the *Provinciales* (Pascal, *Oeuvres*, VI, 292) in a discussion of the art of clarity and conciseness in writing: 'The great Monsieur Pascal had a particular happiness in compriz-

ing much in a few Words: he had a very Mathematical Turn of Thought; and of all things hated an idle Prolixity. You will be pleas'd with an Excuse of his in a certain Case, where he had been guilty of it: 'Tis in the close of one of his Letters, where he begs his Friend to pardon the unusual length of it, by saying, That he really had not time to make it shorter.' Joseph Spence, *An Essay on Mr. Pope's Odyssey* (1737), p. 275.

52 One wonders how Pope would have received the remark of a contributor to the *Christian Observer*, XIV (1815), 355, that his own youthful productions and those of Abraham Cowley bore comparison with the childhood achievements of Pascal.

53 The sources utilized by Pope have been frequently attributed and discussed; for his indebtedness to French writers, see especially Emile Audra, *L'influence française dans l'oeuvre de Pope*. Leading editions of the *Essay* carry frequent references to the works of other writers; see Alexander Pope, *Works*, ed. Elwin and Courthope, II, 341–456, and Alexander Pope, *An Essay on Man*, ed. Mack. Forthcoming references are to Mack's edition.

54 Pope, *Correspondence*, III, 155, 173. See also discussion in Audra, *L'influence française dans l'oeuvre de Pope*, p. 480.

55 For a fuller account of this controversy, see ibid., pp. 87–107, 481–82; also Pope, *Essay on Man*, pp. xv–xxii. The views of both Crousaz and Silhouette quickly became known in English translation. A general analysis of the early French reactions to the *Essay* has been given by R.G. Knapp, 'The Fortunes of Pope's *Essay on Man* in Eighteenth-century France,' LXXXII.

56 Pope, *Correspondence*, IV, 415; see also Audra, *L'influence française dans l'oeuvre de Pope*, pp. 98–104, for discussion and matters relating to the letter's discovery.

57 Pope, *Essay on Man*, pp. 15–17: Pascal, *Oeuvres*, XII, 70–92, sec. 72 (P.R., ch. xxii, and xxxi, para. 23; Kenn., pp. 186–92, and 348–49). See also Audra, *L'influence française dans l'oeuvre de Pope*, p. 483.

58 Pope, *Essay on Man*, p. 26: Pascal, *Oeuvres*, XIII, 88–90, sec. 172 (P.R., ch. xxiv, para. 12; Kenn., pp. 202–203).

59 Pope, *Essay on Man*, p. 35: Pascal, *Oeuvres*, XIII, 196–99, sec. 267, 268, 270, 273 (P.R., ch. v, para. 1, 2, 3, 4; Kenn., pp. 51–52).

60 Pope, *Essay on Man*, pp. 44–45: Pascal, *Oeuvres*, XIII, 78–79, sec. 72 (P.R., ch. xxii; Kenn., p. 190).

61 Pope, *Essay on Man*, pp. 53–56. The metaphor with Pascalian overtones of an isthmus may well have been coined before the published *Pensées* by Abraham Cowley, in the opening lines of his ode, *Life and Fame*. Addison made use of it in the *Spectator*, V, 18 (No. 590, September 6, 1714), and Prior also in all but name in *Solomon*.

62 John Hawkesworth and others, *The Adventurer* (1756), II, 231–32 (No. 63, June 12, 1753); Joseph Warton, *An Essay on the Genius and Writings of Pope*, II, 77–78.

63 (a) Pascal, *Oeuvres*, XIII, 70–71, sec. 144 (P.R., ch. xxix, para. 21;

Kenn., p. 302). (b) Ibid., xii, 85, sec. 72 (P.R., ch. xxii; Kenn., p.
192). (c) Ibid., xiii, 302, sec. 395 (P.R., ch. xxi, para. 1; Kenn., p.
183). (d) Ibid., 339, sec. 431 (P.R., ch. iii, para. 1; Kenn., p. 35). (e)
Ibid., 290, sec. 381 (P.R., ch. xxv, para. 3; Kenn., p. 205). (f) Ibid.,
346, sec. 434 (P.R., ch. xxi, para. 3; Kenn., p. 185).

64 In August 1713, after he had been attending astronomical lectures
by William Whiston at Button's coffee-house, Pope wrote to Caryll:
'Good God! what an Incongruous Animal is Man? how unsettled in
his best part, his soul; and how changing and variable in his frame of
body? The constancy of the one, shook by every notion, the temperament of the other, affected by every blast of wind. What an April
weather in the mind! In a word, what is Man altogether, but one
mighty inconsistency.' Pope, *Correspondence*, 1, 185–86. A month
later he expressed similar thoughts upon man and his place in the
universe again to Caryll (ibid., 190–91), and in a letter to the
Guardian (No. 169, September 24, 1713): Alexander Pope, *Prose
Works*, ed. Ault, 1, 137–40. For the influence of contemporary
astronomy upon aspects of Pope's thought, see Marjorie Nicolson
and G.S. Rousseau, *'This Long Disease, My Life'; Alexander Pope and the
Sciences*, pp. 133–235.

65 Audra, *L'influence française dans l'oeuvre de Pope*, pp. 481–84.
66 Pope, *Essay on Man*, pp. 60–64, 82–83: Pascal, *Oeuvres*, xiii,
215–16, sec. 294 (P.R., ch. xxv, para. 5; Kenn., p. 208).
67 Pope, *Essay on Man*, pp. 87–88: Pascal, *Oeuvres*, xiii, 307, sec. 425
(P.R., ch. xxiv, para. 3; Kenn., p. 199); ibid., xii, 52–65, sec. 139
(P.R., ch. xxvi, para. 1, 2, 3; Kenn., pp. 215–35).
68 Pope, *Essay on Man*, p. 99: Pascal, *Oeuvres*, xiii, 261–63, sec. 347
(P.R., ch. xxiii, para. 6; Kenn., p. 196).
69 Pope, *Essay on Man*, pp. 134–35: Pascal, *Oeuvres*, xiii, 88–90, sec.
172 (P.R., ch. xxiv, para. 12; Kenn., pp. 202–203).
70 Pope, *Essay on Man*, pp. 157–58: Pascal, *Oeuvres*, xiii, 141–55, sec.
233 (P.R., ch. vii, para. 1, 2; Kenn., pp. 58–65).
71 For some comments upon the differences between Pope and Pascal,
see Harry Ransom, 'Riddle of the World: a note upon Pope and
Pascal,' xlvi, 306–11; Austin Warren, *Alexander Pope as Critic and
Humanist*, pp. 213–14; E. L. Tuveson, 'An Essay on Man and "The
Way of Ideas",' xxvi, 378n. For similarities from a Catholic standpoint, see F.B. Thornton, *Alexander Pope: Catholic Poet*, pp. 208–21.
72 Pascal, *Oeuvres*, xii, 86, sec. 72 (P.R., ch. xxii; Kenn., p. 192).
73 Ransom, 'Riddle of the World,' 306–307.
74 Viscount Bolingbroke, *Works*, viii, 465.
75 Voltaire, *Oeuvres complètes*, xxii, 178; Voltaire was recalling a criticism of Pascal he had made in 1739 (ibid., xxii, 44). The passage in
the *Essay* he approved so wholeheartedly in contrast to Pascal's views
consisted of the following lines (Pope, *Essay on Man*, pp. 17–18):
   Presumptuous Man! the reason wouldst thou find,
Why form'd so weak, so little, and so blind!

First, if thou canst, the harder reason guess,
Why form'd no weaker, blinder, and no less! [1, 35–38]

Voltaire's remarks were noted by Warton, *Essay on the Genius and Writings of Pope*, 11, 62–63; see also G.R. Havens, 'Voltaire's Marginal Comments upon Pope's *Essay on Man*,' XLIII, 429–39.

76 In the introduction to his edition of *The Fable of the Bees*, F.B. Kaye has seen Mandeville as having been conversant with Pascal's anti-rationalism and his analysis of human selfishness: Bernard Mandeville, *The Fable of the Bees*, ed. Kaye, 1, lxxix-xc. Lines from Thomson's poem *Summer* (333–38) may recall Pascal's observations upon the two extremes between which man is placed: James Thomson, *Complete Poetical Works*, ed. Robertson, p. 65.

77 Spence, *Essay on Mr. Pope's Odyssey*, p. 275.

78 The shifting composition of Pascal's appreciative English audience is well illustrated by the changing firms who chose to reissue Kennett's translation of the *Pensées*. When the edition of 1727 appeared, it was jointly published by Jacob Tonson and John Pemberton, the latter of whom had recently produced Jesup's *Lives of Picus and Pascal*. Pemberton was also the publisher for the Society for the Propagation of the Gospel, and brought out the third edition alone. In 1741, it was Pemberton and Richard Ware, whose business specialized in bibles, testaments, and books of prayers, who ventured upon a fourth edition.

CHAPTER FIVE

1 Charles Gildon, *The Deist's Manual* (1705), p. x: Pascal, *Oeuvres*, XIII, 197–99, sec. 270, 273 (P.R., ch. v, para. 3, 4; Kenn., p. 52). Gildon's work is briefly discussed in John Hunt, *Religious Thought in England from the Reformation to the End of the Last Century*, 11, 231. For a survey of the varieties of deism and its exponents, Sir Leslie Stephen's *History of English Thought in the Eighteenth Century* remains indispensable.

2 John Tillotson, *Works* (1728), pp. 20, 31; for comment, see H.G. van Leeuwen, *The Problem of Certainty in English Thought*, 1630–1690, pp. 45–46. Some antecedents of the argument of the wager have been investigated by Léon Blanchet, 'L'attitude religieuse des jésuites et les sources du pari de Pascal,' XXVI, 477–516, 617–47. Knowledge of the argument in an earlier form doubtless explains Tillotson's use of it, also its appearance in Sir John Denham's poem, 'Cato Major. Of Old age,' written in the sixteen-sixties; Denham, *Poetical Works*, ed. Banks, pp. 224–25.

The same premises were also being utilized and extended for

other purposes. The mathematician John Craig, who produced his *Theologiae Christianae Principia Mathematica* in 1699, calculated that the ratio of happiness provided in another world to that obtainable here was infinite. Assuming the older the evidence, the more likely it is to be false, he estimated the odds in favour of the truth of the gospel narrative at present stood as equal to that represented by the statement of twenty-eight contemporary witnesses; but, by the year 3144, Craig considered any such grounds for belief would have entirely disappeared.

3 Sir William Dawes, *An Anatomy of Atheisme* (1693): George Berkeley, *Works*, VII, 12 – 13: Pascal, *Oeuvres*, XIII, 147, sec. 233 (P.R., ch. vii, para. 1, 2; Kenn., pp. 57 – 65). Berkeley's familiarity with Mme. Perier's account of Pascal's life has already been mentioned, and it is very likely he possessed copies of the *Lettres provinciales* (Cologne, 1657) and the *Pensées* (Paris, 1679); see René Maheu, 'Le catalogue de la bibliothèque des Berkeley,' III, 187.

4 Earl of Shaftesbury, *Characteristics of Men, Manners, Opinions, Times, etc.*, ed. Robertson, I, 26 – 27.

5 Pascal, *Thoughts on Religion* (London, 1704), Preface of the Translator.

6 Anthony Collins, *The Scheme of Literal Prophecy Considered* (1727), p. 344: Pascal, *Oeuvres*, XIV, 140 – 42, sec. 706, 710 (P.R., ch. xv, para. 1,2; Kenn., pp. 125 – 26). Collins owned the four-language edition of the *Provinciales* (Cologne, 1684), two editions of Daniel's *Entretiens de Cléandre et d'Eudoxe* (1697 and 1700) and a subsequent defence of the *Provinciales* (Delft, 1700), and the *Pensées* (Amsterdam, 1688); *Bibliotheca Antonii Collins* (1731), II, 34, 111, 131.

7 Edmund Law, *Considerations on the Theory of Religion* (1755), p. 132n: Pascal, *Oeuvres*, XIV, 204, sec. 750 (P.R., ch. xvi, para. 8; Kenn., p. 144).

8 John Byrom, *Private Journal and Literary Remains*, ed. Parkinson, II, pt. 1, 96–97. Hartley is best known for his *Observations on Man* (1749), in which he sought to displace the soul as an influence on the formation of ideas in favour of their development through the association of experiences.

9 Joseph Butler, *Works*, ed. Gladstone, I, 5.

10 Some leading comparisons are to be found in Mark Pattison, 'Tendencies of Religious Thought in England, 1685 – 1750,' pp. 286 – 87; Stephen, *History of English Thought*, I, 260; E.C. Mossner, *Bishop Butler and the Age of Reason*, pp. 148, 233 – 35.

11 Byrom, *Private Journal*, II, pt. 1, 99.

12 Mossner, *Bishop Butler*, p. 233.

13 Stephen, *History of English Thought*, I, 260.

14 William Warburton, *Works*, VI, 40 – 41: Pascal, *Oeuvres*, XIII, 226, sec. 302 (P.R., ch. xxxi, para. 11; Kenn., pp. 343 – 44).

15 [William Warburton], *Letters from a Late Eminent Prelate to One of his Friends*, p. 97; Warburton, *Works*, IX, 260.

16 Warburton, *Works*, I, 77. Hurd's preface, where these comments are

found, was written for the first collection of Warburton's writings, published between 1788 and 1794.

17 See his series of sermons, 'An Introduction to the Study of the Prophecies concerning the Christian Church'; Richard Hurd, *Works*, v, 62, 70, 106, 134, 147. In a sermon preached in 1769, Hurd also made use of the argument of the wager (ibid., vi, 300–301), and in 1773 referred to Pascal's remarks on the self-effacement of biblical writers (ibid., vii, 185 – 86).

18 Joseph Addison, *Works*, v, 103n. The material from which Hurd's edition of Addison's writings was published was found among his papers on his death in 1808.

19 C.J. Abbey and J.H. Overton, *The English Church in the Eighteenth Century*, i, 351 – 52; see also C.J. Abbey, *The English Church and its Bishops*, 1700 – 1800, i, 3 – 4.

20 For his *Remarques*, see Voltaire, *Oeuvres complètes*, xxii, 27–61; xxxi, 1–40. See also Blaise Pascal, *Eloge et Pensées. Nouvelle édition commentée, corrigée et augmentée par M. de* *** [Voltaire] (Paris, 1778). For a short account of the range of Voltaire's attacks on Pascal, see David Finch, *La critique philosophique de Pascal au* xviiie *siècle*, pp. 13–38. Leading studies of the nature of the conflict include Jean-Raoul Carré, *Réflexions sur l'anti-Pascal de Voltaire*, and Mina Waterman, *Voltaire, Pascal and Human Destiny*.

21 Voltaire, *Oeuvres complètes*, xxxi, 4.

22 Waterman, *Voltaire, Pascal and Human Destiny*, p. 14.

23 Voltaire, *Oeuvres complètes*, xxii, 51.

24 Ernst Cassirer, *The Philosophy of the Enlightenment*, pp. 144–45.

25 For the *Lettres philosophiques*, see Voltaire, *Oeuvres complètes*, xxii, 75 – 187.

26 Some of the many contributors to this debate have been: Gustave Desnoiresterres, *Voltaire et la société au* xviiie *siècle*, ii, 27–44; Gustave Lanson, 'Voltaire et les Lettres Philosophiques,' iv, 367 – 86; Lucien Foulet, *Correspondance de Voltaire*, 1726–1729; Archibald Ballantyne, *Voltaire's Visit to England*, 1726–1729, pp. 165–67; André Bellessort, *Essai sur Voltaire*, p. 76; Voltaire, *Notebooks*, ed. Besterman; I.O. Wade, *The Intellectual Development of Voltaire*.

27 Voltaire, *Letters concerning the English Nation*, pp. 197 – 255. Lockman (1698 – 1771) translated several other works from French, among them Voltaire's *Henriade* and *Siècle de Louis* xiv.

28 See R.S. Crane, 'The Diffusion of Voltaire's Writings in England, 1750 – 1800,' xx, 261 – 74. The part played by Francklin and Smollett in this edition of Voltaire's *Works* (London, 1761 – 65) appears, however, to have been little more than nominal.

29 Pierre Bayle, *A General Dictionary, Historical and Critical* . . ., ed. Birch and others (London, 1734–41), viii, 172–73. Another translation of the *Dictionnaire* appeared in London between 1734 and 1738, but the entry on Pascal had no real difference from that in the translation of 1710.

30 Ibid., 172; see also Voltaire, *Oeuvres complètes*, xxii, 27 – 28, 33 – 34.

31 The extracts from the *Remarques* appearing in the *General Dictionary* differ in wording from those in the second English edition of Voltaire's *Lettres philosophiques*. The style is freer, resembling that of the other twenty-four chapters of the English *Lettres*; in 1741, 'R.E.M.' followed the French original more literally. One may imagine that Lockman's familiarity with Voltaire's writings caused him to make a partial translation for the *Dictionary* from material newly available to him.

32 L.P. Courtines, *Bayle's Relations with England*, p. 154.

33 *Encyclopaedia Britannica . . . The Second Edition* (1778–81), VIII, 5896.

34 *A New and General Biographical Dictionary* . . . (1784), X, 192.

35 This quotation comes from the second of Juvenal's *Satires* – lines 38–39 of Housman's edition (Cambridge, 1931) – a work much admired by eighteenth-century English writers.

36 These signed engravings are listed among Vertue's works in Horace Walpole, *Anecdotes of Painting in England*, ed. Dallaway and Wornum, III, 1005. The portrait of Pascal was taken from an engraving by Gerard Edelinck made several years after Pascal's death, and published by Desprez about 1686. It provided the eighteenth century with its standard impression of Pascal's appearance. See Ulysse Moussali, *Le vrai visage de Blaise Pascal*.

37 Thomas Lathbury, *A History of the Nonjurors: Their Controversies and Writings*, pp. 406–407. D.A. Stauffer (*The Art of Biography*, II, 193) has suggested 'W.A.' might be the miscellaneous writer, William Ayre, but Lathbury is quite explicit. Andrews' translation was published by James Bettenham, also a Nonjuror.

38 Pascal, *The Life of Mr. Paschal, with his Letters Relating to the Jesuits* (1744), I, Preface to the Reader. Andrews erroneously believed the earlier English translation to have been the last of all versions in foreign languages, which surely indicates his familiarity only with the reprinted edition of 1679.

39 Paul Kaufman, 'Reading Vogues at English Cathedral Libraries of the Eighteenth Century,' LXVII, 666–67; LXVIII, 123. Idem, *Borrowings from the Bristol Library*, 1773–1784, p. 22.

40 William Cole, *A Journal of my Journey to Paris in the Year 1765*, ed. Stokes, p. 255.

41 [Charles Jenner], *Letters from Altamont in the Capital, to his Friends in the Country* (1767). This work contained thirty-five letters and drew from several French authors.

42 Edward Gibbon, *Autobiography*, pp. 72–73. The other two works Gibbon mentioned were *The Life of Julian* by the Abbé de la Bléterie, and Giannone's *History of Naples*.

43 *The Library of Edward Gibbon*, ed. Keynes, p. 214; see also *The Rothschild Library*, I, 244.

44 G.M. Young, *Gibbon*, pp. 17–18. Young also pointed to another instance in Gibbon's description of the formula of Christ in two

natures as 'this momentous particle (which the memory rather than the understanding must retain)'; ibid., p. 151. For similar examples of irony detected, see G.R. Cragg, *Reason and Authority in the Eighteenth Century*, pp. 152 – 53; and Oliver Elton, *A Survey of English Literature, 1730 – 1780*, II, 299.

5　John Brown, *Essays on the Characteristics of the Earl of Shaftesbury*, pp. 27 – 28; Oliver Goldsmith, *Collected Works*, ed. Friedman, V, 346.

6　Laurence Sterne, *The Life and Opinions of Tristram Shandy, Gentleman*, ed. Saintsbury, pp. 299 – 301. The conversation ended: 'But you forget the great Lipsius, quoth Yorick, who composed a work the day he was born: – They should have wiped it up, said my uncle Toby, and said no more about it.' Sterne owned copies of Andrews' translation of the *Provinciales* and an edition of the *Pensées* in French (Amsterdam, 1701), as well as many other French books: *A Facsimile Reproduction of a Unique Catalogue of Laurence Sterne's Library*, ed. Whibley, pp. 41, 83. Another novelist possessing a number of French works, among them the *Pensées* (Amsterdam, 1700), was Henry Fielding: see the auction catalogue of his library (1755) reproduced in E.M. Thornbury, *Henry Fielding's Theory of the Comic Prose Epic*, p. 171.

47　John Mainwaring, *Memoirs of the Life of the late George Frederick Handel* (1760), pp. 5 – 6; see also discussion in Stauffer, *The Art of Biography*, I, 509 – 14.

48　*Anecdotes of Polite Literature* (1764), I, 21. Jean Baptiste Dubos was the author of *Réflexions critiques sur la poësie et sur la peinture* (Paris, 1719).

49　Adam Fitzadam (pseud. for Edward Moore), *The World* (1763), II, 243 – 49; see also *Spectator*, I, 478 – 79. The author of this piece has been identified as Lord Chesterfield. The continuing influence of the *Spectator* in acquainting English opinion with Pascal cannot be ignored. What other explanation could be given to Edmund Burke's writing, at the age of sixteen, the following words in a letter attempting to console a friend?: 'Paschal tells us that nothing engages men to apply [to] business or diversion, but to drown thought to hinder us [from sin]king into ourselves and seeing what an unhappy and f[oolish] condition we really are–would it be amiss to use this remedy [to] dispell a little of that gloominess that Clouds you . . .'; Edmund Burke, *Correspondence*, ed. Copeland, I, 61. It is unlikely he had singled out this reflection from the *Pensées*.

50　Earl of Chesterfield, *Letters*, ed. Bradshaw, I, 73.

51　A.T. Hazen, *A Catalogue of Horace Walpole's Library*, I, 274; II, 58. Mme. du Deffand wrote to Walpole in 1779 that a nightmare had made her understand Pascal's fears of a chasm seeming to open at his feet—a hallucination, Voltaire claimed, resulting from a carriage accident; but there is no record of this having produced any comment: Horace Walpole, *Correspondence*, ed. Lewis, VII, 116 – 17.

52 Berkeley, *Works*, v, 136.
53 Elizabeth Carter, *A Series of Letters between Mrs. Elizabeth Carter and Miss Catherine Talbot, from the Year* 1741 to 1770 . . . , ed. Pennington, I, 168, 179, 184 – 86: Pascal, *Oeuvres*, XIII, 379, sec. 471 (P.R., ch. xxviii, para. 56; Kenn., p. 285).
54 Carter, I, 188 – 89, 191 – 92. Hannah More later considered Mrs. Carter's High Church views had caused her scrupulously to forebear reading books proceeding from any other quarter: 'She would on no account have read even Doddridge or Pascal, two sins of which, to her great regret, I lived in the constant commission.' William Roberts, *Memoirs of the Life and Correspondence of Mrs. Hannah More*, III, 306.
55 Rudolf Mertz, 'Les amitiés françaises de Hume et le mouvement des idées,' IX, 647 – 51.
56 David Hume, *Essays Moral, Political, and Literary*, ed. Green and Grose, II, 303 – 305.
57 Ibid., 94, 101n.
58 Thomas Percival, *Moral and Literary Dissertations* . . . (1784), pp. 130 – 34. For the editing committee's remarks, see Pascal, *Oeuvres*, XII, cxcvii; Kenn., p. liii. For these extracts from Pascal's *prière pour demander le bon usage des maladies*, see Pascal, *Oeuvres*, IX, 323 – 26; P.R., supplement following ch. xxxi; Kenn., pp. 370 – 75. Percival also mentioned Pascal in another paper, 'On Inconsistency of Expectation, in Literary Pursuits,' listing him with Isaac Watts and Pope as authors whose writing had been impeded by frequent illnesses: *Moral and Literary Dissertations* . . . , p. 187.
59 Joseph Priestley, *Lectures on History and General Policy* (1788), pp. 23 – 24. When Priestley's library was sold after his death in America, it contained the first volume of Andrews' translation of the *Provinciales* and a French edition of 1712, as well as several Port Royal grammars: *Catalogue of the Library of the late Dr. Joseph Priestley*, pp. 31 – 32.
60 *Gentleman's Magazine*, LIX (1789), pt. 2, 899 – 901. The parson and his family are clearly imitated from *The Vicar of Wakefield*.
61 Ibid., pt. 2, 974 – 76.
62 In *The Literary Career of James Boswell, Esq.*, pp. 231 – 32, F.A. Pottle thought it certainly possible that Boswell wrote the two letters, being of the opinion that, if the first stood alone, he would 'unhesitatingly pronounce it Boswell's' on account of its style and Boswell's habit of reproducing sermons at length. The second letter, however, 'is not peculiarly Boswellian,' and he remarked on the inconsistency of the views expressed on Pascal with the praise in the *Life of Johnson*. Two essays (LIV, LV) in Boswell's *London Magazine* series, 'the Hypochondriack,' nevertheless form close parallels in their treatment of religion; and Pottle noted that two other essays appearing in the *Gentleman's Magazine* in 1789, opposing and defending strict Sunday observance, were represented as a correspondence between

'Eusebius' and 'Pascal,' their associations leading him to suspect Boswell was probably the author of them as well. Boswell was in Westmorland in the summer of 1789, and, of course, was a Scots Presbyterian; he also not infrequently contributed to the *Gentleman's Magazine*. A practically identical life of Pascal, omitting the final commentary, appeared the following month in the *New London Magazine*, v (1789), 590 – 92; and a more charitable biography was presented in the *Literary Magazine and British Review*, III, (1789), 241 – 49, in October, with an engraved portrait by Anthony Walker.

53 Lady Mary Wortley Montagu, *Complete Letters*, ed. Halsband, II, 73. Young's French translator, Pierre Le Tourneur, was apparently the first to compare Young's poetry with the *Pensées*, seeing likenesses in 'l'energie, la profondeur, les idées du même ordre, & le même tour d'imagination': Edward Young, *Les nuits*, trans. Le Tourneur (1770), I, xxix–xxxi. Other comparisons have been drawn by Walter Thomas, *Le poète Edward Young*, 1683–1765, and W.J. Courthope, *A History of English Poetry*, v, 297–98.

CHAPTER SIX

1 H.W. Turnbull (ed.), *James Gregory Tercentenary Memorial Volume*, p. 91.

2 Sir George Mackenzie, *Essays upon Several Moral Subjects* (1713), p. 410: Pascal, *Oeuvres*, XIII, 70 – 71, sec. 144 (P.R., ch. xxix, para. 21). In *Religio Stoici* (1663), Mackenzie anticipated Pascal's wager by arguing that belief in God was a far safer course than atheism.

3 See Ruth Clark, *Strangers and Sojourners at Port Royal*, especially pp. 230 – 40.

4 Gilbert Burnet, *History of My Own Time*, ed. Airy, I, 244.

5 Dugald Butler, *Life and Letters of Robert Leighton*, pp. 591 – 92. For a comprehensive survey of the rise and flowering of this Scottish school of mysticism, see G.D. Henderson, *Mystics of the North-East*, pp. 11 – 73.

6 Ibid., pp. 260 – 61: Pascal, *Oeuvres*, XIV, 145 – 46, sec. 712 (P.R., ch. xv, para. 12; Kenn., p. 137).

7 Quoted in Henderson, *Mystics of the North-East*, p. 37. Scottish interest in Mme. Bourignon and Quietism has also been discussed by Henderson in *Religious Life in Seventeenth-Century Scotland*, pp. 220–31.

8 Ramsay's rôle in presenting Fénelon to the world has been examined by Albert Cherel, *Fénelon au XVIIIe siècle en France*, 1715–1820. and, more briefly, by G.D. Henderson, *Chevalier Ramsay*, pp. 67–84.

9 Emile Audra, *L'influence française dans l'oeuvre de Pope*, pp. 82–86; Henderson, *Chevalier Ramsay*, pp. 143 – 44.

10 A.M. Ramsay, *The Life of François Salignac De La Motte Fenelon, Archbishop and Duke of Cambray* (1723), pp. 149 – 50; Historical Manuscripts Commission, *Report on the Laing Manuscripts preserved in the University of Edinburgh*, II, 331. Elsewhere, Ramsay compared Pascal with Bossuet in France, and with Samuel Clarke and Henry More in England, as writers whose style possessed the rare qualities of 'l'Esprit mâle'; *Mémoires pour l'histoire des sciences et des beaux-arts*, XXXV (1735), 698 – 99. See also Henderson, *Chevalier Ramsay*, p. 176, regarding this article's authorship.

11 Lord Forbes of Pitsligo, *Essays, Moral and Philosophical, on Several Subjects*, pp. 252 – 54. The passage quoted by Forbes is from Pascal's letter on the death of his father (*Oeuvres*, II, 550 – 51). Extracts from the letter formed the thirtieth chapter of the Port Royal *Pensées*; see also Kenn., p. 324.

12 Forbes, *Essays*, pp. 263 – 64: Pascal, *Oeuvres*, XIII, 367 – 68, 384 – 85, sec. 455, 477 (P.R., ch. xxix, para. 18, ch. ix, para. 5; Kenn., pp. 299–300, 79).

13 Forbes, *Essays*, p. 309, referring to the third chapter of the Port Royal *Pensées*.

14 Ibid., pp. 321, 361 – 62: Pascal, *Oeuvres*, XIII, 86n (P.R., ch. xxvi, para. 4; Kenn., pp. 233 – 35). Another 'Addition' upon the nature of religion quoted Pascal's aphorism that orthodoxy one side of the Pyrenees may be heresy on the other: Forbes, *Essays*, p. 353.

15 Ibid., p. 23: Pascal, *Oeuvres*, XIII, 128 – 29, sec. 210 (P.R., ch. xxix, para. 44; Kenn., p. 312).

16 Forbes, *Essays*, pp. 114 – 15: Pascal, *Oeuvres*, XIII, 74 – 75, sec. 150 (P.R., ch. xxiv, para. 5; Kenn., p. 199).

17 Forbes, *Essays*, p. 133.

18 Ibid., p. 155: Pascal, *Oeuvres*, XII, 9 – 16, sec. 1,2 (P.R., ch. xxxi, para. 2; Kenn., pp. 335 – 39).

19 Forbes, *Essays*, p. 165: Pascal, *Oeuvres*, XIII, 238 – 39, sec. 319 (P.R., ch. xxix, para. 41; Kenn., p. 311).

20 Forbes, *Essays*, Advertisement from the Publisher.

21 Ibid., p. 132.

22 In Albert Maire, *Bibliographie générale des oeuvres de Blaise Pascal*, II, 363, a translation of the *Lettres provinciales* by Thomas M'Crie is listed as having been published in Edinburgh in 1751; but this is a mistake for an edition appearing a century later.

23 For leading accounts of the party's fortunes, see J.H. Overton, *The Nonjurors. Their Lives, Principles, and Writings*, and Henry Broxap, *The Later Non-Jurors*.

24 John Byrom, *Private Journal and Literary Remains*, I, pt. 2, 449; *A Catalogue of the Library of the late John Byrom, Esq . . .*, p. 170. Byrom's copies of the *Provinciales* are listed as being editions of Cologne (1669) and London (1658), also London (1695) – no doubt a misprint; and, of the *Pensées*, Amsterdam (1684 and 1699) and London (1731), Mme. Perier's life of Pascal appearing in the first of these.

25 Byrom, *Private Journal*, I, pt. 2, 577 – 78.
26 John Byrom, *Poems*, ed. Ward, II, pt. 1, 110 – 12: see also Pascal, *Oeuvres*, I, 101 – 102.
27 Clark, *Strangers and Sojourners*, p. 264; H.A. Talon, *William Law: A Study in Literary Craftsmanship*, p. 22n.
28 J.H. Overton, *William Law, Nonjuror and Mystic*, p.20.
29 J.A. Leger, *L'Angleterre religieuse et les origines du méthodisme: La jeunesse de Wesley*, p. 119.
30 William Law, *A Practical Treatise upon Christian Perfection* (1734), pp. 9 – 10, 13.
31 Neither Overton in his study of Law, nor Stephen Hobhouse, editor of *Selected Mystical Writings of William Law*, mention the works or example of Pascal in their analyses of Law's mysticism.
32 Thomas Hearne, *Remarks and Collections*, ed. Doble and others, x, 74. Hearne went on to observe that the *Pensées* were particularly admired by his friend, John Leake, of St. Mary Hall.
33 The influence of Pascal upon the Wesleys has been discussed, *inter alia*, by Edmond Gounelle, *Wesley et ses rapports avec les français*, pp. 77 – 82; T.E. Brigden, 'Pascal and the Wesleys,' VII, 60 – 63, 84 – 88; Leger, *L'Angleterre religieuse*, pp. 114 – 19; Jean Orcibal, 'Les spirituels français et espagnols chez John Wesley et ses contemporains,' CXXXIX, 50–109, and 'L'originalité théologique de John Wesley et les spiritualités du continent,' CCXXII, 51 – 80.
34 Susannah Wesley, 'Mrs. Wesley's Conference with her Daughter,' p. 39: Pascal, *Oeuvres*, XIII, 199, sec. 273 (P.R., ch. v, para. 3; Kenn., p. 52). Leger has examined in detail Mrs. Wesley's use of the *Pensées*, and shown the closeness of her quotations to passages in Kennett's translation: Leger, *L'Angleterre religieuse, pièces justificatives*, pp. 48 – 52.
35 Susannah Wesley, pp. 24–25: Pascal, *Oeuvres*, XIV, 230–33, sec. 793 (P.R., ch. xiv, para. 1; Kenn., pp. 117 – 21).
36 Henry Moore, *The Life of the Rev. John Wesley*, I, 327: Pascal, *Oeuvres*, XIII, 128 – 29, sec. 210 (P.R., ch. xxix, para. 44; Kenn., p. 312).
37 Leger, *L'Angleterre religieuse*, p. 116.
38 Thomas Jackson, *The Life of the Rev. Charles Wesley*, II, 520.
39 Adam Clarke, *Memoirs of the Wesley Family*, II, 217 – 18. It is worth noting that Samuel died suddenly in November 1739, while John Wesley, despite years of travelling, intense work, and hardships of various kinds, was to live until 1791.
40 Leger, *L'Angleterre religieuse*, p. 116.
41 John Wesley. *Letters*, ed. Telford, I, 76: Pascal, *Oeuvres*, XIV, 19, sec. 571 (P.R., ch. x. para 10, 11, 12; Kenn., p. 91).
42 John Wesley, *Works*, XI, 203 – 37; Maximin Piette, *John Wesley in the Evolution of Protestantism*, p. 544n.
43 Charles Wesley, *Journal*, ed. Jackson, I, 47. For Pascal's prayers, see *Oeuvres*, IX, 319 – 40; P.R., supplement following ch. xxxi; Kenn., pp. 369 – 92.

44 Leger, *L'Angleterre religieuse*, pp. 330 – 31.
45 Charles Wesley, I, 75. Pascal's prayer for conversion would most likely be the fourth of his prayers in times of sickness: *Oeuvres*, IX, 326 – 28; P.R., supplement following ch. xxxi; Kenn., pp. 375ff.
46 Charles Wesley, *Journal*, I, 156.
47 George Whitefield, *Journals*, ed. Murray, pp. 429 – 30.
48 John Wesley, *Letters*, I, 207.
49 J.B. Green, *John Wesley and William Law*, pp. 177 – 94; see also discussion in J.E. Rattenbury, *The Conversion of the Wesleys*, pp. 53 – 60.
50 Quoted in Brigden, 'Pascal and the Wesleys,' 86.
51 John Wesley, *Letters*, II, 152 – 53.
52 John Wesley (ed.), *A Christian Library* (Bristol, 1749 – 55), the *Pensées* appearing in XXIII (1753), 3 – 223. Wesley's project was not very successful in spite of efforts to aid the *Library's* distribution, and realized a financial loss. This was partly owing to many of his marks of deletion having been misunderstood by the printers, thus rendering the collection open to charges of doctrinal errors which he had deliberately tried to avoid. His corrections were incorporated into the second edition (London, 1819–27), the *Pensées* appearing in XIII (1821), 35 – 207. For a short account of Wesley's production of the *Christian Library*, see T.W. Herbert, *John Wesley as Editor and Author*, pp. 25 – 31.
53 John Wesley, *Journal*, ed. Curnock, IV, 55. Apparently Wesley was referring to Voltaire's praise for the *Lettres provinciales*, but some knowledge of his criticism of the *Pensées* is surely implied.
54 John Wesley, *Works*, XIII, 416; see also *Arminian Magazine*, IV (1781), 209, and discussion in T.B. Shepherd, *Methodism and the Literature of the Eighteenth Century*, pp. 130 – 31.
55 John Wesley, *Letters*, VI, 205.
56 *Arminian Magazine*, X (1787), 151 – 53, 207 – 209, 256 – 62, 316 – 19; forming ch. xxvi of the Port Royal *Pensées*.
57 J.S. Simon, *John Wesley and the Advance of Methodism*, p. 85. In Philip Doddridge's *Course of Lectures on the Principal Subjects in Pneumatology, Ethics, and Divinity* (1799), I, 455, there appeared a brief reference to the *Discourse of the Proofs of the Books of Moses*, printed at the end of a French edition of the *Pensées*. These lectures were first published in 1763.
58 John Wesley, *Works*, VI, 493: Pascal, *Oeuvres*, XIV, 235, sec. 797 (P.R., ch. xiv, para. 4; Kenn., p. 122).
59 John Wesley, *Works*, XI, 461 – 62.
60 John Wesley, *Letters*, VIII, 218.
61 Bernard Martin, *John Newton*, pp. 170 – 71.
62 It may be worth noting that Cowper's intimate friends at Olney, the Throckmortons, though Catholic, owned a copy of the *Lettres provinciales: Bibliotheca Osleriana*, p. 471.
63 Coming from the French-speaking part of Switzerland, Fletcher no

doubt was familiar with the *Provinciales* and the *Pensées* in their original tongue, and had perhaps absorbed to some degree the style and method of the former.

64 J.W. Fletcher, *Works*, IV, 14. The *Eulogy* was originally written in French, and praised Bacon, Boyle, Newton, and others, besides Pascal.

65 Ibid., IV, 32 – 33: Pascal, *Oeuvres*, XIII, 427 – 28, sec. 543, 544 (P.R., ch. xx, para. 2; Kenn., pp. 167 – 68). Fletcher's first illustrations from Pascal seem more fanciful than genuine.

66 Fletcher, IV, 351. Fletcher was probably referring to passages in the eleventh of Pascal's prayers in times of sickness.

67 Robert Sandeman, *Letters on Theron and Aspasio*, I, 282 – 85; Voltaire, *Oeuvres complètes*, XXII, 33 – 34.

68 To examples already given, we may add the possibility that William Penn used the *Pensées* as a model when he wrote *Some Fruits of Solitude* in 1693; see W. C. Braithwaite, *The Second Period of Quakerism*, p. 169. The library at Sion College contained the *Pensées* (Amsterdam, 1672), the gift of the sometime President, Edward Waple, also the *Lettres provinciales* in English (1679): William Reading, *Bibliothecae Cleri Londinensis in Collegio Sionensi Catalogus* (1724).

69 Elizabeth Rowe, *Works* (1796), I, 67 – 72.

70 Elizabeth Carter, *A Series of Letters between Mrs. Elizabeth Carter and Miss Catherine Talbot*, I, 191.

71 Rowe, *Works*, I, 160 – 62: Pascal, *Oeuvres*, XIII, 53n (P.R., ch. xxvi, para. 1; Kenn., p. 216).

72 Rowe, *Works*, IV, 30 – 31, 68 – 71, 82 – 83.

73 Ibid., 190 – 91; see also, 30

74 John Nichols, *Literary Anecdotes of the Eighteenth Century*, V, 433n. The writer was the Rev. George North, Vicar of Welwyn and a noted numismatist.

75 *The Rule of Life* (1769), p. 176. Pascal was also quoted on the use and insufficiency of human learning (p. 83), the importance of an awareness of immortality (p. 252), and on the Devil's temptation to vice by scorning virtues (p. 274).

76 Lindley Murray, *The Power of Religion on the Mind, in Retirement, Affliction, and at the Approach of Death*, pp. 104 – 109.

77 William Dodd, *Sermons to Young Men*, II, 293 – 94; III, 191 – 92.

78 *Christian's Magazine*, I (1760), 245 – 56, 293 – 95.

79 Samuel Johnson, *Works*, ed. Murphy, V, 119: Pascal, *Oeuvres*, XII, 42 – 43, sec. 33 (P.R., ch. xxxi, para. 32; Kenn., pp. 364 – 65). A variety of parallels and some contrasts between the thought of Pascal and Johnson have been drawn by C.F. Chapin, 'Johnson and Pascal,' pp. 3 – 16.

80 Samuel Johnson, *Letters, with Mrs. Thrales's Genuine Letters to Him*, ed. Chapman, II, 433.

81 *Thraliana: The Diary of Mrs. Hester Lynch Thrale, later Mrs. Piozzi*, ed. Balderston, I, 191. For Pascal's ideas upon infinity, see *Oeuvres*, XII,

70 – 92, sec. 72 (P.R., ch. xxii; Kenn., pp. 186 – 92). For those of Soame Jenyns, see 'A Free Inquiry into the Nature and Origin of Evil,' (1761), II, 208 – 209.

Mrs. Thrale evidently continued an interest in Pascal, for, in 1803, she found his thoughts on human greatness contrasting with her own experience: 'When I am reading Watts or Locke, or Paschal – or La Bruyere – I shut the Book, informed but little, 'tis true; – Yet filled with Admiration of the Authors, & well disposed to reverence Mankind, as little lower than the Angels &c. Oh wondrous Race of wise tho' fallen Beings! I exclaim, – but when I come down Stairs among my Workmen, & hear them talk such Nonsense as they do – I cry What Monkeys are these great Philosophers to think Man was ordain'd for any thing except to beg God's merciful Endurance of their Folly – & gain by Sweat & Toil their daily Bread. . . . These are the People too, not Locke & La Bruyere, for whom y^s World was made, for whom X^t died – if indeed these are not too high a Class among the Ranks of Humanity': *Thraliana*, II, 1039n.

82 Samuel Johnson, *Diaries, Prayers and Annals*, ed. McAdam and others, p. 119.

83 Ibid., pp. 293 – 94.

84 James Boswell, *Life of Johnson*, ed. Hill and Powell, III, 380. No copy of the *Pensées* was listed in Boswell's library following his death, only a French (1738) and the four-language edition of the *Lettres provinciales*: *Bibliotheca Boswelliana*, p. 56.

85 William Roberts, *Memoirs of the Life and Correspondence of Mrs. Hannah More*, I, 211, 278.

86 *Christian's Magazine*, I (1760), 295.

CHAPTER SEVEN

1 Mrs. Carter provides an excellent early illustration of this trend. In her letters to Miss Talbot, she had criticized Pascal for reasons reminiscent of those on which Voltaire had formed his attacks; but, when writing to another friend, Mrs. Vesey, in 1763, she spoke against Voltaire in the strongest of terms:

If I happened to be accidentally in a room with Voltaire, I do not believe I should think it necessary to run out screaming fire and murder; but certainly from every society in which I had a casting vote, such a wretch would be infallibly excluded; . . . A wicked writer is a much worse character than even a wicked man. . . . The present fashionable system of French philosophy, the wisdom of the encyclopedistes, subverts all the foundations of morality, breaks all connexion between earth and heaven, and tries to cheat mankind out of all that is worth living for, and all that is worth dying for. Can any talents of understanding, any treasures of learning, or any brilliancy of wit, reconcile one to the conversation of a person engaged in a scheme to thwart every dispensation of Heaven for human happiness!: Elizabeth Carter, *A Series of Letters between Mrs. Elizabeth Carter and Miss Catherine Talbot*, II, 96 – 97.

2 B.A. Schilling, *Conservative England and the Case against Voltaire*, pp. 296 – 97.

3 See discussion, ibid., pp. 248 – 77.

4 *Monthly Review*, LXI (July-Dec., 1779), 506.

5 *Gentleman's Magazine*, LIX, pt. 1 (1789), 216.

6 *European Magazine*, XXV (1794), 24 – 25: (a) Pascal, *Oeuvres*, XIII, 249, sec. 330; (b) ibid., 93, sec. 177 (P.R., ch. xxix, para. 34; Kenn., p. 307); (c) ibid., XIV, 328, sec. 895 (P.R., ch. xxviii, para. 60; Kenn., pp. 289–90).

7 *Universal Magazine*, CI (1797), 418. In a letter to Mrs. Thrale in 1783, Johnson had written: 'Life to be worthy of a rational Being must be always in progression; we must always purpose to do more or better than in time past. The Mind is enlarged and elevated by mere purposes, though they end as they begin by airy contemplation. We compare and judge though we do not practice': Johnson, *Letters*, III, 912.

8 *Universal Magazine*, CI (1797), 343. For Mme. Perier's description of Pascal's devotions, see Pascal, *Oeuvres*, I, 103; the extract from Bayle is adapted from a passage in his *Oeuvres Diverses*, I, 195.

9 *European Magazine*, XXXIII (1798), 92; Bayle, *Oeuvres Diverses*, I, 194.

10 [William Seward], *Anecdotes of some Distinguished Persons, chiefly of the Present and Two Preceding Centuries* (1795 – 97), II, 209 – 15 (Pascal, *Oeuvres*, I, 97 – 98); III, 328 – 29; supplement, 249 – 50.

11 *Encyclopaedia Britannica... The Third Edition* (1788 – 97), XIII, 794 – 98; see also the fourth edition of the *Britannica* (1800 – 10), XVI, 14 – 18, and exactly the same reference in the fifth (1810 – 17). Very similar articles appeared in Charles Hutton's *Mathematical and Philosophical Dictionary* (1795), II, 202 – 204, and the *Universal Magazine*, CV (1799), 369 – 75. The last carried an engraving by James Hopwood, after the printed portrait of Pascal by George Vertue.

12 *New and General Biographical Dictionary...* (1798), XII, 54.

13 Robert Alves, *Sketches of a History of Literature* (1794), pp. 94 – 95, 291 – 92; Henry Kett, *Elements of General Knowledge*, I, 14 – 15, 60 – 63.

14 Blaise Pascal, *Thoughts on Religion, and Other Important Subjects* (London, 1803), pp. 9, 12 – 13. Chevalier's interest in foreign languages and theology also led him to translate Bossuet's *Discours sur l'histoire universelle* and assist in the production of a polyglot Bible. His edition of the *Pensées* carried as frontispiece a portrait of Pascal after Edelinck by the London engraver, Philip Audinet. Another Baptist interested in the *Pensées* was the Rev. John Foster, who achieved

some fame as an essayist; and we are told the Danish lady who married William Carey in India had been particularly influenced by the *Pensées*.

15 Ibid., pp. 19 – 20, 23 – 24.

16 Ibid., pp. 54, 62.

17 Ibid., pp. 25 – 34.

18 Ibid., pp. 37 – 38.

19 Ibid., p. 64; see also Pascal, *Oeuvres*, I, 98. In fact, Chevalier continued: 'A remark found on one of his papers, and which is inserted in the last paragraph of page 179, discloses one of the grand secrets of the revolution manufactory.' The passage in question, in Chevalier's translation, reads as follows:

The art of overturning states is to discredit established customs, by looking into their origin, and pointing out that it was defective in authority and justice. We ought, say you, to go back to the primitive and fundamental laws of the state, which unjust customs have abolished. This is the sure way to overset every thing. Nothing is right in such a balance: yet the multitude lend an ear to such discourses; they shake off the yoke as soon as ever they begin to feel it; and the great take advantage of it, to ruin both them, and these curious examiners into established customs. But by a contrary fault, men think they may do with justice whatever is not without example. Pascal, *Oeuvres*, XIII, 219–21, sec, 294 (P.R., ch. xxv, para. 5, 6).

20 Pascal, *Thoughts on Religion* (London, 1803), pp. 65 – 67.

21 Ibid., pp. 68 – 69; see also Voltaire, *Oeuvres complètes*, XXII, 28.

22 Pascal, *Thoughts on Religion* (London, 1803), pp. 69 – 71; Blaise Pascal, *Thoughts on Religion, and Other Important Subjects* [trans. Chevalier], (London, 1806).

23 Hannah More, *Works*, X, 296 – 301; from *An Essay on the Character and Practical Writings of Saint Paul*.

24 C.C. Hankin, *Life of Mary Anne Schimmelpenninck*, p. 363.

25 William Roberts, *Memoirs of the Life and Correspondence of Mrs. Hannah More*, I, 204 – 205; see further Ruth Clark, *Strangers and Sojourners at Port Royal*, pp. 265 – 67, regarding Miss More's admiration for Port Royal. For a recent study of her life and relations with the Evangelical party, see M.G. Jones, *Hannah More*. This author's description of 'Miss More,' rather than 'Mrs.,' has been followed here.

26 More, *Works*, XI, 111 – 12, 117 – 18.

27 Roberts, *Memoirs*, III, 234. Miss More's friend, Mrs. Boscawen, had recently left her 'a legacy of about forty volumes, chiefly the Port Royal authors.' Another, very different contemporary who admired such books was the one-time headmaster of Harrow, Samuel Parr, sometimes oddly called the Whig Dr. Johnson. He owned Kennett's translation of the *Pensées* (1749), several Port Royal grammars, and Nicole's *Essais de morale* which he inscribed 'Very excellent indeed': *Bibliotheca Parriana*, pp. 85, 257, 450.

28 More, *Works*, V, 358; VII, 204; X, 23. For the last, see Pascal, *Oeuvres*, XIV, 72 – 73, sec. 631 (P.R., ch. viii, para. 2; Kenn., pp. 75 – 76).

29 Roberts, *Memoirs*, III, 340.

30 More, *Works*, VII, 50 – 52.

31 Roberts, *Memoirs*, III, 277 – 78, 283 – 84.

32 William Wilberforce, *A Practical View of the Prevailing Religious System of Professed Christians . . . (*1797), p. 483n. Remarking on the choice of eternal happiness or misery which the unbeliever must face, Wilberforce commented that Pascal pressed his argument 'with uncommon force.' He also described the *Pensées* as 'a book abounding in the deepest views of practical Christianity'; ibid., p. 339n.

33 Roberts, *Memoirs*, III, 237 – 38. The 'Daubinian school' no doubt bore the name of Archdeacon Daubeny, an extreme High Churchman of that time.

34 *Christian Observer*, I, 15 – 17, 96 – 97; for the three discourses recorded by Nicole, see Pascal, *Oeuvres*, IX, 359 – 73. For other instances of Pascal's appeal to the editors of the *Christian Observer* and its contributors, see III, 746 (similarities in style between the *Pensées* and the recent *Thoughts on the Trinity* by Bishop Huntingford of Gloucester); IV, 269 – 73 (an essay, 'On Indifference in Religion,' inspired by 'the great Pascal'); V, 674 – 75 (Pascal quoted on the effects of melancholy); VI, 718 – 19 (reference to the arguments concerning grace in the *Lettres provinciales*); VIII, 154 – 55 (a generous extract from ch. i of the Port Royal *Pensées* in translation, retitled 'The No-Creed, or practical Reasoning, of a Sceptic'; the contributor thought it might 'illustrate some of your remarks on the character of Mr. Hume') XI, 454 (on the testimony of Pascal and other men 'of undisputed liberality and genius' to the divine inspiration of Scripture); XIII, 3 – 4 (on Pascal's manner of receiving the last sacrament).

35 Ibid., IV, 495. For a further comparison, see the review of Miss More's *Christian Morals*, ibid., XII, 108.

36 Ibid., XI, 579.

37 Ibid., XIII, 710 – 30; this edition was by Antoine-Auguste Renouard, published in Paris in 1812. The review has been attributed to Sir Robert Grant, later a persistent advocate of the removal of civil disabilities for Jews. Similar exceptions to the rest of Catholicism were made in a letter to the editor from a pronounced Evangelical, the Rev. G.S. Faber, who saw Bernard, à Kempis, and Pascal as '*spiritual* members' of the community of true believers, 'although their *bodily* residence was within the limits of the mystic Babylon'; ibid., VI, 151: also by a correspondent writing on 'the distinctive character of Popery' who included Quesnel and Gaston de Renty, seventeenth-century friend of the poor, among that small number; ibid., IX, 353.

38 Ibid., XIV, 349 – 56, 421 – 27, 493 – 98, 565 – 76, 637 – 44, 709 – 15, 781 – 87, 853 – 58. The quotation from Bacon comes from his 'Character of a Believing Christian.'

39 Ibid., XIII, 726 – 27; Amelia Heber, *Life of Reginald Heber, D.D., Lord Bishop of Calcutta*, I, 336.

40 Mary Anne Schimmelpenninck, *Select Memoirs of Port Royal . . .*, II, 238 – 46. This lady's enthusiasm for Port Royal led her prose to take many an imaginative flight.

41 George Eliot, *Middlemarch*, pp. 2, 25; see also *Letters*, ed. Haight, VII, 11.

42 Blaise Pascal, *Provincial Letters, containing An Exposure of the Reasoning and Morals of the Jesuits* (London, 1816), pp. v-xxxii. The revival of the Jesuits gave rise to several original polemics in England, both in opposition and defence. As on earlier occasions, this production shows signs of having been hastily prepared. Its success was probably not very great, a translator thirty years afterwards commenting that it had failed to excite any general interest: Pascal, *The Provincial Letters*, trans. Thomas M'Crie (Edinburgh, 1847), p.x. But, in 1827, Hazlitt wrote of the *Provinciales* having been once more enlisted for combat against superstition and intolerance: William Hazlitt, *Complete Works*, ed. Howe, XVII, 208. In 1822, the *Quarterly Review* (XXVIII, 30–31) found the *Provinciales* 'worse than disingenuous', and Pascal primarily concerned with promoting the interests of his sect.

43 Blaise Pascal, *Thoughts on Religion, and Other Subjects*, trans. Edward Craig (Edinburgh, 1825), pp. vii-xi, 13 – 82. An engraved portrait of Pascal, signed 'W.H. Hearn,' formed the frontispiece. Craig held an Oxford M.A. and was a member of the Wernerian Society, a Scottish society for natural history; Berthou's edition of Pascal's works had appeared in 1819. Craig's translation was published a second time in Edinburgh in 1828, and, in 1829, provided the first American edition of the *Pensées* when it was printed in Amherst, Mass.
    Craig's final remarks surely referred to the reactionary policies of Charles X, who had ascended the French throne in 1824. A curious appraisal of Craig's work appeared in the *Phrenological Journal*, a periodical devoted to the study of human mental faculties and characteristics. Impressed by the standard of Craig's version – 'Pascal may now be considered as naturalized amongst us, and fitted with an English dress which appears to suit him as well as his native costume' – the reviewer discussed Pascal's precocity as a mathematician as evidence for the phrenological belief that men are not born with equal mental faculties. He then endeavoured to make some of Pascal's reflections more understandable by transposing them into 'the language of phrenology,' as in the following extract:
    '"The heart has its reasons, of which reason knows nothing. It is the heart which feels God, and not the reasoning powers." Every one must feel the truth of the sentiment thus beautifully expressed in popular language. To render it phrenological, we must substitute *"moral sentiments"* for *"heart"*; and how far more philosophical and rational is the statement thus rendered!'
    According to this reviewer, 'phrenology affords us a light whereby we can explain many of Pascal's sublime, but often obscure thoughts, and expound the reason of things where, perhaps, he perceived only

the effect': *Phrenological Journal and Miscellany*, IV, 103 – 12.

44 *Wesleyan-Methodist Magazine*, XLVIII, 688.

45 Blaise Pascal, *Thoughts on Religion* (London, 1825). This edition was clearly of Kennett's translation, with its language modernized. It bore no prefaces, and omitted chapters XXIX and XXXI. I have found no mention of it elsewhere, but a copy is in the possession of the library of Harvard University.

46 S.T. Coleridge, *Collected Letters*, ed. Griggs, I, 478 – 79: Pascal, *Oeuvres*, XIII, 346 – 47, 302, sec. 434, 395 (P.R., ch. xxi, para. 1 – 4; Kenn., pp. 177, 183). See also W. Schrickx, 'Coleridge and Friedrich Heinrich Jacobi,' XXXVI, 818 – 19; this same quotation had formed the motto to Jacobi's *David Hume über den Glauben* (1787), which upheld some form of belief as indispensable whenever reason fails.

In the *Edinburgh Review*, XXII, 238, Coleridge's onetime acquaintance, Sir James Mackintosh, described this same observation by Pascal as 'so remarkable for range of mind, and weight of authority, that it seems to us to have a higher character of grandeur, than any passage in human composition which has a mere reference to the operations of the understanding.' See also R.J. Mackintosh (ed.), *Memoirs of the Life of the Right Honourable Sir James Mackintosh*, I, 410 – 11.

47 S.T. Coleridge, *The Notebooks*, ed. Coburn, I (text), entry 1647.

48 H.C. Robinson, *Diary, Reminiscences, and Correspondence*, ed. Sadler, I, 308 – 309, probably recalling Pascal, *Oeuvres*, XIV, 19, sec. 571 (P.R., ch. x, para. 10, 11, 12; Kenn., p. 91). Robinson seems to have carried in his mind a permanent interest in Pascal's understanding of divine grace. On circuit as a barrister in 1817, he recorded a conversation with a Methodist preacher on the doctrines of *grace suffisante* and *grace efficace* in the *Provinciales*, and, in 1839, we find him asking the famous Dr. Arnold for an opinion on the same subject: *Diary*, II, 47 – 48 (see also Pascal, *Oeuvres*, IV, 158 – 75, and VII, 23 – 58); III, 165.

49 S.T. Coleridge, *The Friend*, ed. Rooke, II, 7 – 8.

50 Coleridge, *The Notebooks*, II (text), entry 2598; S.T. Coleridge, *Miscellaneous Criticism*, ed. Raysor, p. 286.

51 Coleridge, *Collected Letters*, II, 994.

52 Coleridge, *The Notebooks*, II (text and notes), entries 2133 – 36; see also II (notes), pp. 397 – 98, for comments on Coleridge's efforts to learn Italian.

53 S.T. Coleridge, MS note on back paste-down of his copy of the *Lettres provinciales* (Cologne, 1684), Coleridge Collection, Victoria College Library, University of Toronto; these notes are printed here by kind permission of the Victoria University Librarian. For an account of Coleridge's experiences abroad, see Donald Sultana, *Samuel Taylor Coleridge in Malta and Italy*.

54 Robert Southey, *Common-place Book*, ed. Warter, I, 344 – 45. The commonplace book of James Mill, historian, economist, and philosopher, also contained extracts from Pascal's writings and from

other leading French authors: Alexander Bain, *James Mill*, p. 465.
55 R.D. Havens, in *The Mind of a Poet*, p. 131, has seen a similarity between Pascal's comment on the reasons of the heart, and Wordsworth's exclamation in *The Excursion*, 'Happy for us that the imaginations and affections in our own despite mitigate the evils of that state of intellectual Slavery which the calculating understanding is so apt to produce'; William Wordsworth, *Poetical Works*, ed. de Selincourt and Darbishire, v, 109, n.16. When Wordsworth's library was sold, it contained no work by Pascal.
56 Sara Hutchinson, *Letters from 1800 to 1835*, ed. Coburn, pp. 274, 316.
57 W.A. Knight (ed.), *Memorials of Coleorton*, I, 185.
58 Hazlitt, *Complete Works*, I, 179; see also Pascal, *Oeuvres*, VI, 292. Another author at this time who appreciated a good quotation from the *Provinciales* was Thomas Mathias. In his preface to his satirical poem, *The Pursuits of Literature*, published anonymously, he recalled a 'pleasant passage' of 'smart and sprightly' dialogue from the fifth letter upon the mistaken ascription of authorship. This, in his opinion, might be 'easily adapted to the Probability Corps on the present occasion'; [T.J. Mathias], *The Pursuits of Literature*, p. xxiii. In his *Autobiography*, ed. Ingpen, II, 51 – 52, Leigh Hunt recalled Charles Lamb's humour as being of the kind practised by Pascal.
59 Hazlitt, *Complete Works*, IX, 58 – 59.
60 *Quarterly Review*, XXII (1819–20), 162.
61 E.J. Morley (ed.), *Henry Crabb Robinson on Books and their Writers*, I, 237.
62 Thomas Thomson, *History of the Royal Society from its Institution to the End of the Eighteenth Century*, pp. 268 – 69; *Edinburgh Review*, XX, 178.
63 *Monthly Magazine*, IX, 3; Roberts, *Memoirs*, II, 450. The *Gentleman's Magazine*, LXXXVIII, pt. 2 (1817), 50, believed the fame of Pascal and the *Provinciales* had been 'too long and too widely established, to require any particular description.'
64 *Encyclopaedia Londinensis*, XVIII, 729 – 31. The author's remarks upon the engraving, which is signed 'T. Dale,' are worth recording for their odd association of Pascal with that famous English ancient, Thomas Parr:

> *Underneath the Portrait which accompanies this article, a hand from heaven is seen filling out of a small phial the lamp of Pascal's short life. We take this opportunity of supplying our omission of explaining the allegorical Entablature which accompanies the Portrait of old Parr, which alludes to a life as much lengthened beyond the usual standard as the other falls short of it: there, Clotho and Lachesis spin on the life of Parr, while Atropos seems totally to forget or to neglect the use of her scissars.*

65 *Monthly Magazine*, XXXIV (1812–13), 44.
66 See, for example, the article in the *General Biography* (1799 – 1815), by John Aikin and others, which found Pascal's opinions on man's condition and divine government 'utterly irreconcileable with just

and rational views of religion, and to reflect dishonour on the
wisdom and benevolence of the Deity.' A broadly similar article in
Abraham Rees' *Cyclopaedia*, gave as its sources Moréri and Bayle.
The *General Biographical Dictionary*, edited by Alexander Chalmers,
was a little more up-to-date, stating it had drawn its material from
Bossut, Mme. Perier, Hutton's *Mathematical and Philosophical Dictionary*, and Thomson's *History of the Royal Society*.
67 See *Encyclopaedia Londinensis*, XVIII, 731, and Pascal, *Provincial Letters*
(1816), p. v.
68 Dugald Stewart, *Collected Works*, ed. Hamilton, I, 165 – 67. Pascal's
opinion on the providential nature of man's condition was shared by
Stewart's younger colleague at Edinburgh, Thomas Brown; *Lectures
on the Philosophy of the Human Mind*, III, 415 – 16.
69 Pierre Bayle, *An Historical and Critical Dictionary* (1826), III, 15 – 17.
70 *Edinburgh Review*, XLVII (1828), 2 – 3.
71 This translation (Glasgow, 1838) was by Jonathan Edwards Ryland,
with an introduction by Isaac Taylor, author of *The Natural History of
Enthusiasm*. Taylor was of the opinion that 'in England, Pascal's
writings, and his Thoughts especially, have always been in favour
among meditative and intelligent religious readers' (p. lxxi).
72 *Edinburgh Review*, LXXXV (1847), 201 – 203. The author of this
lengthy review article was apparently Henry Rogers (1806 – 77), a
frequent contributor and a Christian apologist.

APPENDIX

1 S.E. Morison, *The Intellectual Life of Colonial New England*, p. 135: *A
Catalogue of Curious and Valuable Books, Belonging to the late Reverend
& Learned, Mr. Ebenezer Pemberton* ... (1717), pp. 15, 16, 23: *A
Catalogue of Curious and Valuable Books, (Which mostly belonged to the
Reverend Mr. George Curwin, Late of Salem, Deceased)* ... (1718), p. 14.
2 L.G. Tyler, 'Libraries in Colonial Virginia,' II, 171.
3 Charles Morton, 'Compendium Physicae,' XXXIII, Collections,
51 – 52.
4 Samuel Sewall, 'Diary, 1674 – 1729,' VI, 93 – 94.
5 The stone is described and its epitaph printed in J.L. Sibley and
others, *Biographical Sketches of Graduates of Harvard University*, I,
205 – 206. A correspondent in the *Christian Register*, III, 270, stated
Stoughton's epitaph 'has been repeatedly published, and often admired,' but he was not aware 'that in any publication, it has been
traced to its right origin.' He sought to rectify 'the general, if not the
universal impression . . . that it was the production of our own country' by printing it side by side with the epitaph for Pascal.
No way of illustrating the similarities between the two epitaphs
could be better than to reproduce them in conjunction here:

Blasius Pascalis, Scutarius nobilis,

Hic jacet.
Pietas si non moritur, aeternum vivet.
Vir conjugii nescius,
Religione sanctus,
Virtute clarus,
Doctrina celebris,
Ingenio acutus,
Sanguine et animo pariter illustris;
Doctus, non doctor,
Æquitatis amator,
Veritatis defensor,
Virginum ultor,

Christianae moralis corruptorum acerrimus hostis.
Hunc rhetores amant facundum
Hunc scriptores norunt elegantem,
Hunc mathematici stupent profundum,
Hunc philosophi quaerunt sapientem,
Hunc doctores laudant theologum,
Hunc pii venerantur austerum,
Hunc omnes mirantur;
Omnes ignotum; omnibus licet notum.
Quid plura? Viator, quem perdidimus?
Pascalem.
Is Ludovicus erat Montaltius.
Heu! Satis dixi,
Urgent Lachrymae,
Sileo.
Ei, qui bene precaberis,
Bene tibi eveniat, et vivo et mortuo.
Vixit An. 39, M. 2.
Obiit An. Rep. Sal. 1662, 14 Kal. Sept.
ΩΛΕΤΟ ΠΑΣΚΑΛΙΟΣ,
ΦΕΥ! ΦΕΥ! ΠΕΝΘΟΣ ΟΣΟΝ!
Cecedit Pascalis!
Heu! Heu! Qualis Luctus!

Gulielmus Stoughtonus, Armiger,
Provinciae Massachusettensis in Nova Anglia Legatus,
Deinde Gubernator,
Necnon Curiae in eadem Provincia superioris
Justiciarius Capitalis,
Hic jacet;

Vir conjugii nescius,
Religione sanctus,
Virtute clarus,
Doctrina celebris,
Ingenio acutus,

Sanguine et animo pariter illustris,

Æquitatis amator,
Legum propugnator,
Collegii Stoughtoniani fundator,
Literarum et literatorum fautor celeberrimus,
Impietatis et vitii hostis acerrimus.
Hunc rhetores amant facundum,
Hunc scriptores norunt elegantem,
Hunc philosophi quaerunt sapientem,
Hunc doctores, laudant theologum,
Hunc pii venerantur austerum.
Hunc omnes mirantur;
Omnes ignotum; omnibus licet notum.
Quid plura? Viator, quem perdidimus?
Stoughtonum!

Heu! Satis dixi,
Urgent Lachrymae,
Sileo.

Vixit annos septuaginta,
Septimo die Julii. Anno Salutis, 1701,

Cecedit,
Heu! Heu! Qualis Luctus!

The stone was repaired by Harvard College in 1828. The inscription has also been printed and briefly discussed in the following: J.M. Robbins and others, *History of the Town of Dorchester, Massachusetts*, pp. 276 – 77; J.H. Merriam, 'Historic Burial-Places of Boston and Vicinity,' VII, 401 – 402; W.D. Orcutt, *Good Old Dorchester*, pp. 105 – 106. The attribution of the epitaph to Mather, based upon that for Pascal, is universally made.

For further details regarding Pascal's epitaph, see Pascal, *Oeuvres*, x, 312 – 13.

6 Ebenezer Pemberton, *The Divine Original and Dignity of Government Asserted...* (1710), pp. 1 – 2. Pemberton took as the text for his sermon Psalm LXXXII: 6 – 7: 'I have said, Ye are Gods: and all of you are Children of the most High: But ye shall Die like Men.' His quotation summarized some of Pascal's arguments contained in the *Discours sur la condition des grands* (Pascal, *Oeuvres*, IX, 359 – 73), printed by Nicole in *Essais de morale*.

7 L.B. Wright, 'The 'Gentleman's Library' in Early Virginia: The Literary Interests of the First Carters,' I, 45: C.K. Shipton, 'Literary Leaven in Provincial New England,' IX, 208: Samuel Johnson, *Career and Writings*, ed. Schneider and Schneider, I, 497, 510, 521: Ebenezer Parkman, 'Diary,' ed. Walett, LXXII, 380.

8 F.B. Tolles, 'A Literary Quaker: John Smith of Burlington and

Philadelphia,' LXV, 317: H.J. Cadbury, 'Anthony Benezet's Library,' XXIII, 72.

9 Perry Miller, *Jonathan Edwards*, p. 262.

10 Jonathan Edwards, *Notebook*, MS, p. 4. In the original, the word 'Present' has been scored out. The notebook has been discussed by T.H. Johnson, 'Jonathan Edwards' Background of Reading,' XXVIII, 193 – 222.

11 O.W. Holmes, *Writings*, VIII, 362 – 66: Pascal, *Oeuvres*, XIII, 106, sec. 194 (P.R., ch. i, para. 1; Kenn., p. 10).

12 A.O. Aldridge, *Benjamin Franklin, Philosopher and Man*, p. 10.

13 *A Catalogue of Books Belonging to the Library Company of Philadelphia* (1741), pp. 21, 47.

14 H.M. Jones, 'The Importation of French Books in Philadelphia, 1750 – 1800,' XXXII, 157 – 77; the situation was much the same in New York. Franklin himself arranged the sale of a collection including a copy of Walker's translation of the *Pensées* (1688), in 1744. When the Library Company published a catalogue in 1807, it listed two copies of the *Pensées* translated by Kennett, one of Andrews' translation of the *Provinciales*, and a French *Provinciales*. The Loganian Library in Philadelphia in 1795 possessed the tetraglott edition of the *Provinciales* (Cologne, 1684).

15 W.J. Potts, 'Du Simitière, Artist, Antiquary, and Naturalist, Projector of the First American Museum, with some extracts from his Note-Book,' XIII, 363 – 64.

16 J. Adams, *Diary and Autobiography*, ed. Butterfield, IV, 60.

17 T. Jefferson, *Papers*, ed. Boyd, VIII, 111.

18 *Catalogue of the Library of Thomas Jefferson*, ed. Sowerby, II, 116, 191: J.S. Bassett (ed.), *The Writings of 'Colonel William Byrd of Westover in Virginia Esqr.'*, p. 429.

19 *Catalogue, No. 2, of Books in the Boston Library*, p. 7: *A Catalogue of the Books belonging to the Charleston Library Society* (1826), p. 269: *Catalogus Bibliothecae Harvardianae Cantabrigiae Nov-Anglorum* (1790), pp. 120, 185: *Catalogue of Books in the Library of Yale College*, p. 68: *Catalogue of Books belonging to the Library of Rhode-Island College* (1793), pp. 21, 33.

20 M.-M. H. Barr, *Voltaire in America*, 1744 – 1800, has not listed any reference to Pascal in her comprehensive work on the topic.

21 W. Barton, *Memoirs of the Life of David Rittenhouse*, pp. 606 – 607.

22 Blaise Pascal, *Provincial Letters* (New York, 1828). This would appear to be an American printing of the English edition of 1816.

23 *Christian Disciple*, II, 65 – 66, 177 – 80, 202 – 206; see also Pascal, *Oeuvres*, V, 83 – 108. In the *Massachusetts Missionary Magazine*, I and II, Pascal was the name of a spiritual adviser writing 'letters on solitary devotion' to a young convert, Julia, encouraging her in her habits and manner of prayer. The effectiveness of these 'letters' seems to have been questionable, since Julia's dejection apparently increased, and the series was broken off after twenty-two instal-

ments, in spite of an assurance it would be continued.

24 Benjamin Rush, *Selected Writings*, ed. Runes, p. 226.
25 Benjamin Rush, *Medical Inquiries and Observations upon the Diseases of the Mind*, p. 327.
26 James Madison in 1822 quoted Pascal's excuse from the *Provinciales*, when he wrote that an author he had read had not had time to make his arguments shorter: *Letters and Other Writings*, iii, 261 – 62.
27 *The Adams-Jefferson Letters*, ed. Cappon, ii, 474.
28 Edward Everett, *Orations and Speeches on Various Occasions*, ii, 589: *A Catalogue of the Books of John Quincy Adams Deposited in the Boston Athenaeum*, p. 115: C.F. Adams, *Diary*, ed. Donald and Donald, ii, 103n.
29 C.F. Adams, *Diary*, ii, 190.
30 George Ticknor, *Lectures on French Literature*, MS, vol. iii. For C.F. Adams' comments on these lectures, see *Diary*, i, 383, 385.
31 Blaise Pascal, *Thoughts on Religion, and Other Subjects* (Amherst, Mass., 1829). The translation was that by the Rev. Edward Craig, which had first appeared in Edinburgh in 1825.
32 R.W. Emerson, *Letters*, ed. Rusk, iv, 509. See also R.W. Emerson, *Journals and Miscellaneous Notebooks*, ed. Gilman and others, ii, 390; vi, 39 – 40.
33 H. Melville, *Moby Dick*, ed. Mansfield and Vincent, p. 422.
34 Harry Levin, *The Power of Blackness*, pp. 101, 162: Austin Warren, 'Hawthorne's Reading,' viii, 486: Haldeen Braddy, *Glorious Incense*, p. 83.

Bibliography
(Bibliography for Appendix listed separately at end.)

I   WORKS BY BLAISE PASCAL
(in chronological order)

A   Collected Works

Oeuvres, ed. Charles Bossut, 5 vols. La Haye, 1779.

Oeuvres, ed. Léon Brunschvicg and others, 14 vols. Paris, 1908 – 1921.

Pensées, fragments et lettres, ed. Prosper Faugère, 2 vols. Paris, 1844.

The Physical Treatises of Pascal, ed. I.H.B. and A.G.H. Spiers. New York, 1937.

B   Les Provinciales

Les Provinciales: or, The Mysterie of Jesvitisme, discover'd in certain Letters, written upon occasion of the present differences at Sorbonne, between the Jansenists and the Molinists. . . . London, 1657.

Les Provinciales, or, The Mystery of Jesuitisme. Discovered in certain Letters, written upon occasion of the present Differences at Sorbonne, between the Jansenists and the Molinists. . . . London, 1658.

The Mystery of Jesuitism, Discovered In certain Letters, written upon occasion of the present Differences at Sorbonne between the Jansenists and the Molinists. London, 1679.

The Life of Mr. Paschal, with his Letters Relating to the Jesuits, trans. William Andrews, 2 vols. London, 1744.

Provincial Letters, containing An Exposure of the Reasoning and Morals of the Jesuits . . . *To which is added, A View of the History of the Jesuits, and the Late Bull for the Revival of the Order in Europe.* London, 1816.

The Provincial Letters, trans. Thomas M'Crie. Edinburgh, 1847.

C Pensées

Pensées de M. Pascal sur la religion et sur quelques autres sujets. Paris, 1678.

Monsieur Pascall's Thoughts, Meditations, and Prayers, Touching Matters Moral and Divine, As they were found in his Papers after his Death, trans. Joseph Walker. London, 1688.

Thoughts on Religion, and Other Subjects [trans. Basil Kennett]. London, 1704.

Thoughts on Religion, And other Curious Subjects, trans. Basil Kennett. London, 1727.

Thoughts on Religion, and other Curious Subjects, trans. Basil Kennett. London, 1731.

Thoughts on Religion, And other curious Subjects, trans. Basil Kennett. London, 1741.

Thoughts on Religion, And other curious Subjects, trans. Basil Kennett. London, 1749.

Thoughts on Religion, and Other Subjects [trans. Basil Kennett]. Edinburgh, 1751.

'Thoughts on Religion, And other Subjects,' *A Christian Library*, ed. John Wesley, 50 vols. Bristol, 1749–1755. XXIII (1753), 3–223.

*Eloge et pensées. Nouvelle édition commentée, corrigée et augmentée par M. de * * * [Voltaire].* Paris, 1778.

Thoughts on Religion, and Other Important Subjects [trans. Thomas Chevalier]. London, 1803.

Thoughts on Religion, and Other Important Subjects [trans. Thomas Chevalier]. London, 1806.

'Thoughts on Religion, and Other Subjects,' *A Christian Library*, ed. John Wesley, 50 vols. London, 1819–1827. XIII (1821), 35–207.

Thoughts on Religion [trans. Basil Kennett]. London, 1825.

Thoughts on Religion, and Other Subjects, trans. Edward Craig. Edinburgh, 1825.

Thoughts on Religion, and Other Subjects, trans. Edward Craig. Edinburgh, 1828.

Thoughts on Religion and Philosophy [trans. Jonathan Edwards Ryland], *with an original memoir of the author, and an introductory essay, by Isaac Taylor.* Glasgow, 1838.

Pensées sur la religion et sur quelques autres sujets, ed. Louis Lafuma, 3 vols. Paris, 1951.

II   OTHER WORKS

A Bibliographical Aids

Arber, Edward (ed.), *The Term Catalogues, 1668 – 1709 A.D.; with a Number for Easter Term 1711 A.D. . . .*, 3 vols. London, 1903 – 1906.

Eyre, G.E.B., and Rivington, C.R. (eds.), *A Transcript of the Registers of the Worshipful Company of Stationers; from 1640 – 1708 A.D.*, 3 vols. London, 1913 – 1914.

Hodgson, Norma, and Blagden, Cyprian, 'The Notebook of Thomas Bennet and Henry Clements (1686 – 1719): With some aspects of Book Trade Practice,' *Publications of the Oxford Bibliographical Society*, New Series, VI (1953), 1 – 228.

Lafuma, Louis, *Histoire des Pensées de Pascal, 1656 – 1952*. Paris, 1954.

Leroy, Olivier, *A French Bibliography of Sir Thomas Browne*. London, 1931.

Maire, Albert, *Bibliographie générale des oeuvres de Blaise Pascal*, 5 vols. Paris, 1926 – 1927.

B Library Catalogues, Contemporary and Modern

Bibliotheca Antonii Collins, two parts. London, 1731.

Bibliotheca Boswelliana. London, 1825.

Bibliotheca Burnetiana [London, 1716].

Bibliotheca Digbeiana [London, 1680].

Bibliotheca Hookiana [London, 1703].

Bibliotheca Osleriana. Oxford, 1929.

Bibliotheca Oweniana. London, 1684.

Bibliotheca Parriana. London, 1827.

Bibliotheca Rayana [London, 1708].

Catalogue of the Library of the late Dr. Joseph Priestley. Philadelphia, 1816.

A Catalogue of the Library of the late John Byrom, Esq., preserved at Kersall Cell, Lancashire. London, 1848.

A Catalogue of the entire and valuable Library of Books of the late Henry Fielding, Esq. [London, 1755]; reproduced in Ethel M. Thornbury, *Henry Fielding's Theory of the Comic Prose Epic*. Madison, 1931, pp. 168 – 89.

A Catalogue of the Valuable Library of the late celebrated Joseph

Addison, Secretary of State, &c. . . . . London, 1799.

A Collection of Excellent English Books, . . .*Being the Library of the Most Reverend Father in God, Dr. Tillotson, late Lord Archbishop of Canterbury* [London, 1695].

Deed, Stanley G., *Catalogue of the Plume Library at Maldon, Essex.* Maldon, 1959.

A Facsimile Reproduction of a Unique Catalogue of Laurence Sterne's Library, ed. Charles Whibley. London, 1930.

Harrison, John, and Laslett, Peter, *The Library of John Locke.* Oxford, 1965.

Hazen, Allen T., *A Catalogue of Horace Walpole's Library,* 3 vols. New Haven, 1969.

Le Fanu, T.P., 'Catalogue of Dean Swift's Library in 1715, with an Inventory of his Personal Property in 1742,' *Proceedings of the Royal Irish Academy,* XXXVII (1924 – 1927), Section C, 263 – 75.

The Library of Edward Gibbon: A Catalogue of his Books, ed. Geoffrey Keynes. London, 1940.

Maheu, René, 'Le catalogue de la bibliothèque des Berkeley,' *Revue d'histoire de la philosophie,* III (1929), 180 – 99.

Reading, William, *Bibliothecae Cleri Londinensis in Collegio Sionensi Catalogus.* London, 1724.

The Rothschild Library, 2 vols. Cambridge, 1954.

White, Newport J.D., *A Catalogue of Books in the French Language, Printed in or before A.D. 1715, remaining in Archbishop Marsh's Library, Dublin.* Dublin, 1918.

Williams, Harold H., *Dean Swift's Library. With a facsimile of the original sale catalogue and some account of two manuscript lists of his books.* Cambridge, 1932.

C Contemporary Sources, Manuscripts, and Periodicals

Aaron, Richard I., and Gibb, Jocelyn (eds.), *An Early Draft of Locke's Essay. Together with Excerpts from his Journals.* Oxford, 1936.

Addison, Joseph, *Works,* ed. Richard Hurd and Henry G. Bohn, 6 vols. London, 1901 – 1913.

Aikin, John, and others, *General Biography: or Lives, Critical and Historical, of the Most Eminent Persons of All Ages, Countries, Conditions and Professions* . . . , 10 vols. London, 1799 – 1815.

Aitken, George A., *The Life and Works of John Arbuthnot.* Oxford, 1892.

Alves, Robert, *Sketches of a History of Literature.* Edinburgh, 1794.

Anecdotes of Polite Literature, 5 vols. London, 1764.

[Anon.], *Fair Warning To take heed of Popery, Or a short and true History of the Jesuits Fiery Practises and Powder-Plots, to destroy Kings, Ruin Kingdoms, and lay Cities waste.* London, 1674.

—————————, *The Missionarie's Arts Discovered: or, An Account of their Ways of Insinuation, their Artifices, and several Methods of which they serve themselves in making Converts.* London, 1688.

Arminian Magazine, IV; x. London, 1781; 1787.

[Arnauld, Antoine (?)], *A Journall of all Proceedings between the Jansenists, and the Jesuits: From the first coming abroad of the Provincial Letters to the Publication and the Censures of the Clergy of France and Theological Faculty of Paris passed upon a Book entituled An Apology for the Casuists....* London, 1659.

[Arnauld, Antoine, and others], *To Mystérion tés Anomias: Another Part of the Mystery of Jesuitism or The new Heresie of the Jesuites, publickly maintained at Paris in the College of Clermont...Together with The Imaginary Heresie in three Letters with divers other Particulars relating to this Abominable Mysterie....* London, 1664.

Atterbury, Francis, *Sermons and Discourses on several Subjects and Occasions*, 4 vols. London, 1761.

Barrow, Isaac, *Theological Works*, ed. Alexander Napier, 9 vols. Cambridge, 1859.

[Bastide, Marc Antoine de la], *An Answer To the Bishop of Condom's Book; Entituled, An Exposition of the Doctrin of the Catholick Church, upon Matters of Controversie* [trans. Joseph Walker]. Dublin, n.d. [1676].

Baxter, Richard, *A Key for Catholicks, To open the Jugling of the Jesuits....* London, 1659.

Bayle, Pierre, *The Dictionary Historical and Critical ... The Second Edition, Carefully collated with the several Editions of the Original*, 5 vols. London, 1734 – 1738.

—————————, *Dictionnaire historique et critique. Troisième édition, revue, corrigée et augmentée par l'auteur*, ed. Prosper Marchand, 4 vols. Rotterdam, 1720.

—————————, *A General Dictionary, Historical and Critical*, ed. Thomas Birch and others, 10 vols. London, 1734 – 1741.

—————————, *An Historical and Critical Dictionary*, 4 vols. London, 1710.

—————————, *An Historical and Critical Dictionary*, 4 vols. London, 1826.

—————————, *Oeuvres diverses...contenant tout ce que cet auteur a publié sur des matières de théologie, de philosophie, de critique, d'histoire & de littérature; excepté son Dictionnaire historique et critique* [ed. Pierre des Maizeaux], 4 vols. La Haye, 1727 – 1731.

Berkeley, George, *Works*, ed. A.A. Luce and T.E. Jessop, 9 vols. London, 1948 – 1957.

Birch, Thomas (ed.), *A Collection of the State Papers of John Thurloe, Esq.*, 7 vols. London, 1742.

Bodleian Library, *MS. Rawl. D.* 878.

Bolingbroke, Henry St. John, Viscount, *Works*, 8 vols. London, 1809.

Boswell, James, *Life of Johnson, together with Boswell's Journal of a Tour to the Hebrides and Johnson's Diary of a Journey into North Wales*, ed. G.B. Hill and L.F. Powell, 6 vols. Oxford, 1934 – 1950.

Boyle, Hon. Robert, *Works*, ed. Thomas Birch, 6 vols. London, 1772.

Brown, John, *Essays on the Characteristics of the Earl of Shaftesbury*. Dublin, 1752.

Brown, Thomas, *Lectures on the Philosophy of the Human Mind*, 4 vols. Edinburgh, 1820.

Burke, Edmund, *Correspondence*, ed. T.W. Copeland. Cambridge, 1958-.

Burnet, Gilbert, *History of My Own Time*, ed. Osmund Airy, 2 vols. Oxford, 1897 – 1900.

Butler, Joseph, *Works*, ed. W.E. Gladstone, 2 vols. Oxford, 1897.

Byrom, John, *Poems*, ed. A.W. Ward, 2 vols. Chetham Society, New Series, Manchester, 1894 – 1895.

——————————, *The Private Journal and Literary Remains*, ed. Richard Parkinson, 2 vols., each in two parts. Chetham Society, Manchester, 1854 – 1855.

Carter, Elizabeth, *A Series of Letters between Mrs. Elizabeth Carter and Miss Catherine Talbot, from the Year* 1741 *to* 1770. *To which are added Letters from Mrs. Elizabeth Carter to Mrs. Vesey, between the Years* 1763 *and* 1787 . . . , ed. Montagu Pennington, 2 vols. London, 1808.

Chalmers, Alexander (ed.), *The General Biographical Dictionary: containing an Historical and Critical Account of the Lives and Writings of the Most Eminent Persons in Every Nation* . . . , 32 vols. London, 1812 – 1817.

Chesterfield, Philip Dormer Stanhope, Earl of, *Letters*, ed. John Bradshaw, 3 vols. London, 1892.

Christian Observer, I; III; IV; V; VI; VIII; IX; XI; XII; XIII; XIV. London, 1802; 1804; 1805; 1806; 1807; 1809; 1810; 1812; 1813; 1814; 1815.

Christian's Magazine; or, A Treasury of Divine Knowledge, I. London, 1760.

Clarke, Samuel, *Medulla Theologiae: or The Marrow of Divinity, Contained in sundry Questions and Cases of Conscience, both Speculative, and Practical.* . . . London, 1659.

Clarkson, David, *The Practical Divinity of the Papists Discovered to be Destructive of Christianity and Men's Souls.* London, 1676.

Cole, William, *A Journal of my Journey to Paris in the year* 1765, ed. F.G. Stokes. London, 1931.

Coleridge, Samuel T., *Collected Letters*, ed. E.L. Griggs, 4 vols. Oxford, 1956 – 1959.

————————, *The Friend*, ed. B.E. Rooke, 2 vols. Princeton, 1969.

————————, MS note on back paste-down of his copy of Blaise Pascal, *Les Provinciales* (Cologne, 1684), Victoria College Library, University of Toronto.

————————, *Miscellaneous Criticism*, ed. T.M. Raysor. Cambridge, Mass., 1936.

————————, *The Notebooks*, ed. Kathleen Coburn. New York, 1957-.

Collier, Jeremy, *Essays upon several Moral Subjects: In Two Parts.* London, 1697.

————————, *Essays upon several Moral Subjects: Part III.* London, 1720.

————————, *Essays upon several Moral Subjects: Part IV.* London, 1725.

Collins, Anthony, *The Scheme of Literal Prophecy Considered.* London, 1727.

Condorcet, Marie-Jean Antoine Nicolas de Caritat, Marquis de, *Oeuvres*, ed. A.C. O'Connor and M.F. Arago, 12 vols. Paris, 1847 – 1849.

Craig, John, *Theologiae Christianae Principia Mathematica.* London, 1699.

[Daniel, Gabriel], *The Discourses of Cleander and Eudoxe upon the Provincial Letters. To which is Added An Answer to the Apology for the Provincial Letters.* London, 1704.

Dawes, Sir William, *An Anatomy of Atheisme.* London, 1693.

Denham, Sir John, *Poetical Works*, ed. T.H. Banks. New Haven, 1928.

Dennis, John, *The Critical Works*, ed. E.N. Hooker, 2 vols. Baltimore, 1939 – 1943.

Dodd, Charles (pseud. for Hugh Tootell), *The Church History of England, From the Year* 1500, *to the Year* 1688. *Chiefly with regard to Catholicks* . . . , 3 vols. Brussels, 1737 – 1742.

Dodd, William, *Sermons to Young Men*, 3 vols. London, 1771.

Doddridge, Philip, *A Course of Lectures on the Principal Subjects in Pneumatology, Ethics, and Divinity: with references to the most considerable authors on each subject*, 2 vols. London, 1799.

Donne, John, *Complete Poetry*, ed. J.T. Shawcross. London and New York, 1968.

Dryden, John, *Works*, ed. Sir Walter Scott and George Saintsbury, 18 vols. Edinburgh, 1882 – 1893.

Edinburgh Review, or Critical Journal, XX; XXII; XLVII; LXXII; LXXXV. Edinburgh, 1812; 1813 – 1814; 1828; 1840 – 1841; 1847.

Eliot, George, *Letters*, ed. G.S. Haight, 7 vols. New Haven, 1954 – 1955.

—————————, *Middlemarch*. Oxford, 1947.

Encyclopaedia Britannica; or, A Dictionary of Arts, Sciences, &c. on a Plan entirely New . . . The Second Edition; greatly Improved and Enlarged, 10 vols. Edinburgh, 1778 – 1783.

Encyclopaedia Britannica; or, A Dictionary of Arts, Sciences, and Miscellaneous Literature . . . The Third Edition, 18 vols. Edinburgh, 1788 – 1797.

————————— [The Fourth Edition], 20 vols. Edinburgh, 1800 – 1810.

————————— [The Fifth Edition], 20 vols. Edinburgh, 1810 – 1817.

Encyclopaedia Londinensis, or Universal dictionary of arts, sciences, and literature . . . , 24 vols. London, 1810 – 1829.

European Magazine, and London Review, XXV; XXXIII. London, 1794; 1798.

Evelyn, John, *Diary*, ed. E.S. de Beer, 6 vols. Oxford, 1955.

—————————, *Diary and Correspondence*, ed. William Bray, 4 vols. London, 1850 – 1852.

Fitzadam, Adam (pseud. for Edward Moore), *The World*, 4 vols. London, 1763.

Fletcher, John William, *Works*, 4 vols. New York, 1854.

Forbes of Pitsligo, Alexander Forbes, Lord, *Essays, Moral and Philosophical, on Several Subjects*. London, 1734.

—————————, *Thoughts concerning Man's Condition and Duties in this Life, and his Hopes in the World to Come*. Edinburgh, 1766.

Foster, John, *Life and Correspondence*, ed. J.E. Ryland, 2 vols. London, 1855.

[Gale, Theophilus], *The True Idea of Jansenisme, both Historick and Dogmatick*. London, 1669.

Gentleman's Magazine, VIII; LIX; LXXXVIII. London, 1738; 1789; 1817.

Gibbon, Edward, *Autobiography*. London, 1911.

Gildon, Charles, *The Deist's Manual: or, A Rational Enquiry into the Christian Religion . . . .* London, 1705.

Goldsmith, Oliver, *Collected Works*, ed. A. Friedman, 5 vols. Oxford, 1966.

Gordon, Thomas, *The Humourist: being Essays upon Several Subjects*, 2 vols. London, 1720 – 1725.

Hawkesworth, John, and others, *The Adventurer*, 4 vols. London, 1756.

Hazlitt, William, *Complete Works*, ed. P.P. Howe, 21 vols. London, 1930 – 1934.

Hearne, Thomas, *Remarks and Collections*, ed. C.E. Doble and others, 11 vols. Oxford, 1885 – 1918.

Heber, Amelia, *Life of Reginald Heber, D.D., Lord Bishop of Calcutta*, 2 vols. London, 1830.

Hermant, Godefroi, *Mémoires sur l'histoire ecclésiastique du* XVIIe *siècle*, 1630 – 1663, ed. A. Gazier, 6 vols. Paris, 1905 – 1910.

Historical Manuscripts Commission, *Report on the Laing Manuscripts preserved in the University of Edinburgh*, 2 vols. London, 1914 – 1925.

Hooke, Robert, *Diary*, 1672 – 1680, ed. H.W. Robinson and Walter Adams. London, 1935.

Hume, David, *Essays Moral, Political, and Literary*, ed. T.H. Green and T.H. Grose, 2 vols. London, 1875.

Hunt, Leigh, *Autobiography*, ed. Roger Ingpen, 2 vols. London, 1903.

Hurd, Richard, *Works*, 8 vols. London, 1811.

Hutchinson, Sara, *Letters from 1800 to 1835*, ed. Kathleen Coburn. London, 1954.

Hutton, Charles, *A Mathematical and Philosophical Dictionary*, 2 vols. London, 1795.

Huygens, Christiaan, *Oeuvres complètes*, 22 vols. in 23. La Haye, 1888 – 1950.

Jarrige, Pierre, and others, *A further Discovery of the Mystery of Jesuitisme. In a Collection of severall Pieces, Representing the Humours, Designs and Practises of those who call themselves The Society of Jesus.* London, 1658.

[Jenner, Charles], *Letters from Altamont in the Capital, to his Friends in the Country*. London, 1767.

Jenyns, Soame, *Miscellaneous Pieces*, 2 vols. London, 1761.

Jesup, Edward, *The Lives of Picus and Pascal, Faithfully Collected from the most Authentick Accounts of them. To which is subjoin'd a Parallel between those two Christian Worthies*. London, 1730.

Johnson, Samuel, *Diaries, Prayers, and Annals*, ed. E.L. McAdam, and others. New Haven, 1958.

——————, *Letters, with Mrs. Thrale's Genuine Letters to him*, ed. R.W. Chapman, 3 vols. Oxford, 1952.

——————, *Works*, ed. Arthur Murphy, 12 vols. London, 1816.

Keill, John, *Introductio ad Veram Physicam*. Oxford, 1705.

Kennett, Basil, *Sermons Preached on Several Occasions, to a Society of British Merchants, in Foreign Parts*. London, 1715.

Kett, Henry, *Eléments of General Knowledge*, 2 vols. London, 1803.

Knight, William A. (ed.), *Memorials of Coleorton, being letters from Coleridge, Wordsworth and his Sister, Southey, and Sir Walter Scott, to Sir George and Lady Beaumont of Coleorton, Leicestershire*, 2 vols. Edinburgh, 1887.

The Ladies Library: Written by a Lady: Published by Mr. Steele, 3 vols. London, 1714.

Larroque, Matthieu de, *The History of the Eucharist*, trans. Joseph Walker. London, 1684.

Law, Edmund, *Considerations on the Theory of Religion*. Cambridge, 1755.

Law, William, *A Practical Treatise upon Christian Perfection*. London, 1734.

Literary Magazine and British Review, III. London, 1789.

Locke, John, *An Essay Concerning Human Understanding*, ed. A.C. Fraser, 2 vols. Oxford, 1894.

Lough, John (ed.), *Locke's Travels in France, 1675 – 1679. As related in his journals, correspondence and other papers*. Cambridge, 1953.

Mackenzie, Sir George, *Essays upon Several Moral Subjects*. London, 1713.

——————, *Religio Stoici*. Edinburgh, 1663.

Mackintosh, Sir James, *History of England*, 10 vols. London, 1830–1840.

Mackintosh, Robert J. (ed.), *Memoirs of the Life of the Right Honourable Sir James Mackintosh*, 2 vols. London, 1835.

Mainwaring, John, *Memoirs of the Life of the late George Frederic Handel*. London, 1760.

Mandeville, Bernard, *The Fable of the Bees*, ed. F.B. Kaye, 2 vols. Oxford, 1924.

[Mathias, Thomas J.], *The Pursuits of Literature*, 14th edition. London, 1808.

Mémoires pour l'histoire des sciences et des beaux-arts, XXXV. Trévoux, 1735.

Mengel, Elias F., Jr. (ed.), *Poems on Affairs of State: Augustan Satirical Verse, 1660 – 1714*. New Haven, 1963 –.

Milton, John, *Life Records*, ed. J.M. French, 5 vols. New Brunswick, N.J., 1949 – 1958.

————————, *Works*, ed. F.A. Patterson and others, 18 vols. New York, 1931 – 1938.

Montagu, Lady Mary Wortley, *Complete Letters*, ed. Robert Halsband, 3 vols. Oxford, 1965 – 1967.

Monthly Magazine; or, British Register, IX; XXXIV. London, 1800; 1812 – 1813.

Monthly Review; or Literary Journal, LXI. London, 1779.

More, Hannah, *Works*, 11 vols. London, 1830.

Moréri, Louis, *The Great Historical, Geographical and Poetical Dictionary*, 2 vols. London, 1694.

————————, *The Great Historical, Geographical, Genealogical and Poetical Dictionary*, ed. Jeremy Collier, 2 vols. London, 1701.

Morley, Edith J. (ed.), *Henry Crabb Robinson on Books and their Writers*, 3 vols. London, 1938.

Murray, Lindley, *The Power of Religion on the Mind, in Retirement, Affliction, and at the Approach of Death*, 10th edition. York, 1801.

A New and General Biographical Dictionary; containing an Historical and Critical Account of the Lives and Writings of the Most Eminent Persons in Every Nation . . ., 12 vols. London, 1784.

————————, *A New Edition, greatly enlarged and improved*, 15 vols. London, 1798.

New London Magazine, v. London, 1789

News for the Curious; A Treatise of Telescopes . . ., trans. Joseph Walker. London, 1684.

Newton, Isaac, *Correspondence*, ed. H.W. Turnbull. Cambridge, 1959 –.

————————, *Mathematical Papers*, ed. D.T. Whiteside. Cambridge, 1967 –.

[Newton, William], *The Life of the Right Reverend Dr. White Kennett, Late Lord Bishop of Peterborough*. London, 1730.

Nichols, John, *Literary Anecdotes of the Eighteenth Century,* 9 vols. London, 1812 – 1815.

Nicole, Pierre, *Discourses: Translated from Nicole's Essays by John Locke.* London, 1828.

——————————, *Essais de morale, contenus en divers traitez sur plusieurs devoirs importans,* 4 vols. Paris, 1678 – 1679.

[Nicole, Pierre], *The Pernicious Consequences of the New Heresie of the Jesuites against the King and the State.* London, 1666.

[Nouet, Jacques, and Annat, François], *An Answer to the Provinciall Letters Published by the Jansenists, Under the Name of Lewis Montalt, Against the Doctrine of the Jesuits and School-Divines.* Paris, 1659.

Oldenburg, Henry, *Correspondence,* ed. A.R. Hall and M.B. Hall. Madison and Milwaukee, 1965 – .

Ollion, Henry, and De Boer, T.J. (eds.), *Lettres inédites de John Locke à ses amis Nicolas Thoynard, Philippe van Limborch et Edward Clarke.* La Haye, 1912.

Percival, Thomas, *Moral and Literary Dissertations....* London, 1784.

[Perrault, Nicolas], *The Jesuits Morals.* London, 1670.

Petty, Sir William, *The Petty Papers,* ed. Marquis of Lansdowne, 2 vols. London, 1927.

The Petty-Southwell Correspondence, 1676 – 1687, ed. Marquis of Lansdowne. London, 1928.

Phrenological Journal and Miscellany, IV. Edinburgh, 1826 – 1827.

Pope, Alexander, *Correspondence,* ed. George Sherburn, 5 vols. Oxford, 1956.

——————————, *An Essay on Man,* ed. Maynard Mack. London, 1950.

——————————, *Prose Works,* ed. Norman Ault. Oxford, 1936 – .

——————————, *Works,* ed. Whitwell Elwin and W.J. Courthope, 10 vols. London, 1871 – 1889.

[Pope, Alexander, and others], *Memoirs of the Extraordinary Life, Works, and Discoveries of Martinus Scriblerus,* ed. Charles Kerby-Miller. New Haven, 1950.

Power, Henry, *Experimental Philosophy, In Three Books: Containing New Experiments Microscopical, Mercurial, Magnetical.* London, 1664.

Priestley, Joseph, *Lectures on History and General Policy.* Birmingham, 1788.

Prior, Matthew, *Literary Works*, ed. H.B. Wright and M.K. Spears, 2 vols. Oxford, 1959.

Quarterly Review, XXII; XXVIII. London, 1819 – 1820; 1822 – 1823.

Quesnel, Pasquier, *Correspondance sur les affaires politiques et religieuses de son temps*, ed. A. Le Roy, 2 vols. Paris, 1900.

Ramsay, Andrew M., *The Life of François Salignac De La Motte Fenelon, Archbishop and Duke of Cambray*. London, 1723.

Rees, Abraham, and others, *The Cyclopaedia; or, Universal Dictionary of Arts, Sciences, and Literature*, 39 vols. London, 1819.

Rigaud, Stephen P. (ed.), *Correspondence of Scientific Men of the Seventeenth Century*..., 2 vols. Oxford, 1841.

Roberts, William, *Memoirs of the Life and Correspondence of Mrs. Hannah More*, 4 vols. London, 1834.

Robinson, Henry Crabb, *Diary, Reminiscences, and Correspondence*, ed. Thomas Sadler, 3 vols. London, 1869.

Rowe, Elizabeth, *Works*, 4 vols. London, 1796.

The Rule of Life, 9th edition. London, 1769.

Sandeman, Robert, *Letters on Theron and Aspasio. Addressed to the Author of that Work*, 2 vols. London, 1768.

Schimmelpenninck, Mary Anne, *Select Memoirs of Port Royal, To which are appended Tour to Alet; Visit to Port Royal; Gift of an Abbess; Biographical Notices, &c.*, 2 vols. London, 1835.

Scougall, Henry, *The Life of God in the Soul of Man: or, The Nature and Excellency of the Christian Religion*. London, 1739.

[Seward, William], *Anecdotes of some Distinguished Persons, chiefly of the Present and Two Preceding Centuries*, 4 vols. with supplement. London, 1795 – 1797.

Shaftesbury, Anthony Ashley Cooper, third Earl of, *Characteristics of Men, Manners, Opinions, Times, etc.*, ed. J.M. Robertson, 2 vols. London, 1900.

Southey, Robert, *Common-place Book*, ed. J.W. Warter, 4 vols. London, 1850.

Spectator [by Joseph Addison, Richard Steele, and others], 5 vols., ed. D.F. Bond. Oxford, 1965.

Spence, Joseph, *An Essay on Mr. Pope's Odyssey*. London, 1737.

Sprat, Thomas, *The History of the Royal Society of London, For the Improving of Natural Knowledge*. London, 1667.

Sterne, Laurence, *The Life and Opinions of Tristram Shandy, Gentleman*, ed. George Saintsbury. London, 1912.

Stewart, Dugald, *Collected Works*, ed. Sir William Hamilton, 11 vols. Edinburgh, 1854 – 1860.

Taylor, Jeremy, *The Whole Works*, ed. Reginald Heber and C.P. Eden, 10 vols. London, 1847 – 1854.

Thomson, James, *Complete Poetical Works*, ed. J.L. Robertson. Oxford, 1908.

Thomson, Thomas, *History of the Royal Society from its Institution to the End of the Eighteenth Century*. London, 1812.

Thraliana: The Diary of Mrs. Hester Lynch Thrale, later Mrs. Piozzi, ed. K.C. Balderston, 2 vols. Oxford, 1942.

Tillotson, John, *Works*. London, 1728.

Turnbull, Herbert W. (ed.), *James Gregory Tercentenary Memorial Volume*. London, 1939.

Universal Magazine of Knowledge and Pleasure, CI; CV. London, 1797; 1799.

[Vischard de Saint-Réal, César], *Caesarion, or Historical, Political, and Moral Discourses*, trans. Joseph Walker. London, 1685.

Voltaire, François Marie Arouet de, *Letters concerning the English Nation*. London, 1741.

—————————, *Notebooks*, ed. Theodore Besterman, 2 vols. Geneva, 1952.

—————————, *Oeuvres complètes*, ed. Louis Moland, 52 vols. Paris, 1877 – 1885.

—————————, *Works*, ed. Thomas Francklin and Tobias Smollett, 25 vols. London, 1761 – 1765.

Wallis, John, *Opera Mathematicorum*, 3 vols. Oxford, 1693 – 1699.

Walpole, Horace, *Anecdotes of Painting in England*, ed. James Dallaway and R.N. Wornum, 3 vols. London, 1849.

—————————, *Correspondence*, ed. W.S. Lewis. New Haven, 1937 – .

Warburton, William, *Works*, 12 vols. London, 1811.

[Warburton, William], *Letters from a Late Eminent Prelate to One of his Friends*. London, 1809.

Warton, Joseph, *An Essay on the Genius and Writings of Pope*, 2 vols. London, 1806.

Wesley, Charles, *Journal*, ed. Thomas Jackson, 2 vols. London, 1849.

Wesley, John, *Journal*, ed. Nehemiah Curnock, 8 vols. London, 1909 – 1916.

—————————, *Letters*, ed. John Telford, 8 vols. London, 1931.

_____, *Works*, 14 vols. London, 1872.

Wesley, Susannah, 'Mrs. Wesley's Conference with her Daughter,' *Publications of the Wesley Historical Society*, No. 3. London, 1898.

Wesleyan-Methodist Magazine, XLVIII. London, 1825.

White, Thomas, *A Letter to a Person of Honour*. [Douay?], 1659.

Whitefield, George, *Journals*, ed. Murray. London, 1960.

Wilberforce, William, *A Practical View of the Prevailing Religious System of Professed Christians*.... London, 1797.

Wilson, John, *The Cheats*, ed. M.C. Nahm. Oxford, 1935.

Wood, Anthony à, *Athenae Oxonienses, An Exact History of all the Writers and Bishops who have had their Education in the University of Oxford*, ed. Philip Bliss, 4 vols. London, 1813 – 1820.

[Wood, Anthony à], *The Life and Times of Anthony Wood, antiquary of Oxford, 1632 – 1695*, ed. Andrew Clark, 5 vols. Oxford, 1891 – 1900.

Wordsworth, William, *Poetical Works*, ed. Ernest de Selincourt and Helen Darbishire, 5 vols. Oxford, 1940 – 1949.

Wren, Christopher, *Parentalia: or, Memoirs of the Family of the Wrens*. London, 1750.

Young, Edward, *Les nuits*, trans. Pierre Le Tourneur, 3 vols. Marseille, 1770.

D Secondary Sources

Aaron, Richard I., *John Locke*. Oxford, 1955.

Abbey, Charles J., *The English Church and its Bishops, 1700 – 1800*, 2 vols. London, 1887.

Abbey, Charles J., and Overton, John H., *The English Church in the Eighteenth Century*, 2 vols. London, 1878.

Abercrombie, Nigel J., *The Origins of Jansenism*. Oxford, 1936.

Amoudru, Bernard, *La vie posthume des Pensées*. Paris, 1936.

Ascoli, Georges, *La Grande Bretagne devant l'opinion française au XVIIe siècle*, 2 vols. Paris, 1930.

Audra, Emile, *L'influence française dans l'oeuvre de Pope*. Paris, 1931.

Axtell, James L., 'Locke, Newton and the Two Cultures,' *John Locke: Problems and Perspectives*, ed. J.W. Yolton. Cambridge, 1969, pp. 165 – 82.

Bain, Alexander, *James Mill*. London, 1882.

Ballantyne, Archibald, *Voltaire's Visit to England, 1726 – 1729*. London, 1919.

Beattie, Lester M., *John Arbuthnot, Mathematician and Satirist.* Cambridge, Mass., 1935.

Bellessort, André, *Essai sur Voltaire.* Paris, 1926.

Belloc, Hilaire, *Pascal's 'Provincial Letters.'* Catholic Truth Society, London, 1921.

Bennett, Gareth V., *White Kennett, 1660 – 1728, Bishop of Peterborough.* London, 1957.

Blanchet, Léon, 'L'attitude religieuse des jésuites et les sources du pari de Pascal,' *Revue de métaphysique et de morale*, XXVI (1919), 477 – 516, 617 – 47.

Bonno, Gabriel, 'La culture et la civilisation britanniques devant l'opinion française de la paix d'Utrecht aux Lettres Philosophiques (1713 – 1734),' *Transactions of the American Philosophical Society,* New Series, XXXVIII (1948), pt. 1.

——————, 'Les relations intellectuelles de Locke avec la France (D'après des documents inédits),' *Univ. of California Publications in Modern Philology,* XXXVIII (1955), 37 – 264.

Bordier, Henri L., and Mabille, Emile, *Une fabrique de faux autographes ou récit de l'affaire Vrain Lucas.* Paris, 1870.

Braithwaite, William C., *The Second Period of Quakerism.* Cambridge, 1961.

Bredvold, Louis I., *The Intellectual Milieu of John Dryden.* Ann Arbor, 1934.

Brigden, Thomas E., 'Pascal and the Wesleys,' *Proceedings of the Wesley Historical Society,* VII (1910), 60 – 63, 84 – 88.

Broome, Jack H., *Pascal.* London, 1965.

Broxap, Henry, *The Later Non-jurors.* Cambridge, 1924.

Butler, Dugald, *The Life and Letters of Robert Leighton, Restoration Bishop of Dunblane and Archbishop of Glasgow.* London, 1903.

Carré, Jean-Raoul, *Réflexions sur l'anti-Pascal de Voltaire.* Paris, 1935.

Cassirer, Ernst, *The Philosophy of the Enlightenment.* Princeton, 1951.

Chapin, Chester F., 'Johnson and Pascal,' *English Writers of the Eighteenth Century,* ed. J.H. Middendorf. New York, 1971, pp. 3 – 16.

Charlanne, Louis, *L'influence française en Angleterre au* XVIIe *siècle: La vie sociale – La vie littéraire.* Paris, 1906.

Cherel, Albert, *Fénelon au* XVIIIe *siècle en France, 1715– 1820.* Paris, 1917.

Chinard, Gilbert, *En lisant Pascal.* Lille, 1948.

Clark, Ruth, *Strangers and Sojourners at Port Royal: Being an account of the connections between the British Isles and the Jansenists of France and Holland.* Cambridge, 1932.

Clarke, Adam, *Memoirs of the Wesley Family*, 2 vols. London, 1836.

Conant, James B. (ed.), *Robert Boyle's Experiments in Pneumatics.* Cambridge, Mass., 1950.

Courthope, William J., *A History of English Poetry*, 6 vols. London, 1895 – 1910.

Courtines, Léo P., *Bayle's Relations with England and the English.* New York, 1938.

Cousin, Victor, 'Rapport à l'Académie française sur la nécessité d'une nouvelle édition des Pensées de Pascal,' *Journal des savans*, 1842.

Cragg, Gerald R., *Reason and Authority in the Eighteenth Century.* Cambridge, 1964.

Crane, Ronald S., 'The Diffusion of Voltaire's Writings in England, 1750 – 1800,' *Modern Philology*, xx (1922 – 1923), 261 – 74.

Cranston, Maurice, *John Locke: A Biography.* London, 1957.

Desnoiresterres, Gustave, *Voltaire et la société au xviiie siècle*, 8 vols. Paris, 1867 – 1876.

Dobrée, Bonamy, *English Literature in the Early Eighteenth Century, 1700 – 1740.* Oxford, 1959.

Dunn, William P., *Sir Thomas Browne: A Study in Religious Philosophy.* Minneapolis, 1950.

Eastwood, Dorothy M., *The Revival of Pascal: A Study of his Relation to Modern French Thought.* Oxford, 1936.

Elton, Oliver, *A Survey of English Literature, 1730 – 1780*, 2 vols. London, 1928.

Fairchild, Hoxie N., *Religious Trends in English Poetry*, 5 vols. New York, 1939 – 1962.

Finch, David, *La critique philosophique de Pascal au xviiie siècle.* Philadelphia, 1940.

Fitzmaurice, Lord Edmond, *The Life of Sir William Petty, 1623 – 1687.* London, 1895.

Foulet, Lucien, *Correspondance de Voltaire, 1726 – 1729.* Paris, 1913.

Francis, Raymond, *Les Pensées de Pascal en France, de 1842 à 1942: Essai d'étude historique et critique.* Paris, 1959.

Gillow, Joseph, *A Literary and Biographical History of the English Catholics*, 4 vols. London, 1885 – 1902.

Gladstone, William E., *Studies Subsidiary to the Works of Bishop Butler*. Oxford, 1896.

Goldmann, Lucien, *The Hidden God: A study of tragic vision in the Pensées of Pascal and the tragedies of Racine*. London, 1964.

Gosse, Sir Edmund, *Sir Thomas Browne*. London, 1905.

Goulding, Sybil, *Swift en France*. Paris, 1924.

Gounelle, Edmond, *Wesley et ses rapports avec les français*. Nyons, 1898.

Green, J. Brazier, *John Wesley and William Law*. London, 1945.

Hankin, Christiana C., *Life of Mary Anne Schimmelpenninck*. London, 1859.

Havens, George R., 'Voltaire's Marginal Comments upon Pope's *Essay on Man*,' *Modern Language Notes*, XLIII (1928), 429 – 39.

Havens, Raymond D., *The Mind of a Poet: A study of Wordsworth's thought with particular reference to 'The Prelude.'* Baltimore, 1941.

Hay, Malcolm V., *The Jesuits and the Popish Plot*. London, 1934.

Henderson, George D., *Chevalier Ramsay*. London, 1952.

————————, *Mystics of the North-East*. Third Spalding Club, Aberdeen, 1934.

————————, *Religious Life in Seventeenth-century Scotland*. Cambridge, 1937.

Herbert, Thomas W., *John Wesley as Editor and Author*. Princeton, 1940.

Hobhouse, Stephen (ed.), *Selected Mystical Writings of William Law*. London, 1948.

Hubert, Sister Marie Louise, *Pascal's Unfinished Apology: A Study of his Plan*. New Haven, 1952.

Humbert, Pierre, *L'oeuvre scientifique de Blaise Pascal*. Paris, 1947.

Hunt, John, *Religious Thought in England from the Reformation to the End of the Last Century*, 3 vols. London, 1870 – 1873.

Irving, William H., *The Providence of Wit in the English Letter Writers*. Durham, N.C., 1955.

Jackson, Thomas, *The Life of the Rev. Charles Wesley*, 2 vols. London, 1841.

James, David G., *The Life of Reason: Hobbes, Locke, Bolingbroke*. London, 1949.

Janelle, Pierre, 'Pascal et l'Angleterre,' *Pascal présent*. Clermont-Ferrand, 1963, pp. 147–72.

Jansen, Paule, *De Blaise Pascal à Henry Hammond: Les Provinciales en Angleterre*. Paris, 1954.

Jones, Mary G., *Hannah More*. Cambridge, 1952.

Jovy, Ernest, *Pascal inédit*, 5 vols. Vitry-le-François, 1908 – 1912.

Kaufman, Paul, *Borrowings from the Bristol Library*, 1773 – 1784. Charlottesville, 1960.

_____, 'Reading Vogues at English Cathedral Libraries of the Eighteenth Century,' *Bulletin of the New York Public Library*, LXVII (1963), 643 – 72; LXVIII (1964), 48 – 64, 110 – 32, 191 – 202.

Knapp, Richard G., 'The Fortunes of Pope's *Essay on Man* in Eighteenth-century France,' *Studies on Voltaire and the Eighteenth Century*, ed. Theodore Besterman, LXXXII (1971).

Krutch, Joseph W., *Samuel Johnson*. New York, 1944.

Ladborough, Richard W., 'Pepys and Pascal,' *French Studies*, X (1956), 133 – 39.

Lambin, G., *Les rapports de Bossuet avec l'Angleterre*. Paris, 1909.

Lanson, Gustave, 'Voltaire et les Lettres Philosophiques,' *Revue de Paris*, IV (1908), 367 – 86.

Lathbury, Thomas, *A History of the Nonjurors: Their Controversies and Writings*. London, 1845.

Leavenworth, Isabel, *A Methodological Analysis of the Physics of Pascal*. New York, 1930.

Leeuwen, Henry G. van, *The Problem of Certainty in English Thought, 1630 – 1690*. The Hague, 1963.

Lefebvre, Henri, *Pascal*, 2 vols. Paris, 1949 – 1955.

Leger, J. Augustin, *L'Angleterre religieuse et les origines du méthodisme au XVIIIe siècle: La jeunesse de Wesley*. Paris, 1910.

Leroy, Oliver, *Le Chevalier Thomas Browne, 1605 – 1682: médecin, styliste et métaphysicien*. Paris, 1931.

Leyden, Wolfgang von, 'Locke and Nicole,' *Sophia*, XVI (1948), 41 – 55.

Lough, John, 'Locke's Reading during his Stay in France (1675 – 1679),' *Library*, Fifth Series, VIII (1953), 229 – 58.

Macaulay, Thomas B., *The History of England from the Accession of James II*, ed. T.F. Henderson, 5 vols. Oxford, 1931.

Maclean, Kenneth, *John Locke and English Literature of the Eighteenth Century*. New Haven, 1936.

Maher, Leo D., *Pascal and the Critics of the Pensées*. Unpublished doctoral dissertation in Philosophy, Columbia University, 1957.

Martin, Bernard, *John Newton: A Biography*. London, 1950.

Mathew, David, *Catholicism in England, 1535 – 1935: Portrait of a Minority*. London, 1936.

Mertz, Rudolf, 'Les amitiés françaises de Hume et le mouvement des idées,' *Revue de littérature comparée*, IX (1929), 644 – 713.

Mesnard, Jean, *Pascal: His Life and Works*. London, 1952.

Moore, Henry, *The Life of the Rev. John Wesley*, 2 vols. New York, 1826.

Mortimer, Ernest, *Blaise Pascal: The Life and Work of a Realist*. London, 1959.

Mossner, Ernest C., *Bishop Butler and the Age of Reason*. New York, 1936.

Moussali, Ulysse, *Le vrai visage de Blaise Pascal*. Paris, 1952.

Nicolson, Marjorie, and Rousseau, G.S., *'This Long Disease, My Life'; Alexander Pope and the Sciences*. Princeton, 1968.

Orcibal, Jean, 'L'originalité théologique de John Wesley et les spiritualités du continent,' *Revue historique*, CCXXII (1959), 51 – 80.

————————, 'Les spirituels français et espagnols chez John Wesley et ses contemporains,' *Revue de l'histoire des religions*, CXXXIX (1951), 50 – 109.

Overton, John H., *The Nonjurors. Their Lives, Principles, and Writings*. London, 1902.

————————, *William Law, Nonjuror and Mystic*. London, 1881.

Palmer, Robert R., *Catholics and Unbelievers in Eighteenth Century France*. New York, 1961.

Pater, Walter, *Appreciations. With an Essay on Style*. London, 1910.

Pattison, Mark, 'Tendencies of Religious Thought in England, 1685 – 1750,' *Essays and Reviews*. London, 1861, pp. 254 – 329.

Piette, Maximin, *John Wesley in the Evolution of Protestantism*. London, 1937.

Plumptre, Edward H., *The Life of Thomas Ken, D.D., Bishop of Bath and Wells*, 2 vols. London, 1889.

Pons, Emile, 'Swift et Pascal,' *Les langues modernes*, XLV (1951), 135 – 52.

————————, 'Swift et Pascal: note complémentaire,' *Etudes anglaises*, V (1952), 319 – 25.

Pottle, Frederick A., *The Literary Career of James Boswell, Esq., being the bibliographical materials for a life of Boswell*. Oxford, 1927.

Préclin, Edmond, *L'union des églises gallicane et anglicane*. Paris, 1928.

Price, M. Martin, *To the Palace of Wisdom: Studies in order and energy from Dryden to Blake*. New York, 1964.

Quintana, Ricardo, *The Mind and Art of Jonathan Swift*. London, 1953.

Ransom, Harry, 'Riddle of the World: A Note on Pope and Pascal,' *Sewanee Review*, XLVI (1938), 306 – 11.

Rattenbury, J. Ernest, *The Conversion of the Wesleys: A critical study*. London, 1938.

Ressler, Kathleen, 'Jeremy Collier's Essays,' *Seventeenth Century Studies*, Second Series, ed. Robert Shafer. Princeton, 1937, pp.179 – 285.

Sainte-Beuve, Charles-Augustin, *Port-Royal*, 7 vols. Paris, 1912 – 1913.

Schilling, Bernard A., *Conservative England and the Case against Voltaire*. New York, 1950.

Schlatter, Richard B., *The Social Ideas of Religious Leaders*, 1660 – 1688. Oxford, 1940.

Schlegel, Dorothy B., *Shaftesbury and the French Deists*. Chapel Hill, 1956.

Schrickx, W., 'Coleridge and Friedrich Heinrich Jacobi,' *Revue belge de philologie et d'histoire*, XXXVI (1958), 812 – 50.

Scott, Joseph F., *The Mathematical Work of John Wallis, D.D., F.R.S.* London, 1938.

Shepherd, Thomas B., *Methodism and the Literature of the Eighteenth Century*. New York, 1966.

Simon, John S., *John Wesley and the Advance of Methodism*. London, 1925.

Smith, George, *The Life of William Carey, D.D., Shoemaker and Missionary*. London, 1887.

Spears, Munroe K., 'Matthew Prior's Attitude toward Natural Science,' *Publications of the Modern Language Association of America*, LXIII, pt. 1, (1948), 485 – 507.

——————, 'Matthew Prior's Religion,' *Philological Quarterly*, XXVII (1948), 159 – 80.

——————, 'The Meaning of Matthew Prior's *Alma*,' *English Literary History*, XIII (1946), 266 – 90.

——————, 'Some Ethical Aspects of Matthew Prior's Poetry,' *Studies in Philology*, XLV (1948), 606 – 29.

Stauffer, Donald A., *The Art of Biography in Eighteenth Century England*, 2 vols. Princeton, 1941.

Steinmann, Jean, *Pascal*. Paris, 1954.

Stephen, Sir Leslie, *History of English Thought in the Eighteenth Century*, 2 vols. London, 1902.

Stoughton, John, *Ecclesiastical History of England: The Church of the Restoration*, 2 vols. London, 1870.

Strowski, Fortunat, *Histoire du sentiment religieux en France au* XVIIe *siècle: Pascal et son temps*, 3 vols. Paris, 1907 – 1908.

Sultana, Donald, *Samuel Taylor Coleridge in Malta and Italy*. New York, 1969.

Talon, Henri A., *William Law: A Study in Literary Craftsmanship*. London, 1948.

Taunton, Ethelred L., *The History of the Jesuits in England*, 1580 – 1773. London, 1901.

Thomas, Walter, *Le poète Edward Young*, 1683 – 1765. Paris, 1901.

Thornton, Francis B., *Alexander Pope: Catholic Poet*. New York, 1952.

Torrey, Norman L., *Voltaire and the English Deists*. New Haven, 1930.

Tuveson, Ernest L., 'An Essay on Man *and "The Way of Ideas",'* *English Literary History*, XXVI (1959), 368 – 86.

Vamos, Mara M., *Pascal's Pensées in England*, 1670 – 1776. Unpublished doctoral dissertation in French, Brown University, June, 1961.

————, 'Pascal's *pensées* and the Enlightenment: the Roots of a Misunderstanding,' *Studies on Voltaire and the Eighteenth Century*, ed. Theodore Besterman, XCVII (1972), 7 – 145.

Wade, Ira O., *The Intellectual Development of Voltaire*. Princeton, 1969.

Warren, Austin, *Alexander Pope as Critic and Humanist*. Gloucester, Mass., 1963.

Waterman, Mina, *Voltaire, Pascal and Human Destiny*. New York, 1942.

Webb, Clement C.J., *Pascal's Philosophy of Religion*. Oxford, 1929.

Willey, Basil, *The Eighteenth Century Background: Studies on the idea of Nature in the thought of the period*. London, 1940.

————, *The Seventeenth Century Background: Studies in the thought of the age in relation to poetry and religion*. New York, 1934.

Wright, Harold B., *Matthew Prior: A Supplement to his Biography*. Unpublished doctoral dissertation in English, Northwestern University, June, 1937.

Young, George M., *Gibbon*. New York, 1933.

Bibliography for Appendix

I WORKS BY BLAISE PASCAL

Provincial Letters, containing an Exposure of the Reasoning and Morals of the Jesuits . . . To which is added, A View of the History of the Jesuits, and The late Bull for the Revival of the Order in Europe. New York, 1828.

Thoughts on Religion, and Other Subjects [trans. Edward Craig]. Amherst, Mass., 1829.

II OTHER WORKS

A Contemporary Sources, Manuscripts, Library Catalogues, and Periodicals

Adams, Charles Francis, *Diary*, ed. A.D. and D. Donald, 2 vols. Cambridge, Mass., 1964.

Adams, John, *Diary and Autobiography*, ed. L.H. Butterfield, 4 vols. Cambridge, Mass., 1961.

The Adams-Jefferson Letters; The Complete Correspondence between Thomas Jefferson and Abigail and John Adams, ed. L.J. Cappon, 2 vols. Chapel Hill, 1959.

Bassett, John S. (ed.), *The Writings of 'Colonel William Byrd of Westover in Virginia Esqr.'*. New York, 1901.

A Catalogue of the Books of John Quincy Adams Deposited in the Boston Athenaeum, ed. H. Adams and W.C. Ford. Boston, 1938.

Catalogue, No. 2, of Books in the Boston Library, Franklin Place. Boston, 1819.

A Catalogue of the Books belonging to the Charleston Library. Charleston, 1826.

A Catalogue of Curious and Valuable Books, (Which mostly belonged to

the Reverend Mr. George Curwin, Late of Salem, Deceased) Consisting of Divinity, Philosophy, History, Poetry, &c. . . . Boston, 1718.

Catalogue of the Library of Thomas Jefferson, U.S. Library of Congress, Jefferson Collection, ed. E.M. Sowerby, 3 vols. Washington, 1952 – 1953.

A Catalogue of Books Belonging to the Library Company of Philadelphia. Philadelphia, 1741.

A Catalogue of the Books, belonging to The Library Company of Philadelphia. Philadelphia, 1807.

Catalogue of the Books Belonging to The Loganian Library, 2 vols. Philadelphia, 1795.

A Catalogue of Curious and Valuable Books, Belonging to the late Reverend & Learned, Mr. Ebenezer Pemberton, Consisting of Divinity, Philosophy, History, Poetry, &c. . . . Boston, 1717.

Catalogue of Books belonging to the Library of Rhode-Island College. Providence, 1793.

Catalogue of Books in the Library of Yale College. New Haven, 1823.

Catalogus Bibliothecae Harvardianae Cantabrigiae Nov-Anglorum. Boston, 1790.

Christian Disciple, II. Boston, 1814.

Christian Register, III. Boston, 1823 – 1824.

Edwards, Jonathan, *Notebook.* MS, Yale University, Beinecke Library.

Emerson, Ralph W., *Journals and Miscellaneous Notebooks,* ed. W.H. Gilman and others. Cambridge, Mass., 1960 –.

————————, *Letters,* ed. R.R. Rusk, 6 vols. New York, 1939.

Everett, Edward, *Orations and Speeches on Various Occasions,* 4 vols. Boston, 1850 – 1868.

Jefferson, Thomas, *Papers,* ed. J.P. Boyd. Princeton, 1950 –.

Johnson, Samuel, *Career and Writings,* ed. H. and C. Schneider, 4 vols. New York, 1929.

Madison, James, *Letters and Other Writings,* 4 vols. Philadelphia, 1865.

Massachusetts Missionary Magazine, I. Salem, Mass., 1803 – 1804; II. Boston, 1804 – 1805.

Melville, Herman, *Moby Dick,* ed. L.S. Mansfield and H.P. Vincent. New York, 1962.

Morton, Charles, 'Compendium Physicae,' *Publications of the Colonial Society of Massachusetts,* XXXIII (1940), Collections.

Parkman, Ebenezer, 'Diary,' ed. F.G. Walett, *Proceedings of the American Antiquarian Society,* New Series, LXXII (1962), 329–481.

Pemberton, Ebenezer, *The Divine Original and Dignity of Government Asserted; and An Advantageous Prospect of the Ruler's Mortality Recommended*. Boston, 1710.

Rush, Benjamin, *Medical Inquiries and Observations upon the Diseases of the Mind*. Philadelphia, 1812.

_____, *Selected Writings*, ed. D.D. Runes. New York, 1947.

Sewall, Samuel, 'Diary, 1674 – 1729,' *Collections of the Massachusetts Historical Society*, Fifth Series, v-vii. Boston, 1878 – 1882.

Ticknor, George, *Lectures on French Literature*, 5 vols. MS, Harvard University Archives.

Tyler, Lyon G., 'Libraries in Colonial Virginia,' *William and Mary College Quarterly* (Series 1), ii-ix (1893 – 1901), *passim*.

B Secondary Sources

Aldridge, Alfred O., *Benjamin Franklin, Philosopher and Man*. Philadelphia, 1965.

Barr, Mary-Margaret H., *Voltaire in America*, 1744 – 1800. Baltimore, 1941.

Barton, William, *Memoirs of the Life of David Rittenhouse, LL.D., F.R.S. Late President of the American Philosophical Society, & c.* Philadelphia, 1813.

Braddy, Haldeen, *Glorious Incense*. Port Washington, N.Y., 1968.

Cadbury, Henry J., 'Anthony Benezet's Library,' *Bulletin of Friends' Historical Association*, xxiii (1934), 63 – 75.

Holmes, Oliver W., *Writings*, 14 vols. Boston, 1899 – 1900.

Jaffe, Adrian H., 'French Literature in American Periodicals of the Eighteenth Century,' *Revue de littérature comparée*, xxxviii (1964), 51 – 60.

Johnson, Thomas H., 'Jonathan Edwards' Background of Reading,' *Publications of the Colonial Society of Massachusetts*, xxviii (1930 – 1933), Transactions, 193 – 222.

Jones, Howard M., 'The Importation of French Books in Philadelphia, 1750 – 1800,' *Modern Philology*, xxxii (1934 – 1935), 157 – 77.

_____, 'The Importation of French Literature in New York City, 1750 – 1800,' *Studies in Philology*, xxviii (1931), 767 – 83. ·

Levin, Harry, *The Power of Blackness*. New York, 1967.

Merriam, John M., 'Historic Burial-Places of Boston and Vicinity,' *Proceedings of the American Antiquarian Society*, New Series, vii (1890 – 1891), 381 – 417.

Miller, Perry, *Jonathan Edwards*. New York, 1959.

—————————, *The New England Mind*, 2 vols. Boston, 1961.

Morison, Samuel E., *The Intellectual Life of Colonial New England*. New York, 1956.

Orcutt, William D., *Good Old Dorchester. A Narrative History of the Town*, 1630 – 1893. Cambridge, Mass., 1893.

Potts, William J., 'Du Simitière, Artist, Antiquary, and Naturalist, Projector of the First American Museum, with some extracts from his Note-Book,' *Pennsylvania Magazine of History and Biography*, XIII (1889), 341 – 75.

Robbins, James M., and others, *History of the Town of Dorchester, Massachusetts*. Boston, 1859.

Shipton, Clifford K., 'Literary Leaven in Provincial New England,' *New England Quarterly*, IX (1936), 203 – 17.

Sibley, John L., and others, *Biographical Sketches of Graduates of Harvard University, in Cambridge, Massachusetts*. Cambridge, Mass., and Boston, 1873 – .

Tolles, Frederick B., 'A Literary Quaker: John Smith of Burlington and Philadelphia,' *Pennsylvania Magazine of History and Biography*, LXV (1941), 300 – 33.

Warren, Austin, 'Hawthorne's Reading,' *New England Quarterly*, VIII (1935), 480 – 97.

Wolf, Edwin, 2nd., 'Franklin and his Friends Choose their Books,' *Pennsylvania Magazine of History and Biography*, LXXX (1956), 11 – 36.

Wright, Louis B., 'The 'Gentleman's Library' in Early Virginia: The Literary Interests of the First Carters,' *Huntington Library Quarterly*, I (1937 – 1938), 3 – 61.

Adams, Charles Francis, of Massachusetts, 245
Adams, John, President of United States, 242, 245; letter to Jefferson on Jesuits, 244
Adams, John Quincy, President of United States, 245
Addison, Joseph, 75, 110, 111, 131, 265n61; quotes Pascal on human mortality in *Guardian*, 111; on dignity of human nature, in *Tatler*, 111–12; opinion of Port Royal, 113–14; religion compared with Pascal's, 114, 140, 215. *See also Spectator*
Aemilius Papinianus, 80
Alexander VII, Pope, condemns *Provinciales*, 9
Allam, Andrew, antiquary, 20
Alves, Robert, *Sketches of a History of Literature*, 207
America: knowledge and reputation of Pascal in, 97, 235–47; Pascal's attraction to American readers contrasted with English, 240–41, 246; availability of Pascal's works in libraries, 242, 288n14
Andrews, William, translator of *Provinciales* (1744), 23–24, 94, 111, 150–51, 177, 178, 221
Anglicans, interest in Pascal, 4, 13–14, 19–20, 33, 67, 141, 151, 169, 184, 213, 216
Annat, François, jesuit, *Answer to the Provinciall Letters* (with Jacques Nouet), 6, 9, 18, 23, 24, 26, 31
Antijacobin Review, 216
Aquinas, St. Thomas, 94
Arbuthnot, John, physician and wit, 89, 114, 117–19, 120; Pascal's influence on poem *GNOTHI SE'AUTON Know Yourself*, 117–18
Archimedes, 60, 208
Aristotle, 60, 115
Arminianism, 184, 192, 195
Arnauld, Antoine, Jansenist leader, 1–2, 13, 18, 20, 28, 30–31, 32, 67, 72, 150, 159, 170, 249n7. *See also* Jansenists; Port Royal
Arnauld, Jacqueline, Port Royal reformer, 25
Arnold, Dr. Thomas, of Rugby, 283n48
Atterbury, Francis, Bishop of Rochester, quotes Locke and Pascal, 55–56
Augustine of Hippo, St., 133, 173, 174, 177
Ayre, William, miscellaneous writer, 270n37

Bacon, Francis, Lord Verulam, 36, 60, 218–19, 277n64
Baillet, Adrien, *Jugemens des sçavans*, 148
Ball, J., "virtuoso," 42
Balzac, Jean-Louis Guez de, literary work translated by

Kennett, 76
Baptists, interest in Pascal, 208, 279n14
Barlow, Thomas, Bishop of Lincoln, 21
Barrow, Isaac, mathematician and divine, 38, 40, 57, 187, 254n13
Barruel, Abbé Augustin, *Memoirs Illustrating the History of Jacobinism*, 204
Bastide, Marc Antoine de la, *Answer To the Bishop of Condom's Book*, translated by Walker, 66-67
Baxter, Richard, nonconformist, commends *Provinciales* to Richard Cromwell, 15–16, 251n33
Bayle, Pierre: life of Pascal in *Dictionnaire historique et critique*, 84–88, 111, 165, 204, 207, 245; English translations of *Dictionnaire*, 85, 145, 198, 233; views on Pascal in *Nouvelles de la république des lettres*, 87, 90–92, 206, 239; Voltaire's opinions of Pascal included in *Dictionnaire*, 145–47, 157; influence on English encyclopaedias, 147–48
Beaumont, Sir George and Lady, of Coleorton, 226, 227
Belloc, Hilaire, Catholic apologist, 253n80
Benezet, Anthony, American quaker, 239
Bennet, Thomas, London bookseller, 55, 74
Berington, Joseph, papal vicar-general, corresponds with Hannah More, 215–16
Berkeley, George, Bishop of Cloyne: on Pascal's life, 89–90; on Pascal's argument of the wager, 133; on human nature, 155; compared with Pascal by Hazlitt, 228–29; library, 268n3
Bernard, Edward, astronomer, 40
Bernard, St., 12, 216, 281n37
Bernier, François, talks with Locke on Pascal's discoveries, 49
Berwick, James Fitzjames, Duke of, amused by *Provinciales*, 28–29
Betham, Dr. John, tutor of James,

the Old Pretender, defends *Provinciales*, 28
Bettenham, James, publisher, 270n37
Birch, Thomas, historian and biographer, 147–48
Bishop, Mary, John Wesley recommends *Pensées* to, 189, 202
Böhler, Peter, moravian, and the Wesleys, 182, 185
Boehme, Jakob, German mystic, 180
Boileau-Despréaux, Nicolas, poet and critic, and English readers, 105, 111, 129, 201
Bolingbroke, Henry St. John, Viscount, politician and philosopher, on Pascal, 126, 131; influence on Gibbon, 152
Bond, William, miscellaneous writer, preface to Jesup's edition of Mme. Perier's *Vie de Blaise Pascal* (1723), 90–92, 148
Bossuet, Jacques-Bénigne, Bishop of Meaux, 66, 171; admired in England, 141, 177, 216, 274n10
Bossut, Abbé Charles, editor of Pascal's *Oeuvres* (1779), 99, 104, 204, 207
Boswell, James: alleged author of essays in *Gentleman's Magazine* (1789) condemning Pascal, 161–64, 176, 201, 272n62; Johnson gives *Pensées* to, 163, 200; essays in series "the Hypochondriack," *London Magazine*, 272n62
Bourdaloue, Louis, jesuit, 216
Bourignon, Antoinette, religious enthusiast, 170, 171
Boyle, Michael, Archbishop of Dublin, Walker's dedication of *Answer To the Bishop of Condom's Book* to, 67, 69
Boyle, Hon. Robert: Evelyn's letter to, on Jansenist controversy, 20, 69; investigates Pascal's work in physics, 37, 41–42, 43–47, 63, 236, 255n34; and Pascal's calculating machine, 40; compared with Pascal, 69–74, 82, 140, 153; compared with Alexander

the Great, 72; mentioned, 81, 88, 136, 254n13, 277n64. *See also* Walker, Joseph
Brereton, William, Lord, interest in Pascal's mathematics, 40
Brillon, Pierre Jacques, *Suite des Caractères de Théophraste et des Pensées de Pascal*, 49
Bristol Library, 151
Brouncker, William, Viscount, President of Royal Society, 39; on Pascal's mechanical skills, 47
Brown, John, Anglican clergyman, on Pascal's religion, 153
Brown, Thomas, Scottish philosopher, 285n68
Browne, Simon, dissenting minister, partial insanity compared with Pascal's, 160–61
Browne, Sir Thomas, possible knowledge of Pascal's writings, 57–58
Brunschvicg, Léon, editor of Pascal's *Oeuvres* (1908–21), 99
Budgell, Eustace, remarks on Pascal in *Spectator*, 88-89, 110, 112, 113, 148–50, 153–54, 271n49; their inclusion in Kennett's translation of *Pensées*, 94, 150
Bunyan, John, *Pilgrim's Progress*, 167; *Holy War*, 187
Burke, Edmund, statesman and political thinker, 213; quotes Pascal on man's need of diversions, 271n49
Burnet, Gilbert, Bishop of Salisbury: attacks Jesuits, 19, 251n47; interest in Jansenism, 57, 170, 251n47; mentioned, 187
Bush, David, of Philadelphia, 241
Butler, Joseph, Bishop of Durham: conversation on Pascal with John Byrom and others, 136–38, 178; *Analogy of Religion* compared with Pascal's thought, 137-39, 167, 219
Byrd, William II, of Virginia, 242
Byrom, John, Nonjuror: conversation on Pascal with Bishop Butler and others, 136–37,

138; use of Pascal's prayers for shorthand lessons, 178; purchases *Pensées* with shirts and gingerbreads, 178; verse paraphrase of Pascal's confession of faith, 178–79

Callaghan, John, Irish jansenist, 25
Canillac, Philippe de Montboisier-Beaufort, Marquis de, 233
Caramuel, Juan, cistercian, 12
Carcavy, Pierre de, mathematician, and competition on cycloid, 38–39
Carew, Bampfylde Moore, "king of the gypsies," John Adams forsees Jesuits assuming similar disguises to, 244
Carey, William, Baptist missionary, 279n14
Carter, Elizabeth, poet and translator: corresponds with Catherine Talbot on Pascal's religion, 155–57, 196; views on Voltaire, 278n1
Carter, Robert, of Virginia, 239
Caryll, John, correspondent of Pope, 119–25 *passim*, 266n64
Casimir V, King of Poland, Pascal on, 205
Catholicism, Catholics; *see* Roman Catholicism, Roman Catholics
Cato, 80, 112
Chalmers, Thomas, Scottish preacher, 222
Chambourg, Aimonius Proust de, author of Pascal's epitaph, 236, 260n36
Charles I, King of England, 4; Pascal on, 205
Charles II, King of England, 19, 23, 33, 36; reads Evelyn's work on Jansenist controversy, 21; and Port Royal, 25–26
Charles X, King of France, 282n43
Charron, Pierre, sceptic, 119
Chesterfield, Philip Dormer Stanhope, Earl of: alleged author of essay in *World* (1754)

quoting Pascal, 153–54, 271n49; on Port Royal, 154

Chetwood, Knightly, Dean of Gloucester, and preface to Dryden's *Pastorals*, 261n18

Chevalier, Thomas, translator of *Pensées* (1803): translation, 99, 103, 207–208; on Pascal's life and character, 208–10, 218; on Voltaire's attacks on Pascal, 210–12, 221

Christian Disciple (Boston, Mass., 1814), quotes Pascal on duelling, 243

Christian Observer (1802–15 *passim*), and Evangelical interest in Pascal, 217–19, 281n34, 281n37

Christian's Magazine (1760), biography of Pascal, 198, 201

Christina, Queen of Sweden, Pascal on, 205

Cicero (Tully), 60, 80, 112

Clapham Sect, 213

Clarendon, Edward Hyde, Earl of, interest in Jansenist controversy, 21

Clarke, Samuel, nonconformist and biographer, 14–15, 187

Clarkson, David, anti-jesuit writer, 19

Clements, Henry, London bookseller, 259n20

Cole, William, antiquary, on Pascal's tomb, 151–52

Coleridge, Samuel Taylor: impressed by Pascal's arguments for faith, 224–25, 229; on human nature and Pascal, 225–26; on the French character, 226; pleasure on reading *Provinciales*, 226–27, 231; on Jesuits, 227

Collège des Ecossais, 28, 169

Collier, Jeremy, Nonjuror: edits Moréri's *dictionnaire*, 84; on Pascal's childhood, 88; attack on the stage, 107; adapts Pascal's views on weakness of human reason, 108–109, 113; and deism, 109, 132; interest in *Provinciales*, 109–10; Macaulay's comparison with Pascal, 262n19

Collins, Anthony, deist, attacks

Pascal on prophecies and miracles, 134, 135

Collins, John, mathematician, 40–41, 57, 169, 255n19

Compton, Henry, Bishop of London, and re-issue of *Provinciales* (1679), 19, 23

Condorcet, Marie-Jean Antoine Nicolas de Caritat, Marquis de: edition of *Pensées* (1776), 98–99, 104, 144, 217; revised edition by Voltaire (1778), 142, 211, 227

Conry, Florence, Archbishop of Tuam, and Jansenism, 24

Conybeare, John, Dean of Christ Church, Oxford, promises Charles Wesley to read Pascal, 185

Cousin, Victor, philosopher, 99, 104

Coverley, Sir Roger de, Pascal compared with, 88–89, 150, 154, 263n33. *See also* Budgell, Eustace; *Spectator*

Cowley, Abraham, poet and essayist, 108, 187, 265n52, 265n61

Cowper, William, poet, 191, 201, 229, 247, 276n62

Craig, Edward, of Edinburgh, translator of *Pensées* (1825): translation, 99, 221–23, 282n43; on Pascal's life, 222–24; translation published in America (1829), 246; reviewed in *Phrenological Journal*, 282n43

Craig, John, mathematician, 169, 267n2

Cromwell, Oliver, 18, 25; Pascal on, 26, 111

Cromwell, Richard, son of preceding, 15

Crousaz, Jean Pierre de, of Lausanne, criticisms of Pope's *Essay on Man*, 120, 127, 155

Cudworth, Ralph, Cambridge platonist, 187

Curwin, George, of Salem, Mass., 236

Daniel, Gabriel, jesuit: refutes *Provinciales*, 28–29; work trans-

lated by William Darrell, 29–32
Darrell, William, jesuit: translates Daniel's refutation of *Provinciales* (entitled *Discourses of Cleander and Eudoxe*), 29–32; on English popularity of *Provinciales*, 30–31, 33, 110, 132, 250n26; on Pascal's appeal to Englishwomen, 30, 111, 220
Davies, John, of Kidwelly, translates *Provinciales*(1657), 3
Dawes, Sir William, Archbishop of York, and Pascal's wager, 133
Deffand, Marie, Marquise du, writes to Horace Walpole on Pascal, 271n51
Deism in England, and effect on Pascal's reputation, 106, 109, 114, 126, 129, 131–38; in America, 241
Denham, Sir John, poet, and Pascal's wager, 267n2
Dennis, John, playwright and critic: conflict with Jeremy Collier on the stage, 107, 262n19; quotes Pascal on man's search for pleasure, 107; quotes Pascal on Christ speaking simply, 108
Descartes, René, 29, 40, 60, 101, 115, 192, 226
Deskford, James Ogilvy, Lord, 176
Desprez, Guillaume, publishes Port Royal *Pensées*, 40, 98, 270n36
Diderot, Denis, 144
Digby, Sir Kenelm, courtier and scientist, 38, 62
Diogenes, compared by Hume with Pascal, 158–59, 164
Dodd, William, preacher and forger, quotes Pascal, 198
Doddridge, Philip, dissenting minister, 190, 229, 272n54
Donne, John, poet, 60, 67, 68
Douai, English college at, 32
Dryden, John, poet, 107, 261n17
Dubois, Guillaume, Cardinal, 233
Dubos, Abbé Jean Baptiste, on Pascal's childhood, 153

Edelinck, Gerard, portrait of Pascal, 270n36
Edinburgh Review on Pascal, 229, 233, 234, 262n19, 283n46
Edwards, Jonathan, American theologian and philosopher, 187; knowledge of Pascal discussed, 239–40
Eliot, George, novelist, 220; refers to Pascal in *Middlemarch*, 220–21
Emerson, Ralph Waldo, American transcendentalist, admires *Pensées*, 246
Encyclopaedia Britannica, accounts of Pascal's life, 148, 207, 231
Encyclopaedia Londinensis, account of Pascal with portrait, 229–30
England, knowledge of Pascal in (*See also* Pascal, Blaise, especially incidents in life of, *Provinciales*, and *Pensées*; Perier, Gilberte, *Vie de Blaise Pascal*)

[Part I, *Growth and Course of Pascal's Reputation*; Part II, *Pascal's Life and Character as Presented by English Writers*; Part III, *English Portraits of Pascal*; Part IV, *Pascal Compared with Other Figures*.]

I. *Growth and Course of Pascal's Reputation*. First knowledge of, 1–2, 36–38, 57–63, 74, 83–84; as anti-jesuit writer, 1–34, 221; attraction to Englishwomen, 30, 110–11, 151, 155–57, 182–83, 195–97, 200–201, 213–16, 220–21, 227–28, 277n81; appeal to Protestants though a Catholic, 33, 72, 77–78, 80, 104, 141, 151, 156, 165, 200–201, 209, 215–16, 218, 219, 221–23, 251n33, 281n37; valued for literary style, 33, 105–106, 226; as mathematician and physicist, 35–63, 229; read with other French writers, 50, 105–11, 119; early harmony of achievements, 62–63, 73–74, 106; valued as religious writer, 78–82, 101, 129–30, 168, 175, 195–202; biographical interest in life and genius, 83–96, 141, 152–53, 165; opinions of dictionaries and encyclopaedias, 84–88, 145–48, 207, 229, 231–33; gradual scepticism concerning life and character, 86–88, 148–50, 160–63, 165; popularity in early eighteenth century, 97, 125–26, 127–28; knowledge of *Pensées* restricted to Port Royal edition until late eighteenth century, 100–105; selective appreciation of *Pensées* by early eighteenth-century writers, 106, 128–29; challenged by deists and rationalist opinion, 106, 126–27, 131–41, 155–66; attractions as a moralist, 113–28; divergence of English opinion on, 129–30; attacked by Voltaire, 141–48, 203–204; continuing popularity as a satirist, 150–52; works borrowed from libraries, 151; neglect or rejection of *Pensées* and author in late eighteenth century, 153, 155, 164–66; continuing religious appreciation, 167–69; appeal to Nonjurors, 177–81; valued by Wesley family and Methodist movement, 181–95; newly-discovered appeal during French Revolution, 203–13; approved by Evangelicals for writings and Christian example, 213–24; admired for insights and genius by Romantics, 213, 224–31; emerging Victorian opinions, 231–34

II. *Pascal's Life and Character as Presented by English Writers.* By Walker, 71–73; by Kennett, 77–80; by Jesup, 90–94, 165, 195, 239, 259n31, 267n78; in dictionaries and encyclopaedias, 147–48, 207, 229, 231–33, 279n11, 284n66; by Andrews, 150; by Percival, 160; by Priestley, 161; in *Gentleman's Magazine* (1789), 163, 272n62; in *Christian's Magazine* (1760), 198, 201; by Chevalier, 208–10; in *Christian Observer* (1814–15),

217–19; by Edward Craig, 222; in *New London Magazine* (1789), 272n62; in *Literary Magazine and British Review* (1789), 272n62. *See also* Bayle, Pierre; Moréri, Louis

III. *English Portraits of Pascal.* 6, 150, 229, 270n36, 272n62, 279n11, 279n14, 282n43, 284n64

IV. *Pascal Compared with Other Figures.* Locke, 53, 55 – 56, 140, 189; Sir Thomas Browne, 58; Robert Boyle, 69–74, 140, 153; Aemilius Papinianus, Cato, and Cicero, 80; Sir Roger de Coverley, 88–89, 150, 263n33; Pico della Mirandola, 93–94; Swift, 110; Marcus Aurelius, 113; Addison, 114, 140, 215; Fénelon, 120, 171, 218; Pope, 124–27 *passim*, 265n52, 272n58; Bishop Butler, 137; William Law, 138, 180, 214; Sir Isaac Newton, 140, 207; Huygens, 153; Handel, 153; Diogenes, 158; a Westmorland parson, 161–64; Voltaire, 189, 193–94, 201, 203–204, 211 – 12, 226, 232 – 34; Malebranche, 189; Montesquieu, 189; Cowper, 191; Elizabeth Rowe, 196; Priestley, 205; Dr. Johnson, 205; Erasmus, 214; John Selden, 214; Grotius, 214; Hamlet, 215; Hannah More, 217; Thomas à Kempis, 218; Nicole, 218; Enoch, 218; Thomas Chalmers, 222; Leibniz, 228; Bishop Berkeley, 228; Jeremy Collier, 262n19; Abraham Cowley, 265n52; Isaac Watts, 272n58; Edward Young, 273n63; Bossuet, 274n10; Henry More, 274n10; Samuel Clarke, 274n10; Thomas, "old," Parr, 284n64

Enoch, 218
Epicureans, 117–18, 174
Episcopalians, Scottish, attracted to Pascal, 170–78 *passim*, 221, 223

Erasmus, Desiderius, 127, 214
Escobar y Mendoza, Antonio, jesuit, 7, 23, 233, 252n61
Essex, Arthur Capel, Earl of, sends Oldenburg Pascal's mathematical work, 40
Euclid, 84, 208
European Magazine on Pascal, 205, 206
Evangelicals, interest in Pascal, 202, 212, 213–21, 223–24
Evelyn, John: translates works relating to Jansenist controversy, 20–21, 23, 25; wrongly thought to have translated *Provinciales,*20, 250n10; and Royal Society, 35; on popularity of *Provinciales*, 250n27
Everett, Edward, American orator, 245

Faber, George, religious controversialist, 281n37
Falkener, Everard, English friend of Voltaire, 145, 146
Faugère, Prosper, edits *Pensées* (1844), 99, 234
Fénelon, François de Salignac de la Mothe, Archbishop of Cambrai: Pope's identification with, 120, 127; English reputation, 141, 164; influence in Scotland, 171, 172, 177; attraction to Wesley, 183, 184, 187, 191; opinions of Evangelicals on, 215, 217, 218; admired by Coleridge, 226
Fielding, Henry, novelist, 271n46
Filleau de la Chaise, Jean, *Discours sur les Pensées de M. Pascal,* 48–49, 57, 66, 77, 98; other works by, 66
Fletcher, John William, Vicar of Madeley, 191–92; defends Pascal against Voltaire, 192; appreciation of Pascal's religion, 192–93
Fontenelle, Bernard Le Bovier de, literary style contrasted with Pascal's, 107–108
Forbes of Pitsligo, Alexander Forbes, Lord: on Kennett's translation of *Pensées,* 102; appreciation of *Pensées,* 168, 171–72, 175–76; quotes Pascal on self-love, 172–74; and on means of salvation, 172–74; and on philosophers, 173, 174; and on love of God, 173–74; and on man's need for diversions, 174; and on human mortality, 174; and on pride, 174; and on rôles in society, 174–75; and on human nature, 176; Forbes' kinsmen, 176
Foster, John, Baptist essayist, 279n14
Foxe, John, *Martyrology,* 31
France: effect of *Provinciales* in, 1–2, 5–6, 17–18, 32; interest of English government in French affairs, 20–21, 63; influence of French thought and style on English writers, 47–48, 74, 85, 105–11, 114; reception of *Pensées,* 57, 65; impact of French rationalist philosophy on England, 144, 148, 164–65; links with Scottish religious thought, 169–76 *passim*; effect of Revolution on English opinion, 202, 203–204, 213, 216, 219, 227; French contacts with America, 241–42; American reaction to Revolution, 243
Francklin, Thomas, miscellaneous writer, 145
Franklin, Benjamin, delight in *Provinciales,* 241; mentioned, 246, 288n14
Freeman, R., quotes Pascal's *Discours sur la condition des grands* in *Gentleman's Magazine* (1738), reprinted from *London Journal,* 264n50

Gale, Theophilus, *True Idea of Jansenisme,* 17–18, 33
Galileo (Galilei), 40, 47, 60
Gallican Church, relations with Church of England, 4, 141
Garden, George, of Aberdeen, Episcopalian clergyman, 170–71
Garnett, Henry, jesuit, 23
Gassendi, Pierre, scientist and

philosopher, 43, 49
Gentleman's Magazine on Pascal, 161–64, 204–205, 264n50, 284n63
Gibbon, Edward, historian, influenced by Provinciales, 152, 231, 241; mentioned, 179
Gifford, William, editor of Quarterly Review, 228
Gildon, Charles, Deist's Manual, 132–33
Glasites, 193
Godeau, Antoine, Bishop of Vence, work translated by Kennett, 76
Goldsmith, Oliver, 153; Vicar of Wakefield, 272n60
Gordon, Thomas, reference to Pascal in Humourist, 112–13
Grafton, Charles Fitzroy, Duke of, 90–91
Grant, Sir Robert, advocate of Jewish rights, 281n37
Grattan, Henry, Irish statesman and orator, 262n26
Gregory, James, Scottish mathematician, 40, 169, 255n19
Gregory, Olinthus, mathematician, on Pascal, 217
Grene, Martin, Irish jesuit: translates Nouet and Annat's Answer to the Provinciall Letters, 9, 13, 24, 26, 31; on the Provinciales and England, 9–12, 27–28
Grotius, Hugo, 109, 214
Guyon, Jeanne-Marie de la Motte, quietist, 171, 172, 179, 191, 226

Hale, Sir Matthew, judge, 61
Hamilton, Anthony, Mémoires de Grammont, 25
Hamilton, Sir George, and Port Royal, 25
Hamlet, 215
Hammond, Henry, Anglican divine: responsible for first English publication of Provinciales (1657), 3–4, 13, 19, 81, 141; preface to first English edition, 5–7, 10, 33, 151; preface to second edition (1658), 7–8
Handel, George Frideric, child-

hood compared with Pascal's, 153
Hartley, David, philosopher, 136
Harvard College, Massachusetts, knowledge of Pascal at, 236, 242
Hawkesworth, John, on Pope and Pascal in Adventurer, 123
Hawthorne, Nathaniel, American novelist, and Pascal, 247
Hazlitt, William, essayist, hopes for Pascal's fame, 228–29
Hearne, Thomas, Oxford antiquary, 181
Heber, Reginald, Bishop of Calcutta, opinion of Pascal, 219
Henrietta Maria, Queen of England, 25
Herbert, George, poet, 67
Herbert of Cherbury, Edward, Lord, 132
Herbert, Sir Henry, and Jansenist controversy, 21
Hervey, James, Calvinist controversialist, 191, 193
Hewet, Sir John, and Walker's translation of Pensées, 67–69, 70
Hippocrates, 60
Hobbes, Thomas, philosopher: acquaintance with Pascal and his works, 37, 39, 254n8; disagrees with Pascal's findings on air pressure, 37, 42; mentioned, 60, 254n13
Holden, Henry, English catholic, 3
Holland, early knowledge of Pensées in, 65, 74; and Jansenists, 65, 253n64
Holmes, Oliver Wendell, American author, on Pascal and Jonathan Edwards, 239, 240
Homer, 60; Iliad, and Odyssey, 107, 264n51
Hooke, Robert, scientist, purchases Pensées, 57; interest in Pascal's works, 62–63, 254n13, 257n73
Horace, 107
Hughes, John, quotes Pascal on man's dignity in Spectator, 112, 113
Huguenots, 65, 66, 67, 208
Hume, David, Scottish

philosopher: hostility to Pascal,
157–59, 281n34; compares
Pascal unfavourably with
Diogenes, 158–59, 164; on
miracle of the holy thorn, 159
Huntingford, George, Bishop of
Gloucester, 281n34
Hurd, Richard, Bishop of Worcester: views on Pascal's works and
religious opinions, 140–41;
compares Pascal with Addison,
140
Hutchinson, Sara, reads *Pensées*,
227
Huygens, Christiaan, 39, 43, 153

Innocent x, Pope, condemns Jansenist teachings, 1
Ireland, Jansenist influence in,
24–25, 28; Joseph Walker's
links with, 66–67

Jackson, Daniel, friend of Swift,
262n26
Jacobi, Friedrich Heinrich, German
philosopher, 224, 225
Jacobites, 29, 171, 172, 176, 177,
181
James II, King of England, 23,
177; interest in Jansenism, 26,
28
James, the Old Pretender, 28, 171
Jansen, Cornelius, Bishop of
Ypres, 1, 24, 27
Jansenists (*See also* Pascal, Blaise,
Provinciales; Port Royal): controversy with Jesuits, 1–2, 3, 13,
15–16, 17–18, 20, 26, 31–33,
86, 141, 142–43, 201, 210, 222,
233; teachings, 1–2, 5, 15–16,
31, 101, 140, 143, 216, 283n48;
English sympathy with, 4, 7–8,
10, 14, 18–20, 21, 33, 38, 48,
57, 63, 109, 213, 219; and
British catholics, 24–26, 28, 32;
and Ireland, 24–25, 28; and
Scotland, 28, 169–71, 176
Jarrige, Pierre, anti-jesuit writer,
250n20
Jefferson, Thomas, and Pascal's
works, 242, 244
Jenkins, Francis, English gardener

at Port Royal, 25
Jenner, Charles, *Letters from Altamont*, 152
Jenyns, Soame, philosophical writer, views on infinity compared
with Pascal's by Dr. Johnson,
199
Jephson, Michael, Dean of St.
Patrick's, Dublin, 20
Jesuits (*See also* Pascal, Blaise, *Provinciales*; Roman Catholicism,
English hostility towards): conflicts with Jansenists, 1–2, 25,
32, 35, 63, 142–43, 145, 201;
casuistry, 2, 7, 14, 15–16, 19,
23, 28, 210, 232; treasonable offences, 2, 21, 67, 221; alleged
readiness to murder, 2, 14, 15,
16, 222–23; English hostility
towards, 3, 4, 5–8, 14–16, 17,
19, 20–23, 33, 35, 48, 222–23,
227, 229–31, 235, 249n4; doctrine of probability, 6, 16, 27,
139; leaders mentioned, 7, 23,
60, 233, 252n61; replies to *Provinciales*, 9–13, 29–32; doctrines of equivocation and mental reservation, 15, 17, 28, 30,
33, 109–10; on gluttony,
simony, and abortion, 17; on
papal powers, 20, 27, 151; and
British catholics, 24, 26–28; dissolution of order, 33, 210, 221;
scientific views, 37, 42; and
miracles, 159; restoration of
order, 221, 243, 282n42; and
America, 235–36, 243, 244; on
duelling, 243
Jesup, Edward, edits *Lives of Picus
and Pascal* (1723), 90–94, 165,
195, 239, 259n31, 267n78. *See
also* Perier, Gilberte, *Vie de Blaise
Pascal*
Jewel, John, Bishop of Salisbury,
67
John of the Cross, St., 180
Johnson, Samuel: and *Pensées*,
163, 200–201; Pascal's appeal
to, 198–201; on Pascal's definition of beauty, 198–99; on
Pascal's literary style, 199; on his
comments on infinity, 199;

reads Pascal's life, 200; compared with Pascal, 205, 206; mentioned 195, 213, 214
Johnson, Samuel, of King's College, New York, reads *Pensées*, 239
Julius Caesar, 60
Junius, Letters of, 152
Juvenal, lines from *Satires* introduce Andrews' translation of *Provinciales*, 150

Keill, John, mathematician and astronomer, 47, 169
Keith, James, Scottish physician, 176
Kempis, Thomas à, 177, 180, 184, 191, 198, 218, 281n37
Ken, Thomas, Bishop of Bath and Wells, 20, 177
Kennett, Basil, translator of *Pensées* (1704): translation and its influence, 73, 74–75, 81–83, 97, 105–106, 110, 113, 123, 125, 128, 212, 238; life and works, 75–76; content and style of translation, 76–77, 99–100, 102–103, 104, 105, 121–22, 175–76; admiration of Pascal in preface, 77–80, 131, 133, 135, 151, 221; quotes Pascal in sermons, 80–81; subsequent editions of translation, 82, 90, 91, 94, 103–104, 121, 128, 145, 150, 176, 178, 187–89, 223, 239, 267n78, 283n45
Kennett, White, Bishop of Peterborough, 75–76, 263n35
Kett, Henry, miscellaneous writer, 207
King, William, Principal of St. Mary Hall, Oxford, 181

La Bruyère, Jean de, English readers and opinions of his *Caractères*, 50, 108, 109, 110, 277n81
Ladies Library (published by Steele), recommends Pascal, 110–11, 151
Lafuma, Louis, edition of *Pensées* (1951), 99, 101

Lalouère, Antoine, Jesuit mathematician, 39
Lamb, Charles, essayist, Leigh Hunt compares humour with Pascal's, 284n58
La Placette, Jean, work translated by Kennett, 76
La Rochefoucauld, François, Duc de, English acquaintance with *Maximes*, 50, 107, 119
Larroque, Matthieu de, *History of the Eucharist*, translated by Walker, 66–67, 68
Law, Edmund, Bishop of Carlisle, refers to Pascal on the Jews, 136
Law, John, financier, 233
Law, William, Nonjuror, 130, 138, 178, 198, 214; knowledge of Pascal's thought, 179–81; relations with Wesleys, 182, 184, 185, 186
Leake, John, of St. Mary Hall, Oxford, 275n32
Leibniz, Gottfried Wilhelm, 120, 228–29, 255n19
Leighton, Robert, Archbishop of Glasgow, interest in Jansenism and Pascal, 20, 57, 170
Le Pailleur, François, mathematician, 49
Lessius, Leonard, jesuit, 7
Le Tourneur, Pierre, compares Young's *Night Thoughts* with *Pensées*, 273n63
Line, Francis, jesuit, attacks Boyle's findings on air pressure, 42, 255n26
Lisola, Baron de, imperial diplomat, 70
Locke, John: Pascal's influence on *Essay Concerning Human Understanding*, 36–37, 50–53, 54–55, 56, 113, 133; travels in France, 47–49; interest in Pascal's works and discoveries, 48–49; and in works by Nicole and Port Royal authors, 49–50, 51; compared with Pascal, 53, 55–56, 140, 189, 199; on Pascal's memory, 53–54, 88, 233; *Essay*'s rôle in introducing Pascal to English readers, 55–56, 74; mentioned,

81, 85, 119, 121, 136, 138, 145, 219, 240, 277n81

Lockman, John, translates Voltaire's *Lettres philosophiques* (1733), 145, 147, 269n27

Logan, James, of Philadelphia, 239

Lorimer, William, religious writer, 258n1

Louis XIV, King of France, 26, 233; reads *Pensées* with court, 57

Lowther, Sir John, member of parliament, admires Pascal on methods of reasoning, 59–60, 62

Loyola, St. Ignatius, founder of Jesuit order, 7, 244

Lubbock, Sir John, publishes Kennett's translation of *Pensées*(1893), 104

Macaulay, Thomas, Lord: on *Provinciales*, 2; on careers of Voltaire and Pascal, 233; on Jeremy Collier and Pascal, 262n19

Mackenzie, Sir George, king's advocate, quotes Pascal on human reason, 169

Mackintosh, Sir James, philosopher, on Pascal's thought, 283n46

Madison, James, President of United States, knowledge of *Provinciales*, 242, 289n26

Mainwaring, George, Rector of Church Stretton, on Handel and Pascal, 153

Malebranche, Nicolas de, metaphysician, English admiration of, 107, 189, 226

Malthus, Thomas, *Essay on the Principle of Population*, 228

Manchester, Henry Montagu, Earl of, 67

Mandeville, Bernard, *Fable of the Bees*, 85, 128

Marcus Aurelius, thoughts compared with Pascal's, 113

Marlborough, John Churchill, Duke of, 141

Marsh, Narcissus, Archbishop of Armagh, 20

Mary of Modena, Queen of England, 28

Massachusetts Missionary Magazine (1803–1805), letters by "Pascal," 288n23

Massillon, Jean-Baptiste, preacher, 216

Mather, Cotton, of Boston, Mass., 187, 236, 239, 240; and Pascal's epitaph, 236–38

Mathias, Thomas, satirist, appreciates *Provinciales*, 284n58

Melville, Herman, on Pascal in *Moby Dick*, 247

Mersenne, Père Marin, and *académie libre*, 37, 40

Methodist movement and Pascal, 181–95 *passim*, 202, 223, 240

Mill, James, historian and political economist, 283n54

Milton, John: possibly possessed copy of *Provinciales*, 18, 191; mentioned, 108, 176, 254n13

Mirandola, Pico della, Italian polymath, compared with Pascal, 93–94, 259n31

Mohammed, 136

Molière, Jean-Baptiste Poquelin, known as, English reputation, 60, 105, 129, 226

Molina, Luis de, jesuit, 7

Monkhouse, John, reads *Pensées* with Sara Hutchinson, 227

Monmouth, James Scott, Duke of, educated by Jansenists, 25–26

Montagu, Lady Mary Wortley, on Pascal and Fénelon, 164

Montaigne, Michel de: influence in England of *Essais*, 50, 105, 110, 116, 119, 124, 129; Pascal on, 101, 110, 117, 136

Montesquieu, Charles Louis de Secondat, Baron de, 189, 235

Monthly Magazine on Pascal, 229, 231, 263n33

Montresor, Capt. John, of British Armies in America, 241

Moravians, 182, 185, 220

Moray, Sir Robert, courtier and scientist, interest in Jansenist controversy and in Pascal's physics, 21, 43

More, Hannah: talks with Dr. Johnson on Pascal and Port Royal, 200–201; condemns Voltaire, 213; delights in works by Pascal and Port Royal authors, 213–16, 220, 229, 272n54; and Evangelicals, 217, 219
More, Henry, Cambridge platonist, style compared with Pascal's, 274n10
More, Sir Thomas, 60, 90
Moréri, Louis, life of Pascal in *Grand dictionnaire historique*, 84, 108
Morland, Samuel, his calculating machine, 255n18
Morris, David, secular priest, 27
Moses: laws contrasted with Jesuit teachings, 23; their truths upheld by Filleau de la Chaise, 66, 258n1, 276n57; and by Bishop Warburton, 139
Murray, Lindley, American quaker, recommends Pascal, 197–98
Muskerry, Donogh MacCarthy, Lord, and Port Royal, 25
Mysticism: Pascal's tendencies towards, 58, 101; his attraction to men with such inclinations, 168, 172, 176, 179; William Law's mystical understanding of Christianity, 179–80; its rejection by John Wesley, 186–87, 194; attitude of Dr. Johnson towards, 198; Hannah More on, 214

New and General Biographical Dictionary on Pascal's life, 148, 207
News for the Curious, translated by Walker, 66
Newton, Sir Isaac: Pascal's works known to, 40, 57; on prophecies, 136; compared with Pascal, 140, 207; mentioned, 49, 129, 208, 254n13, 277n64
Newton, John, Vicar of Olney, 191, 201, 251n41
Nicole, Pierre: and publication of *Provinciales*, 3, 5, 6, 28, 32; works on Jansenist controversy, 13, 20, 21, 63; *Essais de morale*, 49, 51, 119, 196, 216, 218, 236,

256n43, 264n50, 280n27, 287n6; eulogy of Pascal, 54; and miracle of the holy thorn, 159; and Pascal's *Discours sur la condition des grands*, 264n50, 287n6
Noël, Etienne, Jesuit physicist, dispute with Pascal on the vacuum, 37
Nonjurors, interest in Pascal, 20, 109, 136, 150, 168, 177–81 *passim*, 184, 270n37
North, George, Vicar of Welwyn, 277n74
Nouet, Jacques, jesuit, *Answer to the Provinciall Letters* (with François Annat), 9, 18, 23, 24, 26, 31

Oates, Titus, instigator of Popish Plot, 18, 23, 31
Oldenburg, Henry, Secretary of Royal Society: and Pascal's competition on the cycloid, 38, 40; and Pascal's works, 40, 41, 63; friendship with Pascal, 253n6
Oldham, John, poet, on Jesuits, 252n61
Ormonde, James Butler, Duke of, 26
Orrery, Roger Boyle, Earl of, and Joseph Walker, 69, 70
Owen, John, Puritan divine, and Jansenist controversy, 18
Oxford, interest in Pascal at, 18, 20, 40, 41, 47, 81–82, 181, 183, 184, 214, 275n32
Oxford Movement, 253n81

Paley, William, religious philosopher, 219
Parkman, Ebenezer, of Westborough, Mass., 239
Parr, Samuel, of Harrow School, 280n27
Parr, Thomas, "old," lifespan compared with Pascal's, 284n64
Parsons, Robert, jesuit, 23
Pascal, Blaise (*See also* England, knowledge of Pascal in; Perier, Gilberte, *Vie de Blaise Pascal*)

[Part I, *Incidents in Life of*; Part

II, *Works (other than Les Provinciales, and Pensées)*; Part III, *Les Provinciales*; Part IV, *Pensées, French editions*; Part V, *Pensées, English translations*; Part VI, *Pensées, Contents and Major Themes of.*]

I. *Incidents in Life of* (for published works, see *infra*). Pseudonym (Louis de Montalte), 1, 6, 9, 15–16, 18, 93, 250n13; supposed authorship of Perrault's *Jesuits Morals*, 18, 31; miracle of the holy thorn, 26, 159, 218; remarkable memory, 31, 54, 56, 87, 88; mathematical and physical discoveries, 36, 37–47, 48, 74, 79, 84, 86, 87, 117, 140, 152–53, 199, 205, 229, 236; education, 37, 85, 198, 208; reaction to the Fronde, 37, 84, 89–90, 206, 210; competition on the cycloid, 38–40; calculating machine, 40, 49, 255n18; and Torricellian experiment, 41–42, 47, 236, 255n34; invention of bellows without vent, 44; charity, 71, 86, 87, 219; on death of father, 80, 172, 274n11; stories of childhood, 84, 85, 88, 89, 119, 148, 153, 160, 208, 218, 233, 240, 265n52; conversion, 86, 240; religious devotion, 86, 186, 191, 193, 196–97, 206, 218; health, 86–87, 89, 96, 148, 160, 163, 183, 209, 218, 219, 220, 272n58; ascetic practices, 87, 148, 156, 158, 160, 161, 163, 183, 190, 197, 198, 206, 207, 209, 219, 245; death, 89, 140, 163, 210, 219, 222–23; tomb, 92, 152, 220; epitaph, 92–93, 198, 210, 223, 236–38, 247, 260n36, 285n5; celibacy, 148, 207; hallucination of a gulf, 148, 207, 247, 271n51; supposed insanity, 160–61, 242, 244; profession of faith, 178–79; forged correspondence with contemporaries, 254n13

II. *Works (other than Les Provinciales, and Pensées).* Discours sur la condition des grands, 217, 238, 264n50, 287n6; *Ecrits sur la grâce*, 24; *Entretien de Pascal avec Saci*, 117; *Expériences nouvelles touchant le vuide*, 37; *Factum pour les curés de Paris*, 8; *Histoire de la roulette*, 38; *Lettres de A. Dettonville*, 39–40, 169; *Prières*, 100, 160, 178, 185, 205, 275n43, 276n45, 277n66; *Second écrit des curés de Paris*, 8; *Traité du triangle arithmétique*, 40, 49, 255n19; *Traitez de l'équilibre des liqueurs et de la pesanteur de la masse de l'air*, 43–46, 49, 84

III. *Les Provinciales.* Appearance, 1–3, 25; condemnation, 2, 9, 32, 87; literary merits, 2, 29, 33, 86, 106, 110, 151–52, 168, 206, 207, 210, 214, 226–27, 241, 245; first English edition (1657), 2–7, 235, 249n2, 250n10; reasons for rapid English translation, 2–4, 14; second English edition (1658), 3, 7–8; on doctrine of grace, 5, 30, 31, 101, 283n48; authorship of, 6, 8, 18, 83, 84, 250n13, 284n58; popularity in England, 7, 13–24, 31, 33–34, 36, 37, 48, 70, 74, 141, 150–52, 169, 229–30, 231–32; sequels to, 7–8, 12, 20–21, 253n81; translation of Jesuit replies, 9–13, 28, 29–32; on various Jesuit doctrines and practices, 14–17, 109–10; second edition reissued (1679), 19, 23, 270n38; translated by William Andrews (1744), 23–24, 94, 111, 150–51, 177, 221; effect on British catholics, 24–33; apology for letter's length quoted, 53, 119, 228, 264n51, 289n26; Bayle on, 86, 87; Voltaire on, 110, 148, 189, 210; translation of 1816, 221, 253n81, 282n42; arrival in America, 235–36; discussion on duelling referred to, 243; first

American edition (1828), 243;
translated by Thomas M'Crie
(1851), 274n22, 282n42

IV. *Pensées, French editions* (*See also*
Port Royal). First edition (*Edition
de Port-Royal*, 1670), 47, 57, 65,
98; manuscript, 65, 98, 211;
miscellaneous editions, 66, 76,
105, 208; contents and special
character of Port Royal edition,
73, 83, 97–105, 106, 109, 123,
125, 129, 134–35, 168, 176,
181, 195, 238, 259n31, 261n9;
limited edition (1669), 98; expanded edition (1678), 76, 98;
Condorcet's edition (1776),
98–99, 104, 217; Bossut's edition (1779), 99, 104, 204, 207;
Faugère's edition (1844), 99,
234; Brunschvicg's edition
(1904), 99; Lafuma's edition
(1951), 99, 101; Condorcet's edition, revised by Voltaire (1778),
142, 211, 227; Renouard's edition (1812), 217, 281n37;
Berthou's edition (1819), 221;
other editions, 260n6, 260n7

V. *Pensées, English translations.*
Early translation of part of ch.
XXXI of Port Royal edition,
58–62; translation by Joseph
Walker (1688), 65–74 (*see also*
Walker); translation by Basil
Kennett (1704), 74–83, 100,
102–103 (*see also* Kennett); later
editions of Kennett's translation,
82, 103–104; translation by
Thomas Chevalier (1803), 99,
103, 207–12 (*see also* Chevalier);
translation by Edward Craig
(1825), 99, 221–24, 246 (*see also*
Craig); Kennett's translation
published in Edinburgh (1751),
103, 176, 187; as published in
John Wesley's *Christian Library*
(1753), 187–89 (*see also* Wesley);
translation by Jonathan Edwards
Ryland (1838), 234, 285n71;
first American edition (1829),
246, 289n31 (*see also* Craig, Edward)

VI. *Pensées, Contents and Major
Themes of.* Plan and reasoning of
work, 36, 78–80, 97–98, 105,
217; literary style, 36, 77,
101–102, 106, 107–108, 112,
113, 129, 141, 171, 199, 212,
227–28; on methods of reasoning, 37, 58–62, 127, 175; on
man's place in the universe, 37,
52–53, 121; argument of the
wager, 50–52, 56, 78, 87, 100,
114, 124, 128, 133–34, 137,
138, 146, 165, 207, 261n11,
261n17, 267n2, 269n17, 273n2;
on God's attributes, 53, 240; on
weakness of human reason, 53,
108–109, 110, 115–16, 122,
123–24, 127, 128, 169, 183,
200, 227; on the pleasures of
pursuit, 53; on faith and reason,
53, 78, 82, 101, 106, 133–34,
173, 175, 182, 189, 192, 198,
201, 212, 214, 224, 225; on
morals and immortality, 55–56,
126, 277n75; on philosophers,
56, 101, 173, 174; on miracles
and prophecies, 78–79, 81,
134–35, 137–38, 140, 143, 159,
164, 170, 178, 200, 219, 225; on
human nature's inconsistencies,
79–80, 101, 112, 113, 114, 115,
122–23, 125, 127, 128, 136,
143, 146–47, 155, 157, 169,
172, 176, 180, 190, 201, 211,
215, 222, 225–26, 231, 234,
245, 246, 266n64, 267n76,
277n81; on religious devotions,
80–81; on man's need for diversions, 88–89, 116, 124, 128,
154, 174, 196, 198, 271n49; on
human dignity, 101, 111–12,
113, 206; on the silence of
space, 102, 234; on self-love,
107, 172–74, 267n76; on self-
effacement in writing, 107,
269n17; on suicide as form of
pleasure, 107; on Christ speaking simply, 108, 190; on human
mortality and death, 111, 156,
174, 183, 244; on infinity, 114,
122, 199, 201; on hope of happiness, 122, 124; on pride, 122,

174; on man as thinking reed, 124; on beauty, 127, 146, 198–99, 201; on biblical authority, 128, 214; on the Jews, 136, 143, 187, 192, 261n11; on the perils of innovation, 139, 227; on the means of salvation, 172–74, 180, 205; on civil disorder, 173, 280n19; on love of God, 173–74, 184, 219; on rôles in society, 174–75; on Mohammed, 187; on royal authority, 205; on false conscience, 205

Pascal, Etienne, father of preceding, 37, 85, 198, 208

Pascal, Gilberte; *see* Perier, Gilberte

Pascal, Jacqueline, Pascal's younger sister, 161, 163

Pecquet, Jean, anatomist, 43

Pell, John, mathematician, 40

Pemberton, Ebenezer, of Boston, Mass., knowledge of Pascal's works, 236, 238, 240

Pemberton, John, publisher, 267n78

Pembroke, Thomas Herbert, Earl of, recommends Pascal on geometry to Locke, 49; Herbert family, 25

Pendarves, Mary, Wesley quotes Pascal in letter to, 183–84

Penn, William, quaker, 277n68

Pepys, Samuel, diarist, possible early translator of passage from *Pensées*, 37, 58–59, 61

Percival, Thomas, physician, on Pascal and partial insanity, 159–61

Perier, Etienne, Pascal's nephew, interest in atmospheric pressure and work on calculating machine, 49

Perier, Florin, Pascal's brother-in-law, publishes Pascal's physical discoveries, 43

Perier, Gilberte, elder sister of Pascal, author of *Vie de Blaise Pascal* (*See also* Pascal, Blaise, incidents in life of): biography as preface to *Pensées*, 54, 56, 66, 73, 77, 83, 98, 165, 200, 206, 239; source for dictionaries and encyclopaedias, 84, 86–87, 148; work known to English writers, 89–90, 153, 178–79, 200; edited by Jesup in *Lives of Picus and Pascal* (1723), 90–94; included by Andrews in his translation of *Provinciales* (1744), 94, 150

Perrault, Nicolas, *Jesuits Morals,* 18, 19, 31

Perrinchief, Richard, Prebendary of Westminster, 19

Petty, Sir William, statistician, correspondence with Sir Robert Southwell on Pascal and methods of reasoning, 37, 59–62, 113, 129

Philadelphia, knowledge of Pascal in, 241, 242–43, 244, 288n14

Philosophes: hostility to Pascal, 131, 144, 148; denounced in England, 203–204, 210, 221, 224, 226; and in America, 243

Pliny the Younger, literary style of, 113, 245

Plume, Thomas, Archdeacon of Rochester, 19

Plutarch, and English interest in biography, 90, 93

Poe, Edgar Allan, and the *Pensées*, 247

Poole, Thomas, correspondent of Coleridge, 224

Pope, Alexander: early knowledge of Pascal's writings, 89, 119, 266n64; Pascal's influence on *Essay on Man*, 106, 119–27, 129, 130, 139, 155, 171; divergence of thought from Pascal's, 114, 125–27, 131, 132, 165; confession of faith, 120–21, 127, 141, 229; compared with Pascal, 124, 265n52, 272n58; mentioned, 195

Popish Plot, 21–23, 27, 31, 150

Port Royal (*See also* Jansenists): community of, 1–2, 13, 24–26, 32, 220, 223, 231, 233, 251n38; English opinions of, 13, 56, 114, 140, 154; and Charles II,

25–26; works proceeding from, 49, 140, 168, 170, 171, 179, 183, 196, 200–201, 213–14, 216, 220, 226–27, 280n27; edition of *Pensées*, 98–105, 168 (*see also*, Pascal, Blaise, *Pensées, French editions*); and Scotland, 159, 169–70
Portman, Sir William, Walker's dedication of *News for the Curious* to, 67
Power, Henry, physician and naturalist, copies Pascal's experiments on air pressure, 42–43, 57
Presbyterians, 4, 161, 169, 176, 193
Preston, Samuel, of Philadelphia, 241
Priestley, Joseph, scientist and political theorist: on Pascal's life and religion, 161; views criticized, 204–205, 243; library, 272n59
Prior, Matthew: influence of *Pensées* on poetry, 114–16, 120; divergence from Pascal's conclusions, 116, 132; mentioned, 195
Puritans, and Pascal, 14–19 *passim*, 24, 33; in America, 235–40 *passim*, 241, 246
Pufendorf, Samuel von, historian and jurist, work translated by Kennett, 76

Quakers, interest in Pascal, 197, 220, 239, 277n68
Quarterly Review on Pascal, 228, 282n42
Quesnel, Pasquier, Jansenist leader, 32, 183, 281n37
Quietism, 171, 172, 175

Rabelais, François, 247
Racine, Jean, dramatist, 111, 159
Racine, Louis, nephew of preceding, criticizes Pope's *Essay on Man*, 120, 171
Ramsay, Andrew, secretary to Fénelon, compares Fénelon and Pascal, 171
Randolph, Peyton, of Virginia, 242

Rapin, René, works of criticism translated by Kennett, 76, 105–106
Rationalism in England: growth, 69, 82; effect on Pascal's reputation, 106, 126, 127, 131, 139, 161, 164, 165–66, 168; contribution of French rationalist thought, 142, 144, 148, 164–65; redefinition of beliefs during and after French Revolution, 202, 203–204, 209, 213, 224, 231
Ray, John, naturalist, 62
Reading, William, librarian of Sion College, *History of our Lord*, 197; *see also* 277n68
"R.E.M." (translates Voltaire's first *remarques sur les Pensées de Pascal*), 102, 145, 261n13, 270n31
Renouard, Antoine-Auguste, editor of *Pensées* (1812), 217, 281n37
Renty, Gaston de, friend of the poor, 281n37
Reynolds, Frances, Dr. Johnson compares her literary style to Pascal's, 199
Rittenhouse, David, Philadelphia astronomer, 242, 244
Roannez, Arthus Gouffier de Boissy, Duc de, 65
Roberval, Gilles de, mathematician, 38, 39, 49
Robinson, Henry Crabb, diarist, 225, 229, 283n48
Rogers, Henry, contributor to *Edinburgh Review*, on Faugère's edition of *Pensées*, 234, 285n72
Roman Catholicism, English hostility towards, 3–4, 23, 36, 63, 67, 141, 151, 165, 177, 212, 215, 229. *See also* Jesuits
Roman Catholics in Britain: reaction to Pascal's works, 12, 24–33, 124, 127, 276n62; proposed emancipation of, 191, 221
Romanticism, 202, 213, 224, 225
Rousseau, Jean-Jacques, 224, 235, 247

Rowe, Elizabeth, poet and letter-writer, high regard for Pascal, 130, 195–97, 220
Royal Society, 21, 47, 57, 70, 106, 147; interest in Pascal's discoveries and thought, 35–36, 43, 58, 61–62, 71, 129, 229, 236
Royston, Richard, publisher of first English editions of *Provinciales*, 4, 7–8, 23
Rule of Life, 197
Rush, Benjamin, Philadephia physician, views on Pascal, 243–44
Ruysbroeck, Jan van, Flemish mystic, 180
Ryland, Jonathan Edwards, translator of *Pensées* (1838), 234, 285n71

Saint-Cyran, Abbé Jean de, director to Port Royal, 24, 170
Saint-Evremond, Charles de, man of letters, 105
Saint-Germain, court of, 28–29, 176
Sales, St. François de, devotional writer, 216
Sandeman, Robert, Glasite and religious controversialist, defends Pascal against Voltaire, 193–94
Schimmelpenninck, Mary Anne, visits ruins of Port Royal, 220
Scotland: Jansenist influence in, 25, 28, 169, 170; knowledge and opinions of Pascal in, 168–77, 221–23
Scougall, Henry, *Life of God in the Soul of Man*, 170, 177, 184, 187, 191
Scriblerus Club, satirizes Pascal as infant prodigy, 89, 119
Selden, John, lawyer, compared with Pascal, 214
Sewall, Judge Samuel, of Massachusetts, 238
Seward, William, anecdotal writer, praises Pascal, 205, 206, 207, 210
Sewell, George, miscellaneous writer, verse translation of Pascal's

epitaph, 92–93, 198
Shaftesbury, Anthony Ashley Cooper, first Earl of, 47, 48
Shaftesbury, Anthony Ashley Cooper, third Earl of, 85, 119, 139; rejects Pascal's argument of the wager, 133–34
Shaftesbury, Margaret, Countess of, Locke dedicates translation of Nicole's *Essais de morale* to, 49
Short, Richard, Catholic physician, 32
Silhouette, Etienne de, translator of Pope's *Essay on Man*, 120, 121
Simitière, Paul du, Philadelphia artist, 241
Sinnich, John, Irish jansenist, 24
Sion College, London, 277n68
Smollett, Tobias, novelist, 145
Solomon, 114–15, 247
Sorbonne, 1, 3, 5, 91
South, Robert, preacher, 187
Southey, Robert, poet, interest in Pascal's writings, 226, 227
Southwell, Sir Robert, diplomatist, corresponds with Sir William Petty on Pascal and methods of reasoning, 37, 59–62, 113, 129
Spalatin, Georg (Spalatinus), Lutheran champion, 23
Spectator: references made to Pascal's life and thought, 88–89, 110–11, 112, 153–54, 165, 271n49; quotation from used to introduce English versions of *Pensées*, 94–96, 148, 187; mentioned, 113, 178
Spence, Joseph, quotes Pascal when writing on Pope's *Odyssey*, 264n51
Spinoza, Baruch, 120
Stebbing, Henry, divine, 139
Steele, Sir Richard, essayist: satirizes Jesuits, 110; recommends Pascal to ladies, 110–11, 151. See also *Spectator*; *Ladies Library*
Sterne, Laurence, novelist: satirizes Pascal's childhood, 153, 271n46; library, 271n46
Stewart, Dugald, Scottish philosopher, judgement of

Pascal's life and works, 231–33, 245
Stillingfleet, Edward, Bishop of Worcester, 19, 20, 57
Stoics, 101, 112–13, 117–18, 174
Stoughton, William, Governor of Massachusetts, epitaph similar to Pascal's, 236–38, 247, 285n5
Strode, Thomas, mathematician, 40
Suarez, Francisco, jesuit, 60, 252n61
Swift, Jonathan, 89, 110

Tacitus, 60
Talbot, Catherine, corresponds with Elizabeth Carter on Pascal, 155–57, 196, 220
Talbot, Peter, Irish jesuit, 26
Tauler, Johann, German mystic, 180
Taylor, Isaac, religious philosopher, introduction to Ryland's translation of *Pensées* (1838), 285n71
Taylor, Jeremy, Bishop of Down: possible knowledge of *Provinciales*, 19; works of interest to Wesley, 184, 187; admired by Dr. Johnson, 198
Thomason, George, London book-collector, 249n2
Thomson, James, *Seasons*, 128
Thomson, Thomas, chemist, 229
Thornton, John, of Clapham Sect, 219
Thoynard, Nicolas, scientist, 49
Thrale, Hester Lynch, later Mrs. Piozzi, 199, 277n81, 279n7
Thynne, Hon. Henry, teaches Elizabeth Rowe French, 196
Ticknor, George, lectures on Pascal at Harvard College, 245–46
Tillotson, John, Archbishop of Canterbury, 20, 187; and argument of the wager, 133
Tindal, Matthew, deist, 134
Toland, John, deist, 85, 134
Tonge, Israel, anti-catholic writer, 18, 31
Tonson, Jacob, publisher of early

translations of *Pensées*, 66, 70–71, 73, 76, 267n78
Torricelli, Evangelista, physicist: experiment with barometer, 41, 47; related experiments by Pascal, Boyle, and others, 41–43, 47, 236, 255n34, 256n36
Townley, Richard, "virtuoso," 42
Trajan, 113

Unitarians, 161, 229
Universal Magazine on Pascal, 205–206, 279n11

Varro, 60
Vasquez, Gabriel, jesuit, 7, 23
Vaughan, Robert, portrait of Pascal, 6
Vernon, Francis, embassy secretary, sends Pascal's works from Paris, 40, 57
Vertue, George, portrait of Pascal, 150, 279n11
Virgil, *Eclogues*, 107
Vischard de Saint Réal, César, *Caesarion*, translated by Walker, 66
Voiture, Vincent, letter-writer, known in England, 105, 111
Voltaire, François Marie Arouet de: compares English authors with Pascal, 55, 110, 120, 126, 266n75; attacks Pascal in *Lettres philosophiques* and other writings as "sublime misanthropist," 102, 126, 142–48, 155, 211–12, 217, 227, 232, 234, 240, 271n51; and eighteenth-century rationalism, 141–42, 144, 226, 232, 235; and Condorcet's edition of *Pensées*, 142, 211, 217, 227; influence on British opinion, 145, 147–48, 152, 157–58, 164–65, 203, 207; attacks on Pascal incorporated in Bayle's *Dictionnaire*, 145–47; praises *Provinciales*, 148, 189, 210; English religious reactions against, 189, 192, 193–94, 201; English unpopularity during and after French Revolution, 203–204,

213, 217, 226, 278n1; attacked
in Chevalier's translation of
Pensées (1803), 208, 210–12;
nineteenth-century comparisons
with Pascal, 233–34; American
opinion of, 240, 242, 243, 245

Walker, Joseph, translator of
Pensées (1688): translation and
its influence, 37, 59, 62, 63,
65–66, 73–74, 99, 105, 151,
212, 238; contents and style of
translation, 66, 72–73, 90, 102,
103, 104, 261n11; life and
works, 66–71; dedication to
Robert Boyle, 69–74, 82
Wallis, John, mathematician,
38–40, 81, 254n13
Walls, George, Locke's travelling
companion in France, 48
Walpole, Horace, knowledge of
Pascal's works, 154–55; letter
from Mme. du Deffand on
Pascal's hallucination, 271n51
Walsh, William, poet and critic,
familiarity with *Pensées*, 107,
108, 112, 113
Waple, Edward, President of Sion
College, London, 277n68
Warburton, William, Bishop of
Gloucester: defends Pope's *Essay
on Man*, 120; changing views on
Pascal, 139–40, 167
Ward, Seth, Bishop of Salisbury,
39, 254n8
Ware, Richard, publisher, 267n78
Warton, Joseph, mentions Pascal's
influence on Pope, 123
Watts, Isaac, divine, 197, 272n58,
277n81
Wesley family, 130, 168, 170, 181,
194
Wesley, Charles: early knowledge
of Pascal's life and works, 181,
183; uses Pascal's prayers,
184–85; Dr. Conybeare of
Christ Church promises he will
read Pascal, 185
Wesley, John: edition of *Pensées* in
Christian Library (1753), 99, 103,
187–89, 195, 208, 223, 276n52;
appeal of Pascal's religion, 140,

187–91, 194–95, 201, 202, 214;
on Voltaire's attacks on Pascal,
142, 189, 193; early knowledge
of Pascal's life and works, 181,
182–84; relations with William
Law, 184, 186, 198; conversion,
185; rejection of mysticism, 186,
187, 194; on Montesquieu, 189;
Arminian Magazine and Pascal,
189–90, 194; and curriculum of
Kingswood School, 190; and
Arminian controversy, 192, 193
Wesley, Kezia, begs Charles Wesley for Pascal's prayer for conversion, 185
Wesley, Samuel, Rector of Epworth, on Port Royal authors
and Pascal, 181, 183
Wesley, Samuel, the younger: on
Pascal's health, 183; John Wes-
ley writes to on mystics, 186
Wesley, Susannah, mother of the
Wesleys: familiarity with *Pensées*,
181, 220; quotes Pascal on faith
and reason when instructing her
children, 182, 195; quotes Pascal
on human mortality, 183
Whiston, William, priest and
mathematician, 266n64
White, Thomas (Blackloe),
Catholic polemicist, 27, 31,
37–38
Whitefield, George, evangelist,
170, 185, 195; knowledge of
Pascal's life, 186
Whole Duty of Man, 197
Wilberforce, William, reformer:
Hannah More writes to on Port
Royal authors, 214; approves
Pensées, 216, 281n32
Wilkins, John, Bishop of Chester,
21
Williamson, Sir Joseph, of *London
Gazette*, early recipient of Port
Royal *Pensées*, 57
Wilson, John, dramatist, uses
Jesuit arguments to satirize
Puritans, 16–17
Winthrop, John, Jr., of Connec-
ticut, 236
Wollaston, William, philosopher
and moralist, 119

Wood, Anthony à, antiquary, and
  first English translation of *Provinciales*, 3, 19
Woolston, Thomas, deist, 134
Wordsworth, Dorothy, on Pascal's
  style, 227–28
Wordsworth, William, 227,
  284n55
World (edited by Edward Moore),
  quotes Pascal on hunting,
  153–54, 271n49. *See also*
  Budgell, Eustace
Wormely, Col. Ralph, of Virginia,
  236

Wren, Sir Christopher: and competition on the cycloid, 38, 39,
  254n8; sees Pascal's calculating
  machine, 40; mentioned, 81,
  254n13
Wyndham, Sir Edward, Walker's
  dedication of *Caesarion* to, 67
Wyndham, Sir Hugh, judge,
  Walker's dedication of *History of
  the Eucharist* to, 67

Young, Edward, *Night Thoughts*
  compared with *Pensées*, 164, 247